Economic Processes and Political Conflicts

Economic Processes and Political Conflicts

Contributions to Modern Political Economy

edited by
Richard W. England

PRAEGER

New York
Westport, Connecticut
London

Library of Congress Cataloging-in-Publication Data

Economic processes and political conflicts.
  Bibliography: p.
  Includes index.
  1. Marxian economics. I. England, Richard W.
HB97.5.E226   1986   335.4′12   86-20465
ISBN 0-275-92451-3 (alk. paper)

Library of Congress Catalog Card Number: 86-20465
ISBN: 0-275-92451-3

First published in 1987

Praeger Publishers, 521 Fifth Avenue, New York, NY 10175
A division of Greenwood Press, Inc.

Printed in the United States of America

The paper used in this book complies with the Permanent Paper Standard
issued by the National Information Standards Organization (Z39.48-1984).

10 9 8 7 6 5 4 3 2 1

Acknowledgments

Earlier versions of Chapters 1, 2, 3, 4, 5, 6, 7, and 13 were presented to the Political
Economy Workshop, University of New Hampshire at Durham.

A longer version of Chapter 8 appeared in the *Review of Radical Political Economics
15*, no. 1 (1983): 71–91. Copyright *Review of Radical Political Economics*. Reprinted
by permission of the Union for Radical Political Economics.

Chapter 9 was originally printed in *Economic Forum 15*, no. 1 (1984): pp. 39–67.
Reprinted with the permission of the publisher.

An earlier version of Chapter 10 was presented at the Eastern Economic Association
Convention, Boston, March 1983.

Earlier versions of Chapter 11 were discussed in the Labor and Political Economy
Workshops, University of New Hampshire at Durham.

An earlier version of Chapter 12 appeared in the *Journal of Collective Negotiations
in the Public Sector 11*, no. 4.

The quotes taken from Karl Marx, *Capital*, vols. I, II, and III (1967 ed.), were
reprinted with the permission of International Publishers, New York, NY.

Dedication

The contributors to this volume would like to dedicate these essays to Dr. Sam Rosen, professor emeritus of economics, University of New Hampshire. Professor Rosen's scholarly research has addressed macroeconomics, business cycles, and Marxian theory. His published works include *National Income: Its Measurement, Determination, and Relation to Public Policy* and *National Income and Other Social Accounts*.

In addition to these scholarly accomplishments, Professor Rosen has also displayed a passionate commitment to civil rights, academic freedom, the trade union movement—and jazz history. For those of us who have known him, Sam Rosen has been a valued teacher or faculty colleague. Just as important, he has also been a cherished mentor, comrade, and friend.

On the occasion of his formal retirement from the University of New Hampshire, we would like to say, "Thanks!" and "Play it again, Sam!"

Contents

Introduction

Let me introduce this collection of essays by reflecting upon the recent history of economic thought in the United States. As recently as the late 1960s, the "grand neoclassical synthesis" dominated economic discourse in the United States, whereas the voices of radical political economy were few and barely heard. This near-silence on the left was in large measure a consequence of the purge of academic Marxists from university life that had occurred during the early years of the Cold War (Ehrenberg 1986). Someone looking for radical interpretations of contemporary capitalism at that time could turn to Sweezy (1942), Baran and Sweezy (1966), or to a few journals like *Monthly Review* and *Science & Society*, but little else was available to those who doubted that "the end of ideology" had arrived.

During the same period, however, many Americans were active in the civil rights, welfare rights, trade union, antiwar, ecological, and feminist movements. Some became dissatisfied with the lack of a theoretical basis for their political practice, and hence, by the early 1970s, radical political economy experienced an intellectual boom. The upsurge in radical theory was reflected in the inauguration of numerous journals that rejected the orthodox interpretation of U.S. society (e.g. *Review of Radical Political Economics, Insurgent Sociologist, Science for the People*).

Since that period 15 years ago, there has been a decline in radical political organization and activity in the United States, perhaps reflecting the effects of higher unemployment, the financial burden of attending college, the end of the military draft, a conservative ideological offensive, and so forth. Political economy has continued to advance theoretically, however, especially in its Marxist variety. This theoretical progress is recorded in a number of compelling critiques of orthodox economic theory (e.g., Harris 1978; Marglin 1984) and in a growing list of Marxist theoretical treatises (e.g., Weeks 1981; Castells 1980; O'Connor 1984). The vitality of Marxian theory in the United States is also reflected in a number of elementary texts inspired by radical political economy (Hunt and Sherman 1986; Bowles and Edwards 1985; Edwards, Reich, and Weisskopf 1986).

This advance of radical political economy has featured three theoretical prongs. The first is the correction of various hypotheses originally proposed by Karl Marx more than a century ago. Considerable effort, for example, has gone into properly specifying the relationship between the values and prices of commodities in capitalist society—the so-called transformation problem. (Some of those efforts are reported in Mandel and Freeman 1984.) The second thrust has entailed the refinement of various Marxian propositions, such as the interpretation of social class structure of capitalist society (Wright 1978). The third is the application of Marx's categories and principles to entirely new domains, some of which Marx could not have imagined in his day. These include the explosive expansion of unproductive labor associated with the rise of the modern corporation (Becker 1977) as well as the persistence of racism in the United States since the Civil War (Reich 1981).

This collection should be seen as part of that broader effort to correct, refine, and extend the domain of radical political economy. Each of these essays reflects the premise that economic phenomena can be understood only within a historical context and that those phenomena are intertwined with political struggles. It is my fervent hope that these theoretical efforts will help to establish a democratic socialist movement in the United States during the years to come. That outcome will be realized, however, only if radical intellectuals manage to link their theoretical work to progressive struggles for economic equality and democracy.

REFERENCES

Baran, Paul and Paul Sweezy. 1966. *Monopoly Capital*. New York: Monthly Review Press.

Becker, James F. 1977. *Marxian Political Economy: An Outline*. Cambridge, England: Cambridge University Press.

Bowles, Samuel and Richard Edwards. 1985. *Understanding Capitalism*. New York: Harper & Row.

Castells, Manuel. 1980. *The Economic Crisis and American Society*. Princeton, New Jersey: Princeton University Press.

Edwards, Richard, Michael Reich, and Thomas Weisskopf. 1986. *The Capitalist System*. Englewood Cliffs, New Jersey: Prentice-Hall.

Ehrenberg, John. 1986. The Left Academy. *Monthly Review* (January): 52–57.

Harris, Donald J. 1978. *Capital Accumulation and Income Distribution*. Stanford, California: Stanford University Press.

Hunt, E.K. and Howard Sherman. 1986. *Economics: An Introduction to Traditional and Radical Views*. New York: Harper & Row.

Mandel, Ernest and Alan Freeman. 1984. *Ricardo, Marx, Sraffa*. London: Verso.

Marglin, Stephen. 1984. *Growth, Distribution, and Prices*. Cambridge, Massachusetts: Harvard University Press.

O'Connor, James. 1984. *Accumulation Crisis*. New York: Basil Blackwell.

Reich, Michael. 1981. *Racial Inequality*. Princeton, New Jersey: Princeton University Press.

Sweezy, Paul. 1942. *The Theory of Capitalist Development*. New York: Oxford University Press.

Weeks, John. 1981. *Capital and Exploitation*. Princeton, New Jersey: Princeton University Press.

Wright, Erik Olin. 1978. *Class, Crisis and the State*. London: New Left Books.

PART 1
Issues of Methodology

Chapter 1

Dialectic of Matter vs. Dialectic of History: A Critique of Lucio Colletti's Materialism

NICHOLAS N. KOZLOV

Over the last three decades, the work of the Italian philosopher Lucio Colletti has been linked with a positivist (or at least "ultra-materialist") tendency in Marxism. This association stems from the recurring claim in Colletti's earlier writing that many Marxists since Marx have treated the notion of dialectic with insufficient care. In particular, Colletti argued that some Marxists merely replaced the names of Hegelian categories (e.g., the Idea) with words that have a more scientific ring (e.g., Matter) *without* transforming the logic of the Hegelian dialectic in any way. Colletti claimed that despite its title such a "dialectical materialism"[1] (the "diamat" of the Soviet philosophy texts) was necessarily idealist, since idealism is in the strongest sense intrinsic to Hegel's dialectic and cannot be expunged by merely substituting materialist words for idealist ones.

Although Colletti's fire was directed primarily at the so-called orthodox espousers of diamat, the *reaction* to Colletti has come largely from "Hegelian" Marxists (no friends of diamat). Not surprisingly the Hegelian Marxists, who stress the dialectical "essence" of Marxism and who see no basic problem in affirming the Hegelian roots of dialectic (Piccone 1972, 1981; Rosdolsky 1977), soon recognized that Colletti's theses represented at least an implicit challenge to their views. Perhaps somewhat surprisingly, however, at least one Marxist (Hillel-Ruben 1975) has argued that Colletti is not materialist *enough* in that he seeks to combine a materialist ontology with an idealist (Kantian) theory of knowledge—a project which at best is incoherent and at worst leads to idealism.

Lucio Colletti himself, however, has traveled a long road since his "ultra-materialist" days and at present no longer even describes himself as a Marxist. Paul Piccone suggests that Colletti came to believe that being "a good materialist . . . rules out being a Marxist" (Piccone 1981: 732). Piccone's observation, however, is little more than a clever barb because it obscures the fact that Colletti abandoned Marxism *not* because of materialism, but because he came to adopt an increasingly *idealist* perspective.

3

In this essay, I will try to explain this paradox by uncovering the problem that propelled Colletti—in very dialectical fashion—from ultramaterialism (with the idealist Kantian tinge identified by Hillel-Ruben) to an ideological quandary, and finally to a neo-Hegelian idealism. While I concur with Hillel-Ruben's welcome defense of the much-maligned reflection theory of knowledge, my aim extends to revealing that particular problem whose unraveling determined the trajectory of Colletti's thought. Before proceeding with this task, it may be worthwhile to indicate why it is necessary. This is best accomplished by briefly examining the nature of the reaction to Colletti.

The attack on Colletti was certainly foreseeable. As Sebastiano Timpanaro (1980: 29) suggested, "perhaps the sole characteristic common to virtually all contemporary varieties of Western Marxism is their concern to defend themselves against the accusation of 'vulgar' or 'mechanical' materialism."[2] While this observation is perhaps too sweeping, it is probably not far off the mark. For confirmation one need only examine the many and varied forms of insurance that are sought in order to avoid the "vulgar" trap: where today is it possible to find a Marxism that is not tempered by the qualification that it is Hegelian (dialectical), or structuralist, or humanist, or overdetermined, and so on? What is of concern in all of this is that in the rush to avoid conceptual crudity, materialism itself is trampled underfoot.

None of this is to deny the possibility of a vulgar materialist interpretation of Marx. Historically, the experience of the Second International is ample demonstration of the possibility. The point, however, is that on the *present terrain* of Western Marxist theory "there is no danger . . . of a revival of vulgar materialism" (Timpanaro 1980: 13). The reasons for such a state of affairs should emerge as implicit themes in this examination of Lucio Colletti's work.

Much of the current interest in Hegelian Marxism owes an intellectual debt to Georg Lukacs and his extraordinary *History and Class Consciousness* (1923). Dialecticians should note, however, that in a 1967 reassessment of that work Lukacs made an important self-criticism (Lukacs 1967) and in a contemporaneous statement declared that he regarded the book as "superseded" (Lukacs 1975). Further contributions to the origin of Hegelian Marxism also came during the interwar period from the theoreticians of the Frankfurt school (the critical theorists) and in his own specific way Antonio Gramsci (Therborn 1978).

The Italian fascists, however, silenced Gramsci. The Frankfurt theoreticians detached themselves from politics and retreated into academic isolation, where they either degenerated into bourgeois apologia (Horkheimer 1966) or remained trapped in professional labors (Lukacs 1938). Consequently, Lukacs and the Frankfurt school never established a decisive influence on the Marxism of their time (i.e., that of the Third International).

This state of dormancy, however, came to an abrupt end after the theoretical sterility of the Stalin years. Interest in Hegelian Marxism was revived by the rediscovery of Marx's early works and exemplified by the efforts to theorize the notion of "alienation." A special continuity between the prewar critical theorists and present-day themes can be found in the texts of Herbert Marcuse, which play heavily on the Hegelian motif. In addition to critical theory, Hegelian influences pervade the work of the Uno-Riron school (Kozo Uno, Thomas Sekine), the Capital Logicians (E. Altvater, B. Blanke), and individual thinkers such as Roman Rosdolsky, Raya Dunayevskaya, Geoffrey Pilling, Rafael Echeverria, and Bertell Ollman.

Some writers, however, fail to recognize these trends. Ronald Kieve (1983: 37), for example, recently made the rather startling claim that "[i]f there is one thing that contemporary Marxists seem to agree on, it is the need to eradicate every trace of the Hegelian dialectic," citing Lucio Colletti and Louis Althusser as examples. It is true that both of these theoreticians stressed (in very different ways) the profound gulf that separates the Hegelian dialectic from Marxism—a gulf that is deeper than that which separates idealism from materialism (if this is possible). But Colletti and Althusser, together with their followers, hardly represent many or most contemporary Marxists. In general Althusser's work has been poorly recieved, while Colletti (prior to his renunciation of Marxism) was not paid any great amount of attention. Kieve's assertion, quite simply, is puzzling.

Colletti's and Althusser's works, each in their own particular way, *do* represent a critique of Hegelian Marxism—Kieve is correct on this point. Like Colletti, Althusser experienced the period of de-Stalinization as an intellectual in the Communist Party. Both writers have remarked on the "positive" consequences of the Twentieth Congress of the Communist Party of the Soviet Union (1956) and their initially high hopes: "I experienced Khrushchev's denunciation of Stalin as an authentic liberation" (Colletti 1978); and "before the Twentieth Congress it was actually not possible for a Communist philosopher, at least in France, to publish texts that would be relevant to politics" (Althusser 1976: 75). Both found, however, that after a short time the obstacles removed by Khrushchev did not provide for a reconstruction of Marxism. Instead, the ideological critique of the "cult of personality" took fundamentally bourgeois forms: "In one sense, the process of renovation for which I had hoped . . . failed to occur—but in another sense it had occurred, in a patently rightward direction" (Colletti 1978); and "the criticism of Stalin's errors was formulated . . . in terms such that there inevitably followed what we must call an unleashing of bourgeois ideological and philosophical themes" (Althusser 1976: 75). Although substantial differences divided Althusser and Colletti, they both agreed that the missing element was a rigorous *leftist* criticism of the Stalin era and its aftermath.

Neither Colletti nor Althusser, of course, invented anti-Hegelian Marxism any more than Hegelian and humanist Marxism originated in the aftermath of the Twentieth Congress. Since it is not my aim to catalogue all writers from the past who have denounced the "Hegelian Rococo ornamentalism" (Rosa Luxemburg) in Marxism, it will be most convenient to begin a discussion of Colletti by briefly noting that in large measure he took the work of his mentor, Galvano Della Volpe (1897–1968), as a point of departure. The latter began by rejecting the commonly held view that Marxism is merely the Hegelian dialectic "stood on its feet" and by seeking to establish that Marx's criticism of Hegel's theory of the state was centered on revealing the unity of idealism and empiricism in Hegel's thought (Editors 1970: 97–98).

In 1950, Della Volpe put forth an argument (later to be associated with Colletti as well) asserting that a consistently materialist standpoint must affirm the primacy of what Hegel termed the "intellect" over that of "reason," that is, precisely the opposite of Hegel's argument for idealism. Della Volpe put forward the principle of non-contradiction (a principle of the intellect) in opposition to Hegel, who defined reality dialectically as the interpenetration of opposites—as contradiction. To forestall any immediate objections, neither Della Volpe nor Colletti seeks to transform Marxism into a system of harmony. They simply distinguish between, in Colletti's terms, a materialist opposition and a speculative contradiction. This will be discussed further below.

The writing of Della Volpe, however, remained relatively obscure. Only recently translated into English, and cramped by the tactical requirements of the Communist Party of Italy (of which he remained a member until his death), Della Volpe's texts were "vitiated by pedantry and prolixity. . . . It has been left to his pupils, above all Colletti, to write a clearer language, which assumes its political responsibilities" (Editors 1970: 99).

Although it is, perhaps, more clear, Colletti's language has not always been understood or taken seriously. Paul Piccone, the self-styled crusader against "Leninist-Stalinist" dogmatism, simply says that

> Colletti was essentially a Kantian who had never successfully digested
> not only the dialectic, but anything faintly reminiscent of Hegel—as his
> book on *Marxism and Hegel* clearly showed. (Piccone 1981: 727)

In an earlier article in which he claims to "critique . . . all the philosophical positions" of Colletti, Piccone is no more substantive. After a "critique" that occupies less than a paragraph, Piccone sweepingly concludes:

> When all is said and done, Colletti ends up by defending all that is useless
> in positivism while discarding whatever is relevant in Marxism: the dialec-
> tic, the Hegelian critique of the understanding, the critique of bourgeois
> science, and the critique of vulgar materialism. (Piccone 1972: 131)

Since Piccone is generally a verbose writer, it is indeed impressive that he was able to show all this in the space of 20 lines of text. Moreover, as will be seen below, Piccone is simply incorrect on at least one point: namely, his claim that Colletti discards the Hegelian critique of the understanding.

Beyond some parting shots along the lines of "the *worst* Romanticism [being] preferable to the *best* positivism," Piccone's comments are not very specific. He resorts to the unfortunate tactic of suggesting that thinking such as Colletti's "usually hides an apology for dogmatic reiterations of obsolete political positions," the latter referring to Leninism and an insufficiently hostile attitude toward the Soviet Union (1972: 130–31). Innuendo is never constructive, particularly when it originates with one so well known for his hostility toward the modes of argument characteristic of the Stalin era.

Ronald Kieve's analysis of Colletti is considerably more substantive and avoids Piccone's vacuous stridency, but it is still at times frustrating. For example, Kieve (1983: 38) ascribes to Colletti the contention "that the Hegelian system involves the reduction of philosophy to an idealist gnoseology which demands the unreality of matter. . . ." In support of this statement Kieve makes reference to an article by Colletti without, however, any indication of a passage or page. It seems that on a point of such importance, and one with so many possible shades of meaning, meticulous documentation is essential. Upon careful examination, it will be seen that Kieve indeed produces a dialectical result: his interpretation is a unity of truth—and error!

Furthermore, when Kieve seeks to affirm "the possibility of a Marxist dialectic," and indeed finds in Hegel a "crypto-materialism," he derives his results from an analysis of the "Doctrine of Essence," which follows the "Doctrine of Being" in Hegel's *Logic*. Of course one could say, along with Lenin, that parts of the Doctrine of Essence seem "remarkably materialistic," (Lenin 1976: 151). But that is precisely Colletti's point: even before the Doctrine of Being (much less the section on Essence), either in the large *Logic* or in part I of the *Encyclopaedia*, Hegel clearly states that the aim of his work is to prove the necessity of idealism in philosophy. Kieve skips (several hundred pages) directly to the section on Essence to discover his "crypto-materialism," but this makes little sense. Was Hegel's genius really so shallow that he failed to see how easy it would be to turn his system into *Unphilosophie*, i.e, materialism?

Lest contentions such as Kieve's be accepted without argument, this essay will seek to reconstruct Colletti's views on the irreconcilability of materialism and Hegelianism and to argue that these views are defensible. The discussion will then shift to another aspect of Colletti's critique of diamat—its neglect of the "subjective factor." Although Colletti was correct to pose the issue, it will be argued here that he posed it incorrectly, and that as a result, an element of tension appeared in his own work. Finally, the chapter will show how the further development of this tension led to a dilemma that culminated in Colletti's rejection of Marxism.

Insofar as Colletti further developed Della Volpe's theses, his early works aimed at producing an orthodox criticism of recent trends in Marxism from a consistently leftist perspective. The most pervasive theme in Colletti's early writings was the effort to establish the scientific nature of Marx's work by stressing its radical break with Hegel's speculative idealism.

In the first two chapters of the *Science of Logic* ("The Doctrine of Being"), Hegel lays out the fundamental principles of his system. It is here that he establishes the necessity of an idealism in philosophy. This proposition is derived by first demonstrating the limitedness of the finite:

> Finite things *are*, but their relation to themselves is that they are negatively self-related and in this very self-relation send themselves away beyond themselves, beyond their being. They *are*, but the truth of this being is their *end*. (Hegel 1969: 129)

For Hegel, "the being of something is determinate; something has a quality and in it is not only determined but limited; its quality is its limit. . . ." As such, the quality of finite things is given by their limit (i.e., their "end"), from which it follows that "non-being constitutes their nature and being."

It now becomes almost self-evident that the finite may not be regarded as real—in fact, reality is a property of the *infinite*, and is established as a consequence of the finite passing over into its opposite:

> The finite . . . sublates itself, ceases to be. But this its result, the negative as such, is its very determination; for it is the negative of the negative. . . . Closer consideration of this result shows the finite in its ceasing-to-be, in this negation of itself has attained its being-in-itself, is *united with itself*. . . . This *identity with itself*, the negation of negation, is affirmative being and thus the other of the finite, of the finite which is supposed to have the first negation for its determinateness; this other is the *infinite*. (Hegel 1969: 136–37)

But the infinite as *real* is not to be understood simply as the unity of finite and infinite, that is, simply as "being . . . distinct and apart from its determinate mode." Rather, the infinite has been established as "being—but not indeterminate, abstract being, for it is posited as negating the negation; it is therefore also determinate being for it contains negation in general and hence determinateness" (1969: 48–49). This determinate (concrete) infinity is *real*, so idealism in philosophy consists of nothing but the denial of "veritable being" for the finite (1969: 154). Elsewhere, Hegel writes that "this ideality of the finite is the chief maxim of philosophy; and for that reason every genuine philosophy is idealism" (Hegel 1978: 140).

Colletti begins by pointing out that this last series of propositions, the "principle of idealism," was in no sense discovered by Hegel or unknown before him. His point was that this principle had never been actualized—Hegel recognized this difficulty and proceeded to transform idealism into reality, which meant that not only must the development of philosophy (idealism) be logically coherent, but that the principle of idealism itself had to be "realized" (Colletti 1980: 8). Although philosophy, according to Hegel, has generally recognized the principle of idealism, it has never been consistently faithful to it due to a defective method:

> Philosophy has adopted, Hegel states, the point of view of the "intellect," the principle of non-contradiction or of the mutual exclusion of opposites. Thinking that the problem of its "actualization" could simply be reduced to one of logical coherence, philosophy has embraced the "perspective" which presumes "that the finite is irreconcilable with the infinite and cannot be united with it, that the finite is utterly opposed to the infinite." (Colletti 1980: 9)

At first glance, this perspective[3] seems best suited for the affirmation of idealism insofar as the intellect requires that the finite be kept separate from the infinite, and that the latter in some sense be absolute or primary. In this way, by making the infinite superior or "more real" than the finite, it appears as though the principle of idealism is being realized.

But Hegel points out that precisely in the separation of the finite and the infinite lies the hitherto contradictory stance of philosophy. By posing the finite and the infinite as coexistent but *separate*, "the infinite, in that case, *is one of the two*; but as *only* one of the two it is itself finite, it is not the whole but only one side; it has its limit in what stands over against it; it is thus the *finite infinite*. There are present only two finites." (Hegel, in Colletti 1974: 112). Rather than being suppressed or negated, the finite is affirmed and thus acquires being and permanence. Instead of idealism, there is *Unphilosophie*, or materialism (Colletti 1980: 10).

Hegel's solution consists not only of denying that the finite is real, but of further establishing that the nonbeing of the finite is its very nature. This negative self-relation of finite things (i.e., that which makes them ideal) also constitutes as the essence of the finite its opposite ("the negative as such, is its very determination . . ."). Finite things, by the very nature of their limitation, tend to display an "indwelling tendency outwards," and thereby to negate themselves: "for anything to be finite is just to suppress itself and put itself aside" (Hegel 1978: 116).

Colletti understands Hegel to mean that the finite is not essentially itself except when it is the other—the infinite. The advantage of this scheme for Hegel is that it allows him to consider the finite not as an absolute, but rather as a self-abstraction (no outside force is invoked) which is "an *objective* movement carried out by the finite itself in order to go beyond itself and thus *pass over* into its essence" (Colletti 1980: 15). This avoids both the finite-infinite dualism, which is the intrinsic flaw of the perspective of the intellect, while at the same time it permits an incorporation of the finite within the system. Thus

> Matter is not negated: it is affirmed by virtue of that which it is not. But . . . it is also clear that this affirmation is in effect a negation; that is, by declaring matter "essential" only as it is in thought, it is *ipso facto* excluded that the former has any reality as it is outside and antecedent to the notion. (Colletti 1980: 17)

The finite is annihilated—not in the sense of ceasing to exist, but rather as becoming merely the illusion arising from an underlying essence; only the latter is real.

Colletti's interpretation of Hegel is consequently not as simplistic as Kieve claims, and it can be defended by unambiguous textual evidence. Contrary to what Kieve states, Colletti clearly perceives that, for Hegel, the finite is certainly real in the sense that it exists; the finite is *not* real in the sense that its essence lies outside itself. Moreover, I am not seeking to defend the traditional interpretation of Hegel, although it is perhaps worth pointing out that it is Colletti's interpretation that seems reasonable, while Kieve's "crypto-materialism" version is rather strange. For example, Kieve (1983: 46) treats Hegel's *concrete* as identical with the *finite*, which of course they are not. The procession from mere *being* (inadequate because abstract) to Absolute Idea (adequate because concrete) does not actually assert the finitude of Absolute Idea.[4]

Although Colletti's purpose may momentarily seem lost amid Hegel's reflections, it reappears with clarity and a vengeance when Colletti declares that this Hegelian "dialectic of matter" has been uncritically adopted by Marxists (specifically Engels, Kautsky, Plekhanov, Lenin, Stalin, and certain contemporary Soviet theoreticians) and transformed into "dialectical materialism" simply by changing the "Absolute Idea" into absolute "Matter" (Colletti 1980: 27; 1974: 70). It might be objected by readers of Lenin's conspectus of the *Science of Logic* that Lenin had very clearly pointed out that "I [Lenin] am in general trying to read Hegel materialistically. . . . I cast aside for the most part God, the Absolute, the Pure Idea, etc." (Lenin 1976: 104). For Colletti, however, that is precisely the point: Lenin "has 'forced' himself to read Hegel 'materialistically' exactly at the point at which Hegel is in fact . . . annihilating matter" and seeking to prove the existence of a god (Colletti 1974: 123). The substitution of *Matter* for the *Idea* has resulted only in a change of name. The Marxian "specific level of historical-materialist analysis" (i.e., determinate, specific abstractions distilled from concrete reality) has been replaced by an unspecified, unhistorical, metaphysical abstraction (Matter) which is therefore antimaterialist (Colletti 1974: 70).

Lenin did not sin alone (Colletti 1974: 68–72), and in fact Colletti holds Engels responsible for the later contaminations of Marxism. The difficulty with Engels, according to Colletti, was his acceptance of Hegel's critique of the intellect as unscientific and dogmatic. For Hegel, the intellect represented the logic of the finite and was a barrier to true understanding since it upheld the materialist principle of non-contradiction. In *Anti-Duhring* and the *Dialectics of Nature* Engels adopts the same position, in Colletti's view, and thus must argue that the "narrow" mode of thinking practiced in the natural sciences must be replaced by a dialectical one if the sciences are to develop and avoid "metaphysics" (Colletti 1980: 41). Colletti claims that

> Engels takes as an element intrinsically related to metaphysical thinking the very principle of non-contradiction which Hegel considered an obstacle to the full elaboration of a metaphysics *per se*. (Colletti 1980: 40)

For Engels and other dialectical materialists, therefore, the "rational kernel" of Hegel's thought was the dialectic method, a revolutionary method they indiscriminately applied to Matter; the "mystical shell" was simply the idealist "system," epitomized by the Absolute Idea (Colletti 1974: 121).

Colletti then offers his interpretation of Marx's assessment of the Hegelian dialectic. Hegel's genuine discovery, according to Colletti, was that "reason" does not assume the form of a negation of every determination (i.e., it is not a monolithic substance), but on the contrary, it is a "unity of opposites, *being* and *non-being* together, a tautoheterology or dialectic." But Hegel did *not* see that "reason" is only an "epistemological principle," one which serves people *only* as reason, *not* as reality (Colletti 1980: 32). The "mystical shell" thus becomes "the immediate translation of reason into a positive moment, its substantification," an outcome that stems from Hegel's earlier indentification of the sublation of the finite (within the Idea) with reality (Colletti 1980: 48).

In short, Colletti feels that dialectical materialism entails a spurious transformation of a valid epistemological principle into a metaphysical ontological statement, which is subsequently accorded supreme status. This represents, in Colletti's view, an idealist error of the first order due to the consequent identification of reason and reality and the abandonment of the materialist and scientific principle of non-contradiction. A further examination of Colletti's work will show a shift in theoretical position that leads him into an ideological quandary.

One of the more disturbing aspects of dialectical materialism for Colletti becomes what he feels to be the necessary denial of a role for the "subjective factor," or conscious human activity. He says that the proponents of dialectical materialism must confront the freedom/necessity antithesis by simply agreeing with Hegel that "freedom is the recognition of necessity" or "freedom is the consciousness of being determined" (Colletti 1974: 69). Even though such a discussion is couched in terms of the "objective" movements of "matter" (Colletti 1974: 71), to Colletti this represents nothing more than the identification of thought and being, whereby historical social working activity (and thought as its reflection) becomes *subsumed* in the immutable movements of a metaphysical Absolute (called *Matter*).

Thus, it appears to Colletti Marx's rectification of the "chief defect of all hitherto existing materialism" (Marx) has been lost. While Marx recognized that the material circumstances of human existence are in a strong sense a cause, it is also true that human working activity transforms these conditions and thereby also acts as a cause in its turn. According to Colletti, the failure to recognize this means that the *social* characteristics of human interaction with nature are forgotten, thereby separating the historical from materialism.

To be sure, Colletti regards humans as the products of "objective material causation," but at the same time he sees the *determined* human as the simultaneous beginning of a new causal series whose "point of departure is no longer the natural environment but the concept, the *idea of man*, his mental project" (Colletti 1974: 66). This second causal series is the *"final causality*, as opposed to the *material causality* in the case of the first process." For Colletti, these two causal series constitute the essence of the Marxian notion of praxis (Colletti 1974: 66–67).

This formulation, although correct for criticizing numerous errors, suffers from an inadequate formulation of social ontology. By arguing that the teleological process (i.e., presumably labor or working activity) represents a final causality, Colletti reduces the relationship between the goal of the teleological process and its actual result to a simple unity, treating this relationship as nonproblematic. In fact, the individual teleological project can exist, can be comprehended, only as part of a complex social structure (Lukacs 1975: 77); goal-oriented activity is only possible in a world with definite causal relationships. More importantly, these causal determinations are in actuality a *sum* of individual teleological projects, but not in any simple sense,[5] for the sum is such that

> the teleological project involved in labor can never take account of the entire set of conditions of the causal series set in motion, so that something must necessarily emerge in the labor process other than what the laborer set himself as his aim. (Lukacs 1975: 18)

An example given by Lukacs of this situation is the (unintended) tendential formation of the general rate of profit in a capitalist economy that is the outcome of the forcible articulation of individual (teleological) efforts, some successful and others not, to obtain surplus profit.

Posing the question in such a manner does not imply a return to primitive materialism, where human activity is seen as merely a special case of the movement of Matter. Lukacs naturally recognizes the effects of a "reverse" causality, which establishes "new objects, forms and connections . . . in society as a consequence of teleological projects" (Lukacs 1975: 77). It is evident in Colletti's position that, considered from a purely epistemological perspective, one is forced to deal with determination and teleology as two distinct and separate moments. If, however, one treats the "epistemological problems . . . as an aspect of ontological ones," teleology does not collapse into causality—the "vulgar" interpretation which Colletti so vigorously opposes—it retains an autonomy while nevertheless presupposing a structure of determinations.

Another flaw in Colletti's approach is found in the reduction of all ontology to social (historical) ontology. This also stems from his critique of the dialectical materialists insofar as he wishes to demonstrate their neglect of the social determinations of human history. Timpanaro (1980: 16) argues that in the course of this approach, Colletti has completely absorbed the physical/biological exigencies of human existence *within* the social aspect:

> In my view, to reduce man to what is specific about him with respect to other animals is just as one-sided as to reduce him (as vulgar materialists do) to what he has in common with them.[6]

In a spirited defense of Engels, Timpanaro (1980: 34) seeks to affirm the importance of "the conditioning which nature *still* exercises on man, and will continue to exercise for the foreseeable future." He argues that Engels' positive achievements in the *Dialectics of Nature*, such as the (rather anti-Hegelian) polemic against Social Darwinism and the recognition of the frailty of human biological existence, are not only relevant but outweigh the unfortunate "Hegelian residues" (Timpanaro 1980: 132).

Timpanaro clearly regards the full elaboration of a Marxist ontology as being of prime importance, and he feels that this ontology must be rigorously materialist—not only in the sense of recognizing "a reality external to the subject" but also in affirming "the physical nature of the subject." He argues that

> true materialism is not merely methodological. Rather, to use a word which horrifies the methodologists, it is a *Weltanschaung*, open to all the rectifications which the progress of scientific research and social practice will make necessary, but not so "open" as to fade into agnosticism. (Timpanaro 1980: 80–81).

Lukacs suggests the need for a comprehensive Marxist ontology, "having three great underlying forms: the inorganic, the organic and the social, " the task being to uncover "the forms of being that new movements of the complex produce." Lukacs' project accords a privileged position to science, which "really facilitates, time and again, the solution of ontological questions" (Lukacs 1975: 21–22, 24).

The contrast between Timpanaro and Lukacs reflects the interesting divergence of opinion among modern Marxist realists, some of whom maintain the imperative of a transcendental realism (i.e., a *Weltanschauung*) while others claim that realism can only be established inductively (i.e., the results of scientific practice provide good grounds for a belief in an independent, structured world).[7]

Thus far, it is inferable from Colletti's work that his aim is to emphasize the scientific (which to him means *materialistic*) basis of Marxism as well as to demonstrate that history is the site of human self-emancipation (an outcome of the subjective side of human working activity). Hence, Marxism is the unity of science and revolution. In attempting to develop this thesis while upholding the centrality of the category *alienation*, Colletti arrives at certain insights but at the same time slips into an ideological quandary.

"As a scientific doctrine, Marxism essentially consists of the discovery of objective causal relationships," says Colletti. Science is first and foremost the recognition of the principle of non-contradiction, "which every scientist knows to be the principle of material determinacy, in addition to being at the same time the principle of coherent discourse" (Colletti 1975: 14).

Although Colletti rejects dialectical contradiction as intrinsically idealistic, this does not mean that he rejects all notions of conflict or movement. Recapitulating and summarizing Colletti's argument somewhat, the dialectic is expressed as a contradictory opposition in which each term "is in itself negative, being simply the *Negation* of the other" (Colleti 1975: 5). As a negation, each term does not contain its essence, and to be *determined* it must exist in unity with its opposite—hence an inclusive opposition (Colletti 1975: 4).

Such a dialectic cannot be a dialectic of *things*, that is, materialist. It is necessarily an idealist dialectic because *things* cannot be negatively determined. There is, of course, opposition (conflict) between real, material things (or relations), but real opposition is an "exclusive opposition" because

> each of the opposites is real and positive. Each subsists for itself. Since, to
> be itself, it has no need to be referred to the other, we have here a case of a
> relation of mutual opposition. (Colletti 1975: 6).

Consequently, real natural or social forces that are in conflict or opposition may be "positive" and "negative" in their relation to one another (else they would not be in conflict), but, "one of the determinations can never be the contradictory contrary of the other" (Kant, in Colletti 1975: 7). A quantity may be "negative" in relation to another quantity, but a "negative quantity is not a negation of quantity" (Colletti 1975: 9).

These formulations had led the young Colletti to pose reality as "non-contradictory" and at the same time to "identify the social and natural sciences" (Colletti 1978: 338). Both of these themes, in fact, were inherited *in toto* from Della Volpe. But doubts began to emerge in Colletti's work. If reality is indeed non-contradictory, how can Marxism affirm the necessity of revolution? Where does alienation (ignored by Della Volpe) come from if it is not the consequence of a reality that is precisely "upside down" or con-tradictory? If Marxism is a science, does that mean that Marx was not also a philosopher? Is Marxism a positivism? Does the knowledge produced by the social sciences have the same status as knowledge produced by the natural sciences?

Colletti, fully aware of the (positivist) risks involved, wishes to uphold the thesis that there is only one type of knowledge—that which is scientific.[8] At the same time, he wishes to argue that "capitalist contradic-tions are undeniably dialectical contradictions"; not "real" oppositions as described earlier herein, but genuinely dialectical contradictions (Colletti 1978: 338). The primal contradiction of capitalism, from which all others follow, is the opposition found in the commodity between use-value and value (or what amounts to the same thing, between concrete labor and abstract labor). This becomes *"externalized* as the contradiction between commodity and money [which] develops in turn into the contradiction be-tween capital and wage-labor," etc. (Colletti 1975: 25). Although it is true that the elements in the development of these couplets have an independent existence (i.e., money as a real object separate from commodity), Colletti argues they are "separated . . . and yet they are inseparable." Elaborating on this:

> Insofar as they are separated, they have taken on a real aspect; but in-
> sofar as they are inseparable, they have become real and independent
> and yet not truly so. They have been made as real as things, while still
> not being things: they are, in short, a product of alienation, they are en-
> tities which are unreal in themselves and yet have been *reified*. (Colletti
> 1975: 25).

It must be clear then that science, since it necessarily (for Colletti) adheres to the principle of non-contradiction, is of no use in understanding this "counterfeit reality" (capitalism). What has been restored? Marxism as philosophy—a philosophy that affirms the necessity of revolution. This necessity is not based on moral ideals, but rather on the very fact of an up-side down reality.

In simpler and more familiar terms, this means that when Marx criticizes Hegel, the economists and all the reality of capitalism, he still has to do it in the name of reality and *on the basis of reality*. The criterion of his critique, in short, cannot be the *ideal*. It must be a criterion drawn from and rooted in reality. (Colletti 1974: 234)

What has *also* been restored is the primacy of philosophy, and although Colletti does not prefer to say so explicitly, this conclusion is inescapable. It is philosophy that enables Colletti to maintain that contrary to *any other aspect of reality*, "contradiction is the *specific* feature of capitalism, the characteristic which singles it out not only with respect to other forms of society, but with respect to all other cosmic phenomena" (Colletti 1975: 27). It is also philosophy that enables Colletti to maintain that "the theory of alienation and the theory of contradiction are now seen as a single [philosophic] theory, one which (we may now add) embraces and encompasses within itself the [scientific] theory of value" (Colletti 1975: 27). Similarly, Colletti writes elsewhere that the law of value must be considered from two perspectives. The first perspective—the scientific one—considers the law of value "to be a 'regulative principle' which allows the explanation of the system's internal functioning" and which shows capitalism "to be a fundamentally balanced organism in which every part is in harmonious correspondence with the others." The second perspective, from which "the law of value is the theory of *fetishism* . . . enunciates the reasons why men must *overthrow* the system . . . " (Colletti 1973: 182–84).

It is finally also philosophy that enables Colletti to posit an initial social "oneness," an "original unity," that was broken in the course of historical social development and was thereby "destined to culminate in capitalism" —further destined, however, to be eventually restored into a unity and reconciled. In Colletti's own words, "the schema of Hegel's philosophy of history blooms again," albeit in "somewhat modified" form (Colletti 1975: 28).

If this is what Colletti came to believe constitutes Marxism, he should at least be given credit for having abandoned it. Colletti's own warnings (1978) have been entirely ignored: science is reduced to a bearer of pseudo-knowledge while philosophy is elevated to the sole source of true knowledge. Philosophy alone is capable of singling out capitalism from "all other cosmic phenomena" as a "false" reality, and philosphy has established that all the work Marxist scientists have done on crisis theory and the process of accumulation has demonstrated only that capitalism is a system characterized by a "harmonious correspondence" of all its parts.

Apart from simply being bizarre, it hardly needs pointing out that Colletti's arguments are themselves profoundly idealist and teleological. To be sure, it is necessary to show the constitutive (and highly positive) role that Marxist philosophy played with regard to the Marxist science of the capitalist economy. The elaboration of that relationship, however, should be sought along a rather different avenue than the one traveled by Colletti. The genuine contributions made by Colletti, such as the critique of dialectical materialism, the insistence on scientific determinate abstractions, and so on, should not stand in the way of a thorough criticism of the idealism that has found its way into his thinking via a speculative philosophy of history.

It may be relevant to close this essay by raising a political problem. Two articles by Paul Piccone (1972, 1981) have been cited herein. Both articles are stridently anti-Soviet, so at least in one respect neither Piccone nor, sadly, the American political scene in general has changed a great deal with the passage of time. The 1972 article, however, contains a virtual hosanna to the political potentialities of the New Left; the 1981 piece is understandably silent on that score. Is it too much to suggest that the idealism inherent in much of New Left politics cannot be held blameless for the political rout suffered by the movements of the 1960s and 1970s, and that Piccone's criticism of Colletti, far from being a materialist critique of *vulgar* materialism, is idealism pure and simple? In other words, is it possible that the necessary rectifications to either Lucio Colletti's ontology or our current political practice will *not* be accomplished by making them less materialist?

ACKNOWLEDGMENTS. I am grateful to members of the Political Economy Workshop, University of New Hampshire at Durham, for their comments. In particular, I wish to thank Val Dusek for his patience with my persistent questioning.

NOTES

1. This chapter will not delve into the rather arcane debates about whether the development of nature and society is governed by the general laws of a materialist dialectic, or whether it is possible to work out a general logic of a materialist dialectic (Norman and Sayers 1980; Marquit et al. 1982; Sayers 1981–2; Russell 1980–81; Gould 1978). It does seem, however, that efforts to inductively prove the existence of dialectical covering laws on the basis of observations of discontinuous processes, qualitative change, unceasing motion, and so forth, would be of doubtful validity. For once, perhaps, Louis Althusser was right when he characterized such efforts as no more than the practice by philosophers of giving new names to things already discovered by scientists (Althusser 1977: 170). The key issue is not whether discontinuous processes, etc., exist in reality, for no doubt they do. Rather, the question is whether these natural and social processes represent some form of proof that a Marxian ontology should be formulated as merely the materialist analog of the Hegelian.

2. Timpanaro's usage of the term "Western Marxism" is clearly geographic, and does not accord with the standard, more restricted identification of Western Marxism with the so-called Frankfurt school.

3. The perspective of the *intellect* or *understanding* upholds the principle of non-contradiction. Roughly speaking, *intellect* may be said to correspond to that stage of thinking that employs the Aristotelian laws of identity, contradiction, and excluded middle, and sticks "to fixity of characters." By contrast, dialectical thought allows "finite characterizations [to] pass into their opposites"; the highest stage, *positive reason*, "apprehends the unity of terms in their opposition—the affirmative" (Hegel 1978: 113–19).

4. A comprehensive critique of Kieve's article would also question (a) his interpretation of Hegel as a realist on the grounds that the latter "granted an independent, objective existence to *ideas* outside the subjective mind of the individual thinker" (Kieve 1983: 39–40, emphasis added); (b) his perplexing claim that Marx at the same time believed "that an objective external world exists independently of the human mind" *and* rejected "the naive dichotomy" between the knowing subject and the known object (Kieve 1983: 53); and (c) his notion that Marx "begins with the concrete" and proceeds to derive "abstract forms" (Kieve 1983: 61).

5. This is something the structuralists and Althusserians, for all the drawbacks of their positions, clearly recognize.

6. Colletti responds by asserting that Timpanaro's work displays an "ingenuous naturalism" (Colletti 1978: 327). In my opinion, this is unfair, since in numerous places Timpanaro specifically seeks to elaborate the specificity and irreducibility of the "social aspect," the historical development of society, and the class struggle (Timpanaro 1980: 11, 16, 40, 43, 82).

7. A good critical survey of the issue can be found in McLennan 1981: 30–38.

8. This is for a very good reason. If social science is accorded a status distinct from natural science, then the respective knowledges produced are qualitatively different. Colletti argues that where this opinion holds, social science tends "to occupy the same relationship towards [natural science] as philosophy used to occupy towards science as such." This position was adopted by the critical theorists, according to Colletti, with the result that social science became the bearer of "true" (or at least superior) knowledge, leaving to natural science only the possibility of developing a pseudo-knowledge (Colletti 1978: 338–39).

REFERENCES

Althusser, Louis. 1976. *Essays in Self-Criticism*. London: New Left Books.

———. 1977. *For Marx*. London: New Left Books.

Colletti, Lucio. 1973. The Theory of the Crash. In, *Towards a New Marxism*, Bart Grahl and Paul Piccone (eds.) St. Louis: Telos Press.

———. 1974. *From Rousseau to Lenin*. New York: Monthly Review Press (first published in 1969).

———. 1975. Marxism and the Dialectic. *New Left Review* no. 93.

———. 1978. Political and Philosophical Interview. In, *Western Marxism: A Critical Reader*, Editors, *New Left Review*. London: Verso.

———. 1980. *Marxism and Hegel*. London: Verso (first published in 1969).

Editors, *New Left Review*. 1970. Introduction to Della Volpe. *New Left Review* no. 59.

Gould, Stephen Jay. 1978. The Episodic Nature of Change Versus the Dogma of Gradualism. Cambridge: Harvard University Dialectics Workshop.

Hegel, Georg Wilhelm Friedrich. 1969. *Science of Logic*. London: Allen & Unwin.
_____ . 1978. *Encyclopaedia*, part I. Oxford: Clarendon Press.
Hillel-Ruben, David. 1975. Materialism and Professor Colletti. *Critique* no. 4.
Horkheimer, Max. 1966. On the Concept of Freedom. *Diogenes* 53.
Kieve, Ronald A. 1983. The Hegelian Inversion: On the Possibility of a Marxist Dialectic. *Science & Society* XLVIII (1).
Lenin, Vladimir I. 1976. *Collected Works* vol. 38. Moscow: Progress Publishers.
Lukacs, Georg. 1938. *The Young Hegel*. Cambridge, Massachusetts: The MIT Press, 1976. (Although written in 1938, this was not published until after the war.)
_____ . 1967. *History and Class Consciousness*. Cambridge, Massachusetts: The MIT Press.
_____ . 1975. *Conversations with Lukacs*. Cambridge, Massachusetts: The MIT Press.
Marquit, E. et al. (eds.). 1982. *Dialectical Contradictions: Contemporary Marxist Discussions*. Minneapolis: Marxist Educational Press.
McLennan, Gregor. 1981. *Marxism and the Methodologies of History*. London: Verso.
Norman, Richard and Sean Sayers. 1980. *Hegel, Marx and Dialectic: A Debate*. Sussex, England: The Harvester Press.
Piccone, Paul. 1972. Dialectic and Materialism in Lukacs. *Telos* no. 11.
_____ . 1981. The Future of Eurocommunism. *Theory and Society* (OS).
Rosdolsky, Roman. 1977. *The Making of Marx's 'Capital'*. London: Pluto Press.
Russell, James. 1980–81. Dialectics and Class Analysis. *Science & Society* XLIV (4).
Sayers, Sean. 1981–82. Contradiction and Dialectic in the Development of Science. *Science & Society* XLV (4).
Therborn, Goran. 1978. The Frankfurt School. In, *Western Marxism: A Critical Reader*, Editors, *New Left Review*. London: Verso.
Timpanaro, Sebastiano. 1980. *On Materialism*. London: Verso.

Chapter 2

Form vs. Content: A Critique of Morishima's Mathematical Marxism

RICHARD W. ENGLAND

For nearly 25 years, Professor Michio Morishima has played an important role in the modern revival of Marxian political economy. Because of his prolific contribution to that revival and because of his professional stature as a mathematical economist, Morishima's interpretation of Marx needs to be inspected carefully and assessed accordingly. This retrospective review focuses on Morishima's later writings on Marx, especially his *Marx's Economics* (1973).[1]

To begin, let us see what Morishima hoped to accomplish in producing still another interpretation of *Capital*. Two of his stated aims hardly seem controversial: "[My] purpose is not to recapitulate his economics but to give it rigorous expression. . . [and] to recognize the greatness of Marx from the viewpoint of modern advanced economic theory" (1973: vii, 5).

Two of his other avowed purposes seem less innocuous, however, even at first glance. Morishima (1973:9) contends that it took

> nearly ninety years of orthodox economists to overcome the initial advantages of Marxian economics in the field of dynamics. Now it is proposed to integrate the growth theories of the two schools into the Marx-von Neumann theory, and a new state of development is about to start.

In addition to explicitly calling for a synthesis of Marxian and orthodox economics on the theoretical plane, Morishima also seems to call for an end to the "disastrous hostilities" that have divided Marxist and orthodox economists for more than a century. (173: 1, 5, 105). Whether such a theoretical and political reconciliation is possible or not is one topic of this review.

How does Morishima go about giving "rigorous expression" to Marx's analytics and attempting a synthesis of classical Marxism and contemporary economic theory? He first tries to identify the intellectual purposes that motivated Marx's theoretical efforts. Stressing the value theory, transformation solution, and reproduction schemes of *Capital*, Morishima concludes that Marx sought "a theory which can describe dynamic movements of the economy, rather than one which can elaborate consumers' preference" (1973: 3). He further contends that trying to demonstrate the necessity of the ultimate breakdown of capitalism is "evidently the essence of Marxism. . . ."[2]

Morishima's reading of *Capital* also uncovered an interest of Marx less historical in character, that is, a desire to distinguish between superficial appearance and underlying reality in the everyday process of reproducing captialism. "In the theory of exchange, Marx's purpose was to recognize the social character of human labour . . . behind the exchange ratios between commodities" (1973: 145). More fundamentally, however, "Marx thought he had successfully removed the mask of capitalism. . . .[The] transformation problem [had] . . .the aim of showing how 'the aggregate exploitation of labour on the part of total social capital' is, in a capitalist economy, obscured by the distortion of prices from values; the other aim [was] . . .to show how living labour can be the sole source of profit" (1973: 85-86).[3]

In attributing intellectual purposes such as these to Marx, Morishima is hardly exceptional. Part of the novelty of his interpretation is the claim that Marx's analytics frequently paralleled or anticipated theoretical efforts by noted *orthodox* economists. For instance, Morishima attributes the simultaneous and independent formulation of general equilibrium analysis to Marx and Leon Walras (1973: 1-2, 105). He also notes a similarity between Marx's reproduction schemes and Leontief's input-output tables (1973: 3, 126, 147) and comments that the reproduction models can serve as "the prototype for the contemporary theory of economic growth," especially that of von Neumann (1973: 8, 164, 167, 178). Finally, Morishima cites Marx's two-department scheme as a pioneering effort in aggregative economics and judges Marx's use of commodity values as aggregators superior to J. M. Keynes' later use of market price-wage ratios for that same purpose (1973: 102-3).

What is one to conclude from these and other such similarities? On the one hand, Morishima concludes that "Marx is still active on the frontier of our science . . . [and that] we all owe the foundation of dynamic general equilibrium theory, the core of economic theory, to Marx" (1973: 3, 8). Despite this apparently complimentary verdict on Marx's analytics, however, Morishima spends a lot of space discussing what he believes are theoretical defects of *Capital*, which become obvious once modern techniques of mathematical economics have been applied to its arguments.[4]

Least serious of all is the failure of Marx to make certain hidden, albeit innocuous, assumptions explicit. For instance, Morishima shows that assuming the positiveness of commodity values, as Marx did, implies certain premises about the level of technological development. In particular, assuming a particular set of technical conditions are met, values are unique and positive if and only if every capital-good industry can produce a net output of its product and at least one capital-good industry requires some current labor input (1973: 2).

More important is Morishima's verification of the formal equivalence of certain concepts that Marx used interchangeably without proof of their equivalence. Morishima detects, for instance, two alternative and possibly inconsistent definitions of commodity values. According to the first, the "amount of labour embodied in one unit of [a] commodity . . . is defined as the sum of the amount of direct labour and the amount of labour embodied in other factors of production used directly in producing a unit of [that] commodity. . . ." According to the second definition, the "value of a commodity is the total amount of labour necessary to produce a unit of that commodity with the method of production prevailing in that society" (1973: 13-15). On inspection, Morishima finds that the two value concepts are identical and hence that Marx's intuition was correct.[5]

Another theoretical limitation of *Capital*, in Morishima's estimation, is Marx's occasional failure to go beyond merely tautological results. In discussing the impact of technical change in relative values, for example, Marx (1967a: 53-54) failed to calculate the impact of changes in the technical coefficients of production of one commodity on the absolute values of other commodities and thus had to resort to ceteris paribus assumptions about the values of those commodities when discussing changes in relative values. Morishima has calculated these effects of technical change in one industry on the values of commodities produced in other industries and thereby arrives at more substantive propositions about relative values (1973: 29-33).

Up to this point, Morishima's criticisms make Marx's analytics more explicit and more substantive and hence tend to strengthen Marxian political economy vis à vis its orthodox critics. But a major theme of Morishima's interpretation of Marx is that many propositions in *Capital* frequently hinge on restrictive empirical assumptions, especially about the character of technology and technical change. This raises the possibility that some of Marx's theoretical results cannot be generalized once those restrictive assumptions are relaxed.

One example is Marx's handling of the impact of technical change on the organic composition of capital. Marx claims in volume I (1967a: 612) that "there is a strict correlation [between] . . . the value-composition of capital . . . [and] its technical composition. . . ." Although Morishima is perhaps too severe in his interpretation of what Marx meant by "a strict correlation," he demonstrates that the precise relation between changes in the physical composition and value composition of capital is hardly simple:

> [Technological] improvement [in some industry] causes a change in the technical composition of capital [in that industry]. But it [also] brings about changes in the values [of commodities] . . . as well . . . so that the value-composition of capital [in that industry] reflects not only the change in [its own] technical composition but also the induced change in the value structure. (1973: 35)

Hence, Morishima charges that Marx implicitly assumed technical change to be "neutral," in the specific sense that relative values of commodities remained unaltered by technical improvements.[6]

Another example of a restrictive technological assumption involves the algorithm for transforming values into prices, which Marx devised in volume III of *Capital*. Although some authors have argued that an assumption of equal organic composition of capitals among industries is required for Marx's transformation method to be correct, Morishima shows (1973: ch. 7) that such an assumption, though sufficient for its accuracy, is not necessary. In fact,

> the condition of identical value-composition of capital may be weakened into . . . the assumption of linearly dependent industries. . . . [Though] still restrictive, it is necessary and sufficient for the correctness of Marx's algorithm. (1973: 77-79).[7]

If this technical assumption does not hold, then Marx's transformation method yields at best an approximate solution unless an iterative process of recomputations is pursued (1973: 77).[8]

Thus, Morishima's writings on Marx have, in effect, challenged Marxian political economists to show that *Capital's* propositions can be generalized in those instances where Marx's original arguments relied on numerical examples or other restrictive premises. During the past decade or so, a number of Marxists have taken up the challenge. What Morishima terms the "fundamental Marxian theorem" (1973: 53), namely, that "the exploitation of labourers by capitalists is necessary and sufficient for the existence of a price-wage set yielding positive profits," has, for instance, been extended by several authors. In one extension, Bowles and Gintis (1977) postulate a variety of distinct labor strata rather than homogeneous, abstract labor and find that the profit rate is positive only if the labor of one or more strata is exploited. In a complementary vein, Roemer (1978) has demonstrated in his Marxian theory of discrimination that equally productive labor divided into strata that are exploited at differential rates poses no problem for the fundamental Marxian theorem.

Still another critical theme of Morishima is that *Capital* is flawed by numerous confusions between physical and price categories, on the one hand, and value categories, on the other. In Morishima's words, "[Marx] often confused an account in terms of values with the corresponding account in terms of price, in spite of the obvious fact that price and value are dimensionally different" (1973: 73). Although the bibliographic evidence offered to support this charge is a bit sparse, Morishima does discuss one important case where Marx confused price and value categories, namely, his theory of investment behavior.

As Morishima points out, "the rate of accumulation, i.e. the ratio of the value of investment to the total surplus value, is one of the central concepts of the theory [of extended reproduction]. It is defined in terms of value and is . . . given exogenously" (173: 145). "This is, however, a very unrealistic assumption because . . . no capitalist makes a decision about accumulation in terms of the surplus value measured in labour-time. . . . Thus capitalists can at best decide a proportion of the profit . . . which is re-invested" (1973: 140).[9] Morishima proposes, and rightly so, that Marxian accumulation models ought to assume a constant, exogenous propensity to invest profits and then permit the rate of accumulation in value terms to be determined endogenously.[10]

All of these criticisms of Marx discussed so far are hardly devastating. Whether the defect is a hidden assumption, special case, or conceptual confusion, Morishima himself demonstrates that a simple correction or generalization of Marx's original presentation will often do. But, having said this, Morishima then turns to what he believes is a fatal flaw in *Capital*—an alleged incompatibility between the labor theory of value and the relaxation of certain key assumptions of Marxian analysis.

Morishima's own proofs of various Marxian theorems—the necessity of exploitation under capitalism and the inevitability of eventual capitalist breakdown, for instance—are often based on a stylized Marxian model embodying a particular set of assumptions. These six premises are that (1) no industry produces joint outputs; (2) each commodity has a single method of production; (3) abstract, homogeneous labor is the only nonproduced input to production; (4) constant capital comes only in the circulating, and not the fixed, variety; (5) all commodities have the same time period of production; and (6) production is of the point-input-point-output type.

Morishima contends that once one tries to generalize Marx's analysis by introducing labor heterogeneity, alternative techniques of production, and joint products, "the labour theory of value is seen to get into difficulties. This means that . . . we cannot admit Marx [to the ranks of rigorous theorists] unless he is prepared to abandon the labour theory of value" (1973: 8).

In one respect at least, however, Morishima's formal indictment of the labor theory is clearly faulty. Two of his own requirements for an acceptable

Marxian value theory, in addition to requiring that values be (1) non-negative and (2) uniquely determined, are (3) that values be independent from market phenomena and (4) that a uniform rate of exploitation prevail once values have been determined by technical data (1973: 181).[11] These latter two criteria, he claims, are inconsistent with one another once one entertains labor heterogeneity within the Marxian framework. The reason is that there can be a single rate of exploitation common to all labor skills if and only if the conversion ratio used to convert hours of any particular labor skill to hours of unskilled, simple labor is equal to the real wage ratio between that skill and unskilled labor. If that were so, however, various categories of skilled labor could not be reduced to homogeneous, abstract labor without reference to labor market phenomena. Thus, a uniform rate of exploitation is inconsistent with independence of values from superficial market phenomena (1973: 190-93).

But this whole argument hinges on the premise that a uniform rate of exploitation is *essential* to Marx's value theory. Morishima claims that it is:

> [As] soon as the heterogeneity of labour is allowed for, the theory of value is seen to conflict with Marx's law of the equalization of the rate of exploitation through society. . . . This is a serious dilemma from the point of view of Marxian economists, because . . . different classes [sic] of workers obviously are not compatible with Marx's view of the polarization of society into two classes, capitalists and workers. (1973: 180-81)

Certainly, contemporary Marxists do not argue that the labor market is so "perfectly competitive" that labor migration among industries and occupations will equalize rates of exploitation.[12]

A careful reading of *Capital* reveals that even Marx himself made no such assumption:

> Such a general rate of surplus-value—viewed as a tendency, like all other economic laws—has been assumed by us for the sake of theoretical simplification. But in reality it is an actual premise of the capitalist mode of production, although it is *more or less obstructed by practical frictions* . . . such as the settlement laws for farm-labourers in Britain. (1967: 175; emphasis added)

Thus, labor heterogeneity seems at first glance to pose a grave threat to Marxian value theory, but that threat turns out to be an empty one. There is no contradiction whatsoever between the view that capitalist society is divided into a working class and an exploiting class and a recognition that there are numerous objective and subjective differences among workers (e.g., the rates at which they are exploited).

This error by Morishima is, I believe, symptomatic of a number of methodological problems with his approach to Marx's thought in particular and social theory in general. A number of these problems stem from his identification of theoretical rigor with the use of sophisticated mathematical techniques to analyze social relations. In his critique of *Capital*, for instance, Morishima points repeatedly to Marx's lack of formal mathematical training as the explanation for its presumed theoretical defects. According to the author,

> If Marx had been more mathematical . . . he could have developed the whole of the von Neumann model independently and a huge short cut might have been made in the history of economic theory. (1973: 167)[13]

Thus, although Morishima conceives of Marx as a pioneering mathematical economist, he sees the intellectual bequest of Marx as a melange of intuitive conjectures and unresolved theoretical problems, a research agenda left unanswered because of inadequate mathematical skills.[14]

Morishima's admiration, it turns out, is actually reserved for John von Neumann, one of the leading mathematical economists of this century. In the author's estimation, von Neumann's model of general equilibrium is "the most satisfactory dynamic economic theory we are now provided with . . . [and] dynamic general equilibrium theory [is] . . . the core of economic theory" (1973: 8).[15] Marx's stature as a social theorist, then, is measured by the extent to which he managed to anticipate the mathematical economics of von Neumann.

There are a number of serious methodological consequences of this preoccupation with mathematical technique on the part of Morishima. First, it leads him to create a mythical "Marx the mathematical economist" whose ideas are independent from the historical, philosophical, sociological, and political aspects of Marx's thought.[16] This tendency to reduce Marx to a mathematical economist instead of addressing his political economy as a whole helps to explain Morishima's utter neglect of the Marxian literature on social classes in capitalist society and hence his simplistic notion of the proletariat as a group of labor input-wage income recipients exploited at a uniform rate.

His preoccupation with mathematical technique leads Morishima, in turn, towards a formalistic interpretation of Marx. In comparing Marx to Walras, for example, he claims that there is a "substantial identity" between Marx's reproduction models and the Walrasian models of general equilibrium (1973: 105). These two theoretical systems are nearly identical in Morishima's mind for the apparent reason that both are sets of interdependent economic relationships, which can be represented by simultaneous equation systems. The major difference between the two, in Morishima's estimation, is that Marx aggregated his microrelations to obtain a two-sector macroeconomic model:

Walrasian microscopic equilibrium theory is rather sterile, since it is too general and complicated to be able to derive definite conclusions. . . . Marx [on the other hand] . . . wanted to derive some definite laws of movement for capitalist society and therefore needed a method of aggregation. . . . (1973: 2)

The problem with this conception of Marx and Walras is that it is purely formalistic and does not address the theoretical *content* of their respective systems of thought. As Maurice Dobb (1973: 203) pointed out, however,

[Despite his] preoccupation with mathematical formalism, . . . [Walras] was quite well aware that the economic interpretation and causal implications of his system were . . . the derivation of product-prices from consumers' wants and of the value of the services of capital-goods and factors from their productive use in the creation of consumers' goods.

Marx, on the other hand, in the course of

revealing the *essence* behind the phenomenal *appearance* of market relations . . . was led progressively into the examination of production and of production relations . . . and of the social and class roots of a society dominated by exploitation and the pursuit of surplus value. (Dobb 1970: 6)

What a fundamental *difference* in content between two conceptual frameworks that supposedly have such an affinity for one another![17]

Morishima's preoccupation with mathematical technique is also reflected in his tendency to emphasize equilibrium quantities within the existing set of social relations of production and to ignore how qualitative developments in those social relations come about. That is, because of his exaggerated concern with the calculation of static and balanced growth equilibria in his stylized Marxian model, Morishima nearly forgets what Marx had to say about the historical process of capitalist development (e.g., the centralization and concentration of capitals, the geographic extension of the capitalist mode of production into new regions of the world, and so on).

At one point in *Marx's Economics*, it appears as though Morishima is sensitive to the historical orientation of Marx's political economy, since he does discuss Marx's theory of capitalist breakdown at some length (1973: ch. 11, 160-63). However, this appearance turns out to be mostly illusory, since Morishima manages to reduce the complex issue of the historical transition from capitalism to socialism to a mechanistic "breakdown model" in which, under certain technological assumptions, a periodically higher unemployment rate leads to "the expropriation of a few usurpers by the mass of the people" (Marx 1967a: 764). He next argues that under alternative, equally plausible technical assumptions, this periodic increase in the reserve army need not occur and then asks, "Can technological development play the role of the saviour of the regime?" (1973: 141).

Morishima's grasp of the Marxian approach to history is more sophisticated than this breakdown parody might suggest, however. In an important article coauthored with George Catephores (1975), Morishima and his colleague advance a provocative thesis about Marx's methodology when they deny that Marx interpreted the transformation from values into prices as an historical process. Friedrich Engels and several recent commentators on Marx have claimed that commodities actually did exchange in proportion to their labor values during a precapitalist epoch of "simple commodity production."[18]

Morishima and Catephores argue quite persuasively that Marx did not intend to describe an actual mode of production predating capitalism, but rather, formulated the notion of simple commodity production in order to make a *hypothetical* comparison between an ideal exchange economy in which laborers own the means of production they require and the actual capitalist mode in which capitalists appropriate all means of production. In other words, Morishima interprets Marx's theorems involving simple commodity production as logical exercises in institutional comparative statics, not as propositions about the actual course of historical evolution.[19]

Whether Marx intended any particular prediction to be an historical forecast or a static comparison of hypothetical situations is certainly open to debate and textual analysis. However, Morishima's reduction of Marxian thought to a sort of "economics" and his reliance on the balanced growth equilibrium method to model social change render him incapable of analyzing the variety of cultural, political, technical, and economic contradictions within the social relations of capitalist society that propel its historical development.[20]

Morishima's disregard for historical specificity is typified by his assertion (1974c: 71) that "Marx regards . . . B [i.e., the subsistence-consumption vector of wage goods per day] as biologically given. . . ." In fact, Marx argued that the subsistence real wage of a worker is "the product of historical developments. . . . In contradistinction therefore to the case of other commodities, there enters into the determination of the value of labour-power a historical and moral element" (1967I: 171). Morishima would do well to reread Paul Sweezy:

> For Marx, social reality is not so much a specified set of relations. . . . It is rather the process of change inherent in a specified set of relations. . . . The process of social change, however, is not purely mechanical; it is rather the product of human action, but action which is definitely limited by the kind of society in which it has its roots. (1968: 20-21)[21]

Despite these methodological flaws in Morishima's approach to political economy, one must still come to grips with his critique of Marx's labor theory of value. In doing so, one must recall the theoretical purpose of value concepts in the Marxian schema. At one point, Morishima asserts that Marx's "labour theory of value has two functions: (i) to explain the equilibrium prices . . . of commodities, around which actual prices fluctuate over time, and (ii) to provide aggregators, or weights of aggregation, in terms of which a large number of industries are aggregated into a small number of 'departments'" (1973:10). At another point, he attributes a somewhat different pair of purposes to Marx. In addition to providing weights of aggregation, the "other purpose of Marx's theory of value is to provide a theoretical foundation for his two-class view of the capitalist society" (1973: 181).[22]

Having attributed these three motives to Marx, Morishima then argues that the labor theory of value is either unable or unnecessary to serve those purposes. Although he assigns to the labor theory of value "a most important part in Marx's economics, since it provides a system of [aggregative] constants," Morishima finds that the ratios of prices of production to the money wage rate "can also play a role in the aggregation problem equivalent to that of values" (1973: 3, 103). Hence, although values might be used as aggregative weights, they are unnecessary for that purpose.

What about the usefulness of values in explaining the equilibrium prices of commodities? Apart from the common criticism that Marx's original solution of the transformation problem was defective, Morishima argues that, once joint products and alternative methods of production are admitted into the Marxian framework, there is no guarantee that the values calculated from technical coefficients of production will be nonnegative and unique (1973: 181-90). Hence, two of his four criteria for the adequacy of the labor theory of value are violated, and there apparently is little point to even attempting to transform values into equilibrium prices. According to Morishima, then, the value concepts of Marx are simply not an adequate foundation upon which to construct a "rigorous general theory" of capitalism (1973: 4, 8, 194).

In order to get around these logical problems posed by joint products (such as used durable capital goods) and their alternative techniques, Morishima has proposed a fundamental revision of Marx's value concept:

> There is an alternate way to formulate the labour theory of value, not as the theory of "actual values" calculating the embodied-labour contents of commodities on the basis of the prevailing production coefficients as Marx did, but as the theory of "optimum values" considering values as shadow prices determined by a linear programming problem that is dual to another linear programming problem for the efficient utilization of labour. (1974a: 615-16)

In other words, the values of commodities are to be redefined as the shadow prices one would compute for those commodities upon solving a linear program that aimed to minimize total employment of labor for a given net output vector. The set of production methods implied by this linear programming solution would not, in general, be the same as those actually adopted by profit-seeking capitalists. Hence, Morishima's revised commodity values are *optimal* from the perspective of labor utilization but also *hypothetical* from the viewpoint of actual capitalist practice.

Morishima himself is apparently pleased with this reformulation, since it has enabled him to introduce durable capital goods into Marxian analysis and to generalize the fundamental theorem that labor exploitation is the origin of capitalist profit and expansion (1947a: sec. 2). However, there is good reason to be skeptical about Morishima's analytic innovation—the prime reason being that he has misread the theoretical purpose of Marx's original value categories.

Contrary to Morishima's interpretation, Marx was not primarily concerned with explaining equilibrium prices or finding weights of aggregation as he went about formulating his value theory. Rather, Marx believed that scientific understanding of any mode of production requires a detailed analysis of its particular social relations of production and that the very theoretical categories one used to undertake such an analysis must be specific to the mode of production under consideration. As Anwar Shaikh has put it, there are

> two crucial elements of the Marxist approach to history. First, that the specific manner in which laborers and means of production are united, and the specific way in which unpaid surplus-labor is extracted from the direct producers, form the 'hidden basis of the entire social structure.' Secondly, that concepts adequate to the analysis of any specific historical epoch, including that of capitalism, must necessarily be derived from these aspects of its social practice. (1974: 5)[23]

Shaikh continues as follows:

> *Capital* is Marx's application of this approach to the analysis of capitalism, and it should be clear . . . why he begins with an analysis of commodity production (the specific manner in which laborers and means of production are combined under capitalism) and then proceeds to surplus-value (the specific form which the extraction of surplus-labor takes under capitalism). (1974: 5)

That is, value categories were the analytical means whereby Marx incorporated the social relations of captialist production into his theory of capitalist development.[24]

Hence, discarding Marx's value concepts (which are rooted in the actual practice of capitalist society) and replacing them with a hypothetical concept of "optimum value" risks blurring his conception of the social relations specific to capitalism. That loss of theoretical focus, in turn, threatens to reduce political economy to a *natural* science (as neoclassical economics already does) in which technological coefficients and subjective preferences inexplicably thrown up by nature are seen as the determining factors in society.[25]

A preferable agenda for those who think political economy should remain a *social* science is the development of a theoretical framework that can produce quantitative predictions about observable social phenomena and simultaneously explain how those phenomena are rooted in historically specific social conditions. Although Marx's *Capital* certainly suffers from errors of commission and omission, it still seems the most promising point of departure for those who are seeking these twin goals.

NOTES

1. For some initial reactions to this book, see the reviews by Nell (1973) and von Weizsacker (1973). For an example of Morishima's earlier work on Marx, see Morishima and Seton (1961).

2. Despite the supposedly essential place in *Capital*, Morishima admits that the breakdown theory was "only briefly discussed by Marx himself" (1973: 4, 132).

3. In a later paper, Morishima asserted that the "central theme" of *Capital* is Marx's hypothesis that the viability and expansion of capitalism depends upon exploitation of labor (1974a: 614). To his credit, Morishima defends Marx repeatedly against the erroneous charge that he tried to demonstrate the equality or proportionality of prices and values in capitalist society (1973: 36, 39, 56-57, 59, 145).

4. The limited extent of Morishima's admiration for Marx is also revealed by this reply to an orthodox critic of *Marx's Economics:* "Since I reserved criticism until the final chapter, the earlier 13 chapters may have given an exaggerated impression of admiration for Marx. . . . My earlier chapters *interpret* Marx . . . [but] my *verdict* is reserved for Chapter 14" (1974b: 388).

5. Morishima sees the theoretical significance of this equivalence as follows: "The identity between the two definitions of value . . . enables us to avoid criticisms . . . that values, unlike prices, are not observable [and hence are] . . . metaphysical concepts. . . . It is clear from the second definition . . . that values are . . . the employment multipliers discussed by Kahn and . . . Keynes, which can be calculated from Leontief's input-output table" (1973: 18-19).

6. For other discussion of Marx's conception of technical change, see Robinson (1978) and Laibman (1976).

7. In a later paper, Morishima argues (1974a: 630-31) that a still more general, but still restrictive, assumption about the structure of input-output coefficients is necessary and sufficient for the correctness of Marx's transformation method.

8. This iterative method was devised simultaneously by Anwar Shaikh (1977).

9. Morishima has stated this point more generally: "In Marx's economics, value calculation plays a role that is entirely different from the one which price calculation does. Decision [sic] of individuals and firms are all made in terms of price calculation, while value calculation gives a technocratic assessment of labor requirement for production" (1974c: 71).

10. In one such model, he finds that, in general, the rate of accumulation will not only differ from the capitalists' fixed propensity to save but will also change from period to period (1973: 152).

11. In a more recent exchange with Ian Steedman, Morishima provided an explanation for the first critierion: "As we all know, the value of a commodity is defined as the total amount of labour power expended directly or indirectly for its production. It should be non-negative. . . . Whatever can be meant by a negative amount of labour?" (1976: 600).

12. For two examples of Marxian analyses based on the premise of labor market segmentation, see Bowles and Gintis (1977) and Roemer (1978). For empirical evidence of the existence of labor market segmentation, see Dickens and Lang (1985).

13. For a somewhat more charitable assessment of Marx's mathematical skills, see Smolinski (1973).

14. See Morishima (1973: 1, 57, 163) and Morishima (1974a: 611-15).

15. Von Neumann's 1932 paper, which went unpublished until the end of World War II, was a substantial accomplishment both because of its original theorems in pure mathematics and also because of its fundamental revisions of orthodox economic theory (e.g., its discarding of marginal utility theory and its solution of various problems in capital theory by treating durable capital goods as joint products of production processes along with their commodity outputs). See von Neumann (1945-46).

16. The reader is forewarned when Morishima says: "[My] approach to Marx is somewhat different from the so-called Marxian economists. . . . We do not discuss Marx in relation to his predecessors . . . and pay no attention to the development of Marxian economics after Marx. We neglect even his works other than the three volumes of Capital, and confine ourselves to assessing . . . his contributions in that book . . . ." (1973: 5). Not surprisingly, the only work of Marx other than Capital cited by Morishima in Marx's Economics is his Matiematitzieskie Rukopisi, a compilation of Marx's mathematical notebooks published in Moscow in 1968.

17. Two other examples of Morishima's formalistic neglect of substantive differences among social theorists are his comparisons of Marx to Leontief and to Hicks. In his judgment, "Marx's theory of reproduction is very similar to Leontief's input-output analysis (1973: 3). This assessment is highly misleading, however, since Leontief's concept of reproduction is limited to an engineering notion of replacement of physical inputs consumed in production, whereas Marx's far richer conception emphasized reproduction of the social relations of production as well. Morishima's silliest comparison (1973: 33-34) is between John Hicks' three propositions about the effect of autonomous changes in consumers' preferences on equilibrium prices and three Marxian propositions about the impact of autonomous changes in technical coefficients on commodity values. The two sets of propositions are mathematically similar, but their content and the models of capitalist society from which they were derived are fundamentally different.

18. Simple commodity production is a social system in which producers own their own means of production (thereby eliminating any compulsion to sell their own labor services) and exchange the products of their labor.

19. A less convincing comparative static interpretation of Capital is Morishima's claim (1973: 155) that Marx's prediction of a falling tendency of the rate of profit was an exercise in comparative balanced growth equilibria under alternate technical assumptions rather than a historical forecast. In any event, Samuelson has pointed out that Morishima's theorem is incorrect, a criticism accepted by its author. See Samuelson (1974: 68).

20. Morishima seems aware that there is a scientific need to analyze the historical evolution of social systems but settles for asserting that Marx was unsuccessful in his attempts to construct such a social science. See Morishima and Catephores (1975: 326-27).

21. For more on the mechanical conception of society that underlies orthodox theory, see Dobb (1973: 168, 173) and Georgescu-Roegen (1971: 1-3).

22. Attributing the desire for a method of aggregation to Marx is actually questionable. Morishima himself admits that Marx was either unclear about or unaware of the usefulness of values as aggregators (1973: 10, 87). It is hard to see, then, how Marx's extensive research into

value theory could have been motivated by a quest for a nondistorting method of aggregation. Morishima handles this objection by predicting that "Marx would have elaborated his value theory as an aggregation theory if he had had a chance to read Keynes' *General Theory*" (1973: 10, 87). This points up another major flaw in Morishima's account of Marx, which is revealed when one reads it as a history of economic thought. Morishima repeatedly claims that Marx would have embraced a particular theoretical position held by some orthodox economist if only he had lived to read that person's work or if only he had received adequate mathematical training to understand it. He predicts, for example, that "Marx would have accepted the marginal utility theory of consumers' demands if it had become known to him." We are offered two reasons for believing this prediction. First, he "knew differential and integral calculus. But it is also true . . . that Marx began his theory of value by characterizing commodities as 'something two-fold, both objects of utility and, at the same time, depositories of value'" (1973: 40). The first reason is irrelevant. (Just because one understands the principle of the transistor, for instance, one does not necessarily formulate an electronic theory of society.) The second reason is unconvincing. Surely Marx was aware that different workers spend their wages on different market baskets of wage goods. It does not follow, however, that he viewed that fact as an *essential feature* of capitalist society requiring a central place in his theorizing. In fact, he was mainly concerned with understanding how it was possible for capitalists and workers to meet as equals exchanging equivalents in the marketplace and yet have workers produce surplus value for their employers. See his *Grund-risse* (1973: 281-318, 321-26, 333-41). To clinch the issue of Marx's potential acceptance of marginal utility theory, Smolinski reports that Marx *was* aware of Jevon's work (1973: 1193).

23. A revised version of Shaikh's paper appears in Schwartz (1977).

24. On the centrality of the social relations of production to Marx's analysis, see Marx (1970: 19-21).

25. This is precisely the path Morishima follows in *Marx's Economics* as he focuses on technological factors throughout and tries to introduce subjective utility into his Marxian model in chapter 4.

REFERENCES

Bowles, Samuel and Herbert Gintis. 1977. The Marxian Theory of Value and Hetero-geneous Labour: A Critique and Reformulation. *Cambridge Journal of Economics* 1: 173-92.

Dickens, William T. and Kevin Lang. 1985. A Test of Dual Labor Market Theory. *American Economic Review* September: 792-805.

Dobb, Maurice. 1970. Introduction. In, *A Contribution to the Critique of Political Economy*, Karl Marx. New York: International Publishers.

———. 1973. *Theories of Value and Distribution Since Adam Smith: Ideology and Economic Theory*. London and New York: Cambridge University Press.

Georgescu-Roegen, Nicholas. 1971. *The Entropy Law and the Economic Process*. Cambridge, Massachusetts: Harvard University Press.

Laibman, David. 1976. "The Marxian Labor-Saving Bias: A Formaliza-tion. *Quarterly Review of Economics and Business* Autumn: 25-44.

Marx, Karl. 1967a. *Capital*, vol. I. New York: International Publishers.

———. 1967b. *Capital*, vol. III. New York: International Publishers.

———. 1970. *A Contribution to the Critique of Political Economy*. New York: International Publishers.

———. 1973. *Grundrisse*. New York: Vintage.

Morishima, Michio. 1973. *Marx's Economics: A Dual Theory of Value and Growth*. New York and London: Cambridge University Press.

———. 1974a. Marx in the Light of Modern Economic Theory. *Econometrica* July: 611-32.

———. 1974b. Marx's Economics: A Comment on C. C. von Weizsacker's Article. *Economic Journal* June: 387-91.

———. 1974c. The Fundamental Marxian Theorem: A Reply to Samuelson. *Journal of Economic Literature* March: 71-74.

———. 1976. Positive Profits with Negative Surplus Value—A Comment. *Economic Journal* September: 599-603.

Morishima, Michio and George Catephores. 1975. Is there an 'Historical Transformation Problem'? *Economic Journal* June: 309-328.

Morishima, Michio and F. Seton. 1961. Aggregation in Leontief Matrices and the Labour Theory of Value. *Econometrica* April: 203-20.

Nell, Edward J. 1973. Review of *Marx's Economics*. *Journal of Economic Literature* December: 1369-371.

Robinson, Joan. 1978. The Organic Composition of Capital. *Kyklos* vol. 31: 5-19.

Roemer, John. 1978. Differentially Exploited Labor: A Marxian Theory of Discrimination. *Review of Radical Political Economics* Summer: 43-53.

Samuelson, Paul. 1974. Insight and Detour into the Theory of Exploitation: A Reply to Baumol. *Journal of Economic Literature* March: 62-70.

Schwartz, Jesse (ed.). 1977. *The Subtle Anatomy of Capitalism*. Santa Monica, California: Goodyear Publishing.

Shaikh, Anwar. 1974. Marx's Theory of Value and the So-Called 'Transformation Problem'. New York: Unpublished paper, New School for Social Research.

———. 1977. Marx's Theory of Value and the 'Transformation Problem'. In, *The Subtle Anatomy of Capitalism*, Jesse Schwartz (ed.). Santa Monica, California: Goodyear Publishing.

Smolinski, Leon. 1973. Karl Marx and Mathematical Economics. *Journal of Political Economy* September-October: 1189-204.

Sweezy, Paul. 1968. *The Theory of Capitalist Development*. New York: Monthly Review Press.

von Neumann, John. 1945-46. A Model of General Economic Equilibrium. *Review of Economic Studies* 13 (1): 1-8.

von Weizsacker, C. C. 1973. Morishima on Marx. *Economic Journal* December: 1245-254.

PART 2
Precapitalist Modes of Production

Chapter 3

Wars Without End: Reproduction of Class Relations Through Predatory Accumulation in Precolonial Bagirmi

STEPHEN P. REYNA

Bagirmi was an eastern, central Sudanic state.[1] Once I asked an aged man what it had been like in Bagirmi before the French came. I was fishing for a denunciation of French oppression. However, the response came back: "we slept with our sandals on." Puzzled, I enquired why, and was informed that there had been a great deal of war before the *nassara* (whitefolk) came. In fact, the gentleman was confirming what commentators had been reporting concerning Bagirmi for 150 years, that the state warred frequently and pugnaciously.[2] Bagirmi was, furthermore, no exception in this regard, for as Urvoy (1949: 7) has noted, the precolonial history of other Sudanic states was one of "kings and battles," which provokes the question: why?

This essay attempts to answer that question. It argues that Bagirmi warfare was part of a process, termed predatory accumulation, reproducing production relations in a tributary mode of production (MP). It further argues that predatory accumulation explained, at least partially, why there was little "development" in regions with such reproductive processes, and that the existence of this process renders the notion of an African MP problematic [Coquery-Vidrovitch 1977].

BEYOND AHOLISTIC HOLISM

Review of the ethnological literature concerning Sudanic states reveals few attempts to explain precolonial warefare.[3] Perhaps this is in part due to the fact that classic accounts of the Sudanic state, such as M. G. Smith's *Government in Zazzau* took a very narrow view of their analytic chores. Smith justified this narrowness on the ground that if government were studied in "isolation" it would achieve the "major advantage" of "a development sequence of the simplest kind," even though he knew government was "interrelated" with other societal structures [1960: 295–96]. This was an aholistic holism—that is, a refusal, in a discipline that defines itself as holistic, to analyze relations between phenomena, even when they are known to exist. Thus, even though war was frequent and important in Zazzau, it could go unanalyzed because it apparently exhibited both political and economic aspects (1960: 96) and was thus neither purely (governmental) fish nor (economic) fowl.

My approach is a structural, Marxist holism influenced by M. Godelier's (1972a) notions of production relations and contradiction, and E. Wolf's (1982) and S. Amin's (1973) formulations of tributary MPs. It starts from the position that approaches, like Smith's, which study structures in isolation, are much like a physiologist studying the heart while ignoring the rest of the circulatory system. I am most interested in the relationship between domestic and state structures. One of the distinguishing characteristics of structural Marxism, as Rey has observed (1973: 103), is an interest in the reproduction of MPs. This is the principal concern of the present analysis. After a few words to provide Bagirmi with a geographic and ethnographic background,[4] I first show that late nineteenth century, precolonial Bagirmi possessed a tributary MP that linked the state to domestic structures both inside and outside its territory. I then argue that predatory accumulation reproduced the class relations in this MP through frequent recourse to warfare. Finally, I explore the implications of predatory accumulation for precolonial underdevelopment in the central Sudan and for the African MP.

Bagirmi is one of the least known societies in the eastern, central Sudan. This area roughly corresponds to the 1,300,000 square kilometers of the present Republic of Chad. The region is divided into bioclimatic bands running from east to west and moving from moister to drier environments from north to south. Chad is hydrologically dominated by the Shari and Logone rivers, which arise in the Central African Republic and Camerouns and which flow in a northerly direction into Lake Chad. It is a largely desert or arid savanna environment, with little precipitation, which is capriciously distributed in space and time.[5]

Just as there was an east-west banding of bioclimatic zones, so there was a rough east-west banding of social formations. In the north in the desert were Muslim camel pastoralists (the Teda and Daza). Immediately south of the desert in sahelian and sudanic zones were a string of states (the Bornu, Kotoko, Bagirmi, Wadai), each composed of different ethnic groups specializing in different economic activities. South of the states in the woodland bioclimatic zone were non-Muslim, tribal or chiefdomship level peoples (the Sara, Tupuri, Massa) whose subsistence depended upon cereal production.[6]

Bagirmi was located in the sudanic portion of the Shari-Logone river system. The state appears to have differentiated early in the sixteenth century. At the end of the nineteenth century it occupied a territory of about 75,000 square kilometers that was populated by perhaps 150,000 inhabitants (Devallee 1925: 10). Members of the Barma ethnic group have always dominated its offices.

Bagirmi was multiethnic. Arabs and Fulani, who by the nineteenth century were the majority of the population, practiced semisedentary, cattle pastoralism. The Barma integrated pluvial and flood recession sorghum and millet production with fishing and tended to reside in walled towns along the Shari and Bahr Erguig rivers. Towns were surrounded by smaller farming hamlets and Arab and Fulani pastoral camps. I term the complex of hamlets and camps surrounding walled towns a local community. Such communities shared different facets of a common habitat and tended to have long histories of common political and economic ties.

Bagirmi participated in a regional trading network that involved all three of the major social formations in the eastern, central Sudan. Its role in this network remains to be described; however, it was "an important center . . .of commerce in the sahel and savanna regions east of Borno . . ." (Cordell 1980: 72) even prior to the nineteenth century. In that century it acquired products (largely slaves) from southern acephalous populations, which, with the assistance of camel pastoralists (Chapelle 1957: 372), were traded in "desert-side" or circum-Mediterranean markets.[7] These trading networks excited theoretical appetites. Coquery-Vidrovitch, for example, believed their existence indicated that there was a distinct, African MP based ". . . upon the combination of a patriarchal-communal economy and the exclusive ascendancy of one group over long-distance trade" (1977: 85). Clearly, commerce was important in the eastern, central Sudan. However, its study in the absence of consideration of its relationship to the productive systems that it served is another aholistic holism—one that ignores production/circulation interactions.[8] This analysis explores the reproduction of class relations that permitted certain Bagirmi to participate in nineteenth century commerce.

CLASS AND CONTRADICTION IN A
TRIBUTARY MODE OF PRODUCTION

The notion of a tributary MP was formulated by Samir Amin (1973) and Eric Wolf (1982). It is found in agrarian societies possessing some form of the state and includes Marx's feudal and Asiatic MPs. Agricultural laborers control their own land in tributary MPs, and the state's agents appropriate products from these laborers by virtue of their superior power and authority over labor. Thus, the greatest volume of surplus products in this MP flows from agricultural producers to officials. Thus, what distinguishes tributary from other MPs are its relations of production based upon "the extraction of surpluses from the primary producers by political or military rulers" (Wolf 1982:79).

My informants have said that there were two types of people in Bagirmi—*tashkipage* and *maladonoge*. The former worked at farming, herding, or fishing. They were direct producers in the sense that it was their labor that actually created products. The latter occupied positions in the state and used their offices to extract these products as surplus labor from the former and from other peoples, especially to the south. If the concept of production relations "designates the functions fulfilled by individuals and groups in the production process and in the control of factors of production" (Godelier 1972a:335); and if class production relations are those "in which unpaid surplus labor is pumped out of direct producers" (Marx 1981:927), then the direct agricultural producers (*tashkipage*) and the officials (*maladonoge*) were the two classes in Bagirmi. Further, because *maladonoge* were "political rulers," Bagirmi may be said to have possessed tributary, class production relations.

I follow Godelier's interpretation of contradiction (1972b:90). Here contradictions are treated as problems in the reproduction of structures that occur as a result of their operation. Structures are organizations of related elements. They have certain processes by which they operate. These impose on structures "limits to their capacity to reproduce themselves" (Godelier 1972b:90). Limits are conceived of as "thresholds" beyond which "a change of structure must occur" [1972b:90]. Two major types of contradictions occur—those within production relations and those between production relations and production forces (Godelier 1972a:77–82).

It should be clear that the official/primary-producer class relations were a structure composed of two elements—*tashkipage*, whose chore in this structure it was to produce, and *maladonoge*, whose task it was to appropriate. The elements of this structure were themselves structures, or, for clarity's sake, substructures, because the *tashkipage* were organized into households and the *maladonoge* into the state. Certain processes of operation of these two substructures are explored below to show the contradictory nature of official/primary-producer relationship, one of its limits, and how frequently that limit was approached.

Households

Households shared certain attributes regardless of whether they consisted of sorghum and millet specialists or semisedentary, cattle pastoralists. What follows is a discussion of their shared features. First, production occurred in families composed of elders and juniors. Elders were normally male. They were normally the fathers or elder brothers in a household. Juniors were descendants or spouses of descendants of elders. Everybody worked in *tashkipage* households, but juniors owed deference to elders, which meant that they tended to acquiesce to the elders' sense of what should be produced as well as when and how. Juniors, regardless of gender, demonstrated their deference by implementing different agricultural activities. Different junior activities were apportioned largely on the basis of gender and age.

Elders tended to appropriate juniors' agricultural products. However, these were then distributed according to cultural norms of food exchange (largely to other kin, who were also food producers). Generally, products went first to household members, then to kin who had on previous occasions contributed products or services to the household, and finally to nonkin, local community members who in the past had provided products or services. Elders, then, appear to have functioned as circulators, not accumulators, of products.

There were marketplaces and markets within the eastern, central Sudan for the sale of both craft and agricultural products. In general, these became smaller and fewer as one went from the states in the north to the acephalous populations in the south. My informants reckoned that very few products in *tashkipage* households were marketed. These same informants could not give hard, quantitative estimates as to how much was marketed. What they did say was that a household would market some of its products for cash, which would then be spent on those products in which the household was deficit. These were exchanges between populations within a local community. Field and stream products, for example, were swapped for pasture products. In this way, Barma cereals and fish were exchanged for Arab and Fulani milk. Often such exchanges involved only barter. Bagirmi households produced crafts, especially textiles [Burkhardt 1968:435; Cordell 1980:71; Nachtigal 1971:67]. However, most of these were manufactured for a household's internal consumption.

Fields and pastures were "owned" by households or other kin (often descent) groups in the dual sense that they controlled how these resources were utilized and that their use-rights were inalienable. The preceding suggests that households operated in a rather "closed" manner, closed in the double sense that they owned the resources from which products were made and that they or other households in their local community consumed these products.

Households put a few tools in the hands of a few laborers and so worked little land—an acre or so—per member. Hence, households had productive capacities that did not greatly exceed their members' subsistence levels. Barma, for example, were estimated to produce about 240 kilograms of cereal per capita in the 1960s (Reyna 1972), which is about the minimum required for adequate nutrition (Clark and Haswell 1961). The northern part of Bagirmi lies in a sahelian climate, where the average annual rainfall lies between 300 and 650 millimeters, with annual deviations from the mean rainfall ranging from 30 to 45 percent. Its southern part is in a sudanic climate, where average rainfall is between 650 and 900 millimeters per year, with annual deviations from the mean ranging from 25 to 30 percent. Annual deviations of such magnitude mean that production is, and was, frequently marked by drought (Matlock and Cockrum 1974:75). Thus, households operated with low productive forces in an environment of high uncertainty.

The State

A description of Bagirmi's geographic organization is necessary in any analysis of the state. Le Cornec observed that Bagirmi consisted of "three concentric circles" involving the "successive degradation of its political influence and its authority" (1963:18). These circles might be termed core, allied, and predatory zones. They may be distinguished by how they were administered. Core areas were "directly" administered by the Bagirmi state. Allied ones were "indirectly" administered, in the sense that their own political structures continued to function, although strictly within parameters defined by the Bagirmi official responsible for them. There was neither "direct" nor "indirect" administration in predatory zones. Bagirmi armies pillaged in this zone, secure in the belief that the inhabitants were *kirdi*—huntable, naked infidels. Competing central Sudanic states had their own core, allied, and predatory zones. There was a tendency for states to enlarge their cores by transforming old allied areas into new cores and old predatory zones into new allied areas. When the concentric circles of states overlapped, as happened in the nineteenth century, competition between states was heightened.

By the late nineteenth century, Bagirmi's core was along the Bahr Erguig and Shari rivers. The major allied area was to the south of Bousso or near the Shari River among Chadic speakers. These included the Saroua, Miltu, Boa, Niellim, Somrai, Ndam, and Toumak. The major predatory zone was south of this region in the wooded bioclimatic zone inhabited by acephalous cereal producers. Officials conducted Bagirmi's affairs in all three of these "circles."

There were two types of *maladonoge*, some of whom had estates to administer.[9] These could be acquired through inheritance or appointment and might include local communities, kin groups, or allied tributaries. Estates were not contiguous territories. Rather, they were usually a portfolio of groups from different "circles" in the state—a local community in the core, an ethnic group in another core place, and an ethnic group in an allied territory. I term officials with estates Great Officials. Those who lacked estates but who executed Great Officials' decisions I term staff. All officials were distinguishable in terms of whether they were of royal, noble, or slave origins because different offices were reserved for officials of different origins.

There were three levels of office in the state hierarchy. At the summit was the sovereign—the *mbang*. He was surrounded by a following of royal, noble, and slave staff (his court) who assisted him in formulating and implementing royal decisions. At the second level were the Great Officials. The important Great Officials of slave origin were the *ngarman, patcha, mbarma, kirema,* and *katourli*. The important noble officials were the *galadima, mbarakudu, ngar birkete, ngar mweymanga, alipha moito,* and *milma*. The important royal officials were the first four sons of the *mbang* (of whom the most important was the eldest, the *tchiroma*) and the *mbang's* wives (of whom the most important was the first, the *gumsu*.) Great Officials were also Court Officials. When they served in the *mbang's* palace helping to conduct the court's business, they were Court Officials. When they addressed the affairs of their own estates, they were Great Officials. The third level of the hierarchy consisted of the officials on the estates of the Great Officials. These officials, whom I term Estate Officials, were also supported by staffs, which communicated directly with heads of villages, hamlets, and pastoral camps throughout the core and allied areas.

The *mbang* was surrounded by perhaps 1,000 officials in his court at the end of the nineteenth century. He had authority over 20 to 30 Great Officials. Great Officials appear to be surrounded by staffs of between 50 to 100 persons. Within the estates of Great Officials were hundreds of Estate Officials.

Policies often emerged from quite informal meetings between the *mbang* and certain of his Great Officials. These were then communicated to the other Great Officials by the *ngarman*, who functioned as the *mbang's* chief executive officer. Bagirmi officials tended to be undifferentiated. However, when information was communicated between levels in the hierarchy, the official who performed this function was called an *agid*. Thus, an *agid*, acting on instructions from the *ngarman*, would inform a Great Official, for example, the *patcha*, about a decision taken in the palace. This official would then, with his or her staff, formulate a plan to execute the palace decision. Great Officials, like the *mbang*, had individuals who acted as their chief administrative officers. Their title was *kadi-* prefixed to that of the Great Official they served. If a decision taken by the *patcha* required that the Great Official utilize his or her estate, the *kadipatcha* would summon an *agid* who would transmit the required information to the Estate Officials. These also had their *kadi's* and *agids* who would, when required, implement decisions at the level of the *tashkipa*. Thus, Court Officials dealt with affairs of state, Great Officials addressed those of their estates, and Estate Officials administered portions of estates.

A Limit to the Reproduction of Class

The preceding analysis suggests that Bargirmi class relations may be likened to two atoms bonded into a larger molecule. Domestic and state structures were the atoms in this molecule. Households were internally structured into elders and juniors—the planners and doers of food production. The state was internally organized into Court, Great, and Estate Officials—the planners and doers of political activity. So that the larger molecule consisted of a single state bonded through its hierarchy to thousands of domestic structures.[10] This bond, however, was often stretched toward its limits.

Nachtigal observed (1883:612) that officials spent most of their time immersed in the affairs "of the court of war." This meant that at all levels in the hierarchy officials and their families couldn't be bothered with producing food. Remember also that domestic structures tended to be closed in the sense that most of the products they produced were consumed either by themselves or within their local community. Officials had to have *tashkipage* products to survive, but so did the *tashkipage*. This meant that the official/direct-producer bond was contradictory.

The weak productive forces, characterized by low output and high uncertainty, meant that there were often very few food products for *tashkipage* and *maladonoge* to consume. This suggests that one limit to the reproduction of official/primary-producer class relations was nutritional, for these relations would be in jeopardy if either class's nutritional level declined beneath the threshold of adequate diet. Mean daily caloric intakes for people resident in the most productive part of Bagirmi's habitat appear to be about 2,090 calories per capita per day in nondrought years (Bascoulergue ND). These intakes plummet below the threshold level of adequate diet for African populations in drought years. Droughts affecting large numbers of people currently occur in some area of Bagirmi at least one year in ten, and were probably frequent in the past. This meant that the molecular bond between officials and direct producers often approached its limits.

Officials thus faced a ticklish situation. When reproducing their class position, they had to "break" into the closed domestic production to survive, but they had to do so in ways that did not sever the bond with the *tashkipage* who nourished them. Thus, officials had to appropriate surplus labor in ways that were sensitive to absolute scarcity and unpredictability. Predatory accumulation was just such a reproductive process.

PREDATORY ACCUMULATION

Permit me an aside to explain why I substitute the term "predatory accumulation" for one currently in the literature. Hindness and Hirst use the concept "tax/rent couple" for surplus labor appropriation in MPs where "the state extracts the surplus products and there is no private property in land" (1975:192). Amin and Wolf would say that such appropriation occurs in tributary MPs. The crucial feature of surplus labor extraction in tributary MPs is that the *state* does it. Hindness and Hirst, by coupling tax and rent, link one term, tax, that does imply state appropriation with another, rent, that does not invariably imply such appropriation. The scholar is, thus, left to wonder if the concept "tax/rent couple" refers to surplus appropriation through *both* state and private means. Since this is, of course, exactly what Hindness and Hirst do not mean, their term is misleading. I suggest that the phrase "fiscal appropriation" may denote processes of state extraction of surplus product with less ambiguity. Predatory accumulation was one type of fiscal appropriation. It was authorized by ideology, included three means of revenue collection (each of which involved some predation) and led to the accumulation of surplus labor.

Ideology

The Barma do not appear to have had a term for their revenue collection system. Rather, when they talked about it, they did so in terms of the verb *tiru*, which meant "to pull." They said of an official who acquired revenues that he or she had "pulled" them. Bagirmi revenues were "pulled" from three sources: taxes, tribute, and pillage. Each form of "pulling" was ideologically sanctioned.

Barma ontological notions and Islamic law authorized officials to "pull" taxes. When I asked *tashkipage* who "owned" land before the French arrived, the response was the *mbang*. He, however, did not own the land in any Western, legal sense. Rather, he was a "divine king," conceived of as part of the supernatural forces that "caused" events to occur (Pacques 1967,1977). Land was the *mbang's* not because he owned it, but because he was part of the supernatural forces that allowed it to bear fruit. The *mbang*, and by extension his officials, appropriated products because these actions were part of the "natural" order of things. Just as the rains fell, or plants grew, so the *mbang* and his officials taxed. Further, as the *mbang* was an Islamic ruler, he had, under Muslim law, rights to certain taxes.

The "pulling" of tribute was sanctioned by a document that has been called a "kinglist." These were written or verbal chronicles of a Sudanic state's sovereigns and their doings. They were lists, in Urvoy's terms, of "kings and battles" (1949:7). Complete Bagirmi "kinglists" have never surfaced. They appear to have existed, however, and the one that pertained to the *mbang* was called the *dabcar*.[11] Yet, when I listened to informants explain the *dabcar*, it became clear it did not exist only to give Bagirmi a history. Rather, it functioned as do genealogies in societies organized on the basis of descent—to justify relations between groups. Genealogies explain the relationship between descent groups in terms of *shared*, apical ancestors. The *dabcar* established relations between Bagirmi and other groups in terms of *shared* wars. If Bagirmi won these wars, then the defeated groups paid tribute to Bagirmi.

If Bagirmi lost, it had to pay the tribute. A family genealogy records parent-child links to establish a relationship. A *dabcar* did the same by recording wins and losses, establishing who were receivers and payers of tribute. Thus, a *dabcar* was an "account" book, which legitimated tribute flows by establishing tributary relationships.

Raiding was against non-Muslims (*kirdi*). Attitudes towards *kirdi* in the 1970s were strong. They were viewed as those who went naked, got drunk, and were ignorant of Allah. Such views had prevailed even more strongly in the past, when Islam treated the pillaging of such infidels as a sign of piety. Thus, Bagirmi ideology legitimated the *maladonoge* "pulling" of taxes, tribute, and booty.

Revenue Collection[12]

Each "circle" of Bagirmi yielded a different form of revenue. Taxes came from the core, tribute from the allied areas, and booty from the predatory zones. Three major taxes were collected according to my informants. The first was the *gugari*, which may be likened to a moveable feast. Each year during the cold season (from approximately December through February), the *mbang* and his court journeyed throughout his domain, stopping for several days at villages along the way. Those villages at which the *mbang* stopped presented him with gifts, which included grain, cattle, goats, and other forms of wealth. Villages only occasionally had to make *gugari* payments.

The Islamic alms tax (*zakhat*) was the second major tax. It was in theory used to provide nourishment for pilgrims undertaking the *hadj* and was supposed to consist of one-tenth of a farmer's harvest. Pastoralists resident in Bagirmi paid it in cattle. My informants said that only the Great Officials paid a regular, annual *zakhat* to the *mbang*, and that the *tashkipage* paid only when their harvests had been successful. The third major tax, the *hadjar,* called by Devallee *bourma* or *marassouba* (1925:64), was collected annually and appears to have been the major fiscal burden on *tashkipage.* Informants' statements as to the amounts of the *hadjar* varied. At first this annoyed me, and I thought they didn't know, or were concealing, the tax rates. Then it became clear that they reported various tax rates because tax rates fluctuated. One informant said a normal *hadjar* might be "*sa koro dukmuta, kad kedi,*" which meant "eat thirty bowls, give one." However, other informants quickly added that *maladonoge* might "pull" less if the growing season had been poor; or they might "pull" more if it had been generous. Hence, food availability on estates, which was in good measure controlled by prevailing climatic conditions, appears to have at least partially influenced how much *hadjar* officials choose to "pull."[13]

Usually the head of a village (in the past called *ngolbe,* now frequently *ngar*) or of an ethnic group collected the *hadjar* and other taxes and gave them to an *agid* who, in turn, gave them to the Great Official to whom he was responsible. Then, an *agid* of the *mbang* came and collected a portion of these taxes and passed them on to his master. Staff were paid a portion of the Great Officials' and *mbang's* taxes. One informant said that of 20 bowls of grain given to the village head, 12 might eventually reach the *mbang,* suggesting that slightly less than one-half of the taxes remained with the Great and Estate Officials.

Tribute was collected in much the same way as was the *hadjar.* Each Great Official might have in his or her estate allied, hence tributary, groups. This official would arrange through his or her staff to collect the tribute and transmit it to the *mbang's* court.

Every year, during the dry season, Great Officials were sent by the *mbang* to *kab kirdi* (to go [after] pagans). Chevalier (1907:356) reports that the following booty was normally acquired in such raids:

> slaves, herds, poultry, millet, honey, other agricultural products. The Sultan keeps for himself most of the slaves, and he gives some of them to the notables who have accompanied him.

I have analysed elsewhere the amounts contributed to the total state revenues by different revenue sources. The results of this analysis were striking. Slaves were the major source of revenues in the late nineteenth century, probably contributing well above 50 percent of the annual total (Reyna 1977).

Predation

Revenue collection required predation. Booty, largely in the form of slaves, was secured only subsequent to raids. Tribute was collected only following protracted conflicts in which the tributary group, thoroughly trounced, consented to pay tribute. Further, once a polity became tributary, it remained so only because of the fear that resistance would result in military calamity. Taxpayers were core *tashkipage* who, usually in some distant past, had occupied tributary status. And *maladonoge* "fairly often" had to "use force" to collect taxes [Devallee 1925:64].

Bagirmi had two institutions capable of applying force. The Barma called officials not only *maladonoge*, but also *deb an sindage*, which meant "peoples-of-horse." New staff were given horses at the time that they joined a Great Official's retinue. Any ritual involving a Great Official, or the *mbang*, involved the performance of a hell-for-leather cavalry charge (*n'ur sinda*). Such charges were practiced incessantly. This, in conjunction with the fact that a staff member was likely to experience combat at least once a year suggests that a Great Official's staff rapidly became seasoned cavalry. Thus, at all times and in any action involving a Great Official, his staff could impose his interests. In so far as this staff operated to maintain law and authority as part of its other duties, it was an undifferentiated police force.

The second coercive institution was the army. Lanier (1925) and Nachtigal (1889) describe an army composed of core and tributary soldiers organized into squadrons. Usually, the *mbang* did not command the army except during civil and holy wars (Pacques 1977:45). Rather, the decision to mobilize the army also specified which of the Great Officials would command it. Tributary squadrons had those chains of command and types of soldiers that were particular to the ethnic group that dominated the allied territory. Each core squadron was commanded by a Great Official. Each tributary squadron depended upon the Great Official who administered the tributary as part of his or her estate. Core squadrons, which consisted of the Great Official's staff, had two major functions. First, they were the liaison officers assuring communications. Second, they tended to be the major assault troops.

There might also be some *tashkipage* soldiers. However, informants insisted that farmers' business was to farm and not fight, and that *tashkipage* serving as soldiers were usually trying to become *maladonoge*. Thus, the army was overwhelmingly composed of and entirely directed by officials. This could only occur if most of the state officials temporarily dropped all functions save for military ones. Army structure, therefore, was state structure temporarily differentiated to administer force.

There does not appear to have been a prohibition against *tashkipage* owning weapons. And, in fact, informants said that in the past, as was the case in the 1970s, any sensible man owned a knife and a lance. The army, however, consisted of cavalry (Lanier 1925:473), and cavalry weapons were extremely expensive. Horses tended to cost several times the annual value of an average farmer's cereal harvest. Quilted and chain mail armor were luxury items usually stored in royal vaults (al Tunisi 1851:166). Cost considerations, then, prevented *tashkipage* from acquiring cavalry weapons. Great Officials acquired their weapons through purchase from merchants or as spoils of war. Staff usually received their first arms as gifts when they entered a Great Official's service. Thus, it is incorrect to insist that the state enjoyed a total monopoly over weapons. It did, however, possess an *effective* monopoly over the decisive ones—those necessary for the calvary.

Concepts of "kinetic" and "potential" violence might be helpful in understanding the use of force in revenue collection. Raiding was conducted in predatory zones by the army and always required combat to secure revenues. Thus, "kinetic" violence was the order of the day when securing booty. War occurred in allied areas and in Bagirmi's and competitor states' core areas. War was often over tribute flows, but not all tribute payments resulted from combat. Rather, war was usually waged to create new or restore old tribute payments. Police actions were used in core areas to maintain tax flows. These, in fact, tended to be relatively infrequent. Consequently, fighting did not occur every time tribute or taxes were collected. However, the potential was always there. So it may be said that "potential" violence was used to generate tax and tribute revenues.

Perhaps the greatest virtue of predatory accumulation from the perspective of officials was that it could help relax the official/direct-producer contradiction, which tended to intensify during drought. However, informants insisted that Great Officials would "pull" little from an area when its rains failed, while doubling taxation, tribute, or pillaging elsewhere. Raiding was especially useful in this regard.[14] Most raiding during the nineteenth century was directed into the southern parts of the Shari-Logone river system. This meant that when harvests were poor in the core and direct producers had little to share, officials raided into southern ecosystems characterized by greater and more certain production. Thus, predatory accumulation relaxed the limits of the official/direct-producer contradiction in one area by shifting the contradiction to other areas. Here *tashkipage* might be expected to "sleep with their sandals on."

Accumulation

Tributary MPs in regions like the eastern, central Sudan extracted increased amounts of booty, tribute, or taxes over time. Hence, predatory accumulation was, indeed, an *accumulation* process. This dynamic resulted from an intersystemic contradiction between states and the effects of predation upon acephalous populations.

Table 3-1 presents nineteenth century data suggesting that four other eastern, central Sudanic states also extracted taxes, tribute, and booty from food producers in their different "circles" through predation, which they

TABLE 3.1 Predatory Accumulation in Four Eastern, Central Sudanic States

	Bornu[a]	Bulala[b]	Wadai[c]	Darfur[d]
Possessed officials and direct agricultural producers (DAPs)	+	+	+	+
Possessed "circles" from which officials extracted different revenues from DAPs	+	+	+	+
Possessed ideological authorization for officials to secure revenues in the form of taxes, tribute, or booty	+	+	+	+
Used warfare, or its threat, to acquire taxes, tribute, or booty	+	+	+	+
Paid officials from the proceeds of state revenues	−	−	−	−

Notes: The "+" symbol indicates that the state during the nineteenth century possessed the traits indicated in the left-hand column. The "−" symbol means the trait was absent.

Sources: [a]Barth: 1965; [b]Carbou: 1912; [c]Nachtigal: 1971; [d]O'Fahey: 1980

used to pay their officials. Thus, they too were tributary MPs practicing predatory accumulation.

A lucrative form of predation was to defeat a state, pillage it, and then exact tribute from it. Generally, the bigger the state, the greater its yield of booty and tribute. Bagirmi was a rather large state poised between two larger states (Bornu and Wadai) and two smaller ones (Bulala and Kotoko). Throughout the nineteenth century Bagirmi warred with all four. It fought Bornu and Wadai to end costly tribute payments it owed them. It fought Bulala and Kotoko to restart lucrative tribute payments it thought were owed it.[15]

These wars were an expression of an intersystemic contradiction. Whereas Marx had identified the intersystemic contradiction between capitalist productive forces and production relations, the type found in the eastern, central Sudan was between production relations in competing tributary MPs. When Bagirmi and another state fought, officials in both states sought to direct tribute from their opponents to their own. Thus, when the MPs went to war, officials in opposing MPs were in a contradictory relationship. It was as if the warring states were competing firms, except that competition was over tribute, not market share.

Predatory forces were strengthened by enlarging the number of a state's officials, thereby increasing the size of its cavalry. New officials had to be paid incomes derived from a portion of a state's surplus products. These surplus products were, of course, derived from earlier rounds of revenue collection. New officials, in turn, participated in police and army actions, which allowed the state to accumulate additional surplus products. If a state did not operate in this manner, it tended to become an object of another state's successful predatory accumulation. Thus, successful tributary MPs would accumulate surplus products in order to accumulate additional forces of predation which would, in turn, give them a capacity to accumulate even more surplus products.

There was a second reason tributary MPs like Bagirmi were motivated to accumulate surplus products. Raiding conducted by Bagirmi and other tributary MPs against acephalous neighbors tended to centralize those populations. This process had been reported by the late nineteenth century in at least seven populations that Bagirmi had raided: Sara Goulaye (Fortier 1982), Sara Madgingaye (Fortier 1982), Sara Nar (Brown 1983), Moundang (Adler 1955), Buduma (Talbot 1911:249), Hadjerai (Vincent 1975:19–33), and Boa (Prins 1900). Those polities once centralized tended to adopt certain of the political institutions of the state or states that raided them. Thus, the Sara groups and Boa were raided by Bagirmi, became tributaries, and borrowed certain features of Bagirmi statecraft. In so doing, they improved their military capacity and became more formidable opponents. Consequently, Bagirmi had to allocate more surplus products than in the past to its own predatory forces to confront the additional military dangers posed by centralizing peoples.[16] Thus, Bagirmi had to accumulate surplus products to accumulate predatory forces in order to address military challenges from centralizing peoples as well as from competing states. The "logic" of this situation was: prey to accumulate, accumulate to prey, and, being pious, pray to prey.[17]

This "logic" appears consistent with events in the eastern, central Sudan. Consultation of local or Arabic chronicles in Kanem/Bornu (Barth 1965:15–35; Palmer 1923, 1926, 1936; Urvoy 1949), Wadai (al Tunisi 1851; Nachtigal 1971:205–29), Bagirmi (Barth 1965:517–74; Nachtigal 1889:692–728), or the Bulala (Carbou 1912:291–321) suggests that when kings sent their officials into battles, they sent them to raise taxes, tribute, or booty. Thus, "war was a profit-making enterprise" [Fisher 1975:69], and as "profits" accumulated, so did the number and size of Chad Basin states. The first state to develop was that of the Sefwa dynasty in the Kanem (c. 1000 AD). By 1400 AD at least three other states had emerged (Bornu, the Kotoko, and the Bulala), and by 1600 AD Bagirmi and Wadai were fully differentiated (Fisher 1977, pp. 232–330). There were also three small states that by this time were tributaries of the larger states. In the nineteenth century, these eight states were joined by the seven centralizing polities.

This state formation meant that more officials extracted more taxes, tribute, and booty from more direct agricultural producers. Hence, an important aspect of the history of the Chad Basin between 1000 and 1900 AD was the growth in the amount of surplus labor accumulated through predatory accumulation. This accumulation dynamic was not one in which an increasing amount of product was extracted from the same number of direct producers. Rather, it was one in which an increasing number of direct producers became subject to taxes, tribute, and raiding. The existence of predatory accumulation in Bagirmi has implications for its status as an African MP and its precolonial underdevelopment. These topics are addressed in the following section.

DISCUSSION

Goody observed that precolonial Sudanic economies were dominated by extensive agriculture (1971:25). This dominance was due to a large "technology gap" between Eurasian and African factors of production (1971:27), which constrained productivity. Abdoulaye Bara Diop has also argued that

> The weakness of the means of production . . . was the factor which prevented the development of large plantations and primitive capital accumulation, with the capacity to induce formation of a superior class. (in Rey 1976:121)

Thus, weak productive forces appear to have helped maintain the underdevelopment of the precolonial Sudan. But why weak productive forces?

Circulation in capitalist MPs, according to Marx, reproduced production relations between capitalists and workers because it threw the latter on a "double mill" (cited in Balibar 1970:266). On the one hand, the worker was required to sell his or her labor to subsist; on the other, in doing so, he or she produced the products that the capitalist in turn sold, thereby realizing the surplus labor necessary for expanded reproduction. Predatory accumulation may have also placed many direct agricultural producers on a different type of "double mill."

Maladonoge used their incomes to acquire food for themselves and their dependents, to secure and maintain weapons, and to purchase sumptuary and other goods required in the performance of their official duties. The costs of cavalry weapons and sumptuary goods (especially different luxury textiles) were high. There is not a single account in the literature or from any informants of a *maladonoge* investing in any productive enterprise except extensive agriculture. This is probably because they had very little income left after meeting food, weapon, and sumptuary good costs.

Tashkipage also had little income to invest. Table 3–2 suggests why this was the case. First, it reports the total estimated cereal production for a five person household in a favored ecological zone around 1900. Then, it estimates the different amounts of this production that would have been used for taxes, food, cloth, salt, tea, and rituals.

The table suggests there was very little left for investment after households met their subsistence and tax requirements. With such small amounts, Al-Tunisi observed, farmers would "buy what they could, a goat here, a sheep there. . . " (1851:360). What al-Tunisi noted during the first part of the nineteenth century was still prevalent in Bagirmi in the 1960s. Farmers invested their meager resources in livestock that was used for sale or consumption during droughts or in rituals.

TABLE 3.2. Estimated Nineteenth Century Household Investment Potential

Income		Expenses		Disposable for Investment
Total cereal production[a]	3,000kgs	Taxes HADJAR[b] ZAKHAT[c]	100kgs 300kgs	100kgs
		Required for Holt's Reproduction		
		food[d]	1,400kgs	
		cloth	100kgs	
		agriculture input food preparation shelter and health costs[e]	1,000kgs	
		Total expenses	2,900kgs	

Notes: [a]This figure is derived from field work. It estimates the mean production of a family of five (with three laborers) under normal rainfall conditions. It is, thus, a generous estimate.

[b]HADJAR=1/30th total harvest

[c]ZAKHAT=1/10th total harvest

[d]This figure assumes that the five individuals consume a mean of 280 kg/year. It is a low estimate.

[e]This figure is based upon field work estimates that *at the minimum* households were obliged to spend 1/3 of their total annual harvests on agricultural tools, cooking utensils, water carrying containers, building materials and furnishing, and medicines and medical rituals.

Thus, predatory accumulation was, in fact, a "double mill." First, it threw *tashkipage* back into extensive farming by removing so much product for state revenues that there was little left to invest in other productive or commercial activities. Second, it circulated these products to officials, providing them with the means they required to continue extracting products from *tashkipage*. This position is quite the reverse of Diop's, in which weak productive forces did not prevent class formation. Rather, predatory accumulation, which reproduced Bagirmi's "superior" class, constrained the development of productive forces.

The existence of predatory accumulation also raises concerns about the utility of an African MP. Coquery-Vidrovitch says there was no "despotism" in precolonial African states (1977:83), following both Suret-Canale (1964) and Godelier (1963). The reason Coquery-Vidrovitch argues that "the African despot exploited his subjects less . . . " is that ". . . long distance trading provided the major part of his surplus . . . " (1977:84). Godelier had earlier expressed his opinion that it was due "to the control by tribal aristocracies of inter-tribal or inter-regional trade . . . " [1963:30]. So that the "superimposed bureaucracy . . . interferes only indirectly with the community . . . (Coquery-Vidrovitch 1977:79).

Coquery-Vidrovitch and Godelier ignore how officials acquired control over the products they traded. Bagirmi officials in the nineteenth century overwhelmingly traded slaves, which had been acquired as tribute or as booty. Thus, the major commodity officials traded was acquired through predatory accumulation, which required that officials use force to extract products from direct producers. A crucial attribute of Coquery-Vidrovitch's African MP is that officials "interfere only indirectly" with direct producers. However, *tashkipage* handed over their products after a fight or the threat of one. It strains credulity to assert that taxes, tribute, and pillage were "indirect." As al Tunisi reported:

> . . . the poor are in . . . the most shocking misery. They suffer the
> tyranny of their governors without relief; on them weigh the exigencies
> of wars, public corvees. Their life is only that of slaves. (1851:360)

Eastern, central Sudanic data suggest that what is wrong with Coquery-Vidrovitch's proposal of an African MP is that it is based upon a premise that something *did not* occur (direct exploitation) when, in fact, it did (in the form of predatory accumulation)—and with a vengeance!

CONCLUSION

In conclusion, predatory accumulation was a process that used "kinetic" and "potential" force to extract taxes, tribute, and booty to reproduce class relations in tributary MPs like Bagirmi. It led to an accumulation of surplus products by states in regions with competing tributary MPs as in the eastern, central Sudan.

A cost of predatory accumulation was the amount of conflict it generated. Raids, police actions against recalcitrant taxpayers, and wars against tributaries or competing states all had to occur for the system to endure. But raided peoples learned to raid. Recalcitrant taxpayers and tributaries revolted. States warred against returned the favor. Thus, predatory accumulation reproduced class relations in tributary MPs by generating "wars. . . without end" (Nachtigal (1872:405).

NOTES

1. The term Bagirmi has two meanings in this essay. It is sometimes used as a shorthand way of referring to the "society of Bagirmi." It is also used to refer to *all* the people of Bagirmi, regardless of their ethnic affiliation. In this latter case it means "people of Bagirmi."

2. The frequency and intensity of Bagirmi war is reported in the 1820s by Denham (1825:215), the 1850s by Barth (1965:564), the 1870s by Nachtigal (1872:405), the early twentieth century by Gaden (1909:3) and Devallee (1925:28), and most recently by Pacques (1977:63).

3. My forthcoming monograph, *Wars without End*, discusses certain theoretical and methodological reasons for the scholarly neglect of Sudanic warfare. The literature that does exist tends to emphasize the instruments of war (Law 1980; Fisher and Rowland 1971). Cohen's (1984) essay is a fine discussion of eastern, central Sudanic warfare. Cohen, however, is largely concerned with the role of war in state formation. My concern is with its reproductive role.

4. The period roughly between 1870 and 1900 is reconstructed for this essay. Data pertaining to this time is derived from the following sources: my own field work with Bagirmi 1969–70, 1973–74, and 1980; published and unpublished accounts of other ethnographers; Islamic scholars; Islamic and European travellers; and colonial soldiers, administrators, diplomats, and scientists. Translations from French, German, Chadian Arabic, tar Barma, or Sara, unless otherwise noted, are my own.

5. There is no "best" source concerning the eastern, central Sudan's environment. Useful introductions, however, can be found in Chapelle (1980:8–17) and Cabot and Bouguet (1974). An analysis of the influence of environment upon agriculture for the entire West African savanna can be found in Matlock and Cockrun (1974:68–150).

6. The classic source concerning the desert pastoralists is Chapelle (1957). Excellent descriptions of the Teda and Daza during the period under consideration are in Nachtigal (1971). There is "unequal development" in the eastern, central Sudanic state literature. There have been a considerable number of studies concerning Bornu, and to acquire some introduction to these the reader might consult Cohen (1967). Brenner has performed a historical analysis of Bornu during the nineteenth century (1973). There is rather less material concerning the other states. However, an introduction to Kotoko can be found in Lebeuf (1959), to Bagirmi in Pacques (1977), and to Wadai in Carbou (1912) and Nachtigal (1889).

7. Lovejoy synthesizes a considerable literature concerning nineteenth century, central Sudanic trans-Saharan and desert-side trade. She reports that these commercial networks remained unincorporated into the capitalist world system until the turn of the twentieth century (1984:109).

8. Coquery-Vidrovitch sensed that the proposal of an African MP might be criticized for emphasizing distribution while ignoring production. The following statement was included in the essay to forestall such criticisms:

> Let us not be reproached for excessively favoring the *mode of circulation* at the expense of the *mode of production*; the fundamental problem was not to transport merchandise but to procure it—in a certain sense to "produce" it. . . . There were two ways of procuring goods: war . . . or peaceful exchanges. (1977:84; emphasis in the original)

I have two observations concerning the preceding statement. First, though Coquery-Vidrovitch realizes that war was important, the essay *never* analyzes war. I think this analysis went unperformed because Coquery-Vidrovitch was convinced that war was far less important than trade as a way of procuring goods. But by not considering war, the essay was hardly in a position to make such a judgment. By ignoring war, Coquery-Vidrovitch missed an opportunity to raise the essay above an aholistic holism.

Second, the above statement equates distribution with production because it asserts that "peaceful exchange" is procurement and that "in a certain sense" procurement is production. Marx had suggested that production and distribution were different parts in a common production process (*Grundrisse* 1973:88–100). To go further and equate production with distribution is a messy proposition.

9. French administrators asserted that Great Officials held fiefs (Bruel 1905:105). However, Weber observed that estates might be acquired through inheritance (as fiefs) or by appointment (as benefices) (1968, p. 1073). My informants said that some Great Officials inherited their estates and that others were appointed to them. Thus, all Great Officials held estates, some of which were fiefs and others benefices.

10. Some *maladonoge* settled slaves in villages to farm for them. On the basis of similar observations made in Nigeria, a claim has been made that nineteenth century Hausa states were characterized by a plantation economy or a slave MP (Lovejoy 1978). This suggestion has been received skeptically because:

> While slavery was very important in strengthening the authority of the ruling class as a whole, it remained clearly subordinated as a production system to the relationship between free *talakwa* and *masu sarauta*. (Shenton and Freund 1978:11)

Talaka and *masu sarauta* are the Hausa terms for direct producer and official, and correspond to the Barma terms *tashkipa* and *maladono*. The situation in Bagirmi was similar to that among the Hausa, because while some officials did settle slaves into villages, these later were far less numerous than the free farmers from whom officials drew the bulk of their taxes. Thus, the dominant production structure was, indeed, the household.

11. Devallee reports the destruction of a "history" of Bagirmi by the Wadaians subsequent to their defeat of Bagirmi circa 1870 (1925:27).

12. Study of revenue systems in precolonial central Sudanic states is in its infancy. Two observations may facilitate their study. First, many accounts of fiscal systems were made by colonial officials in the early twentieth century. These occasionally announce that precolonial revenue systems extracted more from peasants than their colonial counterparts (Lanier 1925:468). Such assertions might be treated with caution. Colonial officials were in the business of justifying their own domination. Second, certain descriptions confuse state revenues with various forms of kin or neighborly reciprocity. Thus, O'Fahey presents 37 different nineteenth century Darfurian revenues (1980:103–4). However, the reader is never informed whether such obligations as *'ana* (assistance) involve transfers of goods to officials

(classifying them as taxes) or to kin (classifying them as reciprocity). It is impossible to analyse revenue systems if such distinctions are not made.

My description of Bagirmi's revenue system is derived from Barth (1965:563-64), Nachtigal (1872:388), Lanier (1925:468), Devallee (1925:64-67), and Pacques (1977:59)—as well as my own informants. I do not mention in the text two sources of state revenues: market taxes and judicial fines. Both were said by informants to be less important than those presented in the text.

13. At least one nineteenth century Darfurian tax was partially responsive to climatic fluctuation. This was the "basic" tax, the *zaka* (O'Fahey 1980:102). No *zaka* appears to have been collected if a household's harvest was beneath a certain amount. However, because harvest size largely depended upon climate, this meant that in poor rainfall years taxation was reduced.

14. Bagirmi defeat by Wadai in 1803 may have ultimately derived from a decision to shift raiding from a less to a more productive environment. Barth mentions a "severe plague" in Bagirmi during the reign of *mbang* Gaurang I, who was to be defeated by Wadai (1965:551). Urvoy reports a "severe epidemic" in Bornu during the same period (1949:86). This suggests that Bagirmi's environment may have become less productive during this time because people were either dead or too weak to farm. Al Tunisi, who resided in Bagirmi at this time and who appears to have had access to both Wadaian and Bagirmi actors in the drama, said that certain of Gaurang's Great Officials provoked the conflict when they told their sovereign to start raiding Wadai and to cease taxing Bagirmi because the latter was "exhausted" and the former had products in "abundance" (1851:129-30).

15. There were seven nineteenth century *mbangs*: Gaurang I (1785-1806), Bira (1806-07), Burkumanda III (1807-47), Abd el Qadar II (1847-58), Ab Sakin (1858-77), Burkumanda IV (1877-80), Gaurang II (1883-97). Bagirmi was not at war with Wadai, Bornu, Bulala, or Kotoko in only one reign, that of Burkumanda IV. There were protracted wars with Waidai in the reigns of the first five *mbangs* (e.g., from 1785-1877). There was what was described as a "direful war of extermination" (Denham 1826:215) between Bagirmi and Bornu during the reign of Burkumanda III, and, then, again in the reign of Gaurang II. Finally, there were wars with the Kotoko during the reign of Burkumanda III and with the Bulala during those of Gaurang I and Abd el Qader II. Wadai, following a successful, war, made Bagirmi its tributary during the reign of Gaurang I. As a result, the *idee fixe* of Bagirmi policy for the remainder of the nineteenth century was to revoke this tributary status, which explains the frequent hostilities with Wadai. Bornu, profiting from a revival during the first quarter of the nineteenth century under *shehu* al Kanemi, fought with and ultimately defeated Bagirmi during Burkumanda III's own reign. Bagirmi lost certain of its own tributaries as a result of these defeats. Bulala went to Wadai, and the Kotoko, for the most part, fell under Bornuan influence. Thus, wars with these two former tributaries were for the most part to reestablish their tributary status.

16. The Boa were located immediately south of Bagirmi. They had adopted predatory accumulation and were said to be able to place 1,000-force cavalry into the field, which they used to create their own tributaries. Hence, by the 1890s they had become "redoubtable adversaries" of Bagirmi, who were only "irregularly" paid their tribute (Prins 1900:182).

17. The royal Bagirmi war preparation ceremonial, which included prayer, is described in Pacques (1977:45).

REFERENCES

Adler, A. 1966. *Les Day de Bouna.* N'djamena: I.N.T.S.H.

Al Tunisi, M. 1851. *Voyage au Ouaday.* Paris: B. Duprat.

Amin, S. 1973. *Le developpement inegale.* Paris: Minuit.

Balibar, E. 1970. The Basic Concepts of Historical Materialism. In *Reading Capital.* L. Althusser and E. Balibar (eds.) New York: New Left Books.

Barth, H. 1965(1857). *Travels and Discoveries in North and Central Africa.* volume 2. New York: Harper & Row.

Bascoulerque, M. ND. *Enqvête Nutritionnelle dans les Régions du Chari-Baguirmi (Bousso) et de Noyen Chari(Kyabe): Février à Avril 1957.* Brazzaville: Séction de Nutrition du S.G.M.M.P.

Brenner, L. 1973. *The Shehus of Kukawa.* London: Oxford University Press.

Brown, E.C.P. 1983. *Mourrir les gens, mourrir les haines.* Paris: Societe d'ethnographie.

Bruel, Georges. 1905. *Cercle du Moyne Logone.* Paris: Comite de l'Afrique Francaise.

Burkhardt, John. 1968(1822). *Travels in Nubia.* Westmead, England: Gregg International.

Cabot, J. and C. Bouquet. 1974. *Le Tchad.* Paris: Hatier.

Carbou, Henri. 1912. *La region du Tchad et du Ouadai.* Paris: Leroux.

Chapelle, Jean. 1957. *Nomades noires du Sahara.* Paris: Plon.

_____ . 1980. *Le people Tchadien: ses racines et sa vie quotidienne.* Paris: Harmattan.

Chevalier, A. 1907. *L'Afrique Centrale Francaise.* Paris: Challamel.

Clark, J. and B. Haswell. 1961. *The Economics of Subsistence Agriculture.* London: Macmillan.

Cohen, R. 1967. *The Kanuri of Bornu.* New York: Holt, Rinehart & Winston.

_____ . 1984. Warfare and State Formation: Wars Make States and States Make Wars. In *Warfare, Culture and Environment,* R.B. Ferguson (ed.) New York: Academic Press.

Coquery-Vidrovitch, C. 1977. Research on an African Mode of Production. In *African Social Studies,* P.C.W. Gutkind and P. Waterman (eds.) New York: Monthly Review.

Cordell, Dennis. 1980. *Dar al-Kuti: A Slave Trading State on the Islamic Frontier in North Central Africa.* Unpublished manuscript. Department of History, Southern Methodist University, Dallas, Texas.

Denham, D. and H. Clapperton. 1826. *Narrative of Travels & Discoveries in Northern and Central Africa.* London: John Murray.

Devallee, J. 1925. Le Baguirmi. *Bulletin de la Societe des Recherches Congolaises,* 7:3–76.

Fisher, H.J. 1975. The Central Sahara and Sudan. In *The Cambridge History of Africa,* vol. 4, R. Gray (ed.) Cambridge: Cambridge University Press.

_____ . 1977. The Eastern Maghgeb and the Central Sudan. In *The Cambridge History of Africa,* vol. 3, R. Oliver (ed.). Cambridge: Cambridge University Press.

Fisher, H.J. and V. Rowland. 1971. Firearms in the Central Sudan. *Journal of African History* XII(2):215–39.

Fortier, J. 1982. *Le couteau de jet sacre.* Paris: Harmattan.

Gaden, Henri. 1909. *La chute de l'empire de Rabah.*

Godelier, M. 1963. La notion de mode de production asiatique et les schemas marxistes d'evolution des societes. Paris: C.E.R.M.

_____ . 1972a. Structure and Contradiction in *Capital*. In *Ideology in Social Science*, R. Blackburn (ed.). Glasgow: Fontana.

_____ . 1972b. *Rationality and Irrationality in Economics*. New York: Monthly Review Press.

Goody, J. 1971. *Technology, Tradition and State in Africa*. London: Oxford University Press.

Hindness, B. and P.Q. Hirst. 1975. *Pre-Capitalist Modes of Production*. London: Routledge & Kegan Paul.

Lanier, H. 1925. L'ancien royaume du Baguirmi. *Reseignements Coloniaux de l'Afrique Francaise* 10:457–74.

Law, Robin. 1980. *The Horse in West African History*. London: Oxford University Press.

Lebeuf, A.M.D. 1959. *Les principautes Kotodo: Essai sur la caractere sacre de l'autorite*. Paris: CNRS.

LeCornec, J. 1963. *Histoire Politique du Tchad de 1900 à 1962*. Paris: Pichon, Durand-Auzias.

Lovejoy, P. 1978. Plantations in the Economy of the Sokoto Caliphate. *Journal of African History* XIX(3):341–68.

_____ . 1984. Commercial Sectors in the Economy of the 19th Century Central Sudan: The Trans-Saharan Salt Trade. *African Economic History* 13:85–117.

Marx, Karl. 1981(1883). *Capital*, vol. 3. New York: Vintage.

_____ . 1973(1939). *Grundrisse*. New York: Vintage.

Matlock, W. and B. Cockrun. 1974. *A Framework for Evaluating Long-Term Strategies for the Development of the Sahel-Sudan Region*. Cambridge: Massachusetts: Center for Policy Alternative.

Nachtigal, Gustav. 1971(1889). *Sahara and Sudan: Wadai and Darfur*, vol. 4. Berkeley: University of California Press.

_____ . 1872. Voyage du Bornu au Bagirmi. *Le Tour du Monde* vol. 50:337–416.

_____ . 1889. *Sahara and Sudan*. Leipzig: F.A. Brockhaus.

O'Fahey, R. 1980. *State and Society in Dar Fur*. New York: St. Martins Press.

Pacques, V. 1967. Origine et caracteres du pouvoir royale au Bagirmi. *Journal de la Societe des Africanists* XXXVII:183–214.

_____ . 1977. *Le roi pecheur et le roi chausseur*. Strasbourg: Travaux de l'Institut d'Anthropologie de Strasbourg. Institut d'Anthropologie.

Palmer, H.R. 1923. *Sudanese Memoirs*, vols. 1–3. Lagos: Government Printing House.

_____ . 1926. *History of the Last Twelve Years of the Reign of Mai Idris Alouma of Bornu (1571–1583) by his Imam Ahmed Ibn Fartua*. Lagos: Government Printing Office.

_____ . 1936. *Bornu, Sahara and Sudan*. London: John Murray.

Prins, P. 1900. Une annee de residence aupres de Mohamed Abd er-Rhaman Gaurang. Sultan de Bagirmi. *La Geographie* 3(13):177–92.

Rey, P.P. 1973. *Les Alliances de classes*. Paris: Maspero.

_____ . 1976. *Capitalisme negrier. La marches des paysans vers le proletariat*. Paris: Maspero.

Reyna, S.P. 1972. *The Cost of Marriage*. Unpublished Ph.D. dissertation. Columbia University, New York.

_____ . 1977. Metapower and Opportunity: A Multi-Level Analysis of Migration in Colonial Bagirmi. Unpublished manuscript. University of New Hampshire, Durham.

Shenton, B. and B. Freund. 1978. The Incorporation of Northern Nigeria into the World Capitalist Economy. *Review of African Political Economy* 13(8):8–31.

Smith, M.G. 1960. *Government in Zazzau* London: Oxford University Press.
Suret-Canale. 1964. Les Sociétés tradiunelles en Afrique noire et le concept du mode de production Asiatique. La Penseé. 177:19–42. London: Heineman.
Talbot, P.A. 1911. The Buduma of Lake Chad. *Africa* XII(9):12–32.
Urvoy, Y. 1949. *Histoire de l'Empire du Bornu.* Memoires de l'IFAN. Paris: Larose.
Vincent, J.F. 1975. *Le pouvoir et le sacre chez les hadjeray du Tchad.* Paris: Anthropos.
Weber, Max. 1968. *Economy and Society,* vol. 3. New York: Bedminster Press.
Wolf, Eric. 1982. *Europe and the People without History.* Berkeley: University of California Press.

Chapter 4

Toward a Marxist Rethinking of Third World Rural Industrialization

LEIGH BINFORD
SCOTT COOK

Marxists assume axiomatically that fundamental transformations in the organization and conduct of production and exchange, of the kind embodied in the concept of "commoditization" or the process of formation of a "commodity economy," necessarily result in the restructuring of social relations along class lines. The axiomatic status of this proposition has been forged and reinforced through generations of study and discourse focused on socioeconomic process in many different societies. Consequently, for Marxists, the analysis of social differentiation under conditions of commodity economy invariably begins with questions like "Where from?" "What kind of?" or "How much?" with regard to capital accumulation, enterprise expansion, and class formation.

More specifically, research undertaken to seek answers to these and related questions concerning the material bases of rural social differentiation—and the ideological and political ramifications of the latter—has long occupied students of underdeveloped and developed capitalist formations. The results of their research crowd the pages of academic publications from the First, Second, and Third Worlds, and have had considerable political fallout—especially in Marxist circles. Teodor Shanin (1980:83) has identified the stimulus for this scholarly activity with the phrase "measuring peasant capitalism" and has insightfully characterized it as follows:

> It has to do with capitalism as a process; it relates the understanding of the origins of our time to the characterization of the tenets of the global system we live in. It is both central and controversial, for, while different schools multiply argument and terminology, none have managed to avoid the issue of peasant differentiation and structural change.

Regardless of their position on the question of peasant differentiation, practically all schools of thought have tended to treat the Leninist and

Chayanovian aproaches as mutually antagonistic and analytically incompatible. In this chapter we reject such a perspective and prefer to follow the lead of Banaji (1976) in viewing Chayanov's arguments and ideas as a fundamental and necessary supplement to Leninist analysis (cf. Cook 1985). It is our view that the life cycle/demographic factor identified by Chayanov as crucial to understanding the dynamics of peasant economy (which he defined heuristically as a "natural economy" in which peasant households produced primarily for own-use without engaging in commodity production or wage labor) is not only reconcilable with Lenin's emphasis on objective socioeconomic factors but, in fact, provides an essential missing link in Lenin's explanation of social differentiation within rural commodity economies.

To anticipate an argument, which we will develop more fully below, it is our contention that the movement of household enterprises from conditions of petty commodity production to those of petty capitalism (which implies a movement from a noncapitalist to a capitalist location in the class structure) is significantly affected by household demographics through their impact on productive capacity and capital accumulation. Family labor contributes critically to capital accumulation in most household units that experience this movement; however, by no means do all petty commodity-producing households that experience such "endofamilial accumulation" (Cook 1984a, 1984b) cross the threshold to petty capitalist production. It is, therefore, a mistake to reduce the dynamics of social differentiation among peasant-artisan producers to household demographics as some recent contributions to the study of rural economy have tended to do.

While almost all petty commodity producing households pass through a demographic cycle, characterized by changing size and consumer/worker ratios, only a minority (larger or smaller according to the specific industry and possibilities for accumulation and investment) achieve a petty capitalist level of production that is reproduced primarily through the appropriation of surplus value from wage labor (usually remunerated by piece rate). The majority of households that do not achieve this level remain either at the level of petty commodity production, enter the rural proletariat, or are characterized by some degree of combination of petty commodity production and proletarian status (usually referred to as "semiproletarian"). Quite apart, then, from household demography and life cycle, there are a series of continuously operating material and ideological conditions that propel or constrain household movements so as to sustain a particular structure of social differentiation.

LENIN, CHAYANOV, AND CAROL SMITH:
AN INCOMPATIBLE THREESOME

For all of the heat and light it has generated, the study of rural social differentiation has been unbalanced and inconsistent. Not only has excessive emphasis been placed upon demographic/life cycle factors as opposed to socioeconomic factors, but it has often been the case that the role of industrial commodity production in social differentiation has been subordinated to an almost exclusive focus on the role of agriculture (Cook 1984c).

There have been some recent contributions that seek to overcome this latter imbalance. While they raise new theoretical problems or reopen old ones, they also perpetuate the Lenin vs. Chayanov opposition. For example, Carol Smith (1984), a prominent student of underdevelopment and rural Guatemala, has written a provocative article dealing with the process of social differentiation among petty industrialists in the Guatemalan municipality of Totonicapan in which she reformulated the concept of petty commodity production to include reproductive dependency on wage labor by its component peasant-artisan domestic units.

This reformulated concept, in effect, subsumes under the rubric of petty commodity production a situation Marx (1967), Lenin (1964), and most subsequent Marxist authors like Dobb (1963) have conceptualized as "petty capitalism," a concept Smith finds troublesome. As she expresses it (1984:82):

> In few cases of petty commodity production is the category of wage labour lacking. . . . Indeed the existence of some group able to expand or contract the family workforce seems a necessary feature of a fully commoditized economy. On the other hand, the producers we describe do not exploit a permanent proletariat, fail to accumulate capital, and do not differentiate into smaller and larger units with different technical requirements for production. The scale of production in all of these systems remains small (or petty). Thus it seems advisable to reconsider the defining feature of petty commodity production (lack of wage labour). I suggest that the defining feature should be the absence of a fully proletarianized, self-reproducing (sic!), labour force.

In order to differentiate petty commodity production from the situation usually referred to as "petty capitalism" Smith asserts that " . . . categories of owners and workers exist . . . but do not reproduce themselves as classes; instead, they reproduce each other through the life cycle" (Smith 1984:60).

Before addressing some of the specifics of Smith's argument, it will be instructive to consider her posture regarding Lenin's contribution and the Chayanovian tradition. To begin with, Smith (1984:61 passim) oversimplifies Lenin's views concerning the problem of class differentiation in capitalist development (as illustrated by her focus on the slogan "commodity economy enriches the few while ruining the masses"). She also rejects Lenin's thesis that capitalism appears historically in simple as well as complex forms and fails as well to deal substantively with his approach to differentiation through rural industrial commodity production (see Hussain and Tribe 1981:35-37 and Cook 1984c:6-9). In an early statement, which is representative of his approach to the problem, Lenin (*Collected Works* 1:217) asserted that " . . . peasant industry, in spite of its comparatively tiny establishments and low productivity of labour, its primitive technique and small number of wageworkers, is capitalism." He went on to criticize the Russian populists for their failure to "grasp the point that capital is a certain relation between people, a relation which remains the same whether the categories under comparison are at a *higher or lower level of development*" (emphasis in original). Lenin did not argue, as Smith's rendition of his views implies, that the presence of industrial or agricultural wage labor in the rural Russian economy was indicative of a process of class differentiation that depended for its rate of development on the *absolute dispossession* of the peasants (as Smith construes his argument in her repeated references to a "free proletariat" as the hallmark of capitalism and to the metaphorical proletarianization slogan). Rather than the growth of a *landless* proletariat, Lenin keyed upon the emergence of peasant-artisan households with *insufficient* land (Hussain and Tribe 1981:35).

For Smith the early twentieth century Russian "differentiation of the peasantry" literature (which she cavalierly dismisses as having "factual" but not "theoretical" significance, 1984:61) is less relevant to understanding the phenomenon in the "complicated world economy" of today than is the literature on U.S. "family farmers." Just as Friedmann (1978:96 passim) posits wage labor dependency as a temporary phase in the developmental cycle of Great Plains wheat farming households (and not necessarily symptomatic of a separate working class), so Smith posits wage labor as a temporary phase in the household cycle of Totonicapan weavers and not indicative of a "fully proletarianized, self-reproducing, labour force" (Smith 1984:82). Moreover, as mentioned above, she proposes that the presence of temporary, cyclical wage labor should become the generic defining feature of petty commodity production—though in doing so she is simply codifying a thesis already clearly proposed by Friedmann (1978:95, cf. 96).

We think that this abstract concern with the nature of petty commodity production in general—or, if you wish, the petty commodity mode of production (Cook 1977)—is analytically unrewarding. This is especially true in view of the previous efforts by several students of contemporary peasant artisans to conceptualize in operational terms the multiple potential involvements of peasant-artisan domestic units in value-creating and monetary circuits—including production for own-use, production for exchange, and wage labor (e.g., Cook 1978, 1982:ch. 8; Deere and de Janvry

1979; Palerm 1980). We believe that it is counterproductive to encumber the concept of petty commodity production with a reproductive dependency on wage labor for several reasons, among which two are prominent: (1) it wrongly conceives of petty commodity production as a creature of capitalism with no precapitalist history, and (2) it ignores the fact that, in reality, the extent to which peasant-artisan domestic units within capitalist formations participate in wage labor—not to mention the consequences of that participation—is always a matter for empirical determination.

The empirical record for peasant artisans in any contemporary Third World capitalist formation will show considerable intra- and intercommunity variation regarding participation in the labor market. When Smith encounters peasant-artisan households whose participation in labor is occasional, minimal, or nonexistent, she would claim that such units had been in the past, or will be in the future, in a different demographic situation—one in which they would not be capable of meeting their labor needs internally. So, her reformulation of petty commodity production as entailing wage labor dependency is drawn at the *industry* level; it is enough for some production units (those with domestic labor shortage) to hire labor (from households with a surplus or from new households without means of production) in order for *all* units to be designated as petty commodity producers. By contrast, we argue that it is untenable to assert that petty commodity production in all social formations across time and space is reproduced through wage labor. On the contrary, wage labor might better be taken as an index of capitalist production and its appearance in petty commodity enterprises as potential evidence of their transformation into petty capitalist enterprises. (We will examine this issue in more detail below.)

Smith's emphasis on a fully developed, "self-reproducing" proletariat, which implies that class self-reproduction is a *conditio sine qua non* of capitalism, seems to be derived from Chayanov's (1966) position that peasant households in the "family economy" were self-reproductive. However, to reiterate, Chayanov assumed for heuristic purposes that the typical peasant-artisan domestic unit was the "fully natural family farm" (or "family labor unit," Chayanov 1966:10-13) in which noncommodity activities, value forms (1966:27), and relations prevailed, and did not consider all rural households in the modern world to fit into this category. He accepted the Marxist thesis of social differentiation as valid for that sector of the rural social-economy in which commodity production and wage labor prevailed, although he emphasized the importance of household demographics in rural social differentiation.

Smith, like Chayanov, understands that the regional peasant-artisan population she is studying is inserted in a national and world capitalist economy. However, unlike Chayanov, Smith characterizes her Guatemalan peasant-artisan households as petty commodity producing units fully in-volved in capitalist circuits and markets—including, most importantly, the labor market. Under conditions of the prevalence of the wage category and wage relations within the commodity sector, it is quite clear that Chayanov would be less insistent about the operation of the labor-consumer balance or other equilibrating forces (1966:222-23), which he posited as nourishing the dominance of demographic factors in the development trajectories of peasant-artisan commodity-producing households (1966:244-49). Under such conditions, as is unmistakeably clear from his writings, Chayanov was in-clined to accept that Marxist scenario of class differentiation. In effect, Smith, then, has employed a Chayanovian explanation for an empirical situation that fails to exhibit the criteria for Chayanovian analysis. Consequently, whereas Smith quite correctly points to the importance demographic/life cy-cle factors may have in differentiating peasant-artisan households socioeco-nomically, she is wrong: (1) in denying that the capital/labor relations established among peasant artisans are, indeed, capitalist in nature and (2) in insisting that only household demographic/life cycle factors generate and reproduce such relations.

Finally, Smith's insistence that capitalism operates only through a per-manent, free proletariat, (1984:89-91 passim) not only ignores capitalism's pre-and proto-history (i.e., capitalism did not drop from the sky with its class relations "fully developed") but flies in the face of findings from a growing body of research on the "informal sector" in contemporary world capitalism that indicates that its structural funcion is to "alleviate, from the point of view of firms, consequences of the proletarianization process" (Portes 1983:163). This tendency of many advanced capitalist firms to "deproletarianize" labor in order to bring down its cost (e.g., bypassing minimum wages and fringe benefits via subcontracting household labor) parallels the earlier tendency of proto-industrial capital to employ rural or semirural household (especially female) labor (e.g., Tilly and Scott 1978; Goody 1982; Kriedte, Mednick and Schlumbohn 1981; Mednick 1976, 1981).

Similar tendencies are manifest today not only in the capitalist metropolis (e.g., Katz and Kemnitzer 1983) but throughout the Third World (e.g., Novelo 1976:214 passim; Ong 1983; Tai-Li 1983; Alonso 1983) and characterize multinational as well as national capital, advanced capital as well as "backward" capital (Portes 1983:161). Indeed, Wallerstein (1983:21-40) in explicating his concept of "historical capitalism" convincing-ly argues that the tendency toward the "commodification" or pro-letarianization of labor may not be as indicative of the needs of capitalist enterprise as semicommodified or semiproletarianized labor, which can be employed for lower wages and, therefore, *ceteris paribus* may be subjected to higher rates of exploitation. The past, the present, and future of capitalist industrial enterprise—whether small-, medium- or large-scale—is, according to Wallerstein, geared toward the employment of cheap labor, and labor is clearly purchased cheaper under semiproletarianized than it is under fully proletarianized conditions (1983:39).

While one may disagree with particular aspects of these arguments by Wallerstein and others, they are correct to emphasize that the types and conditions of labor that capital exploits are as variegated and changing as are the types and conditions of capital itself (e.g., Froebel, Heinrich, and Kreye 1978, 1980; Nash 1983). In sum, Smith's mechanistic identification of capitalism with *complete* proletarianization and her teleological insistence that capitalist accumulation requires *complete* rather than partial proletarianization are unacceptable.

In what follows, we demonstrate, through the analysis of field data gathered in the Oaxaca Valley in southern Mexico, how it is possible to construct an alternative view of petty commodity production and its relationship to petty capitalism.

THE CHAYANOVIAN APPROACH AND THE OAXACA VALLEY DATA

Since prehispanic times the Oaxaca Valley, located some 350 road miles south of Mexico City in the central highlands of the state of Oaxaca and surrounding its capital city, has had an intercommunity division of labor and specialization with widespread industrial commodity production (Blanton et al. 1981; Blanton and Kowalewski 1981; Kowalewski and Finsten 1983). While some commodities (e.g., metates) were produced in the prehispanic or colonial periods in the same communities in which they are produced today, others (e.g., bricks, cloth produced on treadle looms) are of either postcolonial origin or have assumed new forms in the postcolonial period. With few exceptions, valley settlements are also substantially involved in agriculture on lands communally or privately possessed, though private ownership is predominant over communal or ejidal forms of tenure (see Beals 1975; Cook and Diskin 1976; Cook 1982:6-18, 1984a:4-14, 1984b, and 1984c for more information on the society and economy of the Oaxaca Valley).

The results of research conducted in 23 villages and towns in the Oaxaca Valley between 1977 and 1981 in the Oaxaca Valley Small Industries Project yield a different view of the dynamics of petty industrial commodity production from that presented by Smith for Guatemala (see Cook 1984a:207-10 for a review of the Oaxaca Valley Small Industries Project). Our findings, based upon interviews with 1,008 households and the employment and entrepeneurial histories of selected informants in various rural industries, generally support the thesis that petty commodity producers may accumulate capital and, concomitantly, transform the nature of their enterprises and of the local social-economy in which they participate. Unlike Smith's thesis of the "undifferentiating" and "expanding" nature of petty industrial commodity production, our findings suggest that the latter both generates social differentiation in the form of class relations and involves capital accumulation together with investment to expand enterprise scale (if not to introduce "technological innovation"). In short, we find that petty commodity production in some industries has been and is providing a seedbed for capitalist development.

Three specific propositions, among others, have emerged from the analysis of the Oaxaca Valley materials: (1) the fact that peasant-artisan households aim for subsistence does not mean that they cannot also aim for capital accumulation, nor is their subsistence aim incompatible with new investment in commodity-producing operations; (2) household industrial enterprises may expand by supplementing or replacing unpaid family labor by hired labor together with investing capital in acquiring means of production that may not be technologically innovative but that do, nonetheless, increase productive capacity; and (3) there is a tendency for *certain* petty commodity producing enterprises to develop into petty industrialist enterprises that regularly employ wage labor but do not develop into medium- or large-scale capitalist enterprises.

The first of these propositions leads us directly into a confrontation with Chayanov and his quasi-Marxist supporter, Carol Smith, whose work we have critiqued above. Before introducing selected materials from the Oaxaca Valley, it is appropriate to summarize in a more systematic fashion our view of the relationship between the Chayanovian and Marxist approaches to rural capitalist development.

Chayanov was the leading proponent of the "organization and production school" (or Neo-Populists) approach to the analysis of rural social economy in late nineteenth-early twentieth century Russia and presented an analysis that ran counter to that of the "Agrarian Marxists" (Shanin 1980:88-98; Cox and Littlejohn 1984). Both groups agreed that there was inequality in the Russian countryside, but they sought to explain that inequality in ways that, if not mutually exclusive, are quite different in their respective emphases and implications. As Harrison (1977:332-37) notes, the Marxists related the aggregate data on inequality to trends toward socioeconomic differentiation, whereas the Chayanovians emphasized levelling mechanisms that counteracted such trends.

Chayanov's views were more complex than we can discuss here, and they were by no means void of internal contradiction, but there were two features of great significance for the problem at hand: (1) the role of the biological life cycle, which for Chayanov conditioned the ratio of working to nonworking household members and thus the intensity of labor workers would have to realize in order to reproduce the household (workers plus nonworkers) at any given level of consumption and (2) a theory of peasant consciousness, informed by the utility theory of marginalist economics, in which it was maintained that labor effort would continue until the marginal utility of the product was counterbalanced by the marginal disutility of the drudgery of work. For Chayanov the point of intersection or equilibrium always occurred somewhere around a socially defined consumption standard, which varied from community to community (Chibnik 1984:336). The impact of this, of course, was to deny the possibility of accumulation, since families with an advantageous consumer/worker ratio (which would be expected when previously dependent children become old enough to work outside the household or to contribute unpaid labor to household production enterprises) would opt for a reduced work load (labor intensity) in lieu of maintaining a work intensity that might generate an investible savings.[1]

The material in table 4-1 and table 4-2 provides little or no support for Chayanov's theory of "peasant consciousness." These tables are based upon the statistical analysis of interviews with 654 households engaged mainly in rural agriculture and craft production (with no separation of exclusively artisan households from peasant-artisan households). Among the most important figures are the highly significant negative correlations between both the number of family dependents (FAMDEPS) and the consumer/worker ratio (CWRATIO), on the one hand, with per capita annual household income (CASH), on the other. CASH is a measure of household income obtained by estimating the total value of all household products and wages and then dividing this result by the number of consumers (FAMSIZE). Since it corrects for family size, it provides a sound basis for comparing households with respect to their reproduction and investment potential. If Chayanov had been correct, then one would predict absolutely no relationship between consumer/worker ratio and per capita household income, since for him the level of household reproduction is fixed a priori by the community standard, and variations in consumer/worker ratio are compensated for by increases or decreases in labor intensity (measured by income per worker or WORKING). In fact, labor intensity (WORKING) has only a small positive (.14) correlation with the consumer/worker ratio.[2]

When the cases are divided into "stages" and the data are reanalyzed, as in table 4-2, we observe that, with the exception of stage 1 households (single/married with children) of which there are only 8 cases, the income per worker (WORKING) shows no consistent variation from stages 2 (all

TABLE 4.1. Spearman Rank-Order Correlation Coefficients: Variables for 654 Oaxaca Valley Households

	FAMSIZE	NUMFAM	FAMDEPS	CWRATIO	INCOME	WORKING	CASH
FAMSIZE	1.00						
NUMFAM	.43 (.0001)	1.00					
FAMDEPS	.82 (.0001)	−.10 (.01)	1.00				
CWRATIO	.44 (.0001)	−.55 (.0001)	.84 (.0001)	1.00			
INCOME	.08 (.03)	.18 (.0001)	−.01 (.86)	−.08 (.05)	1.00		
WORKING	−.10 (.01)	−.21 (.0001)	.02 (.61)	.14 (.0005)	.90 (.0001)	1.00	
CASH	−.28 (.0001)	.00 (.96)	−.31 (.0001)	−.25 (.0001)	.91 (.0001)	.90 (.0001)	1.00

children less than 5 years old) through 5 (all household members over 30 years), despite the fact that there is a steady decline in the consumer/worker ratio. It is on the basis of results such as these that we reject the utility approach and the theory of peasant consciousness that is derived from it.

On the other hand, we believe that Chayanov's views regarding the constraints imposed by household demography (which in and of themselves have nothing to do with "peasant consciousness") can become a valuable addition to the general Marxist model of rural social differentiation. Table 4-2 indicates that one consequence of maintaining work intensity in the face of declining consumer/worker ratios in stages 2 through 5 is a steady increase in the median per capita household income from 61 dollars to 120 dollars. In effect "mature" households (stages 4 and 5) are confronted with choices that are not available to those households with few workers and many nonworking dependents. Such households are in the position of being able to choose between elevating their levels of consumption—through the purchase of consumer items that were previously beyond their means—or, alternatively, foregoing additional purchases in order to save and invest earnings in the purchase of means of production. Where such purchase leads to the employment of outside wage labor, the household may cross the threshold from petty commodity production to petty capitalism. Whether this in fact occurs cannot be determined from the synchronic data, which we have analyzed thus far, and so for a deeper insight into the process of social differentiation in the Oaxaca Valley, we examine case study material from the treadle-loom weaving industry.[3]

TABLE 4.2. Demographic and Income Variables by Stage in the Household Development Cycle

Stage	(N)	FAM-SIZE	NUM-FAM	FAM-DEPS	C/W	INCOME	WORK-ING	CASH
1	8	2.2	2.0	0	1.0	607	249	249
2	368	6.7	2.0	4.0	2.5	388	143	61
3	164	5.7	3.0	3.0	2.0	423	168	81
4	58	3.9	3.0	1.0	1.4	382	165	107
5	54	2.0	1.0	0	1.0	213	131	120

PRODUCTION AND VALUE DISTRIBUTION
IN TREADLE-LOOM WEAVING

That capital accumulation and associated social differentiation are oc-curring within the rural petty commodity sector of the Oaxaca Valley can be illustrated through a consideration of the weaving industry. Production data for five household enterprises selected from one community are presented in table 4-3. Elsewhere we have presented comparable data for the brick industry (Cook 1984a; Cook and Binford 1985).

Whereas the five weaving units in our subsample (from the village of Xaagá) are smaller in scale than Smith's Totonicapan units—averaging, for example, only three regular employees per unit vs. eight per unit in her sample— we are prepared to argue on the basis of case study data that these five units deserve to be considered to represent petty capitalism rather than petty commodity production.

Xaagá is located 5 kilometers east of Mitla in the district of Tlacolula; it is an ex-hacienda community with all of its land controlled through the ejidal tenure regime. Among the 55 households randomly surveyed (in a community of 191 households), 84 percent participated in craft production. The craft occupation with the highest number of participants was shawl finishing (by patterned tying of loose ends of woven shawls), which was practiced in 36 percent of the households; 32 percent of the households had weavers, and 20 percent had sewing machine operators (i.e., seamstresses). About 90 percent of the seamstresses resided in weaving households, a fact that will be discussed below.

Xaagá weavers employ the treadle loom as their principal instrument of production. Their principal product is cotton and synthetic cloth, which is cut and sewn into polo shirts, blouses, dresses, shawls, and jackets. A few weavers produce and sell only cloth, but most of them weave cloth and then transform it into one or more of the above-mentioned products—either in their own home workshops or through a putting-out system employing female outworkers paid by piece-rate. The female jobs of seamstress and shawl-finisher are completely integrated within production units run by male weavers (or ex-weavers). Indeed, the typical production unit in the weaving industry consists of the tandem couplings: loom/male loom operator and sewing machine/seamstress. It is through skillful performance in organizing and managing production units comprised of one or more of these tandem couplings that a petty capitalist may be distinguished from a petty commodity producer in weaving. This skillful performance entails the regular employment of pieceworkers in combination with or in lieu of family labor to generate profit (cf. Cook 1985).

Of 28 weaving households surveyed in Xaagá, 10 had self-employed weavers who do not employ pieceworkers, 9 had self-employed weavers who do regularly employ pieceworkers (from which 5 cases have been

TABLE 4.3. Production Data, Treadle-Loom Weaving, Oaxaca Valley (all values in dollars)

Case No.	No. of Workers		Means of Production (MP)	Raw Materials	Wages (W)	Value of Output	Profit (P)	P/W	P/(MP+W)
	Family	Hire							
1.	0	3	387	64	42	156	50	1.19	.15
2.	1	2	265	177	124	368	67	.54	.17
3.	2	5	1,184	193	147	578	238	1.62	.18
4.	1	3	1,100	237	142	512	133	.94	.11
5.	1	3	1,117	171	118	533	244	2.07	.20
Subtotal	5	16	4,053	842	573	2,147	732		
Mean	1	3.2	811	168	115	429	146	1.27	.16
Median	1	3.0	1,100	177	124	512	133	1.19	.17

selected as our subsample in table 4-3), and 9 had weavers who were full-time pieceworkers (*operarios*). The average weekly income of the weavers was much higher than that of the seamstresses or the shawl-finishers. Most shawl-finishers (young girls or old women) earned less than $2.20 weekly, whereas seamstresses earned from 3 to 12 dollars weekly. Weaving pieceworkers, by contrast, earned 12 to 20 dollars weekly, whereas the average weekly net income for self-employed weavers (including both employers and non-employers) was 30 dollars.

A relative devaluation of female, as opposed to male, labor power is operative here. Male weavers were paid 3 pesos per meter for the standard type of cotton cloth and wove an average of 3 meters per hour (24 meters in an 8-hour day). Seamstresses were paid 2 pesos per shirt and sewed an average of 4 shirts per hour—most of them work only 4-hour days because of the need to perform domestic tasks. So the average weaver's wage was 9 pesos (40 cents) per hour or 72 pesos ($3.20) per 8-hour day compared to the average wage for a seamstress of 8 pesos (30 cents) per hour or 32 pesos ($1.40) per 4-hour day. Shawl-finishers, on the other hand, earned only 4-7 pesos per shawl (2 hours work) or the equivalent to an hourly wage of 3 pesos (13 cents). The issue of the devaluation of female labor power does not end here however. An important contributory factor to the viability of the weaving enterprise is not *low* wages but *no* wages; the household enterprise is nourished by unwaged female labor power ideologically construed as "helping out" (*ayuda*) rather than "work" (*trabajo*) (Cook 1984a:169; cf. Deere and Leon de Leal 1981:349).

Turning now to the employer units (see table 4-3), it is worth noting that their male proprietors are young (average age 30 years), that their employer status was recently achieved (average of 2.4 years prior to interview), and that they all had long prior experience (average of 9 years) as weaving pieceworkers in the workshops of the nearby town of Mitla. There were mixed incentives underlying their transitions from pieceworkers to independent operators: two explained their decisions to become independent in terms of the inconvenience of the daily commute to Mitla (either on foot or bicycle), another cited disagreements with his last Mitla employer, and still another expressed his rationale as seeking to make more money by selling his own products. Two of these individuals, prior to establishing their own workshops, had temporarily withdrawn from the craft—both citing various physical ailments and exhaustion from long hours spent on the loom. One of them spent the entire year out of weaving working full time as a peasant cultivator, while the other spent a somewhat longer interval as a goat trader. Yet, during this period of withdrawal, he admitted to "having in mind the idea of getting my own loom—but I couldn't figure out how to get the money."

The initial money capital required to purchase a complete loom outfit was accumulated by savings from pieceworker earnings in three cases; in others it was obtained through goat trading, a wife's inheritance, or a loan. Following this initial investment subsequent purchases of additional looms, sewing machines, and other equipment were made, in most cases, with saved earnings. In one case a sewing machine was already owned by the household prior to the purchase of its first loom, and in another a sewing machine was purchased simultaneously with the first loom; in all other cases sewing machines were purchased after looms had been in operation for a year or longer. The expansion of home workshops by these independent weaver-employers was steady and rapid. For example, case no. 3 (table 4-3) in 1977 was a one loom/no sewing machine/no employee operation, but by 1979 (at the time of our study) it had evolved into a 5 loom/2 sewing machine/4 employee operation. In 1980 this proprietor purchased a used pickup truck for $2,200, again from saved earnings—and in doing so became the first Xaagá weaving household to acquire a motor vehicle (and to follow a path already traversed by many Mitla weaver-merchants). Without exception, the other employer units in Xaagá have experienced comparable (if less dramatic in some cases) success in capital accumulation over the same period. (In Mitla and Teotitlan del Valle, there are many cases involving the development of substantially larger weaving enterprises than those recorded here in Xaagá, Beals 1975.) Enterprise histories such as these provide strong backing for our interpretation of synchronic data and our view that, given an appropriate economic environment, rural petty industrial commodity-producing units are fully capable of developing (by no means irreversibly) into petty capitalist enterprises.

Why did the development of units like those in our subsample involve the recruitment and regular employment of wage labor when it had not done so in many other employer units? One likely explanation lies in the division of labor by sex and household demographics or, more specifically, the composition of the in-house workforce. As already emphasized, in Xaagá there was a rigid sexual division of labor that exclusively channeled females away from weaving and into sewing and shawl-finishing, and males away from sewing and shawl-finishing and into weaving. There were no exceptions to this pattern. (This sexual division contrasted with the situation in two other principal treadle-loom weaving communities in Tlacolula, Teotitlan del Valle and Santa Ana del Valle, respectively, where household surveys did disclose some female involvement in weaving.) Consequently, households without, or with a shortage of, working age males are more likely to employ piecework weavers than those with more males. As it turns out, all five of the households in our subsample lacked sufficient personnel to expand weaving operations without resorting to hired labor. The fact that they are all relatively young households suggests that as underage family members mature, they will potentially displace hired workers.

However, it is equally plausible—and, indeed, had occurred in case no. 3—that new family entrants into the labor force do not displace hired workers but, on the contrary, may lead to additional hiring (e.g., a daughter is trained as a seamstress to work alongside her mother and a hired seamstress, giving the enterprise more sewing capacity, which necessitates the acquisition of an additional loom and the hiring of an additional weaver).

Before examining more closely the dynamics of the expansionist units, it is instructive to briefly consider the issue of nonexpansion. More specifically, why do self-employed weaver units, which have similar objective capabilities for expansion to those of expansionist units, fail to expand? There is no single answer to this question. In some cases, the units in question were recently established and had not had time to expand (e.g., five were one year old or younger at the time of the study). In other cases, weaving was looked upon by the weaver-proprietor, who was also a peasant cultivator, strictly as a part-time, seasonal occupation. In still other cases, the weaver-proprietors were unusually skilled and opted to increase earnings by weaving high quality products exclusively with family labor because they felt that quality would be sacrificed if workers were hired. Finally, one weaver-proprietor explained his decision not to purchase an additional loom and hire an employee in terms of his dislike for spending time looking for new customers, buying materials, and in effect, managing a business rather than working at a craft.

A comparison of ten self-employed weaving units in Xaagá (data not shown here) which have no employees with the five employer units (table 4-3), shows that the nonemployee units average 2.3 family workers each compared to only 1.0 for the employer units. This deficit in family workers is offset by an average investment in means of production by the employer units that is more than double that of the nonemployee units. This higher investment in means of production in combination with the employment of wage labor results in a monthly production value for the employer units that is 2.3 times greater than that for the nonemployee units. While these figures do not shed any light on the means or the reasons for the expansion of petty commodity producing enterprises, they do suggest that the results of such expansion bring substantial material benefits.

Their own long experience as exploited pieceworkers in Mitla sweatshops taught the Xaagá weavers the value of labor power long before they became employers themselves. But the viability of their own operations, in a market controlled by Mitla wholesale buyers, hinges significantly on their ability to produce with unwaged family labor—especially that of their seamstress wives and daughters—in combination with hired pieceworkers. The following statement by one of the two most successful employers underlines the importance of family labor:

In weaving one can benefit and help oneself substantially when one's wife and children cooperate. I am convinced that if my wife didn't help me I couldn't continue; this help is an important factor in the trade and in the home. There is work that one cannot do alone, so it's necessary that the family cooperate. I have observed that there are families where the husband works hard but where his wife doesn't collaborate, . . . and that's where there is little progress. Let's assume that my wife earned two pesos for each shirt she sewed; if we sold only our cloth without sewing it into shirts, those two pesos would pass into the hands of the merchant who buys the cloth to make shirts. I have thought about this and have analyzed that those two pesos benefit one's own household. The man or the weaver weaves, and the woman is the confectioner ("*El hombre o el tejedor teje y la mujer confecciona*") and is the one who goes to market—that's the foundation of it.

This is a clear-cut statement of the petty bourgeois strategy of "endofamilial" accumulation, which is employed by weavers like those in Xaagá as well as by brick producers in the Santa Lucia brick industry, analyzed by Cook (1984a). In other words, the achievement of their current employer status and its continued viability hinge significantly upon their use of nonwaged family labor. On appearances, then, there would seem to be real opportunities for some of today's pieceworkers to join the ranks of tomorrow's successful employers.

There is a larger reality in the Xaagá situation that places serious constraints on its approximating an idyllic petty bourgeois scenario, namely, the hegemony of Mitla merchant capital over the Xaagá industry. What confronts us here is a situation of capital accumulation by proxy, which has evolved through the partial de-industrialization of weaving in Mitla. Unlike their counterparts in late medieval/early modern England, the Mitla worker-owners turned piecework sweatshop operators appear to have rejected the path of "rationalization," which could have conceivably led them from workshop to manufactory to factory, and have opted to gradually disband their workshops—which were increasingly dependent on imported labor from Xaagá—to sell their well-used looms and accessories to their ex-*operarios*, and to concentrate on redeploying their capital toward the consolidation of their local monopoly over the sale of thread and other raw materials as well as over the marketing of locally produced textiles. Accordingly, the ex-*operario* from Xaagá, as neophyte shop proprietor, becomes essentially an engager of labor power in his own village labor pool for Mitla merchant capitalists who were willing to retreat from the field of production so as to exploit the cheap labor of Xaagá by proxy.

From this perspective, the Xaagá industry can be considered as being comprised of "castaway shops," which are held hostage by monopolistic merchant capital centered in Mitla. The burdens of proprietorship and managership of the means and process of production are increasingly being borne by the new Xaagá employers, but the lion's share of the profits flow in the Mitla direction. Only time will tell whether or not the Xaagá industry (or some of its enterprising representatives) will be able to break these bonds of subregional dependency, simply accomodate itself to them, or, perhaps, through persistent endofamilial and petty capitalist accumulation or outside help, drive Mitla capital into greener pastures outside of weaving.

PETTY COMMODITY PRODUCTION, ENDOFAMILIAL ACCUMULATION, AND PETTY CAPITALIST ACCUMULATION: IMPLICATIONS OF THE OAXACA VALLEY DATA FOR AN UNDERSTANDING OF PROVINCIAL CAPITALISM

It is clear from our Oaxaca Valley study that capitalist development is not occurring uniformly in the rural petty industrial sector. Indeed, there are several industries in which it is not occurring at all, others in which its trajectory is capricious and indeterminate, and in no case is its trajectory either unambiguously lineal, much less irreversible. In all cases its structuration is dynamic and its subjects'/agents' social locations are subject to change. Enterprises persist intergenerationally. There is turnover in personnel both on the capital and labor sides (some participate for lifetimes, others participate for shorter periods) just as there is differential time and labor commitment (full time vs. part time, seasonal vs. annual). But this dynamism should not be mistaken for the absence of capitalist production relations and forms of enterprise. After all, such dynamism is clearly characteristic of advanced capitalism as well, within which competition and declining rates of profit are dealt with through reorganizational strategies and capital redeployments that keep labor divided and on the defensive, profits flowing, and capitalist hegemony intact (e.g., Frobel, Heinrichs, and Kreye 1978; Portes 1983; Nash and Fernandez-Kelly 1983).

If one accepts a dynamic, processual view of capitalism, it is logical to interpret objective measures of differential economic status and performance by enterprises—patterned to show inequality with a tendency toward permanency in the employment of wage labor within the industry (as, for example, Smith's data on Totonicapan weavers does)—as indicative of petty capitalist development. Once it is shown that capital is being accumulated between turnover periods, that it is being reinvested in production (in a way that raises productive capacity, even if not in a technologically innovative way that raises labor productivity), that wage labor is regularly employed by piece-rate in the profit-taking enterprises, and that the value created by that labor is unequally distributed, then it is logical to assume that some form of capitalism, and not of petty commodity production, is indicated. This is confirmed ideologically when the piece wage nexus divides employers (*patrones*) from employees (*operarios* or *destajeros*) in people's social consciousness (as it does, for example, in the treadle-loom weaving industries in Totonicapan and in the Oaxaca Valley), when one's cash share of the value produced is conceptualized as "profit" or "wage," respectively, and where these relative shares are subject to ongoing negotiation (as they are in industries like brickmaking and treadle-loom weaving in the Oaxaca Valley).

Before peasant industrial capitalism can be measured, it must be recognized that there is not one but many phenomenal forms of capital. This is a recognition that appears to be absent from the approach of Smith (and others, like Friedmann), who adheres to a highly abstract, formalist model of capital as an articulated combination of particular sets of forces and relations of production, which presents itself phenomenally just as it is conceived theoretically, namely, with high levels of technology and a tendency toward labor-saving technological innovation, large-scale enterprises, completely polarized social classes, incremental profit-taking, and so on. While Smith attempts to view underdevelopment in Guatemala in historical perspective, she does not view the development of capitalism processually or comparatively. By implication, for her the specific histories and evolutionary dynamics of commodity production in Third World countries were forever preempted by the world-historical trajectory of commodity production in eighteenth and nineteenth century Europe, which culminated in the emergence of industrial capitalist production. In other words, capitalism from that point on can emerge in the Third World only from external colonial and neocolonial sources. Smith's adherence to this view only shows, of course, the extent to which she has been influenced by the dependency and world systems schools of thought.

We argue, contrary to this prevailing view, that it is mistaken to assume that in Third World countries like Mexico and Guatemala—where commodity production has strong precolonial as well as colonial roots—petty or incipient forms of capital cannot emerge as they did during the proto-industrial period in Europe (without assuming that their developmental potential or trajectory can or will replicate those of European proto-industrial capital). In other words, just as petty commodity forms historically generated petty capitalist forms in various branches of European industry, comparable developments can occur (and are occurring) in underdeveloped regional economies of the contemporary Third World.

The key to distinguishing between petty commodity production and petty capitalist production in a given household enterprise revolves around the conditions of value-creating labor. As Chayanov recognized, capital is necessarily accumulated for replacement, and also possibly for investment, in household production units dependent exclusively upon nonwaged family labor. In other words, in Chayanovian analysis (and also in Chevalier's recent analysis, 1983:178-79) capital accumulation is held to occur as a regular process within the "peasant family economy" (or peasant or petty commodity mode of production, defined to exclude wage labor). This process, the dynamics and outcome of which are a direct function of household demographics, has been analyzed by Cook (1984a, 1984c, and 1985) as "endofamilial accumulation." Discrete production units cross a threshold from petty commodity production and endofamilial accumulation into the realm of petty capitalist production when, among other things, wage laborers are *regularly* employed in lieu of or to supplement family laborers. The crossing of this "threshold" also implies that the petty commodity producers who cross it enlarge their stock of means of production and "treat the latter as means of profit accumulation" (Chevalier 1983:179).

More specifically, from an operational point of view (necessary for the conduct of theoretically informed empirical research) a commodity-producing unit (or enterprise) in a provincial underdeveloped economy like that of the Oaxaca Valey can be identified as "petty capitalist" when the following conditions are met: (1) the means of production are owned or controlled and the enterprise is managed by an individual or surrogate, (2) wage labor is regularly employed either in lieu of or to supplement family or reciprocal labor to the degree that it produces more than half of the value of unit output per turnover period, (3) the purpose of production for each turnover period is to generate a net cash return (profit) in excess of input costs, (4) the individual proprietor spends at least as much time in management and marketing as participating directly in production, and (5) over time the unit invests profits in the replacement as well as in either the improvement or expansion of means of production for the purpose of maintaining or increasing productive capacity (and possibly raising labor productivity) and, consequently, profit.

It is possible, in any given situation, that the capitalist threshold can be crossed at the enterprise level without being associated with a permanently polarized structuration of social classes at the community, industry, or regional levels. However, the capitalist threshold may be crossed at, for example, the industrywide level, even though only a minority (say, 10 percent) of the enterprises regularly employ wage labor (and meet the other criteria of capitalist performance) intergenerationally, provided that the value of their aggregate output accounts for more than half of the value of the total output of their industry. This may or may not be accompanied by a structural tendency toward such polarization, which will be expressed in the status or social location of individual households at any given time. Capitalism, more than any other economic system, is characterized by the possibility of short- and long-term agent mobility; the performance trajectories of discrete enterprises fluctuate, and competitively unsuccessful ones tend to dissolve just as the class position of individuals may change over time. This is most likely to be the case in provincial Third World regional economies dependent upon metropolitan capital for raw material and/or final product markets. Nevertheless, agent mobility does not rule out—it is rather indicative of—capitalist structure.

Household demographics may operate to propel specific enterprises across the capitalist threshold through high levels of endofamilial accumulation and subsequently force a retreat back into petty commodity production as endofamilial accumulation, for whatever reason, diminishes, or if levels of petty capitalist accumulation cannot be sustained. However, at the industry level the structural conditions underlying the possible transformation of individual enterprises remain in place. The retreat of some enterprises back into petty commodity production may be counterbalanced by the movement of others across the threshold into petty capitalism. Furthermore, despite the shifting mix of family/hired labor—linked among other things to changing household demographics—a certain proportion of petty capitalist enterprises is likely not to experience the retreat. Then, the problem of analysis becomes to explain why petty capitalist accumulation does not lead to more advanced forms of accumulation. This, of course, is quite a different problem (and much more legitimate) from the ill-conceived one posed by writers like Smith as to why the threshold of capitalist production is not crossed in the first place.

Needless to say, it is less difficult empirically to identify a particular enterprise as capitalist than is to so identify an industry, a branch of production, or an economy. Moreover, it is quite possible to identify capitalist enterprises within a noncapitalist industry. If we grant Smith the possibility that the weaving industry in Totonicapan may not be capitalist (according to the formula outlined above), it seems to us clear that many individual enterprises (e.g., Smith's 15 "successful" weaver units) are demonstrably so.

It is appropriate, before closing, to briefly address the following question: Beyond considerations of academic discourse or a scientific concern with the production of valid knowledge, why should the problem of relationship between commodity production and class differentiation in the Third World countryside continue to hold our attention? From our perspective the answer lies in politics and policy making—or, more specifically, in the space where they overlap. This is because, as Lenin's contribution demonstrated, a central "task of analysis in Marxist investigation . . . is the formation of a basis for political work" (Ennew, Hirst, and Tribe 1977:301) and also because of our appreciation ex post facto of the political ramifications of the running debate generated by this problematic in late nineteenth/early twentieth century Russia where scholarly careers and lives were jeopardized or sacrificed in its pursuit. Another factor that has influenced our thinking is the extreme social conflict, the cycle of state-sponsored violence and popular counter-violence that pervades many Third World polities at the present conjuncture, and of the need for devising counter-hegemonic strategies that serve the political interests of the direct-producing, popular majorities.

In the case of Guatemala, for example, are we to assume—following Smith's lead—that neither an original nor continuing basis of indigenous peasant-artisan participation in popular revolt throughout the Western highlands lies in their experiences in the small industrial sector of the commodity economy? Is not Smith's denial of a linkage between the production of value, its unequal distribution, and class differentiation among petty Guatemalan industrialists tantamount to precluding the possibility that the conditions in which many rural Guatemalans live and work may be related directly or indirectly to their political involvement or inclinations? Whether intentional or not, these inferences do follow inevitably from Smith's interpretation of her field data. In opposition to her interpretation, we propose that industrial commodity production, together with agriculture and commerce, has contributed to the differentiation of highland Guatemalan Indian society into "incipient social classes" (Wasserstrom 1975:478) and that the differentiation process has possibly had a significant political impact—at least since the period of Arbenz—that both crosscuts and injects class content into the endemic ethnic hatred usually emphasized by anthropologists (e.g., Siegel 1954) in attempts to explain the pathology of Guatemalan politics. It remains the task of future analysts to examine and evaluate in Guatemala and elsewhere the socioeconomic, ideological, and political significance of peasant-artisan household involvement in industrial commodity production—a task that has been either neglected or poorly performed since Lenin's seminal contribution.

NOTES

1. It is clear from reading Chayanov that he was inconsistent in his handling of capital accumulation by peasant-artisan household enterprises. He acknowledged the possibility of saving and investment (in addition to capital replacement) in the short run but seemed to deny it in the long run. Short-term flexibility was necessary in order for the supply of non labor inputs to expand and to meet the needs of growing households. Consequently, where the supply of consumers and workers was increasing, there would have to be both a savings fund and an investment fund, regardless of the consumption standard (cf. Harrison 1977:330). Against this, however, long-run capitalization was simply ruled out. In short, we agree with Patnaik that, 'The analysis of . . . 'capital accumulation' . . . is the point where the contradiction between class reality and Chayanov's classless model appears most glaring" (1979:391).

2. Of the 1,008 households in the total sample there was adequate information to estimate CASH (annual per capita household income) for 685 households or 67.5 percent, among which there were peasants, artisans, peasant-artisans, and a mixed category of professionals, waged employees, etc., accounting for only about 30 cases. An additional 31 cases with values equal to or less than zero were deleted as untrustworthy, leaving 654 cases (64.5 percent) in the sub-sample. NUMFAM refers to the number of workers in the family. FAMDEPS refers to the number of nonworkers. CWRATIO is calculated by dividing the number of resident household members (equals FAMSIZE) by the number of workers (NUMFAM). INCOME refers to estimated annual household income. WORKING estimates income generated by the average worker and is obtained by dividing INCOME by NUMFAM.

3. The values for FAMSIZE are means; values for all other variables are medians. IN-COME, WORKING, and CASH are in dollars. Stages 1-5 in the household developmental cycle were borrowed from Murphy and Selby (1981) and are defined as follows: 1—single/married without children; 2—all children less than 5 years old; 3—all children 5 years or older; 4—all children 15 years or older; 5—all household members over 30 years of age.

REFERENCES

Alonso, J.A. 1983. The Domestic Clothing Workers in the Mexican Metropolis and Their Relation to Dependent Capitalism. In *Women, Men and the International Division of Labor*. J. Nash and M. Fernandez-Kelly (eds.). Albany: State University of New York Press.

Banaji, J. 1976. Chayanov, Kautsky, Lenin: Considerations Towards a Synthesis. *Economic and Political Weekly*, October 2:1594-607.

Beals, R. 1975. *The Peasant Marketing System of Oaxaca, Mexico*. Berkeley and Los Angeles: University of California Press.

Blanton, R. and S.A. Kowalewski. 1981. Monte Alban and After in the Valley of Oaxaca. *Supplement to the Handbook of Middle American Indians*. J. Sabloff (ed). Austin: University of Texas Press.

Blanton, R. et al. 1981. The Valley of Oaxaca. In *Ancient Mesoamerica, a Comparison of Three Regions*. London: Cambridge University Press.

Chayanov, A.V. 1966. *The Theory of Peasant Economy*. Homewood, Illinois: Irwin.

Chevalier, J. 1983. There Is Nothing Simple About Simple Commodity Production. *Journal of Peasant Studies* 10: 153-186.

Chibnik, M. 1984. A Cross-Cultural Examination of Chayanov's Theory. *Current Anthropology* 25 (3): 335-340.

Cook, S. 1977. Beyond the Formen: Towards a Revised Marxist Theory of Precapitalist Formations and the Transition to Capitalism. *Journal of Peasant Studies* 4 (4): 360-89.

_____ . 1978. Petty Commodity Production and Capitalist Development in the "Central Valleys" Region of Oaxaca, Mexico. *Nova Americana* I: 285-332.

_____ . 1982. *Zapotec Stoneworkers*. Lanham, Maryland: University Press of America.

_____ . 1984a. *Peasant Capitalist Industry*. Lanham, Maryland: University Press of America.

_____ . 1984b. Rural Industry, Social Differentiation, and the Contradictions of Provincial Mexican Capitalism. *Latin American Perspectives* 11 (43): 60-85.

_____ . 1984c. Peasant Economy, Rural Industry and Capitalist Development in the Oaxaca Valley, Mexico. *Journal of Peasant Studies* 12 (1): 3-40.

_____ . 1985 (forthcoming). Entrepeneurship, Capital Accumulation, and the Dynamics of Simple Commodity Production in Rural Oaxaca, Mexico. In *Entrepreneurship*. S. Greenfield and A. Strickson (eds.). Lanham, Maryland: University Press of America.

Cook, S. and L. Binford. 1985. Commodity Economy and Capital Accumulation Without Social Differentiation? A Critique of Quasi-Chayanovian Marxism. Unpublished manuscript. University of Connecticut, Department of Anthropology.

Cook, S. and M. Diskin (eds.). 1976. *Markets in Oaxaca*. Austin: University of Texas Press.

Cox, T. and G. Littlejohn (eds.). 1984. *Kritsman and the Agrarian Marxists.* Special Issue, *Journal of Peasant Studies* 11 (2).

Deere, C. and A. de Janvry. 1979. A Conceptual Framework in the Empirical Analysis of Peasants. *American Journal of Agricultural Economics* 61: 601-611.

_____ . and M. Leon de Leal. 1981. Peasant Production, Proletarianization, and the Sexual Division of Labor in the Andes. *Signs* 7 (2): 338-360.

Dobb, M. 1963. *Studies in the Development of Capitalism*. New York: International.

Ennew, J., P. Hirst, and K. Tribe. 1977. Peasantry as an Economic Category. *Journal of Peasant Studies* 4 (4): 295-322.

Friedmann, H. 1978. Simple Commodity Production and Wage Labour in the American Plains. *Journal of Peasant Studies* 6 (1): 71-100.

Froebal, F., J. Heinrichs, and O. Kreye. 1978. The New International Division of Labor. *Social Science Information* 17 (1): 123-142.

_____ . 1980. *The New International Division of Labor*. London: Cambridge University Press.

Goody, E. (ed.). 1982. *From Craft to Industry*. London: Cambridge University Press.

Harrison, M. 1977. The Peasant Mode of Production in the Work of A.V. Chayanov. *Journal of Peasant Studies* 4 (4): 323-36.

Hussain, A. and K. Tribe. 1981. *Marxism and the Agrarian Question, Vol. 2, Russian Marxism and the Peasantry 1861-1930*. Atlantic Highlands, New Jersey: Humanities Press.

Katz, N. and D. Kemnitzer. 1983. Fast Forward: The Internationalization of Silicon Valley. In *Women, Men and the International Division of Labor*. J. Nash and M. Fernandez-Kelly (eds.). Albany: State University of New York Press.

Kowalewski, S. and L. Finsten. 1983. The Economic Systems of Ancient Oaxaca: A Regional Perspective. *Current Anthropology* 24 (4): 413-42.

Kriedte, P., H. Mednick, and J. Schlumbohm. 1981. *Industrialization Before Industrialization*. London: Cambridge University Press.

Lenin, V.I. 1927. *Collected Works, Vol. 1*. New York: International Publishers.

Lenin, V.I. 1964. *The Development of Capitalism in Russia*. Moscow: Progress.

Marx, K. 1967. *Capital*. New York: International.

Mednick, H. 1976. The Proto-Industrial Family Economy: The Structural Function of Household and Family during the Transition from Peasant Society to Industrial Capitalism. *Social History* 1 (3) 291-315.

———. 1981. The Proto-Industrial Family Economy. In *Industrialization Before Industrialization*. P. Kriedte et al (eds.). London: Cambridge University Press.

Murphy, A. and H. Selby. 1981. A Comparison of Household Income and Budgetary Patterns in Four Mexican Cities. *Urban Anthropology* 10 (3): 247-67.

Nash, J. 1983. The Impact of the Changing International Division of Labor on Different Sectors of the Labor Force. In *Women, Men and the International Division of Labor*. J. Nash and M. Fernandez-Kelly (eds.). Albany: State University of New York Press.

Nash, J. and M. Fernandez-Kelly (eds.). 1983. *Women, Men and the International Division of Labor*. Albany: State University of New York Press.

Novelo, V. 1976. *Artesanías y Capitalismo en México*. Mexico, D.F.: SEP-INAH.

Ong, A. 1983. Global Industries and Malay Peasants in Peninsular Malaysia. In *Women, Men and the International Division of Labor*. J. Nash and M. Fernandez-Kelly (eds.). Albany: State University of New York Press.

Palerm, A. 1980. *Antropología y Marxismo*. Mexico: Editorial Nueva Imagen.

Patnaik, U. 1979. Neo-Populism and Marxism: The Chayanovian View of the Agrarian Question and Its Fundamental Fallacy. *Journal of Peasant Studies* 6 (4): 375-420.

Portes, A. 1983. The Informal Sector: Definition, Controversy, and Relations to National Development. *Review* VII (1): 151-74.

Shanin, T. 1980. Measuring Peasant Capitalism. In *Peasants in History*. Oxford University Press.

Siegel, M. 1954. What Will the New Regime Offer as its Own? *New Republic* July 19: 11-13.

Smith, C. 1984. Does a Commodity Economy Enrich the Few While Ruining The Masses? Differentiation among Petty Commodity Producers in Guatemala. *Journal of Peasant Studies* 11 (3): 60-95.

Tai-Li, H. 1983. The Emergence of Small-Scale Industry in a Taiwanese Rural Community. In *Women, Men and the International Division of Labor*. J. Nash and M. Fernandez-Kelly (eds.). Albany: State University of New York Press.

Tilly, L. and J. Scott. 1978. *Women, Work, and Family*. New York: Holt, Rinehart and Winston.

Wallerstein, I. 1983. *Historical Capitalism*. London: Verso Editions.

Wasserstrom, R. 1975. Revolution in Guatemala: Peasants and Politics under the Arbenz Government. *Comparative Studies in Society and History* 17: 443-78.

PART 3
Profit, Accumulation, and Crisis

Chapter 5

Accumulation and Crisis

KENT A. KLITGAARD
VALARIE D. ELLIS

When one looks into the possibility of crisis within the capitalist system, one is led to the process of capital accumulation, or the self-expansion of capital, if the analysis chosen is one that encompasses not only the sphere of exchange (the seamy realm of bourgeois economics) but also the process of production. This is the method selected by Karl Marx in explicating the "laws of motion" of capitalist society. Crises do not fall from the sky (as William Stanley Jevons would have us believe in his infamous sunspot theory) but rather are endemic to the capitalist system. Marx's analyses of the accumulation of capital and the possibility of crisis are derived from the theory of value, technological change, and the competition of capitals, as well as an analysis of the historical evolution resulting in the capitalist mode of production.

In the pages of his major work, *Das Kapital*, Marx did not set down a systematic theory of crises. Rather, there are bits and pieces of a crisis theory throughout the work at varying levels of abstraction. However, one thing is certain. An adequate analysis of capitalist crisis entails dealing with capitalist production as a whole, including not only the immediate process of production but also its interrelation with the circulation sphere. This point is crucially important because on the level of the individual capitalist a theory of generalized crisis would make little sense. It is only from the interaction of the multitude of capitalists—the social capital—that a theory of accumulation and crisis can be derived. Since the interactions of the social capital entail the exchange, not only of finished commodity outputs, but also commodity inputs, one must analyze the process of circulation among capitalists as well as a between capitalists and workers. Marx accomplished this level of abstraction in volume III of *Capital*, where most of what is termed his crisis theory is found. However, an analysis of accumulation must start with the production process of the individual capitalist.

This chapter will begin with the labor theory of value as the key to unlock the mystery of capitalist production. It will posit certain historical events. The first is that the era of primitive accumulation has already taken place and industrial capitalists have situated themselves in the position of the ruling class. The working class has been stripped of its privately owned means of production and must make its living only by selling its labor power to the capitalist as a commodity. The level of technology has developed to the large-scale use of machinery. With this advent of modern industry, capital is able to expand surplus value relatively. This last point is crucial to the theory of technological change, which is, in turn, integral to the Marxian theory of accumulation.

Production is carried on under a specifically capitalist process; that is, commodities have been produced by the interaction of wage labor and capital. They have not appeared miraculously as the "manna" endowments of the Walrasian general equilibrium framework, nor have they been produced by independent artisans and brought to market to be exchanged for different use values. The circuit of capital, M–C–M', is production for profit, with the use value of the commodity serving as an intermediate step:

> The objective content of the circulation we have been discussing—the valorization of value—is his (the capitalist) subjective purpose, and it is only in so far as he functions as a capitalist, i.e., as capital personified. . . . Use values must therefore never be treated as the immediate aim of the capitalist; nor must the profit on any single transaction. His aim is rather the increasing movement for profit making. (Marx 1976:988)

Having posited the assumptions necessary for capitalist production and accumulation, it becomes necessary to analyze some limits to capital accumulation. Marx demonstrated that these limits fall from the nature of the accumulation process. However, at the same time, he did not deny that capitalism could reproduce itself. Part III of volume II shows exactly how, given correct action on the part of the capitalists, the possibility of "general equilibrium" exists. In the chapter on "simple reproduction" in volume II, Marx sets the equilibrium condition for reproduction as I v + s = II c. For the rest of the chapter, he outlines why this equilibrium condition for simple (and later expanded) reproduction is not likely to be met.

Early in the first volume, while analyzing the circuit of commodities, Marx asserted that the possibility of crisis exists as soon as there is a break in the circuit. In volume II this point is carried further; breaks in the process of circulation set the objective possibility of crisis because they can keep commodity values from being realized at their full value. The mechanics and value relations of these realization crises (as compared to their objective possibility) are analyzed in volume III of *Capital*, subtitled "The Process of Production as a Whole."

The basic tenets of the labor theory of value should be familiar and therefore need not be developed in detail here. Marx defines value as the socially necessary labor time embodied in the production of a commodity. In an era of specifically capitalist production, these commodities are produced by a work force that has also sold its labor power to the capitalist as a commodity. Since at this level of abstraction it is assumed that commodities exchange at their values and no cheating is taking place, how is it that the capitalist can accumulate? How can M–C–M′ take place?

Accumulation takes place by the production and extraction of surplus value—a concept carefully developed by Karl Marx. Since labor power is a commodity, it has a value—the value of the socially necessary commodity bundle that enables workers to reproduce themselves and their families and return to the workplace in a condition in which they are able to perform labor. The workers have exchanged labor power for wages. Owning no means of production themselves, the workers have given up their control of the labor process to the capitalists. Given the advent of machinery, division of labor, and specialization, workers can produce their value in less than a working day (the day being Marx's unit of measurement).

Throughout volume I of *Capital*, Marx usually assumed for mathematical simplicty that half of the work day would be spent reproducing the worker's needs (i.e., paid labor) and that during the other half of the day the worker would labor for the capitalist free of charge. Marx called the ratio, *unpaid labor/paid labor*, the rate of surplus value or the rate of exploitation.

From the point of view of the capitalist, the relevant calculation is somewhat different—calculated in terms of capital advanced and received. Given variable capital or the value of money advanced by the capitalist for wages, and surplus value or the free labor appropriated by the capitalist, then s/v = unpaid labor/paid labor = rate of surplus value.

At the end of a specified labor process, a unique effect has occurred. When the capitalist productively consumed this labor power, combined with means of production, the creation of value in excess of labor power and means of production resulted.

Here the mystery of accumulation is solved, albeit at a most abstract level. Accumulation can occur when commodities exchange at their values because this productive consumption of labor power created additional value: surplus value. In the immediate process of production this surplus can become capital because "the process of production of commodities is the immediate unity of the processes of labor and valorization" (Marx 1976:978-79). To valorize her or his capital, the capitalist takes realized surplus value and reinvests it into the production process. This larger mass of capital now creates a larger mass of surplus value at the end of the process. M′ is greater than M, and accumulation has taken place.

The assumption concerning relative surplus value now becomes crucial. The way a capitalist increases his or her rate of accumulation at this stage is to increase the rate of surplus value, s/v. When this is done relatively, the goal is to decrease v or decrease the average amount of socially necessary labor time embodied in wage goods (Marx 1976:436-37).

The question now becomes one of finding the method of increasing labor's productivity. Before the advent of capitalist production, great advances in productivity had been occasioned by the division of labor and cooperation among workers. Under capitalist production, advances in labor productivity were made possible by the use of machinery. The machine, which connected a tremendous power force to several tools, replaced the hand as the motive force of industry. Strength and stamina requirements were greatly altered. By changing the motive force from the hand to automation, the work of hundreds of humans could be done by a single machine.

> The steam hammer works with an ordinary hammer head, but of such weight that Thor himself could not wield it. . . . It is mere child's play for it can crush a block of granite into powder, yet it is no less capable of driving a nail into a piece of soft wood with a succession of taps. (Marx 1976:507-8).

Although the machine and technological innovation made the remaining labor much more productive, many workers were completely displaced. While much of this displacement belonged to the epoch of the transition to modern industry, the substitution of constant capital (c) in the form of new and more productive labor-saving machinery would still displace workers through technological unemployment. In observing this historical and empirical phenomenon, Marx was able to formulate his theory of the labor supply in the reserve army of the unemployed, as well as the "general law of capitalist accumulation."

If an individual capitalist could innovate with a new form of constant capital and lower the unit cost of his or her particular commodity, while selling it at the prevailing price, a larger profit could swell the accumulation fund of the particular capitalist. The incessant drive for more and more profit on the part of the capitalist leads, however, to a twofold contradiction. The first is the tendency of the rate of profit to fall. Only living labor can create new value. The productive consumption of constant capital will only transfer the value consumed to the price of the commodity. As the capitalist innovates by introducing new constant capital, there is relatively less living labor to create new value. New capital, however, can make labor more productive, which is why it is introduced in the first place. This is an important counteracting effect on the fall in the rate of profit. Given the existence of counteracting effects within the capitalist accumulation process, Marx chose to formulate the fall in the rate of profit as a tendency rather than as an ironclad law.

To elucidate the analysis, Marx needed to introduce the notion of the composition of capital, which was to be understood in a twofold sense.

> As value it is determined by the proportion which it is divided into constant capital, or the means of production, and variable capital, or the value of labor power, the sum of total wages. As material, as it functions in the process of production, all capitals divided into means of production and living labor power. . . . I call the former the value composition and the latter the technical composition of capital. There is a close correlation between the two. To express this I call the value composition of capital, in so far as it is determined by its technical composition and mirrors the changes in the latter, the organic composition of capital. (Marx 1976:507-8)

As a capitalist invests in labor-saving constant capital and displaces living labor, the technical composition, or the ratio of capital to labor in the physical sense, as well as the organic composition, rises.

What now becomes of the all important rate of profit, defined as surplus value divided by total capital advanced, $s/c + v$? Given less value-creating living labor (expressed through the organic composition c/v), it logically follows that the rate of profit should fall. If the ratio is divided through by v, the relation becomes clearer:

$$\frac{s}{c + v} = \frac{s/v}{(c/v) + 1}.$$

If c/v increases, the denominator of the fraction increases and the entire ratio falls. Unchecked, capital accumulation will tend to lower the rate of profit. However, since an increase in labor productivity also increases the rate of exploitation, an important counteracting effect is built directly into the accumulation process. This effect, combined with conscious class struggle on the part of both capital and labor, tends to make the rate of profit fluctuate.

Another important question waits to be asked. What is the effect of the growth of capital on the working class? As capital accumulates, the demand for labor in the accumulating sectors rises, and wages tend to increase if the composition of capital remains the same. But eventually this rise in wages can have a dampening effect on the ability of the capitalist to accumulate (Marx 1976: 771).

However, the technical composition of capital does not remain the same. Rather, living labor is displaced by dead labor in the form of machinery:

> Since the demand for labor is determined not by the extent of the total capital but by its variable constituent alone, that demand falls progressively with the growth of total capital, instead of rising in proportion to it, as was previously assumed. (Marx 1976:781)

Those set "free" by technological unemployment function as a relative surplus population or the industrial reserve army of the unemployed. The existence of a large mass of unemployed places downward pressure on wages as well as functioning to dissuade labor from shop floor struggles over working conditions. If workers complain about those conditions, they can be replaced by members of the reserve army:

> The over-work of the employed part of the working class swells the ranks of its reserve, while conversely, the greater pressure that the reserve by its competition exerts on the employed workers forces them to submit to over-work and subjects them to the dictates of capital. (Marx 1976:781)

The reserve army is recruited from those thrown out of work by the introduction of constant capital and those who have been rendered redundant by their role in a specific production process. The existence of the reserve army, occasioned by the accumulation of capital itself, is a most important check on the growth of wages and working class power. Such a check is an important weapon in capital's arsenal for the battle of self-expanding value.

Up to this point it has been established that under capitalist production the accumulation of capital leads to a tendency for the rate of profit to fall with an increase in the organic composition of capital. This process also creates a reserve army of the unemployed. Marx identified this tendency as an important "law of motion" of capitalism. While the classical political economists also believed that the rate of profit would fall with accumulation, their theory was based on agricultural, and not industrial, capitalism. The classicals (especially Ricardo) envisioned productivity increases on available land as fixed within narrow limits and anticipated an eventual end to accumulation.

Marx, on the other hand, ties his theory of accumulation to industrial capitalism. While constant capital displaced value-creating living labor, and thereby created a tendency for the profit rate to fall, it also helped initiate vast productivity increases, which caused the mass of profit to rise. Instead of the stationary state, Marx envisioned a "decennial cycle." Capital was still capable of self-expansion, but the limits of accumulation would assert themselves at various stages of the process. Instead of the eventual stagnation of society, Marx offers a theory of recurrent crises.

Until this point it has been assumed that commodities are realized at their full values and that surplus value has been capitalized. To fully grasp the complexities of crises, it is necessary to include the process of circulation. This will establish the basis for an analysis of the competition of capitals, the driving force in the tendency for the rate of profit to fall, as well as the second law of motion of capitalism, the concentration and centralization of capital.

When capitalists compete with each other and utilize the circulation process, the rate of profit tends to equalize among capitals. During the process of competition, capital flows in search of the highest rate of profit from sectors with a high organic composition to those with a low organic composition. Since some capital is fixed in immobile plant and equipment, the equalization of the profit rate takes place during the time when capitalists make new investments; that is, it takes place during accumulation.

The individual capitalist does not earn a profit on his or her own advanced capital, but rather by interrelating with other capitalists, receives a share of the aggregate surplus value produced:

> Average profit is the basic conception, the conception that capitals of equal magnitude must yield equal profits in equal time spans. This, again, is based on the conception that the capital in each sphere of production must share pro rata to its magnitude in the total surplus value sqeezed out of the laborers by the total social capital; or, that every individual capital should be regarded merely as a part of the total social capital, and every capitalist actually as a shareholder in the total social enterprise, each sharing in the total profit pro rata to the magnitude of his share of capital. (Marx 1967b: 789-90)

While the rate of profit tends to equalize through competition, the dialectical nature of Marx's *Capital* also shows the opposite tendency—the disequalization of profit. To analyze this apparent contradiction, we must delve into the motive force of capitalist competition—that of technological change. Technological change is brought about as each individual capitalist tries to raise his or her profit rate by lowering unit costs of production. There are both technical and social aspects to this change.

The technical aspects entail the linking of a motive force to a number of tools and the application of the principles of science to the production process. These are important in two major ways. First, the new machinery, by replacing the hand as the motive force, greatly increases labor's productivity on the physical level. Second, the standardized machinery allows for the separation of conception and execution of labor. This is where "scientific management" got its start (Braverman 1974: 85-121).

Changes in the production process entail changes in the labor process. Labor can now be differentiated into universal labor, that which is charged with the application and direction of the new technology (i.e., middle and lower echelon managers, technicians, etc.) and operative labor, which is a mere appendage of the machine.

The division of labor and specialization are the backbones of capitalist production. This means that in order to obtain his or her productive inputs, the capitalist must depend on the market. Although a capitalist may control her or his production process, she or he stands external to the sphere of circulation. Few capitalists are in the position to generate internally all their own technical innovations. In order for capitalists to obtain the needed equipment to lower their unit costs and compete effectively, they must purchase constant capital from the capitalists in department I who produce means of production as commodities.

The sale of new technologies on the commodity market is a key to both their generalization and their expansion. With a new technology a capital-goods producer can carve out a new market sphere, the innovating capitalist reaps an extra benefit. Once the technology is adopted by other innovating capitalists, this windfall profit disappears as the technique is generalized. This long-run phenomenon of generalization is, of course, due to the interaction of the social capital.

The system can benefit the individual inventor who has created a commodity useful to capital. An individual inventor may create and patent a new technique but must sell it on the commodity market. Patent laws help in the standardization of techniques and can provide others with technical information. Since the most efficient techniques have a beneficial effect on the rate of profit, it is in the self-interest of the capitalist to introduce and generalize these techniques. It must be noted, however, that since this is done through the mediation of the market, the technologically competing capitals become structurally interdependent (Bischak 1978: 4).

Given this structural interdependence of the social capital, technological change forms the foundation of the laws of motion of capitalism. Forced to compete with its rivals, a firm would want to introduce a new technology if it could lower the unit cost of output or decrease the turnover time of capital. To lower the production costs a new technique should economize on either constant or variable capital and thereby reduce the value of the commodity in relation to prevailing techniques. This often means the introduction of expensive capital equipment, which increases the organic composition of capital and hence tends to drive down the rate of profit.

Although capitalists would not willingly lower their rate of profit, in a competitive situation they have little choice. If they do not introduce new machinery to increase labor's productivity and lower the value of their commodities, they are soon producing with relatively high unit cost and find themselves prime candidates for being eliminated from the market place by their lower cost competitors.

The price relationships derived from this competition would differ depending upon demand conditions. If demand were expanding at a rate sufficient to absorb the increased output, the innovating capitalist would sell at the going price and realize a higher profit. That is, profit would be realized from a lower cost price. However, demand conditions may not be expanding proportionately with output capacity. This leads capitalists to cut prices in an attempt to increase their market share, which leads to Marx's second law of motion—that of the concentration and centralization of capitals.

If demand is not growing, the innovating capitalist with a higher profit margin could lower unit costs and squeeze capitalists with higher unit costs from the market. In the extreme, efficient producers can lower their commodity prices below the cost prices of their higher cost competitors, thereby eliminating them from competition (Bischak 1978: 5).

When demand is falling during periods of crisis, high cost producers are forced from the market and bought up at bargain prices by their more efficient competitors. This is the mechanism by which capital concentrates and centralizes: It is a process of competition and technological change. Hence, the concentration and centralization of capital, as well as the tendency of the rate of profit to fall, develops from the dynamics of capital accumulation itself.

Yet, Marx had noted that no individual capitalist would voluntarily implement a technique of production that would lower his or her rate of profit (Marx 1967b: 263). A problem for the capitalists exists, however: the process of competition and capital accumulation is independent of individual wills and belongs to the realm of the social capital, or the interaction of many capitals. And competition "establishes the necessity for the reduction of production costs" (Shaikh 1978: 240-41). By introducing superior machinery, the capitalist increases productivity of labor, and the value of the commodity falls. So, too, does the unit cost of production. Those capitals that are able to innovate reap the benefit of added profits or increased market shares (depending upon demand conditions). Conversely, though, by executing such actions, the individual capitalists lower the socially average rate of profit.

It is also by this process that the rate of profit is equalized by a continual series of disequilibrium positions. Once an equalized profit rate is obtained, it does not remain at some magically static level from which it exhibits no tendency to move. Rather, competition and technical innovation continue, thereby increasing constant capital still further and pressuring the rate of profit downward. When the average rate of profit is pushed low enough to limit the potential self-expansion of capital, a crisis ensues.

> The crises are always but momentary and forcible solutions of the existing contradictions. They are violent eruptions which for a time restore the disturbed equilibrium. (Marx 1967b: 249)

While the rate of profit has been falling due to the increase in the organic composition of capital, the mass of profit has been rising due to increased labor productivity. This mass of profit has also been, once again, redistributed towards ·those who have the larger amounts of capital advanced. Inefficient producers are purged, capital equipment lies unutilized, and capital values are destroyed. The conditions are set for an increase in the rate of profit and a return to "prosperity," but at a more concentrated level. There is yet another apparent contradiction here: "A lower production cost per unit output is achieved by means of a greater investment cost per unit output" (Shaikh 1978: 242). And it is this increased investment that diminishes the rate of profit.

The preceeding exposition has looked at several effects of the accumulation process of capital. However, to grasp the full impact of accumulation on bourgeois society one must look to the other side of the dialectic—to the effects of accumulation and technological change upon the working class. Throughout volume I, Marx stresses the social nature of the labor process (a point too often forgotten in some of the more technical writings on crisis theory). It is in the earlier chapters of *Capital* that Marx traces an increase in productivity made possible by the application of better machinery to a labor force that is social in nature (i.e., where many cooperating workers produce only part of the finished commodity). Here, too, is found the reaction of the working class against the dominion of capital. Worker responses varied from the Luddite movement to the later petitioning of Parliament that resulted in the English Factory Acts.

It was technological change—directed by the capitalist class—that contributed to overcoming some of the difficulties facing capital accumulation as a result of these responses of the working class. Large-scale application of machinery made it possible to separate the functions of conception and execution. No longer did the worker need to have the skill to conceptualize the job; that was embodied in the machine itself. Where machinery was introduced, it could dictate the conditions of operative labor. The operative labor became an appendage of the machine, feeding it raw materials and handling the product when the machine had finished its work. From the point of view of the working class, their skills eroded and wages fell. Technological change also resulted in "structural unemployment." From the point of view of the capitalist, surplus value increased and the variable capital advanced fell.

In this manner the dual nature of mechanization can be seen, a nature that operates on both the levels of the creation and valorizaton of surplus value. In other words, mechanization impacts both the individual capitalist and the social capital. For the individual capitalist, mechanization not only raises the possibility of short-term "technological rents" but also facilitates extraction of surplus value by permitting greater control over the labor process.

A useful analytical tool for viewing this twofold nature of mechanization is Marx's theoretical notion of the real subsumption of labor to capital. Marx had defined the real subsumption of labor to capital as the labor process upon which specifically capitalist production is based. In this form of capitalist production, labor power is purchased as a commodity, the labor process is controlled by the capitalist, and "production for production's sake" becomes not only possible but a competitive imperative (Marx 1976: 1034-37).

Yet, a contradiction develops. To increase the rate of exploitation and (the capitalist hopes) realize a greater rate and mass of profits, the capitalist mechanizes the point of production. If the rate of surplus value grows faster than the organic composition of capital, the rate of profit will rise. The first of an industry's capitalists to innovate and mechanize will reap the advantages of driving his or her individual cost of production below the socially prevailing value. However, as the techniques are generalized, the rate of profit tends to fall with the increase in the organic composition of capital that accompanies a general increase in mechanization.

Yet, a dilemma arises for the individual capitalist that stems from the interrelation of the individual and social capitals. The individual capitalist cannot choose to extract surplus value relatively. The extraction of relative surplus value is a social phenomenon. It is brought into being by a reduction in the value of labor power and the cheapening of wage goods. But this is a social and not an individual phenomenon. No one capitalist can reduce the value of variable capital expended by that capitalist.

However, one capitalist can mechanize, and the individual capitalist can really subsume labor to capital. While the distinction is subtle, the theoretical concept of the real subsumption of labor to capital ties the individual and social levels together and links the process of mechanization to the labor and valorization processes.

In Marx's analysis, social capital depended upon a social labor process that was able to self-expand and accumulate. However, the very process of accumulation served as an obstacle to further self-expansion. Marx saw the "historical mission" of capitalism as one of developing the technological forces necessary to increase human productivity. In doing so it created the potential for its own limits—largely via the class struggle engendered by the proletariat and the tendency of the rate of profit to fall. The falling rate of profit was formulated as a "tendency" rather than an iron-clad law because there were important counteracting influences, some built directly into the accumulation process and some dependent upon direct action of the capitalists. It is to these counteracting influences that this essay now turns.

Viewed from the perspective of the labor process, the possibility of operative labor and removal of many strength requirements by machinery allowed capitalists to substitute the labor of women and children for that of men. Since the value of labor power was calculated on the basis of the reproduction costs of male labor, the amount of variable capital advanced for production fell. Also, aided by machinery, child and female labor could be as productive as male labor (if not more so, since women and children were excluded from early trade unions and offered less organized resistance). They were also paid less, and the amount of surplus value accruing to the capitalist rose. This was an important offset to the tendency of the rate of profit to fall.

From the valorization perspective, a decline in profitability is the result of the overproduction of capital, and there are several ways capitalists can act to overcome this difficulty.

For the capitalist, from both cost and profit standpoints, it is useful to lower the value of constant capital used. In the area of direct production it is the use value of capital that is important. So a production technique that is less costly, in that it lowers the value of constant capital and hence the organic composition of capital, at the same time making labor more productive will both increase the rate of surplus value and forestall the tendency of the rate of profit to fall.

This could partly be accomplished by finding better sources of raw materials. Many of the struggles of imperialism have been to conquer or colonize regions of the world (be they through military effort or unequal exchange) in search of better and cheaper sources of raw materials.

Another way of cheapening the elements of constant capital is to lower the value of fixed capital. This is accomplished in part by the process of accumulation. Means of production are produced as commodities by means of social labor. As technical innovations occur in department I, the socially necessary labor time embodied in the produced means of production decreases. Therefore, their value (and hence their cost price) will fall, even though constant capital employed may itself rise dramatically. As a result, the organic composition may fall:

> Although their absolute value increases, it falls in comparison to the increasing extension of production and the magnitude of the variable capital, or the quantity of labor power set in motion. (Marx 1967b: 82)

Perhaps the best known offsetting tendency to the falling profit rate is the increase in the rate of surplus value. In the early days of capitalism this was accomplished largely on the level of the individual capitalist by lengthening the working day, speeding up or intensifying the labor process, or by lowering wages below their value (Sweezy 1942: 98-99). However, these tactics were prone to limits imposed by the proletariat through class struggle. The working day in England was eventually limited by acts of Parliament. Working people, especially skilled craftsworkers, often found ways of limiting the amounts of the commodities they produced. This drove no less a spokesperson for capital than Andrew Ure to complain:

> By the infirmity of human nature, it happens that the more skillful the workman, the more self willed and intractable he is apt to become, and of course the less fit of a component of a mechanical system in which . . . he may do great damage to the whole. (Ure, quoted in Marx 1976: 490)

Also, the lowering of wages below their value would run into long-run problems of reproduction of labor power: Inadequately fed workers tend to be less productive.

Capital managed to transcend these limits with the advent of machinery, technological change, and specifically capitalist production. Machine production allowed the increase in the rate of surplus value by the cheapening of wage goods (thereby lowering the value of variable capital advanced) while simultaneously removing the will of the independent skilled worker, which served to block productivity increases. As skill and strength requirements fell, women and children were increasingly employed, and wages could be lowered with less drastic effects on the reproduction of the labor force.

Since "the battle of competition is fought by the cheapening of commodities," this increase in the rate of surplus value did not stop after the Industrial Revolution. Rather, it characterizes the epoch of modern capitalism. Whether or not the increase in the rate of surplus value offsets the increase in the organic composition is a question of magnitude. Both processes have limits. The overproduction of capital limits the increase in c/v, while class struggle (in the form of productivity decline) limits the rise of s/v.

So capitalists turn to yet another arena to increase their profit rates, that of decreasing the turnover time to produce and sell commodities. In volumes II and III of *Capital*, Marx discussed how decreasing the turnover time could increase the rate of profit. Turnover is defined as the time necessary to produce and circulate a given commodity. In the process of getting commodities to market, some capital remains idle, sometimes in the form of stocks of raw materials or money capital, and sometimes in the form of unsold commodities:

> The shorter the period of turnover, the smaller this idle portion of capital as compared with the whole, and the larger, therefore, the

appropriated surplus value, other conditions remaining the same. (Marx 1967b:70)

Capital must be advanced for both production and circulation. Let capital A be turned over twice in one year, while capital B turns over only once. Capital A will have a more continuous production process. To produce the same amount of value, capital B will have to advance new and additional capital to circulate the commodity. On the other hand, capital A will have already circulated and realized the surplus value embodied during its productive use. With a more continuous flow, capital A is able to begin a second round of production by turning the money capital received from the sale of its commodities back into productive capital without having to advance more capital.

Two things happen. First, the means of production of capital A do not lay idle waiting for the capitalist to find some new source of funding. Rather, the proceeds of the previous sale flow directly through the circuit of commodity capital into money capital and back into productive capital. Second, less new capital needs to be advanced by A and so does not add to the downward pressure on the rate of profit.

How is this accomplished? "The chief means of reducing the time of production is higher labor productivity, which is commonly called industrial progress" (Marx 1967b: 71). When an innovating capitalist introduces a new technique that increases labor productivity, the resulting technological rents received are due in part to the increased number of turn overs.

In volume II, Marx points out that time of production and time of circulation are mutually exclusive; therefore, each contains its own identifiable characteristics. Reflecting upon this, Marx wrote: "During its time of circulation capital does not perform the functions of productive capital and therefore produces neither commodities nor surplus-value" (Marx 1967a: 124). In the abstract, the process of production, and hence the self-expansion of capital, is interrupted so long as capital value exists in the realm of circulatory capital. The length of circulation time becomes a crucial component of turnover time. If the circulatory phase can approximate zero, then capital may function more productively and increase the rate of self-expansion of value. "A capital's time of circulation therefore limits, generally speaking, its time of production and hence its process of generating surplus-value" (Marx 1967a: 125).

To summarize Marx briefly, the essential activity of the circulatory phase is to convert commodities into money. It is an "ever-recurring condition" of reproduction. Use values, which are in the form of finished commodities, must achieve entry into productive or individual consumption in order for exchange value to be realized. Managers have emerged in contemporary capitalism to act as instrumental agents to facilitate the hastening of circulation time, that is, to increase the rate of turnover. It is imperative to recall, however, that Marx claims that such activity is intrinsically unproductive. It creates neither value nor a product, however efficacious it has proven itself to be under modern capitalism.

Marx's theory of the tendency of the rate of profit to fall can be modified and wedded to theories developed by observers of twentieth century capitalism. Current theoreticians such as James F. Becker and James O'Connor contend that "orthodox Marxism" neglects the rise of the "middle class" or, more specifically, the institution of the "salariat" as a buffer between the working and capitalist classes (Becker 1977: 220). Its prominent roles are that of: (1) embracing ideology that is most conducive to exerting control over workers and thereby making accumulation and reproduction possible and (2) promoting the development of the circulatory mechanism. The number of unproductive workers belonging to the salariat has doubled since World War II (O'Connor 1984: 123). This expansion of social abstract labor is related to the real subsumption of labor to capital and the continuing centralization and concentration of capital. Its activities entail countervailing the tendency of the rate of profit to fall, and contiguous with Marxist theory, it creates inherent contradictions while attempting to realize its goal.

According to Becker (1977: 256), the rising middle class is bifurcated into subgroups. Each lies within the "second approximation of class structure." The manager or "new executive" acts functionally as an entrepreneur but under the paternal, proprietary auspices of the capitalist. His or her job revolves around "the custody of property, its valuation and extension" (Becker 1977: 247). As overseer of a variety of administrative as well as production activities, the manager appropriates the products and services rendered by the industrial working class (Marx's traditional proletariat) and that of administrative labor. The latter is the second subgroup of the middle class that Becker takes pains to define as subordinate to the managerial class.

Administrative labor proper is composed of clerical laborers as well as those involved in educating labor power. "Educators" are not just teachers, but those who labor within the sociocultural sphere—journalists, doctors, social scientists, and men and women of arts, letters, and science. Administrative labor "produces products and services useful for social coordination by virtue of the technique it embodies, a technique that is reproductively useful (Becker 1977: 252) Administrative labor is, however, often aware that unequal relations of power exist in the office. This consciousness surfaces as nascent struggle and conflict between these unproductive workers and management: teachers becoming unionized, journalists fighting state censorship, and so on. For Becker, modern capitalism has transformed class relations. Conflict now arises within the productive sphere (the industrial laborers) and the unproductive sphere (the administrative laborers). Both groups are subject to the exigencies of capitalism. They are subordinate to capital while employed and join the reserve army of labor when unemployed.

James O'Connor has also given considerable thought to the role of management or, using his term, "salariat." It is the "technical brain," which exercises authority over the industrial working class by controlling the planning of work and coordinating functions that previously were the activities of the direct producers. The salariat therefore dominates the "mind of labor over the productive forces" (O'Connor 1984: 113). Concurrently, the salariat is also the "political brain," which excercises a formalized authority. It appropriates the planning, coordination, and control functions in the interest of increasing the rate or mass of surplus value. To this degree, then, the salariat acts to hegemonically control production and dominate the worker.

But its control, as O'Connor argues, is subtle and is exercised under the Lockean guise of the sacredness of individualism: " . . . In American history, and postwar U.S. capitalism in specific, the dominant national ideology was individualism. It was precisely the cultural deification of the 'self' which underwrote ideologies of individualism and individualist practices in U.S. capitalism generally and the production process in particular" (O'Connor 1984: 120). The crucial essence of this ideology lies in seducing workers to believe that they "control" their own destinies and that this control can be expressed through individual consumerism.

O'Connor stresses that Marx's concept of commodity fetishism helps to explain capitalism's powerful grip on the mind of the worker. Via consumerism, workers attempt to personify their "individualism." Workers are aware that they only possess such control of their own consumption because it is required that they implicitly consent to exchange their labor power for wages; that they exchange real creative, direct productive control for alienation; and that they exchange equal distribution of power for hierarchical control. The process of capitalist development creates both commodities and hierarchies. Control of often trivial commodity choices replaces control of the labor process, and the salariat's role is to promote the premise that workers and capitalists are "partners". Workers, however, can only succeed if they accept the capitalist system and as long as they accept competitive relationships with one another. "Capital in this way attempted to unite what was 'naturally' divided and divide what was united" (O'Connor 1984: 123).

The internal structure of these ideologies gives way to inducting workers into an "industrial citizenship," which further individualizes workers' needs and problems and serves to mask class conflict at the point of production. This "individualistic" form of control of the workers, which is maintained and nurtured by the salariat, is indispensable for capitalist reproduction.

A contradictory scenario begins to unfold as workers, so fully convinced of the importance of the individual self, demand a greater share of society's wealth. Coalescence of individuals into specific interest groups has become common during the last 25 years. O'Connor cites the civil rights movement, feminism, environmentalism, and industrial unions as particular examples. Unions, especially, have led the fight for job security in the labor market, as well as struggling against greater intensification of the labor process, and have challenged the role of supervisory authority on the shop floor. All these forms of resistance use collective means to advance individual ends and tend to add more means of subsistence to workers' consumption baskets, thereby putting more pressure upon the capitalist class to discover new forms of control with which to cap the resistance. This, in turn, leads to the increased use of unproductive salariat labor and intensified bureaucratic forms of control. Consequently, the capitalist class must confront the ever-recurring crisis situation in which the tendency of the rate of profit to fall continues to assert itself.

The need to counteract this tendency results in the use of methods that have the potential to exacerbate the process. Capitalists may postpone the crisis, but their techniques do not offer a final solution. Increasing the rate of turnover, appropriating planning and coordination, and supervising a fragmented work force necessitates a greater number of clerical workers and supervisors. Combatting collective action by responding to individualized workers' consumption "needs" creates legions of salesworkers.

The editors of *Monthly Review* have, indeed, shown that the "recovery" of 1983-84 was driven by increases in sales of office automation equipment and automobiles for business use. While investment in these areas may well boost the components of aggregate demand, the aforementioned technical aids to unproductive labor will hardly set the conditions for sustained prosperity (Magdoff and Sweezy 1985: 3-5). As the percentage of unproductive workers increases, the value creating potential of the labor force threatens to diminish. Herein lies the social and economic contradiction of contemporary capitalism.

CONCLUSION

Starting with the tendency of the rate of profit to fall and accounting for several counteracting forces, Marx developed his major laws of motion of a capitalist economy: concentration and centralization of capital, relative surplus population, and periodic crises developing out of competition. As such, Marx was able to forge a profound analysis of the dynamics of capitalist development. This theory envisions a unity of the valorization process and the labor process.

This chapter has attempted to explore that unity. All too often, Marxian value theorists treat the labor process superficially in their analysis of the competition of capitals. Just as often, those who study the nature of work in different capitalist industries have an incomplete knowledge of the process of capital accumulation. Marx himself was not a victim of such a detailed division of labor. Instead, he recognized the unity between the labor process and the valorization process in forming "capitalist production as a whole." One can only hope that an understanding of this unity will aid in the much larger task that faces us: to create a world for ourselves and our children where the law of value is subordinated to human needs.

REFERENCES

Becker, James. 1977. *Marxian Political Economy: An Outline.* Cambridge: Cambridge University Press.

Bischak, Gregory. 1978. The Process of Technological Change in Craft Production, Specifically Capitalist Production, Simple Cooperation and Manufacture. Unpublished Manuscript. New School for Social Research, New York.

Braverman, Harry. 1974. *Labor and Monopoly Capital.* New York: Monthly Review Press.

Magdoff, Harry and Paul Sweezy. 1985. The Strange Recovery of 1983-1984. *Monthly Review* October.

Marx, Karl. 1967a. *Capital,* vol. II. New York: International Publishers.

_____ . 1967b. *Capital,* vol. III. New York: International Publishers.

_____ . 1976. *Capital,* vol. I. New York: Pelican.

O'Connor, James. 1984. *Accumulation Crisis.* New York: Basil Blackwell.

Shaikh, Anwar. 1978. Political Economy and Capitalism: Notes on Dobb's Theory of Crisis. *Cambridge Journal of Economics* no. 2.

Sweezy, Paul. 1942. *Theory of Capitalist Development.* New York: Oxford University Press.

Chapter 6

Technical Change and Profitability: The "Law of the Tendency of the Rate of Profit to Fall" Reconsidered

BENIGNO VALDES

INTRODUCTION

Whenever capitalism undergoes a serious economic recession, economists and politicians are quick to point out the reason, namely, that the rate of investment is lower than it used to be. When capitalists are asked why that may happen, their answer is always the same: the rate of investment is lower because so is the profit rate. Therefore, economic crises appear to be the result of falling profitability. The question is, how does this fall in profitability occur? Basically, there are two contending explanations. One asserts that falling profitability is the result of a rising wage bill. The essential argument is this: During periods in which the strength of the labor movement increases greatly, wages tend to rise faster than productivity and hence the share of profits in national income tends to be "squeezed" by the rising share of wages. Thus, the rate of profit falls because wages rise too much. This explanation is called the "profit-squeeze" theory of crisis."[1]

The alternative explanation sees the cause of falling profitability in the profit-seeking nature of capitalism. The basic argument is as follows. The urge for profit causes capitalists to engage in competition against each other. In the struggle, the immediate goal of each participant is to drive his or her rivals from the field and capture their share of the market. Different methods, such as advertising and some forms of sabotage, are used with that intention. In the end, however, one capitalist can secure a larger share of the market only by selling more cheaply than the other competitors, and to do so without suffering losses, by producing more cheaply. This is achieved by raising the productivity of labor with the continual mechanization of production.[2] The problem is that the cheapening of commodities does not come for free: mechanization, while lowering the cost of production, also raises the unit investment cost. For the capitalists who move

107

first to adopt the new technique, the lower cost of production, the lower price, and the larger market share may compensate for the higher unit investment cost. However, those advantages force the rival capitalists to introduce the same machines, and once the adoption of the new technique becomes universal, the combined increase in investment results in a lower average rate of profit. Profitability falls, therefore, because workers become more rather than less productive. This is Marx's "law of the falling tendency of the profit rate" (LFTRP).

The dispute between these two crisis theories has far-reaching political implications. On one hand, if the "profit-squeeze" argument provides the correct explanation of the problem, two interesting questions arise, namely: (1) Will the lessening of class struggle, by government redistribution of income for instance, ensure economic stability in capitalism? (2) If so, when the economy goes into depression, should workers be held "responsible" for it? On the other hand, if the LFTRP provides the correct explanation, one must conclude that in capitalism economic crises are unavoidable: to survive, capitalism needs mechanization, and mechanization itself creates the condition for economic downturns.

In recent years, the validity of the LFTRP argument has been questioned by the Okishio theorem (Okishio, 1961), which says that the introduction of cost-reducing techniques is incompatible with a lower average rate of profit. However, this result applies only to an economy from which fixed capital is absent, and it has been suggested (Shaikh, 1978a) that the theorem breaks down in the presence of fixed capital. This essay provides a confirmation of that claim.

PRICES OF PRODUCTION IN THE MARXIAN SYSTEM

In *Capital*, volume III, Marx (1967:157) provides an unambiguous definition of price of production in the presence of fixed capital. Price of production is "cost-price" (the per unit cost of production evaluated at ruling prices) plus a percentage π (the average rate of profit) of the unit investment *laid out* (not merely consumed) in production.[3] This definition allows us to formulate the price system for a capitalist economy in the following manner. Consider a two-sector economy producing "consumer goods" (sector 1) and "capital goods" (sector 2). For this economy, let us define terms as follows:

P_i = the price of production of commodity i ($i = 1, 2$)
a_{2i} = the input coefficient of raw material in sector i ($i = 1, 2$)
l_i = the labor input coefficient in sector i ($i = 1, 2$)
w = the real wage rate
π = the average rate of profit
Ω_i = the physical amount of fixed capital laid out in sector i ($i = 1,$ 2) at time $t = 1$
T_i = the life of Ω_i

It follows from these definitions that the monetary value of the fixed capital laid out in sector i ($i = 1, 2$) at time $t = 1$ is $P_2\Omega_i$. Suppose this equipment can turn out N_i units of output in each of its T_i years of life. Then the "average depreciation per unit" in sector i ($i = 1, 2$) is $P_2\Omega_i/T_iN_i = P_2\theta_i$. This means that in sector i ($i = 1, 2$) one unit of output "absorbs" an amount $P_2\theta_i$ of fixed capital. It also absorbs an amount $P_2a_{2i} + P_1wl_i$ of "circulating capital." Hence, the cost-price is given by $P_2\theta_i + P_2a_{2i} + P_1wl_i$.

The unit investment laid out in production consists of two elements: the "circulating capital" and the "fixed capital advanced per unit." The former we already know. To determine the latter, notice that in sector i ($i = 1, 2$) an amount $P_2\Omega_i$ of fixed capital is advanced at the beginning of year $t = 1$ in which N_i units of output are produced. This means that in that sector and year an amount $P_2\Omega_i/N_i$ of fixed capital is advanced per unit of output. That amount drops to $(P_2\Omega_i/N_i)[(T_i - 1)/T_i]$ in year $t = 2$, since $P_2\Omega_i/T_i$ of the original fixed capital depreciates during the first year, and so on. Over the T_i years of life of Ω_i, unit advancements of fixed capital decline as summarized in table 6.1.

Notice that for any one year except the last (which in any case is irrelevant because, properly speaking, there is no fixed capital in it) the amount of fixed capital advanced per unit is greater than the depreciation per unit. Thus, the average of the annual advances of fixed capital is also greater than the unit depreciation. Using that average $[P_2\Phi_i$ ($i = 1, 2$)] as a measure for the "amount of fixed capital advanced per unit,"[4] we can express the "unit investment laid out in production" as $P_2\Phi_i + P_2a_{2i} + P_1wl_i$ ($i = 1, 2$). Hence, the price of production in sector i ($i = 1, 2$) is given by $P_i = (P_2\theta_i + P_2a_{2i} + P_1wl_i) + \pi(P_2\Phi_i + P_2a_{2i} + P_1wl_i)$.

DETERMINATION OF THE AVERAGE RATE OF PROFIT

The above definition of price of production can be used to formulate the price system. Since for our present purpose it is not necessary to know

TABLE 6.1. Annual Advances of Fixed Capital per Unit of Output

$t = 1$	$(P_2\Omega_i/N_i)$
$t = 2$	$(P_2\Omega_i/N_i)\,[(T_i-1)/T_i]$
$t = 3$	$(P_2\Omega_i/N_i)\,[(T_i-2)/T_i]$
.	
.	
$t^5\,T_i$	$(P_2\Omega_i/N_i)\,(1/T_i)$

the absolute prices, we may use the consumer goods as numeraire ($P_1 = 1$). We have

$$1 = (P_2\theta_1 + P_2a_{21} + wl_1) + \pi(P_2\Phi_1 + P_2a_{21} + wl_1) \tag{1.a}$$

and

$$P_2 = (P_2\theta_2 + P_2a_{22} + wl_2) + \pi(P_2\Phi_2 + P_2a_{22} + wl_2) \tag{1.b}.$$

The solution $\{\pi, P_2\}$ of this system provides the average rate of profit and the relative price of capital goods under the ruling technique of production $\{\theta, \Phi, a_{2i}, l_i\}$. In order to find that solution, let us write equations (1.a) and (1.b) in the form

$$\pi = \frac{1 - (P_2\theta_1 + P_2a_{21} + wl_1)}{P_2\Phi_1 + P_2a_{21} + wl_1} \tag{2.a}$$

and

$$\pi = \frac{P_2 - (P_2\theta_2 + P_2a_{22} + wl_2)}{P_2\Phi_2 + P_2a_{22} + wl_2} \tag{2.b}.$$

In the appendix to this chapter it is shown that: (1) equation (2.a) intersects the P_2 axis at $(1 - wl_1)/(\theta_1 + a_{21})$ and the π axis at $(1 - wl_1)/wl_1$, (2) equation (2.b) intersects the P_2 axis at $wl_2/[1 - (\theta_2 + a_{22})]$ and the π axis at -1, and (3) equation (2.a) is monotonically decreasing and equation (2.b) is monotonically increasing. In addition, for the system to be viable (in the sense that it yields a positive rate of profit) it must be the case that $[(1 - wl_1)/(\theta_1 + a_{21}) > \{wl_2/[1 - (\theta_2 + a_{22})]\}$. Therefore, one can derive the solution depicted in Figure 6.1.

FIGURE 6.1.   Determination of the average rate of profit

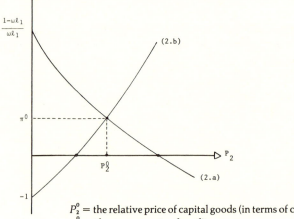

P_2^0 = the relative price of capital goods (in terms of consumer goods)
π^0 = the average rate of profit

Hence, under the ruling technique the average rate of profit is π°, and the relative price of capital goods is P_2°.

THE EFFECTS OF MECHANIZATION UPON THE RATE OF PROFIT

Suppose a technique $\{\theta^*, \Phi^*, a^*, l^*\}$ that is cost-price reducing at ruling prices is introduced in sector i ($i = 1$ or 2, or $i = 1$ and 2). If the innovation occurs in sector 1, we have

$$P_2^\circ\theta_1^* + P_2^\circ a_{21}^* + wl_1^* < P_2^\circ\theta_1 + P_2^\circ a_{21} + wl_1 \tag{3}.$$

Multiplying by -1, adding 1 to both sides, and dividing the resulting inequality by $P_2^\circ\theta_1^* + P_2^\circ a_{21}^* + wl_1^*$, we have

$$\frac{1 - (P_2^\circ\theta_1^* + P_2^\circ a_{21}^* + wl_1^*)}{P_2^\circ\Phi_1^* + P_2^\circ a_{21}^* + wl_1^*} > \frac{1 - (P_2^\circ\theta_1 + P_2^\circ a_{21} + wl_1)}{P_2^\circ\Phi_1^* + P_2^\circ a_{21}^* + wl_1^*} \tag{4}.$$

If mechanization does in fact raise the investment cost per unit of output: i.e., if $P_2^\circ\Phi_1^* + P_2^\circ a_{21}^* + wl_1^* > P_2^\circ\Phi_1 + P_2^\circ a_{21} + wl_1$, then $P_2^\circ\Phi_1^* + P_2^\circ a_{21}^* + wl_1^*$ can be replaced with $P_2^\circ\Phi_1 + P_2^\circ a_{21} + wl_1$ in the right hand side of (4) to yield

$$\frac{1 - (P_2^\circ\theta_1^* + P_2^\circ a_{21}^* + wl_1^*)}{P_2^\circ\Phi_1^* + P_2^\circ a_{21}^* + wl_1^*} \gtreqless \frac{1 - (P_2^\circ\theta_1 + P_2^\circ a_{21} + wl_1)}{P_2^\circ\Phi_1 + P_2 a_{21} + wl_1} \tag{5}.$$

That is,

$$\pi^* \text{ for } P_2 = P_2^\circ \gtreqless \pi^\circ \tag{6}.$$

This expression indicates that in sector 1, the "transitional rate of profit" (i.e., the rate of profit the innovative capitalist would obtain at ruling prices between the moment in which the introduction of the new technique occurs and the moment in which competition brings about a new average rate of profit) may be equal, greater, or lower than the ruling average rate of profit. In terms of the mathematics of the argument, expression (6) simply says that in the new price equation of sector 1, the rate of profit at the ruling prices may be equal, higher, or lower than the ruling rate of profit. Referring once again to figure 6.1, this means that the introduction of the new technique does not move (2.a) in a determinate direction. Hence, a position such as (2.a)* in figure 6.2 is possible, and it entails a *lower* average rate of profit.

FIGURE 6.2.   Effect of sector 1's mechanization upon the average rate of profit

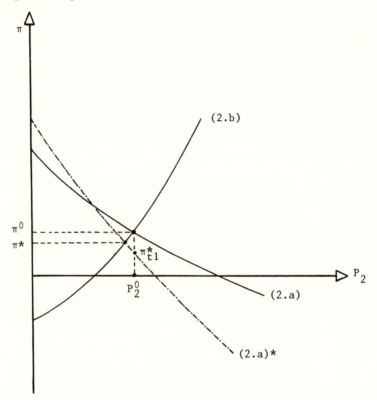

π^0 = ruling average rate of profit
π^*_{t1} = π^* for $P_2 = P^0_2$, i.e. the transitional rate of profit (sector 1)
π^* = new average rate of profit

If the innovation occurs in the capital goods sector ($i = 2$), we have $P_2{}^{\cdot}\theta_2{}^* + P_2{}^{\cdot}a_{22}{}^* + wl_2{}^* < P_2{}^{\cdot}\theta_2 + P_2{}^{\cdot}a_{22} + wl_2$, and similar steps to those followed above[5] lead to the same conclusion: i.e., the average rate of profit may fall. Finally, as indicated in figure 6.3, if the innovation occurs in both sectors simultaneously, the same result applies. (This case is a mere combination of the preceding two). Hence we have the following theorem:

> In the presence of fixed capital, the effects of mechanization upon the average rate of profit are theoretically indeterminate. Therefore, the Okishio theorem is false.

FIGURE 6.3. Effect of a general mechanization
upon the average rate of profit

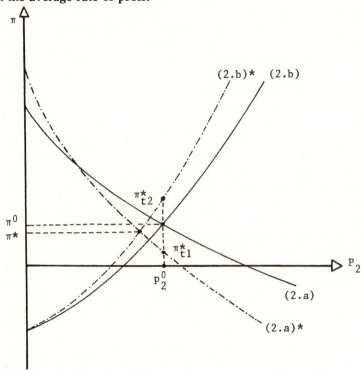

π^0 = ruling average rate of profit
π^*_{ti} = the transitional rate of profit in sector i (i = 1, 2)
π^0 = new average rate of profit

ON THE CAPITALIST CRITERION FOR MECHANIZATION: A LOWER COST OF PRODUCTION OR A HIGHER TRANSITIONAL RATE OF PROFIT?

Simple inspection of figures 6.2 and 6.3 reveals the (necessary) condition under which mechanization results in a lower average rate of profit. That condition can be stated as follows:

> For mechanization to lower the average rate of profit, it must also lower some or all of the transitional rates of profit.

Is there any possibility that this condition will be met in the real world? Traditional teachings suggest that there is none, because those teachings assume that it would be "irrational" for any capitalist to introduce a more mechanized technique so long as it reduces her transitional rate of profit. However, the idea of rationality that permeates this belief is too narrow. To see why, consider the case of a technique $\{\theta^*, \Phi^*, a^*, l^*\}$, which, in relation to the ruling one $[\{\theta, \Phi, a, l\}]$, lowers the unit cost of production and the transitional rate of profit. According to the traditional teachings, no capitalist should ever consider adopting such a technique.

Suppose, however, that one "irrational" capitalist introduced it and began to cut prices. Now the others must follow, or else they will be driven from the market. (Accomplishing that outcome is precisely what the innovative capitalist had in mind. Moreover, since she did lower the price first, she might have won some market share from her dormant rivals.) Obviously, there is a limit (determined by P_i for $\pi = 0$) below which prices cannot be cut without incurring a loss. That limit, however, is not the same for everyone. It is lower for the ("irrational") innovator because, with $\pi = 0$, the price is the cost-price, and this is lower for the new technique. It follows that the innovative capitalist can lower her price to a level rival capitalists cannot match without incurring a permanent loss. Hence, they must begin to behave "irrationally" and introduce the new technique, or else they will be driven from the field, either because they ruin themselves or because they lose their markets to the innovator. It thus seems that the traditional wisdom has got its idea of rationality reversed.

CONCLUSION AND IMPLICATIONS

It may be useful to clarify what has and has *not* been shown in this chapter. It has *not* been shown that the Marxian LFTRP is necessarily correct and hence that Marx was right in saying that in capitalism economic crises are unavoidable. It *has* been shown, however, that the most appealing critique of the LFTRP, namely, the Okishio theorem, does not hold once the existence of fixed capital is taken into consideration. Therefore, the LFTRP remains uncontested.

This result has important implications. On one hand, the Marxian tradition that explains capitalist economic crises in light of the LFTRP must be given the theoretical legitimacy denied to it in recent years. On the other hand, the idea that economic crises are for the most part the consequence of class struggle (i.e., the result of workers' high wage demands) is open to question. This thesis is used as a political weapon against organized labor whenever the economy goes into recession. Somehow the implication is that if workers were to limit their wage demands, economic instability would be eliminated. The possibility that the LFTRP rules the actual process of accumulation makes that claim less persuasive. Perhaps it is not "unreasonable" wage demands but the continual accumulation of capital imposed by the competitive nature of capitalism that periodically throws the economy into recession. In other words, it may well be that the very foundations of the capitalist economy are not as benign as traditional teachings would lead us to believe.

Acknowledgements. I wish to thank Richard England and Paul Wendt for their comments. Needless to say, the responsibility for whatever errors remain is mine.

APPENDIX

From (2.a) it follows that $\lim\limits_{P_2 \to 0} \pi = (1 - wl_1)/wl_1$. Hence, (2.a) intersects the π axis at $(1 - wl_1)/wl_1$. Also, for $\pi = 0$ it is $P_2 = (1 - wl_1)/(\theta_1 + a_{21})$. Hence, (2.b) intersects the P_2 axis at $(1 - wl_1)/(\theta_1 + a_{21})$. In addition, $d\pi/dP_2 < 0$ trivially, since as P_2 increases, the numerator of (2.a) decreases, and the denominator increases; so the entire ratio (π) must decrease. Similarly, it follows from (2.b) that $\lim\limits_{P_2 \to 0} \pi = -1$. Hence, (2.b) intersects the π axis at -1. Also, for $\pi = 0$ it is $P_2 = wl_2/[1 - (\theta_2 + a_{22})]$. Hence, (2.b) intersects the P_2 axis at $wl_2/[1 - (\theta_2 + a_{22})]$. In addition, $d\pi/dP_2 = [(1 + \Phi_2 - \theta_2)wl_2]/[P_2(\Phi_2 + a_{22}) + wl_2]^2 > 0$, since $\Phi_2 > \theta_2$.

NOTES

1. See, among others, Glyn and Sutcliffe (1972).
2. "One capitalist can drive another from the field and capture his capital only by selling more cheaply. In order to be able to sell more cheaply without ruining himself, he must produce more cheaply, that is, raise the productive power of labor as much as possible. But the productive power of labor is raised, above all, by a universal introduction and continual improvement of *machinery*. . . .The more gigantic the scale on which machinery is introduced, the more does the cost of production proportionately decrease, the more fruitful is labor. Hence, a general rivalry arises among the capitalists to increase. . .machinery. . . .

If, now, . . .by the utilization of new machines and their improvement. . . .one capitalist has found the means of producing with the same amount of labor. . .a greater amount. . .of commodities than his competitors, . . .how will this capitalist operate?

He could continue to sell. . .at the old market price; this would, however, be no means of driving his opponents from the field and of enlarging his own sales; . . .consequently, our capitalist will sell his [product] more cheaply than his competitors.

. . .He attains the object he wishes to attain, if he puts the price of his goods only a small percentage lower than that of his competitors. He drives them from the field, he wrests from them at least a part of their sales, by *underselling* them. . . .

However, the *privileged position* of our capitalist is not of long duration; other competing capitalists introduce the same machines, . . .introduce them on the same or on a larger scale. . . .

The capitalists find themselves, therefore, in the same position relative to one another as *before* the introduction of the new means of production. . . .On the basis of [the] new cost of production, the same game begins again. More. . .machinery . . .And again competition brings the same counteraction against this result.

We see how in this way. . .*the application of machinery is necessarily followed by still greater application of machinery. . . .*

That is the law which again and again throws bourgeois production out of its old course—. . .the law which gives capital no rest and continually whispers in its ear: 'Go on! Go on!' . . .

However powerful the means of production which a capitalist brings into the field, competition will make these means of production universal and from the moment when it has made them universal. The only result of the greater fruitfulness of his capital is that. . .he must sell perhaps a thousand times as much as before in order to outweigh the lower selling price by the greater amount of the product sold. Because a more extensive sale is now necessary. . .and because this mass sale becomes a question of life and death not only for him but also for his rivals, the old struggle begins *all the more violently the more fruitful the already discovered means of production are. . . .The application of machinery, therefore, will go on anew on an incomparably greater scale.*

. . .While, therefore, competition continually pursues him with its law of the cost of production and every weapon that he forges against his rivals recoils against himself, the capitalist continually tries to get the better of competition by incessantly introducing new machines, more expensive, it is true, but producing more cheaply, . . .and by not waiting until competition has rendered the new ones obsolete.

. . .We have portrayed above, in a hasty sketch, the industrial war of the capitalists among themselves" (Marx 1977: 22–24).

3. "The price of a commodity which is equal to its cost-price plus the share of the annual average profit on the total capital invested (not merely consumed) in its production is called its price of production. Take, for example, a capital of 500, of which 100 is fixed capital, and let 10 percent of this wear out during one turnover of the circulating capital of 400. Let the average profit for the period of turnover be 10 percent. In that case the cost-price of the product created during this turnover will be 10_c for wear plus $400_{(c+v)}$ circulating capital = 410, and its price of production will be 410 cost-price plus (10 percent profit on 500) 50 = 460" (Marx 1967: 150).

4. The questions may be asked: (1) Why the use of linear depreciation? and (2) Why measure the amount of fixed capital advanced per unit by the average of the actual annual advances? The answer is that no matter what formula for depreciation we use, and no matter whether we measure the fixed capital advanced per unit by its actual annual values or by the average of those values, it is nonetheless true that the fixed capital advanced per unit is greater than the unit depreciation, and this, as we shall see, is the relevant aspect in our argument.

5. Multiply $P_2{}^{\cdot}\theta_2{}^* + P_2{}^{\cdot}a_{22}{}^* + wl_2{}^* < P_2{}^{\cdot}\theta_2 + P_2{}^{\cdot}a_{22} + wl_2$ by -1, add $P_2{}^{\cdot}$ to both sides, and divide the resulting inequality by $P_2{}^{\cdot}\Phi_2{}^* + P_2{}^{\cdot}a_{22}{}^* + wl_2{}^*$. This yields π^* for $P_2 = P_2{}^{\cdot} \gtrless \pi^{\cdot}$.

REFERENCES

Glyn, Andrew and Bob Sutcliffe. 1972. *British Capitalism, Workers, and the Profit Squeeze*. London: Penquin Books.

Marx, Karl. 1967. *Capital: A Critique of Political Economy*, three volumes. New York: International Publishers.

———. 1977. Wage Labor and Capital. In *Marx-Engels Collected Works*, volume 9, pp. 197–228. International Publishers: New York.

Okishio, Nobuo. 1961. Technical Change and the Rate of Profit. *Kobe University Economic Review* 7:85–99.

_____ . 1977. Notes on Technical Progress and Capitalist Society. *Cambridge Journal of Economics* 1:93–100.

Shaikh, Anwar. 1978a. Political Economy and Capitalism: Notes on Dobb's Theory of Crisis. *Cambridge Journal of Economics* 2:233–51.

_____ . 1978b. An Introduction to the History of Crisis Theories. In *U.S. Capitalism in Crisis*. New York: URPE.

Chapter 7
Ecology, Social Class, and Political Conflict

RICHARD W. ENGLAND

During the past dozen years or so, concepts like "ecology" and "environment" have entered popular consciousness around the world. In the United States, for example, there is growing awareness of a wide variety of environmental issues posed by human activities. These ecological issues range from toxic wastes in the soil and water supplies of specific communities to acid rain affecting forests and fisheries in the Northeast to chemical contamination of the nation's food supply. Many environmental issues extend far beyond a particular country's borders—a prime example being accumulation of carbon dioxide in the world's atmosphere.

Human beings are, of course, problem-solving animals, and the identification of a wide variety of environmental threats during recent years has prompted a search for solutions. Nations as disparate as the United States and the Soviet Union have passed environmental legislation and created administrative agencies charged with managing environmental quality within their borders. In the United States, for example, the 1970 Occupational Safety and Health Act mandated federal efforts to prevent accidents and diseases that result from hazardous conditions in the workplace environment and created the Occupational Safety and Health Administration (OSHA) to regulate those conditions.

Although economists have not played much of a role in identifying these environmental problems, they have been increasingly active in analyzing their origins and in proposing specific remedies. The consensus among orthodox economists is that deteriorating environmental quality within a capitalist context arises from a failure to "internalize externalities," that is, from a failure to account properly for all the costs of production, including disposal of wastes.[1]

In an economy based on private ownership of productive wealth and the profit motive, each business organizes its productive activities in order to keep its own private production costs to a minimum. In the absence of public regulation or profit incentives, corporate owners and managers normally ignore the social costs (or externalities) of the production processes of their firm because it is in their financial interest to do so. The total costs of production include environmental losses borne by society, and hence total production costs exceed the costs incurred by the individual firm. Orthodox economists normally view these social costs of economic activity as a residual, small by comparison with private costs. Consequently, the presumed solution to the environmental crisis consists more in patching up the existing system than in redesigning basic institutions.

The solution to the ecological crisis proposed most frequently is simply a new federal excise tax. Orthodox economists advocate that government environmental agencies be instructed to measure the amount of pollution discharged into the environment by both producers and consumers and that a pollution or "effluent" tax be levied on each unit of pollution. The tax rate for each type of pollution would depend on the expected severity of its environmental effects. Those who discharge mildly obnoxious gases would, for instance, be taxed lightly, whereas those who dump highly toxic materials would be taxed at very high rates. Neoclassical economics predicts that three complementary effects would result from such a pollution tax. First, the higher prices of private goods that generate significant social costs would induce some people to buy smaller quantities of these pollution-creating products. Second, business firms would invent and adopt cleaner production techniques in an attempt to reduce their pollution tax payments. Third, the revenue from the pollution tax could be earmarked to reduce pollution at its source, clean it up once it is in the environment, or financially reimburse those who suffer its effects. Ideally, the economists' solution would reduce the total amount of pollution to an "optimal" level, where the benefits of further pollution abatement would not justify the costs of further pollution control.

On the surface this diagnosis and prescription may appear sound. The administration of a pollution tax seems to be simple, at least in principle, and apparently requires a minimal amount of change in existing political and economic institutions. If implemented, such a tax would force a realignment of market prices so that the price of every item produced reflected its full cost of production.[2]

On further investigation, however, this orthodox economic analysis of the environmental question turns out to be seriously inadequate. As I shall argue in the remainder of this essay, the orthodox approach tends to reduce ecological threats to purely *technical* or *administrative* problems awaiting solution by the engineer and manager. As a result, it neglects the economic, political, and social dimensions of the ecological crisis we face.

In particular, the orthodox approach obscures the political *conflicts* inherent in solving environmental problems. It tends to downplay the *global* dimensions of the crisis and look for solutions from individual national governments. It is *utopian* in ignoring the political realities of capitalist societies and, in particular, the influence of corporate leaders on environmental policy. And finally, it ignores several ecological *irrationalities* of capitalist production and consumption that contribute directly to degradation of the environment. Only a broader analysis that looks at the social organization of production and consumption on a global scale, especially the extreme *inequalities* that persist within and among capitalist nations, will help us avoid worsening ecological disasters in the years to come. It is my belief that political economy provides a framework for that broader analysis of society and nature.

SOCIAL CLASS AND ENVIRONMENTAL QUALITY

Of all families in the United States in 1982, the poorest fifth received less than 5 percent of total family income, whereas the richest fifth received nearly 43 percent of all family income. The very richest families in the United States—the top 5 percent—received 16 percent of the total (U.S. Census 1984). These income inequalities reflect, to a great extent, the highly unequal ownership of private wealth in the United States and the resulting concentration of most income from owning wealth in relatively few hands. Professor Edward Wolff (1983: 139–41) estimates that nearly one-half of the total net worth in 1969 of all U.S. households was owned by the wealthiest 5 percent. During that same year, nearly 42 percent of all households owned no income-producing wealth at all. Hence, income inequalities in the United States largely reflect the division of the population into *two broad social classes*: those who rely on income from work and those who rely on income from private ownership of capital.[3]

This division of the population into social classes is mirrored in the unequal exposure of the wealthy and the less affluent to various environmental pollutants. It is clear, for example, that economic necessity forces many working people to live in relatively harmful environments. This is especially true for the urban poor who cannot flee to less polluted surburban neighborhoods because of housing prices beyond their reach, a problem compounded for racial minorities by discrimination in suburban housing. Professors Peter Asch and Joseph Seneca reached the following conclusion after using 1972 data to analyze air quality differences between 284 U.S. cities:

> The evidence . . . points to a simple conclusion. Exposure to particulate matter is relatively higher in cities with low-income characteristics.

. . . While this is not surprising, the consistency of the relationship, . . . over the wide geographic coverage of 23 states, is noteworthy. (1978: 282)

In a more detailed analysis of differences in air quality between neighborhoods within Chicago, Cleveland, and Nashville, these same authors found that residents of poorest neighborhoods tended to suffer heavier airborne concentrations of nitrogen and sulfur dioxides as well as soot compared to residents of richer neighborhoods in the same city.

A direct result of their greater exposure to various pollutants is that the urban poor are more likely to suffer from chronic medical disorders, a condition that helps to reproduce their poverty. In a study of Buffalo, New York, for instance, a team of public health researchers found that children living in low income sections of that industrial city were more likely to be hospitalized for asthma and eczema, diseases probably resulting from the poorer air quality in their neighborhoods (Sultz et.al. 1970).

Those working people who have suffered limited educational opportunities or hiring discrimination because of race or sex also face relatively few *occupational* options. As a result, they often have to bear heavy social costs of pollution on the job. The Appalachian coalminers who breathe coal dust, the southern textile workers who inhale cotton fibers, and the California farmworkers who are exposed to high dosages of pesticides all work in debilitating environments.

The true extent of occupationally related diseases is hard to measure, of course, but it is certainly large. In 1978, for instance, epidemiologists from the National Cancer Institute and other federal agencies estimated that as much as two-fifths of all cancers in the United States might be due, at least in part, to occupational exposure to cancer-causing substances. However, as one author has pointed out,

It should be made clear . . . that all the studies of cancers resulting from industrial chemicals have been made on chemicals used for many years. No one can predict the effects that the great boom in organic chemical production, which began around 1945, . . . will have on cancer incidence in the future. (Loechler 1980: 14)

Hence, although OSHA presently recognizes and regulates fewer than two dozen chemicals as human carcinogens, the National Institute of Occupational Safety and Health lists more than 2,000 chemicals currently in the workplace as possibly carcinogenic. Persistent exposure to this large and growing list of cancer-inducing substances will certainly result in more cases of occupational disease in the United States during the next several decades.

The environmental situation facing corporate owners and executives, on the other hand, is strikingly different from that of the less affluent majority. As far as residential exposure to pollutants is concerned, the wealthy can afford to live in relatively clean suburban neighborhoods or else move to dirtier urban neighborhoods but then purchase air-conditioned condominiums and superb health care and vacations in healthful environments to compensate, at least partially, for the environmental quality they face in the city. In the corporate headquarters, the business leader can avoid the environmental risks of the workplace he manages and still appropriate the profits that accrue to private ownership of factory, mill, and mine. Hence, although everyone in society is ultimately threatened by environmental decay, the wealthy can avoid most of the immediate effects of environmental pollution while reaping short-term benefits from free disposal of wastes in the environment.

What this discussion points out is that the orthodox distinction between the "private" and "social" costs of production actually confuses several issues. Some of the environmental costs of pollution are borne within business firms and are shifted from the owners of these firms to their own workers. Unlike true social costs, which are dispersed widely among a variety of social classes and groups, the effects of in-plant pollution are concentrated within particular occupations and industries. Even those pollution costs that are shifted to groups outside business firms are seldom "social costs." Because of their unequal distribution among social classes, most pollution costs are "class costs" imposed on the poor and other working people.

ECOLOGICAL CONTRADICTIONS

Not surprisingly, then, government policies to regulate air and water quality and to control workplace hazards have reflected conflicting interests and have provoked political battles. Although recognition of social class divisions in U.S. society is essential to understanding these often bitter environmental conflicts, the issues are far more complex than "worker versus capitalist" or "big business versus big government." Looking at the historical record, one finds that environmental policy is not dictated by any particular social class. Rather, it is determined in the political arena as social classes and fractions of those classes battle on their own behalf—albeit with unequal endowments of political power. It is even difficult to identify the self-interest of any particular worker or business owner because, within the constraints of capitalist society, each and every person is caught in a web of contradictory tendencies.

Most corporate leaders, for example, now accept the *principle* of government regulation of environmental quality because they know that environmental anarchy would result in worsening ecological disasters and threats to the legitimacy of capitalism itself. This tendency emerged in a 1970 survey by *Fortune* magazine of 270 chief executives of top U.S. corporations. *Fortune* concluded that,

> [T]he way a large number of business leaders see it, substantial voluntary action on behalf of a single company is wasteful of corporate assets and ineffective in cleaning up the environment. They believe action on pollution must be collective. (Diamond 1970: 119)

So we see that many corporate leaders recognize the need for political action of some sort in order to manage the pace and forms of environmental decay.

Recourse by large corporations to public regulation is nothing new, "free enterprise" ideology notwithstanding. As James O'Connor has observed:

> By the turn of the [twentieth] century, and especially during the New Deal, it was apparent to vanguard corporate leaders that some form of rationalization of the economy was necessary. And as the twentieth century wore on, the owners of corporate capital generated the financial ability, learned the organizational skills, and developed the ideas necessary for their self-regulation as a class. (O'Connor 1973:68)

Some individual corporations and their owners even stand to profit handsomely from government environmental regulations since enforcement of those regulations creates markets for the pollution control devices they sell. If the Environmental Protection Agency (EPA), for example, were to require the installation of flue-gas scrubbers on the 50 largest coal-burning U.S. power plants in order to substantially lower sulfur dioxide emissions and thereby reduce acid rain, then General Electric and several other scrubber manufacturers would reap extra sales of roughly $5 billion (*New York Times* 1983:D1).

However, most corporations are not in a position to construct or manufacture pollution control facilities and devices for profitable sale. Rather, EPA and OSHA standards force many corporations to undertake costly investments, which reduce waste emissions and workplace hazards but do not produce commodities those same firms can then sell in the marketplace. This helps to explain the ambivalence the corporate elite has felt about the environmental movement right from its beginning:

> When it comes to remedial action, a dominant sentiment is caution. The [corporate] executives [surveyed by *Fortune*] are concerned that government, in response to public pressure, will dictate the immediate spending of huge sums, which . . . will sap the financial vigor of their companies. . . . It may come as quite a surprise that the elite of business leadership strongly desire the federal government to step in, set the standards, regulate all activities pertaining to the environment, and help finance the job with tax incentives.

To be specific, 74 percent of the corporation executives surveyed in 1970 believed that accelerated depreciation allowances, investment tax credits, and government grants for corporate abatement projects would be the "most effective" environmental protection measures (Diamond 1970: 172). In effect, they wanted Treasury subsidies and Internal Revenue Service tax cuts in return for not debasing the environment.

Thus, the corporate elite is caught in a political bind. On the one hand, a lack of environmental regulation would result in ever-worsening ecological catastrophes in the years to come. This deterioration of environmental quality, in turn, would *eventually* disrupt corporate profitability because of worsening public health and declining productivity of biological resources. Events such as these could ultimately threaten the legitimacy of capitalist institutions. Recognizing these dangers, corporate leaders have accepted environmentalism to a degree. On the other hand, strict government regulations to maintain environmental quality and ensure workplace safety are typically resented by business leaders, since they see enforcement of those regulations as an *immediate* threat to their profitability unless public subsidies and price hikes compensate for their extra costs.

In a similar fashion, capitalist economic relations put working people in a contradictory position vis-à-vis environmental regulation. As we have already seen, workers and their families bear the brunt of environmental pollution and hazardous working conditions, and hence they stand to benefit greatly from improvements in environmental quality and workplace safety. In fact, the research of Peter Asch and Joseph Seneca suggests that urban workers in the United States did enjoy substantial improvements in air quality during the 1970s:

> Sulfur dioxide levels in urban areas decreased by 30% between 1970 and 1975. . . . [M]ajor progress in air quality has occurred in particulate matter. . . . The change in particulate matter [in Chicago] between 1972 and 1974 appears to have been distributed progressively [since improvements were greater in poorer neighborhoods]. (1978: 190–91)

These changes in air pollution probably reflect a number of causes, but federal efforts to clean up the environment are certainly a major one.

At the same time, however, employed workers are often nervous about proposed environmental regulations because they know that capitalism seldom provides enough jobs for its work force and that corporate decisions to close up shop rather than comply with particular EPA or OSHA standards could throw them into the ranks of the unemployed. Employment insecurity helps to explain, for example, the divisions among labor unions in the United States concerning commercial nuclear power. The United Mine Workers of America (UMWA) has opposed nuclear power from its inception because of the threat it poses to employment in the nation's coal mines. Opposition by union members to nuclear power extends well beyond the UMWA, however. A Lou Harris poll in 1979 found that 42 percent of union members and their families in the United States opposed building more nuclear plants. This suggests that, although preserving one's own job is an important consideration to individual workers, there are other, perhaps broader, issues that are also important to working people in the United States.

The AFL-CIO building and construction unions, on the other hand, have been staunchly pronuclear power, since employment in the construction industry is highly cyclical and since the building of a single nuclear plant can provide 5,000 person-years of employment (Logan and Nelkin 1980:7–10). This suggests that antinuclear power activists must face the issue of unemployment squarely if they want to broaden popular support for their cause. As Jeff Pector (1978: 31) has phrased the issue:

> Nuclear workers cannot be expected to oppose nuclear power when their livelihoods depend on it and no alternatives are available. . . . The "Stop Nuclear Power Now" protests at the workplace entrance often tend to make . . . [antinuclear] unity more difficult to attain.

Fear of unemployment is not the only feature of capitalist society that helps to undermine the proenvironmental tendencies of workers, however. The methods commonly used to *finance* environmental protection measures play a similar role, since their economic burden falls relatively heavily on working families. Although federal grants for construction of municipal sewage treatment plants and other environmental projects have been financed by a mildly progressive federal tax system, much of the expense of environmental protection in the United States has been paid for by regressive price increases that shift corporate antipollution costs to consumers. For example, the absence of adequate public transportation in many U.S. cities has meant that workers have been forced to pay substantially higher prices for new cars that comply with federal exhaust emission standards. A study by two researchers at Resources for the Future suggests that the overall economic impact of the Clean Water Act of 1972 and Clean

Air Act of 1970 has been highly regressive. Leonard Gianessi and Henry Peskin (1980: 99–100) estimate that U.S. families with incomes below $3,000 paid 4.4 and 8.2 percent of their incomes in the early 1970s to safeguard water and air quality, respectively, whereas families with incomes greater than $25,000 paid only 1.7 and 1.8 percent to protect the water and air. Hence, although the urban poor and other workers have borne a disproportionate share of environmental disamenities, they have also shouldered a burdensome share of the costs of environmental protection.

ENVIRONMENTAL POLITICS WITHIN THE METROPOLIS

These contradictory situations of corporate owners and working people are reflected in the zigzag course of environmental policy in the United States during the past 20 years. The original acceptance of government environmental regulation by corporate leaders was, in large part, a response to several environmental disasters of the 1960s and the popular reaction that followed. An acute four-day pollution crisis in New York City during 1966 caused 80 deaths and resulted in a National Air Pollution Conference. This conference, in turn, provided some of the impetus for the enactment of the 1967 Air Quality Act (Baumol and Oates 1979:324). During that same period, as John Mendeloff (1979:17–18) has pointed out,

> The November 1968, Farmington, West Virginia, blast that killed seventy-eight miners precipitated a new wave of support for stricter enforcement of coal mine safety laws. Encompassing that disaster was the emergence of a grass roots movement to aid the victims of black lung. The organization generated by that movement. . .led [to] wildcat strikes and sent thousands of miners to the West Virginia statehouse to demand coverage of black lung in the state's workers' compensation program. . . .

This militant rank-and-file movement within the UMWA won passage of the 1969 Coal Mine Safety Act, which, in turn, paved the way for the Occupational Safety and Health Act of 1970. Thus, highly visible disasters during an era of worker militancy and campus rebellion prompted business leaders to tolerate federal efforts to regulate environmental pollution and workplace hazards.

But, although they accepted the principle of government regulation, corporate executives and owners were never indifferent to the *forms* and *degree* of strictness of environmental regulation. Business opposition to OSHA, for example, has been heated right from its birth. Part of the reason, of course, is that OSHA regulations force corporations to spend their investment dollars in a way that tends to depress their profits. The U.S. Chamber of Commerce has reached the (perhaps exaggerated) conclusion that complying with OSHA standards cost U.S. business an average of $3.5 billion annually from 1972 to 1979.

However, corporate hatred of OSHA has been so deep and widespread that other issues must be lurking beneath the surface. One such is that the

> establishment of the legal right to a healthy and safe work environment, even if poorly enforced, is a [political] gain for workers. . . . In bringing health and safety to the union agenda, OSHA has stimulated organizing drives across the country. (*Dollars & Sense* 1981a)

An episode that must have been threatening to corporate leaders was the 1973 strike by the Oil, Chemical, and Atomic Workers Union against Shell Oil over issues of worker health and safety. This strike was supported by 11 national environmental groups, an act of grass-roots unity that called into question management's right to control the work environment.

Another reason that OSHA has been a target of business criticism from its inception is that, until recently, it was relatively insulated from corporate influence in its rule-making process. During the 1970s, OSHA was overseen by congressional committees whose members were somewhat responsive to the AFL-CIO union federation, and this gave OSHA's rule makers some opportunity to actually regulate hazards in the corporate workplace. Although OSHA standards have never been either strict or strictly enforced, its civil servants have long resisted the argument that they should take the costs of their regulations into account while setting health and safety standards for workers. This resistance to formal cost-benefit analysis at OSHA has angered many business leaders because they fear that the "financial vigor" of their enterprises might be sacrificed if saving human lives is OSHA's unqualified goal.[4]

Not surprisingly, then, both OSHA and the EPA have always been under strong corporate pressure to avoid "excessive" regulatory standards and timetables—even if stricter standards and deadlines would save many lives. This way of thinking was well expressed in 1976 by Arthur Burns, when he commented,

> We must now seek ways of bringing unemployment down without being engulfed by a new wave of inflation. . . . [G]overnmental efforts are long overdue to encourage improvements in productivity through larger investment in modern plant and equipment. This objective would be promoted by overhauling the structure of federal taxation . . . [and] by stretching out the timetables for achieving our environmental and safety goals. (Burns 1976:10)

This comment turned out to be remarkably prophetic. The near depression of 1981–82 created an opportunity for a reactionary shift in federal environmental policy. On the one hand, it intensified the desire of U.S. business leaders for weaker OSHA and EPA regulation so that corporate profitability could be quickly restored. On the other hand, more than 12 million workers in the United States lacked jobs at the depths of that severe recession, and corporate demands for pay cuts, tax cuts, and weaker federal regulation were difficult to resist.

In this depressed economic environment, Ronald Reagan and his conservative congressional allies took the political offensive. In addition to cutting personal taxes on wealthy individuals and practically eliminating the federal tax on corporate profits, the Reagan administration has moved to restrain environmentalist pressures upon and within the federal government.

One Reagan proposal has been to restore the profitability of commercial nuclear power by expediting the licensing of new reactors by the Nuclear Regulatory Commission (NRC):

> Nunzio Palladino, . . . [Reagan's] appointee to head up the NRC, has been trying to get Congress to streamline nuclear licensing procedures. As the regulations stand now, utilities have to go through the NRC certification process twice—once to get permission to build a reactor and again . . . to get permission to operate it. Palladino wants to condense this process down to . . . the initial construction permit. (*Dollars & Sense* 1983)

If successful, this effort would expedite the completion of nuclear power plants and thereby reduce their construction costs, but it would also reduce popular participation in the regulatory process and give the NRC less time to discover hazardous reactor design and construction defects.[5]

Another political initiative to restore the profitability of nuclear power has involved the federal government in trying to solve the acute waste disposal problems of the nuclear industry. Each nuclear power reactor generates roughly 30 tons of highly radioactive spent fuel each year, and since there are presently no disposal sites licensed to receive this radioactive garbage, nuclear power plants are simply accumulating their own hazardous wastes. The Nuclear Waste Policy Act of 1983 promised that the U.S. Department of Energy would find a safe disposal site by 1987, but it is now acknowledged that a federal nuclear waste repository might not be operational before the end of the century (Wald 1984). Hence, the U.S. Congress and the President have fostered the *illusion* that nuclear power does not pose a serious waste disposal problem so that the licensing and commercial operation of power reactors can proceed. This shift in nuclear regulatory policy during the early 1980s has been noted by Robert Pollard, of the Union of Concerned Scientists:

> "We all know the political winds have shifted," N.R.C. Commissioner, Victor Gilinsky, told an industry audience [in 1982]. . . . The N.R.C. staff certainly senses a different mood: some of the very same senior N.R.C. officials who were outdoing each other [after the nuclear accident at Three Mile Island] . . . in proposing new safety regulations are now competing to eliminate such requirements. (Pollard 1983: 569)

Efforts by the Reagan administration to restrain environmentalism are not restricted to nuclear power, however. OSHA's regulation of the work environment has also been a target:

> Reagan's OSHA appointees are pushing to apply "cost-benefit analysis," a supposedly objective economic test, to all regulations. The idea is that they weigh the cost . . . of complying with a regulation against the benefits of the regulation. . . . Thus any cost-benefit analysis of OSHA regulations involves placing a dollar value on human life and death—often, as it turns out, an outrageously low value [of several hundred thousand dollars]. (*Dollars & Sense* 1981a)

If cost-benefit logic prevails within OSHA, then millions of workers in the United States will be routinely and *legally* exposed to hazardous chemicals and other materials because protection of their health has been deemed "inefficient" on economic grounds. As a result, productivity and profitability will be enhanced in the short run as corporations shift their money to more "productive" investments such as industrial robots, but with the longer-term social consequence that even more workers in the United States will eventually suffer cancer and other occupational diseases.[6]

CAPITALIST GROWTH AND ECOLOGICAL IRRATIONALITIES

What this brief history of U.S. environmental policy suggests is that the contradictions of capitalist society continuously undermine governmental efforts to prevent environmental decay. The focal point of these contradictions is the process of capitalist economic growth. Since its infancy, capitalism has been a powerful engine for accumulating personal fortunes and for increasing both the volume and range of consumer goods available to individual workers. At the same time, however, it has always been subject to alternating periods of economic boom and bust, since successive years of business expansion invariably lower capitalists' profits, thereby setting the state for a business downturn and an interruption of economic growth.

Since the Great Depression of the 1930s, national governments in advanced capitalist nations have become more and more deeply involved in trying to manage, if not entirely eliminate, the roller-coaster path of capitalist growth. From the perspective of liberal politicians and corporate leaders, macroeconomic policy is necessary in order to relieve poverty and maintain political stability, given the unequal distribution of income and wealth in capitalist society. One of the most candid statements of this thesis was the (rather sanguine) assertion by Eugene Rostow (1959: 19) that,

> [T]he ideas of liberal planning [i.e., full employment and rapid growth via macroeconomic policy] give capitalism every reason to expect even more spectacular progess in the future than in the past, *without disturbing the basic conditions of property ownership and control.* (emphasis added)

Ever since the election of John F. Kennedy in 1960, high rates of corporate investment and rapid economic growth have been priority goals of federal policy in the United States. As Walter Heller (1966:79–81) has reflected,

> Among the interlocking shifts in liberal Democratic policy in the early 1960s was the increased emphasis on investment relative to consumption, on tax cuts relative to [government] expenditure increases, on cost-price stability relative to demand expansion, and on international relative to domestic considerations. . . . Emphasis on high levels of investment . . . is here to stay. It is essential to the economic growth and well-being of the nation.

Although economic growth in the United States has actually been quite sporadic since the 1960s, the commitment of national politicians and economic planners to stimulating private investment has not waned since the Kennedy-Johnson years, witness the "supply-side" tax cuts of Ronald Reagan during the early 1980s. This commitment to the "financial vigor" of large corporations does not necessarily reflect political corruption or indifference to environmentalists and the poor. Rather, it stems from a recognition that corporate executives presently control most investment decisions in the United States and that economic crisis will result if government policy destroys the "business confidence" of corporate investors. This means that federal policy makers are under constant political pressure to avoid tax laws, public spending programs, or government regulations that threaten corporate profitability. As a result, capitalist growth is inevitably accompanied by greater harm to the environment than is technologically necessary and socially desirable.

But the imperatives of capitalist growth affect not only government policy but also the structure of the private economy itself. The large oligopolistic firms that dominate many industries do not normally engage in spirited price competition. Each corporation recognizes that price cutting in the pursuit of additional sales would provoke immediate retaliation by its rivals and that all firms in the industry would suffer financially as a result. These corporations do, however, engage in various forms of nonprice competition: Advertising campaigns, frequent styling and model changes, minor product improvements, and packaging changes are all calculated to increase a firm's share of the market and to expand the market itself.[7] Developing and marketing products that put a premium on durability and long service life is counterproductive from the point of view of the individual oligopolist and also contrary to the needs of a recession-prone economy.

An immediate consequence of this behavior is that relatively high rates of production and environmental costs are necessary (*ceteris paribus*) in order to maintain and expand stocks of durable goods, at the same time that relatively large quantities of goods are junked or discarded each year. For example, suppose it were desirable to maintain an operating stock of ten million motor vehicles. If cars and trucks had an average life of five years, it would be necessary to produce two million new vehicles a year and to dispose of two million junked vehicles per year. If, on the other hand, the economic life of motor vehicles were extended to ten years, current production and disposal requirements would fall to one million cars and trucks per year. Although pollution and congestion resulting from the operation of the vehicles might remain substantially the same, resource depletion and pollution resulting from the production of motor vehicles would fall significantly.

In addition to rapid obsolescence and depreciation of commodites, other ecological irrationalities plague modern capitalism. Corporations that promote *atomistic* or individual, rather than *social*, consumption also contribute to the environmental crisis. In a famous account of the ways advertising agencies influence individual consumption, Vance Packard described "hidden persuaders" who spend vast amounts of time and money to popularize the taste for private consumption. Packard also quoted a marketing consultant who declared in the *Journal of Retailing*,

> Our enormously productive economy . . . demands we make consumption our way of life, that we seek our spiritual satisfactions, our ego satisfactions, in consumption. . . . We need things consumed, burned up, worn out, replaced, and discarded at an ever increasing rate. (Lebow 1955: 7)

The notion that each nuclear family *needs* its own single-family dwelling complete with a two-car garage and two late-model cars is an important cultural prop for the modern corporate economy. First, it helps to stimulate total consumer spending and thereby relax the restraints on consumer markets imposed by income and wealth inequalities. In so doing, it also discourages personal saving by working-class families and prevents their escape from wage employment via the small-business route. Second, individual consumerism provides an outlet for employees who find themselves nearly powerless and alienated in the workplace. This individualistic escape valve also discourages collective political activity by working people to improve their lot, whether through union organizing or the ballot box.

When the government fails to provide and foster alternative social forms of consumption, an ideological norm such as individual consumption becomes an actual necessity. The most notorious example is the development of urban transport in the United States during the post–World War II period. Massive public expenditures on expressways and arterial highways have encouraged popular dependence on private automobile transport in urban areas. This has led to a deterioration of commuter rail and bus service in many metropolitan areas, thereby compounding reliance on the private automobile. In this manner, the corporate economy not only promotes a popular taste for private auto transport but also eliminates alternative social modes of urban transportation. This type of example has been repeated in the housing sector where federal mortgage subsidy programs, municipal zoning and building codes, and the scarcity of public housing funds favor suburban, single-family-dwelling construction.

An economic consequence of the emphasis on private, rather than social, consumption is that relatively large stocks of durable goods are necessary in order to provide a given stream of consumer services, or use values. There are several reasons for this heavy capitalization of consumption. First, most forms of consumer wealth in advanced capitalist economies are substantially underutilized. Most private autos, for instance, are not in use at a particular moment and consequently are not generating transportation services. These unutilized autos, instead, create severe storage problems in urban areas. Every single-family dwelling has its own complement of household appliances, which are also used only periodically. Second, the emphasis on atomistic consumption prevents the realization of substantial economies of scale in consumption. The continuing suburbanization of North American cities, for example, makes the provision of water and sewage treatment systems extremely costly.

Clearly, therefore, the ecological destructiveness of capitalist society is not simply a consequence of its failure to ration the waste-assimilating capacity of the natural environment. That failure explains only the large quantity of pollutants created and discharged per unit of aggregate output. Oligopolistic rivalries and atomistic consumption compound the problem;

rapid product obsolescence, underutilization of consumer durables, and the failure to realize scale economies via social consumption result in relatively high rates of current production per unit of consumption service. Even if a pollution tax were to result in more careful waste control and disposal, other structural characteristics of modern capitalism would tend to perpetuate depletion and pollution of the environment. Thus, the optimistic claim of many orthodox economists that a federal pollution tax would, if enacted, solve environmental problems is hopelessly utopian because it neglects the contradictions of environmental politics and the structural needs of capitalist accumulation and growth.

INTERNATIONAL CAPITALISM AND ENVIRONMENTAL QUALITY

Capitalist expansion has never stopped at national boundaries, and, since the end of World War II, Western European, Japanese, and North American corporations have extended their profit-seeking operations to the far corners of the world. But ecological processes are international, and even global, in scope as well. Thus, looking for the roots of ecological decay at home is only part of the quest for harmony between humanity and nature: The international dimensions of environmental crisis must be addressed as well.

One of these dimensions is the depressing effect that international trade competition has on the environmental protection efforts within each trading country. If the U.S. government, for example, imposes especially strict regulations on the use of pesticides and the discharge of industrial wastes at home, then the prices of U.S. agricultural and manufactured products will tend to rise compared to those of its foreign trading rivals. If Canadian, European, and Japanese enterprises are not subject to similarly stringent environmental regulation, then the U.S. balance of trade will tend to deteriorate as its exports shrink and its imports rise.

Conservative members of the business community within each nation therefore have an economic issue that can be used to mobilize popular sentiment against measures to protect the environment. Warnings about potentially adverse effects on a nation's balance of trade can be used to undercut domestic support for "overly strict" environmental standards. This argument is likely to be especially persuasive in those industrial nations, like Japan, that depend heavily upon export sales to generate jobs and profits. This prospect was recognized by Hans Dietrich Genscher, the former West German interior minister, when he remarked,

> We must. . .avoid a situation in which individual countries exclude themselves from making investments for environmental protection,

> thereby securing competitive advantages for their own economy vis-a-vis those countries who do meet their responsibilities. (quoted in Russell and Landsberg 1971: 1310)

Of course, international negotiation to coordinate the strictness of national environmental policies would avert this competitive outcome, but reaching international consensus is not easy, particularly during periods of economic recession when each industrial capitalist nation is tempted to pursue its own immediate self-interest without regard for the longer-term consequences.

The environmental impact of international capitalism has not been restricted to the more affluent industrial nations, however. There is some evidence that multinational corporations based in North America, Western Europe, and Japan have sponsored a particularly chilling sort of international "solution" to the pollution problems of their home countries—the export of hazardous products and production processes to the poor nations of the Third World. As Narindar Singh pointed out in the mid-1970s,

> [T]he Diebold Institute lists as many as seven fairly good reasons why multinationals would actually prefer to undertake manufacturing in the Third World countries these days. The very first of these is that they would like "to escape strict standards against pollution" within the metropolises. (Singh 1976: 51)

U.S. investors building manufacturing plants at home found that 10.7 percent of each investment dollar went for pollution control in 1976, whereas the comparable percentage for foreign investments was only 4.8 percent. This international difference probably made environmental standards at home seem "too strict," at least from the investor's point of view (Castleman 1979: 4).

Is there evidence that multinational export of both capital *and* pollution to the Third World has actually occurred as a result of weaker foreign standards? Although I am not aware of a comprehensive study of this question, the recent history of Brazil suggests that the answer is yes. Following a military coup in 1964, which ended a period of democratic and nationalist politics in Brazil, the government aggressively courted multinational investments in order to rapidly develop the Brazilian economy. This development strategy was explicitly antienvironmental, as the following comment of Joao Paulo Velloso, the military junta's planning minister, clearly indicates: "Brazil can become the importer of pollution. . .We have a lot left to pollute. . .And if we don't do it, some other country will." (quoted in Novitski 1972)

This open-door invitation to foreign polluters, together with Brazil's rich natural resources and the military junta's repressive antilabor measures, created a "positive investment climate," and Brazil enjoyed a highly touted economic growth "miracle" for a number of years. But what were the environmental, social, and even economic consequences of this period of rapid capitalist growth? By 1973, one account of São Paulo's industrial suburbs described the environment as "unlivable": "The air is said to contain tons of sulfur dioxide. . . . Fifty percent of the children given medical treatment suffer from diseases of the respiratory tract. . . ." (Baumol and Oates 1979: 205). Cubatao, a major Brazilian industrial city, has recorded the highest level of acid rain ever measured.

By 1983, one observer pointed out that even the economic "miracle" had turned out to be a mere illusion:

> Engulfed in the worst economic crisis in its history, Brazil . . . [has a] $90 billion foreign debt, $55 billion of which is held by U.S., European and Japanese banks. . . . [R]eal wages have plummeted 20 percent in the last year, and . . . Brazilian factories . . . have had to lay off millions of workers. There is no social cushion for such calamities, since Brazil has neither unemployment insurance nor welfare. (Lernoux 1983: 434–35)

Thus, multinational investment and capitalist growth have provided Brazilian workers neither economic security nor a healthful environment. Is it surprising, then, that nearly 200 supermarkets were looted in São Paulo and Rio de Janeiro by hungry mobs during this 1983 economic crisis?

Puerto Rico provides still another example of Third World environmental decay resulting from capitalist economic growth. During recent decades, the Puerto Rican economy has undergone rapid industrialization as U.S. investors have built pharmaceutical, electronics, and other manufacturing plants on fields where sugar cane used to stand. These corporate investors have been attracted by generous tax breaks, ample labor at low wages, and neocolonial political ties to the U.S. government.

But the political jurisdiction of federal agencies on the island has not prevented widespread contamination of the island's water supply. Concern about water quality has been growing since 1982 when the U.S. Geological Survey found that most of the 57 wells it sampled in highly populated areas had been contaminated by industrial pollutants such as trichloroethylene. Since then, the Commonwealth's Department of Health has shut down more than a dozen wells, out of a total of 300 that supply the island's fresh water. Luis Bonilla, scientific adviser to the Puerto Rican legislature, has ventured the following conclusion:

> The major problem is underground water contamination caused by inadequate disposal of hazardous wastes. For more than 10 years, these industries have been disposing of waste in sanitary landfills in a region where the underground is basically permeable to liquids. (quoted in Stuart 1984)

Relocating industrial plants to Third World countries in order to avoid domestic pollution standards is only one tactic among several, however, multinational corporations have used to augment their profits. Another rewarding tactic has been the *export* of hazardous products whose use is prohibited or severely restricted at home. Exporting pesticides such as DDT is a prime example. For U.S. firms, pesticide sales abroad have nearly quadrupled in the last two decades. The chemical industry now exports 20 percent of the pesticides it produces, shipping some 400,000 tons a year to the Third World.

The weakness or even absence of environmental regulation in most Third World nations means that these hazardous imports have serious environmental repercussions:

> On the plantations in northern Mexico that grow tomatoes for U.S. consumption, for example, a pesticide-related death occurs every day. The workers live in huts in the fields alongside the irrigation canals, which receive all the pesticide runoff. They use the canals to wash themselves . . . and to collect drinking water. . . . (*Dollars & Sense* 1981b: 6)

Farmworkers in the Third World are not the only victims of pesticide misuse in their countries, however. According to the U.S. Food and Drug Administration, approximately 10 percent of food imported into the United States contains illegal pesticide residues, thereby completing a profitable "circle of poison" traced by multinational investment.

With anger recently mounting in the United States because of the discovery of a growing number of toxic waste dumps, still another international business opportunity has been seized by some hearty entrepreneurs—finding foreign dump sites for part of the 100 billion pounds of toxic chemicals and nuclear wastes generated domestically each year. According to the EPA, three Texas companies exported PCBs—a well-known carcinogen—to Mexico, South Africa, and the Dominican Republic for disposal during 1980 (McLeod 1980: 27–28). How extensive this practice has become is hard to say, but it seems that multinational corporations are happy to export capital, products, and even toxic wastes to the Third World, whatever the environmental consequences might be.

POPULATION, HUNGER, AND THE ENVIRONMENT

This characterization of the environmental problems facing Third World countries is not the one typically favored by political and intellectual leaders in the West. Rather, it has been far more common in the wealthier capitalist nations to argue that Africa, Asia, and Latin America suffer from *overpopulation* relative to the productive capacity of the land and other natural assets and from excessive rates of *population growth*. Hunger and depletion of natural resources, not pollution, are said to be the environmental spectres haunting the Third World.[8]

This neo-Malthusian claim has a certain ring of plausibility to it, at least upon its first airing. As Ansley Coale has calculated, there is an unavoidable need to *eventually* stabilize the world's population because, at the present global rate of population growth, there would literally standing room only within six or seven centuries (in Baumol and Oates 1979: 129). It is also clear that birthrates in most Third World nations are currently very high relative to those in the United States and other developed countries. The United Nations estimates, for example, that the birthrate in India during the late 1970s was more than double the U.S. rate, whereas the Mexican birthrate was more than two and a half times that north of the border (United Nations 1980: table 9). With birthrates such as these, as much as 90 percent of the world's population growth during the remainder of this century will occur in the poor nations of the Third World (Castro 1983: 171–72).

After citing these demographic trends, many neo-Malthusians then proceed to comment on the persistent hunger and periodic famine that plague the Third World. In India alone, perhaps 200 million people are malnourished. The United Nations estimates that during 1975 chronic hunger affected 22 percent of the African population, 27 percent in the Far East, 13 percent in Latin America, and 11 percent in the Near East (Castro 1983: 96, 177). Chronic malnutrition throughout the Third World is occasionally punctuated by outright famine in some countries, as in Ethiopia during 1985 and Bangladesh in 1974.

The fundamental error in the neo-Malthusian view of Third World poverty is not that these factual observations are wrong, but rather that they are badly misinterpreted. Whereas neo-Malthusians see overpopulation and natural calamities as the *causes* of Third World hunger and famine, a far better interpretation of the facts is that the extreme political and economic *inequalities* that exist within the capitalist world produce both widespread hunger and rapid population growth in the Third World. This perspective was offered by Fidel Castro in his 1983 report to the seventh summit conference of the nonaligned countries:

> It must not be forgotten . . . that the population phenomenon . . . cannot be seriously and rigorously analyzed if . . . the social and economic factors that are the basis and the main cause of that growth are not taken into account. The peoples of the underdeveloped countries are not poorer or hungrier . . . as a result of their high birth rates. The

> uncontrollable growth of the population . . . is, above all, precisely the
> product of the social, economic, and cultural conditions to which our
> peoples have been subjected. . . .

There is abundant evidence to support this radical perspective on Third
World population and hunger. It is clear, for example, that there is no
global food shortage that could account for the 40 million cases of starvation the United Nations estimates occur around the world every year
(Castro 1983: 175–77). Enough grain is now produced to provide every
man, woman and child on earth with roughly 3,000 calories a day. That is
more than the average level of consumption in the United States and about
50 percent above a minimum acceptable level of daily caloric intake (*New
York Times* 1981). Hence, it must be the *unequal distribution* of an adequate world food supply among and within nations, not a general scarcity
of food, that results in widespread hunger and starvation.

On what basis is food distributed among the world's people? The exact
answer to that question varies among societies and through history, but certainly in rich capitalist nations, and increasingly in the Third World as well,
food is produced for market sale and is sold to those who have personal incomes or assets with which to pay. A similar point has been forcefully made
by Amartya Sen (1981: 1) as follows:

> Starvation is the characteristic of some people not *having* enough food
> to eat. It is not the characteristic of there *being* not enough to eat.
> . . . Leaving out cases in which a person may deliberately starve, star-
> vation . . . [raises issues about] ownership of food by persons. In order
> to understand starvation, it is, therefore, necessary to go into the struc-
> ture of ownership.

By concentrating on income and wealth inequalities instead of "overpopulation," one can begin to understand why roughly half of the 160
billion tons of 1981 food exports from the United States went to feed foreign
cattle and hogs and why seven of the top ten importers of U.S. farm exports
were *developed* countries (*Dollars & Sense* 1982). The populations of West
Germany, Japan, and the Soviet Union are relatively affluent and can afford to consume meat by importing U.S. feed grains, while the poorest in
the Third World cannot compete in world markets for those same grain
shipments. Hence, although many of the less developed nations have
become increasingly dependent on grain imports from North American during recent decades, their ability to command part of the grain surpluses of
the United States and Canada is severely limited by their state of economic
underdevelopment.

But why are the nations of the Third World unable to feed themselves?
Doesn't their increasing dependence on grain imports demonstrate that they

have become "overpopulated" and are suffering the Malthusian consequence? It is undeniable that agriculture in Africa, Asia, and Latin America faces serious obstacles. In the early 1970s, arable land per capita in the poor nations was two-thirds the per capita acreage in the developed countries (Castro 1983: 110). Although larger crops per acre could compensate for this agricultural disadvantage, increasing agricultural yields takes improved seeds, more fertilizer, and other technological inputs. Unfortunately, many farmers in the Third World are short of both land and technological resources. The less developed nations were a net importer of fertilizer in 1980, for example, and yet their per capita consumption of fertilizer was less than one-sixth that in the affluent capitalist countries (Castro 1983: 100).

Despite these disadvantages, the primary obstacle to agricultural development in the Third World is not demographic or technological. As the recent experience of the Green Revolution has shown in India, Mexico, and eslewhere, it is the *social organization* of farming and food distribution that is the fundamental barrier to expanding food production and eliminating hunger in the poor countries. Perhaps the most important feature of Third World agriculture is the highly unequal distribution of private land ownership. In the early 1970s, for example, fewer than 8 percent of all Latin American farms accounted for *80 percent* of all agricultural land in that region. Although the degree of inequality was less severe in other parts of the Third World, a similar pattern of unequal land ownership prevailed (Castro 1983: 112).

As Ann Crittenden (1981:1) has noted, the introduction of Green Revolution technology into this situation of extreme rural inequality has led to perverse results:

> A decade ago, when the "green revolution" produced "miracle" wheat and rice, crop yields jumped dramatically throughout the developing world. But because the new seed required the heavy use of costly fertilizer, the wealthiest, large-scale farmers and their urban customers were the main beneficiaries, while the poorest peasants remained as destitute as before.

Crittenden's assessment is actually too mild, however. The increases in farm productivity promised by Green Revolution technology attracted money lenders, military officers, merchants, and multinational corporations, who bought up farmland. As land values rose, so did rents, pushing many tenants and sharecroppers into the ranks of the landless. Landlords also evicted tenants and fired farmworkers as they mechanized their farms. In India, to pick one example, the fraction of the rural work force that is landless has *doubled*—to more than one-third—since the dawn of the Green Revolution (*Dollars & Sense* 1980: 12).

Landless farmers are unable to grow their own food and, unless the dispossessed are able to find steady jobs in the countryside or the city, they are not able to buy very much food in the marketplace, either. This acts to restrain the domestic market for the crops of commercial farmers. Hence, as C. P. Timmer has concluded,

> Highly skewed rural incomes contribute both to widespread hunger, especially among the landless and near-landless, and also to stagnating food production. Without question, basic poverty—the lack of adequate purchasing power among consumers. . .is the most important cause of [Third World] hunger. (*New York Times* 1981: 1)

Is it surprising, then, that despite the introduction of high-yield agricultural methods into various Third World countries, hunger persists among the poor, and agricultural output grows more slowly than population in many cases? At the same time, ought one be surprised that the urban and rural elites in the poor nations eat extremely well despite their Third World citizenship?[9]

The problem of Third World hunger cannot be attributed entirely to social class divisions within the poor nations, however. Multinational investment and superpower politics sometimes play a role as well. The famines in Ethiopia and Bangladesh during the early 1970s provide two shocking examples. As Amartya Sen has shown, the famine in the Wollo region of Ethiopia cannot be explained by the drought that hit that part of the country during 1972–73. Other parts of Ethiopia had above-normal crops during that period, and food output fell 7 percent, at most, for the country as a whole. Food was available for the hungry of Wollo, but the "invisible hand" of the market actually *exported* food from that region during the famine since many of its residents had lower incomes and they could not afford to pay for much food. The group within Wollo who suffered the most from starvation were the nomadic herdsman of the region:

> [T]he pastoralists, particularly of the Afar community, were affected not merely by the drought. . .but also by the loss of grazing land owing to the expansion of commercial agriculture. About 50,000 hectares of good land. . .were "developed" during 1970–1. . .by a few big companies—mostly foreign-owned. . . .The land thus developed had been among the best of the grazing land available to the Afar pastoralist during the long dry season. . . .(Sen 1981: 86–104)

Thus, those who died were not the victims of a purely natural disaster. They were also the victims of the "invisible hand" of the domestic marketplace and multinational investment.

The Bangladesh famine of 1974 offers a variation on this theme. Severe flooding in the northern districts of the country is often cited as the natural cause of the famine. However, the per capita availability of rice and wheat in Bangladesh was *higher* in 1974 than during the three previous years. How is it possible, then, that perhaps a million people starved? The largest group of famine victims were wage laborers, both urban and rural, and during 1974 the average wage of laborers fell relative to the price of rice, thereby pushing many below subsistence. This decline in real wages came about partly because of decreased employment opportunities associated with the floods, but another cause may have been a loss of jobs in the jute industry because of shrinking export markets and U.S. foreign policy:

> The U.S. threatened to cut off food aid in September 1974. At that time the American ambassador called upon [the government of Bangladesh to]. . .cease exporting jute to Cuba. Under PL480, a recipient country cannot trade with blacklisted countries such as Cuba. . . . .The government of Bangladesh cancelled further exports of jute to Cuba at a time when competition from Indian jute and low world market prices had substantially eroded its foreign exchange earnings. (Sen 1981: 135–36)

Hence, it appears that the social class structure within Bangladesh and the political economy of international capitalism, not just natural phenomena, contributed to the starvation of perhaps a million people.

But, the neo-Malthusian might ask, is it not true that high birthrates and rapid population growth also tend to perpetuate hunger and poverty in the Third World? Possibly so, but the most pressing need is to understand that these demographic features of the poor nations are rooted in social class divisions and economic insecurity, not in a natural or cultural propensity to reproduce. As Mahmood Mamdani (1981: 48) has testified,

> The slums of São Paulo and Santiago, of Bombay and Calcutta, of Dakar and Nairobi are all testimony to the rise of this social group—the appropriated masses—in the urban centers of underdeveloped capitalism. . . .[Why] do marginal employment and high population growth go hand in hand? The marginal employment available. . .is daily casual labor. . . .But, most important, this employment is skewed in favor of child labor. Children shine shoes, open car doors or clean cars, and most of all they beg. . . .In slum populations it is not unusual to find whole families who are supported by the children.

That is, unequal land ownership in the countryside has encouraged rapid urbanization in the Third World, and, since adult unemployment is widespread in the cities, poor families are actually encouraged to bear children so that their households can beg and scrounge a subsistence income.

Widespread unemployment for adults is not the only economic feature of many Third World countries that encourages large families. Another is the paucity of government welfare programs to sustain the disabled and elderly. As Karen Michaelson (1981: 113) found during her research in Bombay,

> Children are wanted, additionally, for security: in old age, in sickness, or in case of some unnamed disaster. Women, in particular, are anxious for sons to care for them in old age. . . .The more children born, the more chance that at least one will survive and be able to support aged parents. This phenomenon is common not only in India. . . .

It is for economic reasons such as these that the efforts of Indira Gandhi to reduce India's birthrate by imposing sterilization on the Indian population met with stiff political resistance and had to be abandoned after 1976. Unless the economic issues of mass unemployment, poverty, and social insecurity are first addressed, birthrates in Third World countries will remain high.

In sum, the social and environmental problems of the Third World are rooted in a different terrain than the prophets of a "population bomb" have claimed. The roots of population growth, poverty, hunger, and pollution are the extreme inequalities of wealth ownership within most Third World societies and the dependence of their economies on multinational corporations.

SOCIALISM AND ECOLOGY

How can these environmentally destructive effects of capitalist growth and development be brought under control? Because the social costs of corporate production and individual consumption will continue to rise, the ecological contradictions and political tensions within capitalist societies are bound to become more acute. The resolution of these dilemmas and conflicts will lie in *socializing* those economies, not in imposing new government regulations or effluent taxes on corporate polluters.

Historically the argument for socialism has been grounded in criticism of the social inequality, exploitation of labor, and frequent economic crises that characterize capitalist societies. The socialist prescription to end these ills has traditionally included collective ownership of productive resources by the entire population, not just by a wealthy minority, and democratic planning of the use of those resources, not the "anarchy" of profit-seeking investments by private corporations.

In recent times, the problem of ecological decay and the need for environmental protection have actually strengthened this classic case for democratic socialism. If poverty and unemployment tend to produce high birthrates in the Third World, then more egalitarian distribution of consumer goods via income redistribution measures and full employment via economic planning can help to defuse the long-run "population bomb." If the ups and downs of the capitalist business cycle tend to weaken popular support for pollution control, then eliminating that economic roller coaster via democratic planning of investments can help to protect the environment. If competition among large, oligopolistic corporations promotes atomistic consumption and rapid product obsolescence, then socialism can offer environmentally sounder forms of consumption such as convenient public transport and widespread participation in sports.

But the skeptic might point out that this is mere socialist *theory* and that it is misleading to compare socialist visions with capitalist realities. Fortunately, however, we have the historical *practice* of several socialist countries to look at as we compare the ecological effects of capitalism with those of socialism. The Soviet Union was the first nation to adopt socialism, and its historical record reveals a mixture of environmental gains and losses.

On the positive side, the greater emphasis on *communal* consumption in the Soviet Union has reduced the stocks of physical goods necessary to achieve planned flows of consumer services to Soviet citizens. As Daniel Fusfeld (1982: 619–20) has observed,

> Soviet citizens are eating better and are better clothed than earlier generations. . . .The most striking changes [however] have taken place in communal consumption. Heavy government expenditures are made on education, health care, and support of the aged. The Soviet government reports that in 1970 the value of free consumer services and other benefits amounted to a little over one-third of average earnings per person. If that estimate is correct, about one-fourth of all consumption has been "socialized."

This political commitment to communal forms of consumption has helped to alleviate urban air pollution in the Soviet Union. McIntryre and Thornton (1974) point out that many Soviet cities tend to have serious air quality problems during winter months because of heavy space heating requirements and frequent atmospheric temperature inversions. That tendency has been mitigated, however, by the Soviet commitment to *centralized* combustion facilities to provide heat, hot water, and electricity to apartment buildings and public facilities in urban areas. These combustion plants display a high degree of thermal efficiency and "would seem to be a wise deviation from the home heating practices of most of the rest of the world" (p. 117).

Soviet ideology and practice have been less positive in a number of other respects, however. For many decades, the Communist Party leadership has been committed to the goal of rapid industrial development and has used central planning of investment projects to achieve that goal. Although the economic results have been impressive, there have also been environmental costs associated with rapid industrialization in the Soviet Union.[10] Water pollution has been a problem, for example, as Philip Pryde (1983: 275) has pointed out:

> Lake Baikal. . .has had its extraordinary clean and transparent waters deteriorated by effluents from two large paper mills built on its shores. Although advanced treatment plants have been built,. . .the treated effluent that enters the lake is far from being as clean as the exceptional lake water itself.

The rapidly growing number of trucks and private cars in the Soviet Union is also contributing to urban air pollution problems, especially since each Soviet-built vehicle apparently emits far more pollutants than its U.S. counterpart (Pryde 1983: 276). This increasing reliance on auto transport is also ominous since it tends to undermine political support for communal forms of consumption within the Soviet Union. However, McIntyre and Thornton (1974: 117) report that Soviet planners have attempted to offset these tendencies:

> Expensive and large scale pedestrian underpasses have been built in congested urban areas in order to produce a steady traffic flow and thereby reduce automobile discharges. . . .The use of leaded gasolines has either been prohibited or restricted within certain major population centers, resulting in a remarkably low level of ambient lead and oxidants. . . .Heavy Soviet dependence on railroads rather than motor vehicles to move. . .freight also serves to reduce air pollution.

The rapid expansion of nuclear power in the Soviet Union raises still more questions about the impact of socialist economic growth on environmental quality. In 1970, the Soviet Union had only four nuclear power plants, but by 1980 that total had risen to 22 plants. The Five-Year Plan for 1981–85 called for almost *tripling* nuclear megawattage by the end of that planning period. Although this heavy investment in atomic energy is apparently intended to avoid extra emissions from fossil-fuel-fired electric plants and although Soviet reactors are apparently more safely designed in some respects that U.S. reactors, the siting of these new reactors near cities in the European area of the country raises serious issues about the potential hazards of nuclear accidents in heavily populated areas.[11]

Some anti-Soviet critics in the West have welcomed examples such as these in order to argue that socialism is not environmentally sounder than capitalism. Marshall Goldman for example, has charged that

> a study of pollution in the Soviet Union suggests that abolishing private property will not necessarily mean an end to environmental disruption. In some ways, state ownership. . .may actually exacerbate. . .the situation. (Goldman 1970: 37).

This argument is faulty for several reasons, however. First, it is simply not true that *all* private property has been nationalized in the Soviet Union. Many consumer goods are privately owned and individually used, whereas most productive assets, farmland and factories, for example, are state owned. More important, however, Western critics of the Soviet Union's environmental record typically fail to identify the particular social roots of its ecological problems. It is not state ownership of productive resources and economic planning per se that are at fault but, rather, the limited degree of democratic participation in that planning process that is to blame. If the Soviet state permitted more popular participation in economic decision making, issues of environmental protection and workplace safety would probably receive far more attention within the country than they presently do.

The People's Republic of China provides a more recent, but similarly important, example of socialist development during the twentieth century. China is an especially interesting case because it offers insights into the relationships between food production and distribution, population growth, and environmental quality. More than three decades after a peasant-based socialist revolution came to power on its mainland, China is still a relatively poor, largely agrarian society. Four-fifths of its people live in rural villages instead of cities. In such a society, producing enough food and avoiding malnutrition are major economic and political issues.

What is truly amazing is that, despite its enormous population and despite the fact that its arable land area is roughly two-thirds that of the original 48 states in the United States, China has virtually eliminated hunger and is essentially self-sufficient in food supply. This socialist success—which contrasts sharply with the present situation in most Third World nations—is the result of both expanded domestic food *production* and more equitable *distribution* of that domestic supply of foodstuffs. Grain production in China, for example, expanded from about 113 million tons in 1949 to 174 million tons by 1974. Increases in agricultural output have been obtained by extensive double and triple cropping of farmland, creation of new farmland by terracing and irrigation projects, and increased use of fertilizer.

The elimination of starvation from China has involved more than increases in farm output, however. Socialist principles of egalitarian distribution have played a role, too, as Amartya Sen (1981: 7) has pointed out:

> The elimination of starvation in socialist economies—for example in China—seems to have taken place even without a dramatic rise in food availability per head, and indeed, typically the former has *preceded* the latter. The end of starvation reflects a shift. . .in the form of social security and—more importantly—. . .guaranteed employment at wages. . .adequate to avoid starvation.

That is, socialism in China has meant that food is distributed within the population so that no one starves.

But what have been the environmental effects of agricultural development in revolutionary China? There is evidence to suggest that the Chinese have consciously attempted to limit the ecological effects of expanding food production. In a fascinating account of Chinese agricultural practices, Robert Metcalf and Arthur Kelman (1981) have pointed out that protecting crops from pest attack is an obvious way to increase food supply without undertaking expensive investments in irrigation schemes or fertilizer plants. Recognizing this possibility, the Chinese have pioneered in the development of *integrated pest management*, an approach that utilizes natural insect predators, insect-specific diseases, light traps, and other nonpolluting means to control pest populations. As a result of this comprehensive approach to pest control, the Chinese were able to virtually abandon aerial spraying of insecticides by 1975 as well as the use of DDT and other especially hazardous chemical means to control agricultural pests. Another ecologically sound practice of the Chinese revolution has involved extensive efforts to reforest areas not suitable for farming (Orleans and Suttmeier 1970: 114).

But won't these impressive economic and environmental gains be threatened if China's already large population continues to grow? That would eventually be the case if the Chinese population were growing at a rate like those in the rest of the Third World; but, in fact, socialism in China has contributed to a dramatic fall in the Chinese birthrate. According to U.N. data, that rate was 37 births per 1,000 people in 1952, shortly after the Chinese revolution came to power, but it had fallen to less than 18 by 1979 (United Nations 1965: table 12; United Nations 1980: table 9). As a result of this greatly reduced birthrate, the rate of population growth in China had fallen to a modest 1.2 percent per annum by 1978, and the Chinese government hopes for zero population growth by the end of this century (Wiltgren and Herschede 1982: 22).

Do these demographic trends reflect the use of authoritarian methods by the revolutionary government of China? The simple reply to that question is no. Starting in 1962, the government in Beijing did begin to promote the distribution of contraceptives within China. By 1973, possibly one-third of the relevant Chinese population was practicing some form of family planning. More recently, several economic incentives have been introduced to encourage smaller families. In Beijing, for example, a couple with only one child receives preferential treatment in earlier admission of the child to nursery school and easier access to housing (Wiltgren and Herschede 1982: 25).

But government measures to control population growth could not have been implemented without provoking political resistance unless the Chinese revolution had already laid an economic foundation for smaller families. Socialist measures to increase employment opportunities and reduce poverty have done precisely that. These accomplishments of revolutionary socialism in China contrast sharply with the path of capitalist development in India, and those economic differences help to account for the marked difference in birthrates between the two countries.[12] In summary, the People's Republic of China has provided an impressive example of how hunger can be eliminated and population growth reduced even though a nation's economy is still underdeveloped.

A final example of socialist development that offers some interesting lessons can be found in the Caribbean. Socialist revolution came to Cuba in 1959, and the subsequent changes in Cuban society have been dramatic. Following the end of the Batista dictatorship, Cuba's revolutionaries reduced the unemployment rate sharply. Whereas nearly 12 percent of the work force had been unemployed in 1958, the rate of unemployment had fallen to less than 1.5 percent two decades later. The Cuban revolution has also reduced poverty and economic insecurity by introducing unemployment benefits equal to 70 percent of one's previous wage and a liberal system of pensions for the elderly. As Claes Brundenius (1981: 1086) has concluded, "It is no exaggeration to claim that Cuba has the most advanced social security system in Latin America."

In revolutionary Cuba, food and beverage consumption per capita increased 25 percent from 1958 to 1978, and the distribution of that food supply was equalized to a substantial degree by greater equity in income distribution and egalitarian rationing.[13] As a result of these economic changes and the increased participation of Cuban women outside the home, the birthrate in Cuba has shown a downward trend similar to that in revolutionary China. The Economic Commission for Latin America (ECLA) estimates that the Cuban birthrate was 30–34 births per 1,000 people at the time that Batista's pro-U.S. dictatorship crumbled. By 1979, Cuba's birthrate had fallen to 14.6, less than half that found in the Dominican Republic and almost one-third the rate in Haiti during the late 1970s (United Nations 1965: table 12; United Nations 1980: table 9).

Is there evidence that the Cuban revolution is committed to protection of the environment? There are bright spots to report, but a few ominous ones as well. In 1981, Cuba held its first national ecology meeting and adopted a resolution calling for a Commission on Natural Resources and the Environment with both monitoring and enforcement powers. The Cuban government has already declared that 4 percent of the island's land area will be reserved for conservation purposes, and in his 1980 report to the Communist Party Congress, Fidel Castro commented that more than 300 million seedlings had been planted during recent years in a major effort to reforest parts of the nation (Levins 1981: 30–32). This is in stark contrast with the present situation in much of Central America, where the region is being rapidly *deforested* by a combination of commercial logging, expansion of export-oriented beef ranches, and the efforts of landless peasants to carve subsistence farms from the jungle (Nations and Komer 1983: 12–13).

Several aspects of Cuban development during recent years are less progressive, however, from an ecological point of view. The increase in herbicide use from 11,500 tons in 1975 to 16,000 tons in 1980 was intended to increase agricultural productivity but also introduced potential pollutants into the island's soil. Fidel Castro's description of plans for Cuban energy development during the 1980s is an environmental mixed bag:

> A nuclear research center will soon be built and work must be done to develop solar and other energy sources. . . .[W]ork will continue on the Juragua nuclear-powered electric power plant. . . .(Levins 1981: 32)

Despite some environmentally questionable practices, I believe one has to conclude that socialist development in Cuba has been fundamentally sounder from an ecological perspective than capitalist development in Brazil or Central America.

CONCLUSION

As interesting as these historical sketches of the Soviet Union, China, and Cuba might be, they do not provide a socialist blueprint for other countries. Each nation needs to draw upon its own historical heritage and take account of its own present circumstances as it faces the future. In nations already affluent, socialism will differ greatly from the socialist experiments already underway in some of the world's poorer nations. The United States, for example, already has a highly developed economy and hence democratic socialism in the United States could afford to concentrate more on environmental protection and less on industrialization than the poorer socialist countries have been forced to.

Socialism is not on the immediate horizon in the United States, however, and thus one needs to ask what political actions might serve the cause of environmentalism until an ecologically saner society can be built. No one person, of course, can lay out a political program for ecological sanity, but let me make a few suggestions about future directions for the environmental movement in the United States. First, there is a crying need for a federal "right-to-know" law that would guarantee that employers fully inform their workers about the substances being used in the workplace. This would help to protect workers from occupational disease and would also encourage worker involvement in the planning of new production technologies. Another plank of a proenvironmental platform should be rejection of bureaucratic cost-benefit calculations to assess OSHA and EPA livesaving regulations. Whether saving human lives is economically "efficient" or not should be decided democratically by those whose lives are at risk, not by technocrats whose computations accept existing social inequalities as ethical criteria for deciding public policy.

Safeguarding the environment also raises issues of military and foreign policy. The U.S. government has to return to a foreign policy of detente with the Soviet Union and negotiate an end to the nuclear arms race. If the present course of political and military confrontation is not reversed, then both the United States and Soviet Union will waste enormous amounts of economic resources on arms production instead of protecting the global environment, and the risk of ecological collapse following a nuclear holocaust will continue to rise.[14] How the U.S. government reacts to socialist movements in the Third World is another geopolitical issue with environmental overtones. If the White House and Pentagon continue to label every revolutionary government in Africa, Asia, and Latin America as a "Soviet pawn" and "threat to U.S. national security," then efforts to eliminate poverty and economic insecurity within the poor nations will be impeded and stabilization of the world's population will be postponed.

Energy policy is another area where environmentalists must continue to exert political pressure. In particular, we must reject the false dichotomy promoted by corporate energy monopolies—expansion of nuclear power *or* intensified development of domestic coal and offshore oil deposits. Nuclear power produces serious hazards from radioactivity, and the consumption of fossil fuels contributes to acid rain and carbon dioxide buildup in the world's atmosphere. A third path of domestic energy development, which would be ecologically less destructive, would emphasize production of energy conservation devices, cogeneration equipment, and solar energy systems.

These strategic suggestions are far from comprehensive, but they hopefully embody a general principle that can be applied more broadly. As Narindar Singh (1976: 150) has stated,

> The essential question, then, is one of the relation between man and man and not one between man and nature. This is *not* to say that we can afford to be indifferent towards our habitat, but to submit that we can look after it properly. . .only when we cease to exploit our fellow-men below us, and refuse to be exploited by those. . .above.

Although Professor Singh's remark falsely assumes that all people are of the same gender, he is correct in concluding that the division of societies into antagonistic social classes is the fundamental threat to the world's natural environment and to the survival of humanity as well.

NOTES

1. By "orthodox economists," I mean those economists who operate within a neoclassical theoretical framework, e.g., supply and demand, subjective utility, marginal productivity, perfect competition, etc. For examples of neoclassical analysis applied to the issue of environmental quality, see Ruff (1970) and Dales (1968).

2. Even some orthodox economists, however, doubt whether it is possible to calculate and enforce an "optimal" set of pollution tax rates. This has led some to advocate that *physical* discharge standards be imposed and that these ceilings be allocated among producers and consumers by competitive bidding. See Baumol and Oates (1971).

3. This formulation abstracts from social groupings that cannot be easily categorized as either capitalist or proletarian. For a more detailed theoretical and empirical analysis of class divisions within the United States, see Wright et al. (1982). Unfortunately, research on wealth ownership does not receive a very high priority in capitalist countries, so Wolff's 1969 data are among the most recent.

4. OSHA's reluctance to employ cost-benefit analysis has also provoked criticism by a number of orthodox economists who are all too willing to place a dollar value on workers' lives. Their methods for doing so involve measuring individuals' "willingness to pay" to reduce the risk of death or, alternatively, the additional wages those workers might earn if they live longer. Both of these approaches take the existing social class divisions and income inequalities of U.S. society as technical data that are not to be questioned.

5. The need for *stricter* federal inspection of reactor design and construction is pointed out by the Diablo Canyon case. In September 1981, the NRC gave Pacific Gas and Electric Co. a temporary startup license for its new nuclear plant. Then it was discovered that the plant's anti-earthquake structures had been built backwards because of a blueprint mixup. The NRC had to suspend the plant's license for several years while corrective measures were undertaken. Diablo Canyon received a regular operating license from the NRC in August 1984 and began commercial operation during May 1985.

6. According to a 1985 report by the U.S. Office of Technology Assessment, the Reagan administration has already weakened enforcement of existing OSHA regulations. OSHA workplace inspections have declined substantially during the 1980s, and the average penalty for health or safety violations proposed by OSHA is less than $200! (*Wall Street Journal* 18 April 1985). Whether an OSHA plan to broaden the range of firms subject to spot checks, announced in early 1986, will improve workplace safety remains to be seen.

7. Compare Bain (1959) and Baran and Sweezy (1966).

8. Paul and Anne Ehrlich were leading academic proponents of this viewpoint during the 1970s as the following passage from their *Population, Resources, Environment* indicates:

"The people of the UDCs [i.e., under-developed countries] will be unable to escape from poverty and misery unless their populations are controlled. Today these countries have larger populations than they can properly support, given their physical and biological resources" (1970: 2), Notice that this opening passage of their book tends to confuse population *density* with the rate of population *growth*.

9. A reflection of the social class divisions within contemporary India is the recent growth in the production of cookies, a luxury food. Between 1978 and 1982, cookie production increased nearly 50 percent. This apparently reflects the emergence of a middle-income group of managers and executives, engineers, government officials, and skilled blue-collar workers (*New York Times*, 14 August 1983).

10. Although the Soviet economy grew relatively slowly during and immediately after World War II and although economic growth has been relatively slow during recent years, the Soviet Union has had a record of prolonged economic expansion since the introduction of central planning in 1928 (Fusfeld 1982: 610).

11. On these points, compare Pryde (1983: 277) and Spence (1983: 92).

12. Chinese population policy is not a complete success, however. There is evidence that, despite government efforts to discourage the practice, some couples are engaging in female infanticide so that they can have both small families and male children. The economic roots of male chauvinism have apparently not yet been destroyed in China. See Mirsky (1983).

13. Brundenius (1981) reports that the bottom fifth of Cuban society received 2.1 percent of total income in 1953 and the top fifth 60 percent. Two decades later, the bottom fifth enjoyed 7.6 percent, whereas the top fifth received 35 percent. Hence, Cuba is not an egalitarian utopia, but real progress in that direction has been made.

14. For a chilling account of the probable ecological effects of a "nuclear exchange" between the United States and the Soviet Union, see Turco et al. (1983).

REFERENCES

Asch, Peter and Joseph J. Seneca. 1978. Some Evidence on the Distribution of Air Quality. *Land Economics* 54 (3): 278–97.

Bain, Joe S. 1959. *Industrial Organization*. New York: John Wiley & Sons.

Baran, Paul A. and Paul M. Sweezy. 1966. *Monopoly Capital*. New York: Monthly Review Press.

Baumol, William J. and Wallace E. Oates. 1971. The Use of Standards and Prices for Protection of the Environment. *Swedish Journal of Economics* 73 (1): 42–54.

————. 1979. *Economics, Environmental Policy, and the Quality of Life*. Englewood Cliffs, New Jersey: Prentice-Hall.

Brundenius, Claes. 1981. Growth with Equity: The Cuban Experience (1959–1980). *World Development* 9 (11/12): 1083–96.

Burns, Arthur. 1976. The Real Issues of Inflation and Unemployment. *Challenge* 18 (6): 6–11.

Castleman, Barry. 1979. The Export of Hazardous Factories to Developing Nations. *International Journal of Health Services* 9 (4): 569–606.

Castro, Fidel. 1983. *The World Economic and Social Crisis*. Havana: Council of State.

Crittenden, Ann. 1981. Gains for Latin American Crops Called No Help to Small Farmers. *New York Times* May 4, 1981.

Dales, J. H. 1968. *Pollution, Property, and Prices*. Toronto: University of Toronto Press.

Diamond, Robert. 1970. What Business Thinks. *Fortune* 81 (2): 118.

Dollars & Sense. 1980. The Production Myth. *Dollars & Sense* no. 56: 12–13.

———. 1981a. Deregulating Workers' Health. *Dollars & Sense* no. 70: 3–5.

———. 1981b. Pesticides Create a "Circle of Poison." *Dollars & Sense* no. 67: 6–7.

———. 1982. Amber Waves of Grain. *Dollars & Sense* no. 79: 7–9.

———. 1983. Red Ink Stains Atomic Age. *Dollars & Sense* no. 83: 12–14.

Ehrlich, Paul R. and Anne H. Ehrlich. 1970. *Population, Resources, Environment*. San Francisco: W. H. Freeman and Co.

Fusfeld, Daniel R. 1982. *Economics: Principles of Political Economy*. Glenview, Illinois: Scott, Foresman and Co.

Gianessi, Leonard and Henry Peskin. 1980. The Distribution of the Costs of Federal Water Pollution Control Policy. *Land Economics* 56 (1): 85–102.

Goldman, Marshall. 1970. The Convergence of Environmental Disruption. *Science* 170: 37–42.

Heller, Walter. 1966. *New Dimensions of Political Economy*. Cambridge, Massachusetts: Harvard University Press.

Lebow, Victor. 1955. *Journal of Retailing* 31 (1).

Levins, Dick. 1981. Meeting the People's Needs. *Science for the People* 13 (2): 29–33.

Lernoux, Penny. 1983. Brazil, the Banks, the Third World. *The Nation* 237 (14): 434–35.

Loechler, Ed. 1980. Cancer and the Workplace. *Science for the People* 12 (3): 14–15.

Logan, Rebecca and Dorothy Nelkin. 1980. Labor and Nuclear Power. *Environment* 22 (2): 6.

Mamdani, Mahmood. 1981. The Ideology of Population Control. In *And the Poor Get Children: Radical Perspectives on Population Dynamics*, K. Michaelson (ed). New York: Monthly Review Press.

McIntyre, Robert and James Thornton. 1974. Environmental Divergence: Air Pollution in the U.S.S.R. *Journal of Environmental Economics and Management* 1 (2): 109–20.

McLeod, Christopher. 1980. Dumping for Dollars. *Science for the People* 12 (5): 27–28.

Mendeloff, John. 1979. *Regulating Safety: An Economic and Political Analysis of Occupational Safety and Health Policy*. Cambridge, Massachusetts: M.I.T. Press.

Metcalf, Robert and Arthur Kelman. 1981. Integrated Pest Management in China. *Environment* 23 (14): 6–13.

Michaelson, Karen. 1981. Population Policy, Family Size, and the Reproduction of the Labor Force in India: The Case of Bombay. In *And the Poor Get Children: Radical Perspectives on Population Dynamics*, K. Michaelson (ed). New York: Monthly Review Press.

Mirsky, Jonathon. 1983. The Infanticide Tragedy in China. *The Nation* 237 (1): 12–14.

Nations, James and Daniel Komer. 1983. Rainforests and the Hamburger Society. *Environment* 25 (3): 12–20.

New York Times. 1981. Poverty, Not Scarcity, Called Chief Cause of World Hunger. *New York Times* December 7, 1981.

New York Times. 1983. Acid Rain and Pollution Curbs. *New York Times* November 7, 1983.

Novitski, Joseph. 1972. Brazil Shunning Pollution Curbs. *New York Times.* February 13, 1972.

O'Connor, James. 1973. *The Fiscal Crisis of the State.* New York: St. Martin's Press.

Orleans, Lee and Richard Suttmeier. 1970. The Mao Ethic and Environmental Quality. *Science* 241: 109-14.

Pector, Jeff. 1978. The Nuclear Power Industry and the Anti-Nuclear Movement. *Socialist Review* 8 (6): 9-35.

Pollard, Robert. 1983. At N.R.C. It's Safety Last. *The Nation* 236 (18): 569-72.

Pryde, Philip R. 1983. The "Decade of the Environment" in the U.S.S.R. *Science* 220: 274-79.

Rostow, Eugene. 1959. *Planning for Freedom.* New Haven: Yale University Press.

Ruff, Larry. 1970. The Economic Common Sense of Pollution. *The Public Interest* no. 19: 69-85.

Russell, Clifford and Hans Landsberg. 1971. International Environmental Problems: A Taxonomy. *Science* 172: 1307-14.

Sen, Amartya. 1981. *Poverty and Famines.* Oxford: Oxford University Press.

Singh, Narindar. 1976. *Economics and the Crisis of Ecology.* Delhi: Oxford University Press.

Spence, Martin. 1983. Soviet Power: Nuclear Energy in the U.S.S.R. *Capital & Class* no. 21.

Stuart, Reginald. 1984. Puerto Rico Finds Water Is Victim of Development. *New York Times* February 21, 1984.

Sultz, Harry, et al. 1970. An Effect of Continued Exposure to Air Pollution on the Incidence of Chronic Childhood Allergic Disease. *American Journal of Public Health* 60 (5): 891-900.

Turco, R. P., et al. 1983. Nuclear Winter: Global Consequences of Multiple Nuclear Explosions. *Science* 222: 1283-92.

United Nations. 1965. *Demographic Yearbook.* New York: United Nations.

———. 1980. *Demographic Yearbook.* New York: United Nations.

U.S. Bureau of the Census. 1984. *Current Population Reports,* Series P-60, No. 142. Washington: U.S. Government Printing Office.

Wald, Matthew. 1984. No Nuclear Dump Sites in Sight Yet. *New York Times* January 29, 1984.

Wiltgren, Richard and Fred Herschede. 1982. Marxism and Chinese Population Policies. *Review of Radical Political Economics* 14 (4): 18-28.

Wolff, Edward N. 1983. The Size Distribution of Household Disposable Wealth in the United States. *Review of Income and Wealth* 29 (2): 139-41.

Wright, Erik Olin, et al. 1982. The American Class Structure. *American Sociological Review* 47 (6): 709-26.

PART 4
Gender and Class

Chapter 8

From Home Production to Wage Labor: Women as a Reserve Army of Labor

MARILYN POWER

One striking and important change in women's economic role in the twentieth century has been the proletarianization of ever-increasing numbers of married women. To understand women's work under capitalism, we must be able to explain this movement of married women into the *wage* labor force. Further, any understanding of women's economic roles requires an examination of their work in the labor force, their work in the home, and the interrelationships between these two spheres. The purpose of this essay is to develop an analytic framework for understanding why married women have entered the wage labor force, especially in the latter half of the twentieth century, by looking at change in their work in the home, which made them available for wage labor, and the development of capitalism, which created wage jobs for them. In brief, capitalism's invasion of women's work in the home over the course of the nineteenth and early twentieth centuries gradually changed women's home work from predominantly *production* to predominantly *maintenance*, thereby eliminating women's ability to provide for support of themselves and their families through work outside the sphere of capitalist production. Married women become a *latent* reserve army of labor, to be drawn into wage labor with the development of the capitalist economy.

This argument builds upon feminist theoretical writings of the past decade and at the same time takes issue with some of the theoretical directions that have been taken in recent years. In specific, this analysis will take issue with the concept of women as a *permanent* marginal labor force under capitalism, stress the importance of understanding *changes* as well as *continuities* in women's work in the home, suggest that the existence of the "family wage" was always more ideological than actual, and emphasize the importance of *contradictions* rather than mutual accommodation between capitalism and patriarchy.

In order to develop the argument that married women became a latent reserve army of labor in the twentieth century United States, this essay will begin with a brief discussion of Marx's theory of the industrial reserve army of labor. The next two sections will constitute the main body of the chapter. The first will discuss the historical transformation of women's work in the home from predominantly production to predominantly maintenance and explain the implications of this change for women's economic role, their transformation into a latent reserve of labor. The second will describe the movement of this latent reserve into the active labor force in the course of capitalist development, particularly the expansion of the clerical and service sectors. Finally, I will elaborate upon the theoretical implications of this analysis for feminist political economy. Before beginning this discussion, however, it is necessary to summarize the data on the movement of married women into the wage labor force.

THE ISSUE: MARRIED WOMEN IN THE LABOR FORCE

The movement of married women into the labor force in the twentieth century has been steady and dramatic, particularly since World War II, and perhaps most striking in the last 10 to 15 years. Labor force participation rates of married women rose from an estimated 5 percent in 1890 for paid work *outside* the home (Smuts 1971: 23) to 21.6 percent in 1950, 30.6 percent in 1960, and 49.4 percent in 1979 (Bureau of Labor Statistics 1980: 22). By 1960 the majority (57 percent) of women workers were married with husbands present (Bureau of Labor Statistics 1980: 22). Even among women with preschool children, 44 percent are in the labor force. In short, it is now "normal" for married women to participate in wage labor, and increasingly fewer of them are taking time out even when their children are small.

This movement into the wage labor force constitutes a significant change in the economic role of married women. It has frequently been pointed out (Smuts 1971; Jensen 1980) that the methods used to measure labor force participation have undercounted women's economic contributions through work for pay in the home, especially before 1940.[1] Much of my argument will focus on a discussion of the nature and significance of these contributions. It is important, however, to distinguish them from women's participation in the labor force, for two reasons. First, women's labor force participation as conventionally measured takes place *outside of* and *separate from* the home and family. Thus, the growth in the labor force participation of married women is likely to have considerable effects on relations within the family. Second, while their economic contributions in the home were often *outside* or only peripherally connected to capitalist production, married women's entrance into the labor force constitutes, for the vast majority, a complete integration into capitalist wage labor.

This essay will argue that we can understand this movement of married women into wage labor as a result of capitalist development, which first transformed them into a latent reserve army of labor and has gradually incorporated them into the active labor force in the twentieth century. In order to develop this argument, it is necessary to summarize Marx's analysis of the reserve army of labor (RAL) as it is developed in volume I of *Capital*.

THE CONCEPT OF THE RAL

In order for the self-expansion of capital to proceed successfully, there has to be at all times a large enough pool of labor to meet capital's needs. In modern industry, Marx argued, accumulation only sporadically runs up against a limitation in the supply of labor, because the growing organic composition of capital results in a greater quantity of labor being continuously set "free" than is required for the expansion of capital. When total capital is increasing, the absolute amount of variable capital will increase, but in decreasing proportion. Hence, the demand for labor falls in proportion as total capital increases. Through this process laborers are continuously being "freed," either by actually losing their jobs in a given sphere, or simply not being absorbed in that sphere as rapidly as previously. This process holds for all sectors of capitalist development, but it is possible for different sectors to be in different phases of development at the same moment, some absorbing large amounts of labor while others are "freeing" labor into the reserve army.

This possibility of simultaneously different phases is one reason that the reserve army is crucial to capitalist development, in fact, according to Marx, a "condition of existence of the capitalist mode of production" (Marx 1967: 632). It means that capitalist development need not depend on the rate of growth of population but is continuously generating surplus labor independently, to be used for the sudden and immediate needs of the self-expansion of capital. As capitalism develops, its "power of self-expansion" grows as well, and it becomes crucial that "there must be the possibility of throwing great masses of men [and women] suddenly on the decisive points without injury to the scale of production in other spheres" (Marx 1967: 632).

As Simeral (1978: 165-67) points out, there is both a secular and cyclical function for this industrial army. It may be used to allow the long-term development of new branches of industry and the expansion of old branches. And, the cycles of economic activity, which alternate periods of average economic activity with periods of high production and of stagnation, are reflected in and depend upon the formation of the reserve army:

> The course characteristic of modern industry, viz., a decennial cycle (in-
> terrupted by small oscillations), of periods of average activity, produc-
> tion at high pressure, crises and stagnation, depends on the constant for-
> mation, the greater or less absorption, and the re-formation of the in-
> dustrial reserve army or surplus-population. (Marx 1967: 632-33)

The phrase "reserve army of labor" conjures up a very concrete image
of a specific and specifiable army of people who are moved in and out of the
work force at the will of capital. But Marx did not specify—or intend to
specify—the reserve army as a group separate from the mass of workers. As
Anthias (1980: 50) argues, Marx's discussion is on a higher level of abstraction. He is developing the "absolute general law of capital accumulation"
(Marx 1967: 640): that capital accumulation constantly produces a relative
surplus population; the laboring population produces, along with the accumulation of capital, the means by which laborers themselves become increasingly superfluous. The reserve army, thus, should not be seen as a
separate and discrete group; as Marx notes, the relative surplus population
exists in "every possible form," and every laborer is part of it whenever she
or he is unemployed or only partially employed (Marx 1967).

However, Marx does offer some more concrete categories of the
relative-surplus population, which exist at any point in the recurrent cycles
of capitalism. The *floating* and *stagnant* categories of the reserve army do
not concern us here; we will focus on the *latent* reserve. The latent reserve is
created when capitalism, in the course of its expansion, invades and takes
over sectors of precapitalist production. In Marx's time, the major source of
this reserve was the agricultural sector. As agriculture began to take the
form of capitalist production, the demand for agricultural workers fell absolutely, as labor was replaced in agricultural production without any com-
pensating increase in demand for agricultural workers (unlike in the industrial sector). As a result, there was a pool of agricultural labor that could
be drawn into industrial production. This pool was "latent" because, while
it was "constantly on the point of passing over into an urban or manufacturing proletariat, and on the lookout for circumstances favorable to this
transformation," its existence and numbers were not evident until the opportunity arose, until "its channels of outlet open(ed) to exceptional width"
(Marx 1967: 642). While Marx referred specifically to agricultural labor as
the latent reserve of labor, I will argue that this concept is useful in
understanding the movement of American women into the labor force after
World War II.

As should be clear from this summary, Marx's categories of the reserve
army were general, not intended to describe specific groups of people. As
Hartmann (1979b: 8) has noted, Marxian categories are "sex blind" and also,
we may note, race blind. In order to analyze the experience of specific groups,
it is necessary to look at that experience in its concrete social formation

(Anthias 1980: 51). This entails an examination of the historical, political, and ideological, as well as economic, forces that impinge upon that group. For the case of women, we must look concretely at the context in which, and the processes by which, they have been drawn into employment, and especially into certain categories of employment, in the twentieth century. Further, while this chapter argues that capitalist development had specific effects on women as a *group*, women must also be located in terms of their class and race, which partially determine the timing, intensity, and outcome for each individual of capitalism's invasion of women's productive work.

CHANGES IN THE CONTEXT OF HOUSEWORK: THE "FREEING" OF WOMEN

The expansion of capitalist production changed the content of women's work in the home over the course of the nineteenth and early twentieth centuries. This change occurred unevenly and at varied rates: in addition to race and class, residence in a rural or urban area, occupation (especially farm or nonfarm), and geographic area of residence (e.g., West vs. East) all affected the speed with which capitalism invaded and changed women's work in the home. We can explain the changes by examining two aspects: the change in the content of the work from predominantly *production* to predominantly *maintenance* and the elimination of production for *exchange* from the home.[2]

Production involves the transforming of raw or unfinished materials into finished goods (e.g., growing food, weaving cloth); maintenance involves the care and maintaining of the family and its possessions (e.g., caring for the ill, cleaning house, shopping). Both production and maintenance have historically been aspects of women's work in the home, included in the general category "housework", but over time the mix has changed, with increasing emphasis on maintenance work and a corresponding limiting of women's ability to contribute to family support through their work in the home. That is, production housework provided goods for the support of the family *outside of and independent from* capitalist production. Maintenance housework does not provide such support and may, in fact, increase the family's dependence on wage labor, as cash income is required to provide the appliances and other products used in maintenance. This is not to say that maintenance housework is unimportant for subsistence (reproduction of labor power)—keeping the house clean and family members healthy are necessary to reproduction (and the socially determined level of subsistence includes the possession of a certain quantity of commodities, which need to be purchased and maintained)—but maintenance housework provides no means of support separate from capitalist production.

In the preindustrial United States, women's work time was largely taken up with production housework. Women grew much of the food consumed by the family, gathered wild foods and herbs, and cared for chickens and other domestic livestock. They dried, salted, pickled, and preserved food for winter use and made soap and candles. They were responsible for the production of clothing, starting, in many cases, with raising the sheep or growing the flax used for the yarn. Women performed these tasks with the aid of their children and often servants; an affluent woman may have spent most of her time supervising the production work of servants. Further, the amount of household manufacture was probably less in towns, especially trading towns, than it was in rural areas, since towns had access to cloth and other finished goods from Britain (Reid 1934: 37-39). Nevertheless, even town women had kitchen gardens, chickens, and often cows; all engaged in the preserving of food for the winter; and spinning, knitting, and sewing were performed by town as well as rural women (Earle 1910: 167).[3] Through their production, women contributed significantly to the support of the family, both in towns and in the countryside; it was hardly possible, especially, for a farm to survive without the labor of a woman, and her children as well.[4] Further, women contributed to the household's small but necessary cash income, through such activities as selling extra butter and eggs, and by spinning and weaving cloth for sale (Cott 1977: 27).

As industrial capitalism developed, it increasingly eliminated spheres of petty commodity production and production for use in the home; the forces of competition and accumulation meant that capitalism gradually incorporated (and continues to incorporate) any production that could be made to produce profit. Petty commodity production was eliminated because the capitalist organization of production in factories substantially cheapened the production of commodities; petty commodity producers in the home were immediately affected by this process. For example, textile production was incorporated into the capitalist sector in the first wave of industrialization. The price of factory cloth was substantially lower than that of handwoven cloth, and women gradually lost their market for home-produced textiles (Dublin 1979: 5). One offshoot of industrialization for this aspect of home production was the movement of many young, single women into the textile mills. By the Civil War, according to Jensen (1980: 16), few women did any spinning or weaving except on the frontier.

Production for *use* also tended to be removed from the home through this cheapening of commodities by capitalist production. That is, a woman could choose to continue producing cloth, for example, for her family's use, despite the fact that factory cloth was cheaper. However, this activity no longer made sense as a *survival strategy* for herself and her family.[5] In addition, as the price of land rose and industrialization increased urban density, fewer families, especially of the working class, had access to the most important means of home production, land. Families turned increasingly to the market for goods that women had previously produced at home.

However, this transformation occurred only gradually: textile production moved out of the home very early, but capitalist penetration of other areas of home production developed over the entire course of the nineteenth century. Home production was replaced by capitalist production in urban areas more quickly than in rural areas, and sooner in more "settled" parts of the country. Both access to land and to capitalist markets played a role in determining the rate of change. There is some evidence that working class households turned to the market somewhat before petit bourgeois households, which often had more land, a less urgent need for married women to work *outside* the home, and, often, servants to aid in the work of home production (Lynd and Lynd 1929: 169).

The gradual nature of this transition from home production to capitalist production must be stressed. Home production for use and for exchange continued to contribute significantly to family support into the twentieth century even in urban areas. A study by the U. S. Commissioner of Labor of 2,500 families living in the principal coal, iron, and steel regions in 1890 shows that about half the families had livestock, poultry, vegetable gardens, or all three. Nearly 30 percent purchased no vegetables during the year except potatoes (Smuts 1971: 11).

A common pattern for working class households by the late 1800s was for men to engage in wage labor in the factories while the women engaged in domestic production, producing much of the family's food. Thus, families continued for a long time to cushion their dependence on wage income; in times of layoffs or strikes, they could at least partially subsist from their garden plots, allowing them a modicum of independence from capital.[6]

By the 1920s, use of market substitutes for home production was widespread; the era of the "mass market" had begun. Urbanization and the expansion of capitalist production of food and clothing had effectively eliminated women's ability to provide direct support through domestic production. For example, U. S. Department of Agriculture figures show an increase in the apparent annual consumption of canned vegetables from 15 pounds per person in 1909 to 21 pounds in 1921 and 26 pounds in 1931 (Bell 1967: 18-19). The Lynds, in their 1929 study of a small midwestern city, found that 70 percent of the city's bread was commercially baked, compared with 25 percent in 1890 (Lynd and Lynd 1929: 155). Backyards were shrinking, and vegetable gardens were disappearing (Lynd and Lynd 1929: 95). With the demise of the backyard garden went the decline of canning and preserving.

Production for exchange was also gradually eliminated from women's work in the home. As described above, women in the preindustrial United States had contributed to the family's small cash income through selling such products as surplus butter and eggs, cloth, and clothing sewn at home.

Although capitalism invaded textile and clothing production early, limitations on transportation and storage facilities meant that markets for home-produced butter, eggs, and other fresh produce continued for most of the nineteenth century, except in major urban areas. In rural areas these markets were not penetrated by capitalist production until the early twentieth century. Jensen (1980: 18) cites a study in Texas in 1928-30 that found that between one-fourth and one-third of farm women engaged in domestic production for exchange.

In urban areas many women (especially immigrants) did piecework at home, performing such tasks as finishing sewing on factory-made clothing and rolling cigars; their children, in many cases, worked alongside them. But urban women also engaged in home production *outside* the capitalist sector. They did laundry and sewing for their neighbors and, especially, took in boarders. Taking in boarders was extremely common in late nineteenth and early twentieth century working class households, and often contributed significantly to household income. Jensen (1980: 19) offers the example of a study of urban areas in 1892 that found that 27 percent of the women took in boarders, and that this income from boarders averaged 42.6 percent of their husband's incomes. After the 1920s boarding was gradually eliminated as a source of income, however, largely through the curtailment of immigration.

In sum, by the 1920s, the expansion of capitalist production had eliminated most direct production for exchange and direct production for use from the home. Some production housework remains—for example, food preparation involves the transformation of unfinished into finished products for use and thus is a production task. However, most production housework, as we have seen, was removed from the home to the capitalist sector, and even the content of tasks such as food preparation changed. Such activities as grinding flour, preserving foods, and baking bread have essentially been removed from the home, while cooking involves far less use of raw foods produced by the woman and her family.

We can see a reflection of this trend if we contrast data from one of the earliest studies of time-use in housework, done by Maude Wilson in Oregon in 1926-27, with a time-use study by Kathryn Walker in Syracuse, New York, in 1967-68. Farm women in Wilson's study spent an average of 3.3 hours per day on food preparation, compared with Walker's results of 2.3 hours per day by women not employed outside the home (Wilson 1929: 68; Walker and Woods 1967: 50-51). Wilson noted that one reason for the quantity of time spent by farm women in her study on food preparation was that 53 percent of them baked all or most of their own bread. It is true that 1926-27 is late for our purposes, since capitalist development was widespread by this time. Nevertheless, these farm women in Oregon lived in an area where the capitalist markets were not as pervasive as in more industrialized areas and thus may have retained many of the production tasks of an earlier era. It may be indicative that 43 percent of these households had neither electricity nor plumbing (Wilson 1929: 14, 36).

Those few productions tasks that *have* remained in the home do not contribute in any significant way to the family's support. Further, women are no longer able to produce goods within the home for exchange. Women's ability, then, to contribute directly to the *support* of themselves and their families through their work at home was gradually eliminated by the expansion of the sphere of capitalist production over the course of the nineteenth and early twentieth centuries. During the Depression of the 1930s there was some return to home production, as women attempted to supplement the family's diminishing cash income (Milkman 1976), but in general the 1920s and 1930s mark the transition of women from household production to wage labor: lacking the ability to provide support for their families through their production in the home, married women increasingly began entering the wage labor force.

Although capitalism gradually eliminated women's production work at home, this does not mean that capitalism eliminated *housework*, or that women's role in the production and reproduction of the labor force became less significant. As production work left the home it was replaced by maintenance housework. Women became responsible for the household's greatly expanding consumption of commodities; they became "purchasing agents" for the family. Further, the family's gradually expanding stock of possessions required care and maintenance. In short, as production housework left the home, it was replaced by consumption and maintenance, and housework continued to require long hours.

We can illustrate this transition from production to maintenance housework by once again referring to the Wilson and Walker studies. The Oregon farm women averaged 7.4 hours per day on housework; to this they added 1.6 hours per day of farmwork for a total work day of 9.0 hours. Urban women in Wilson's study spent 7.3 hours per day on housework, while women in Walker's 1967-68 study who were not employed outside the home spent 8.0 hours per day on housework. Hours spent on housework had actually *increased* somewhat over the 40 year period. Further, the mix of tasks had changed, with a decrease in food activities but an increase in maintenance tasks of house and clothing care, in performing and recording the family's purchases, and in care of family members.[7] (See table 8-1.)

This transformation of the content of women's work in the home from predominantly production to predominantly maintenance tied the family far more closely into capitalist production. Maintenance housework may be seen as a substitute for the purchase of services, but it cannot provide a source of use-values for the support of the household separate from capitalist production (maintenance involves the preserving of existing use-values, not the creation of *new* use-values. Further as Fox (1980:190-91) has

TABLE 8.1. Time-Use in Housework Activities: Farm Women and Urban Women in Oregon in 1926-27 and Full-Time Houseworkers in Syracuse, New York in 1967-68 (hours per day)

	1926-27		1967-68
Activity	Farm (n=288)	Urban (n=154)	(n=979)
All housework[a]	7.4	7.3	8.0
food activities	3.3	2.8	2.3
care of house	1.2	1.3	1.6
care of family members	0.5	1.2	1.8
marketing and recordkeeping[b]	0.1	0.4	1.0

Notes: [a]For 1926-27 farm women, includes tasks not listed separately.

[b]For 1926-27 farm women, category is entitled "purchasing for household."

Sources: Wilson 1929: 68; Walker and Woods 1967: 50.

pointed out, the *means* of household production have increasingly become commodities. This is true of both production and maintenance work since to the extent that women still engage in production tasks such as canning and sewing, the raw materials they transform are frequently purchased as commodities, while increasing maintenance work requires the purchase of appliances, cleaning fluids, and even automobiles. Thus, the transformation of housework from production to maintenance activity reflected an increasing dependence on the capitalist market both for the acquisition of use-values and for their maintenance.

Women continued to perform housework in the home, but with a crucial difference: they could no longer contribute directly to family support through this work, probably for the first time in history. They could, of course, turn their attention to economizing and thereby make the "breadwinner's" pay check stretch further, but they could no longer themselves provide bread. For women of the petit bourgeoisie this dependence began by the mid-1800s (Ryan 1979: 154), but for most women the early twentieth century marks the final step in the transition to economic dependence that began with industrialization. These changes had the result that women lost their ability to contribute to the support of themselves and their families through their work in the home. In Marxist terminology, they had become a latent reserve army of labor.

THE MOVEMENT OF MARRIED WOMEN INTO WAGE LABOR

There is no one answer to the question of why married women had not entered the wage labor market force earlier in the nineteenth century. A complex of factors, both economic and ideological, is involved. The ideology of the nineteenth and early twentieth century was emphatic that women's true sphere was home and family (Ryan 1979). Further, there were legal barriers to women's access to many jobs. Hartmann 1979a suggests that protective legislation, demanded by the patriarchal male working class, was an important force because it effectively excluded women from many important sectors of industrial wage labor. Sen (1980) argues that the role of patriarchy, while important, is overstressed in Hartmann's analysis. The difficulty women faced in combining their responsibilities for household production and child care with industrial labor, particularly given the long hours of nineteenth century factory work, were likely to discourage women from entering wage labor unless they were economically desperate:

> The contradictions between wage labor, infant care, and domestic work provided a strong enough impetus for mothers to stay at home, quite apart from their husbands' patriarchal drives. (Sen 1980: 83).

My analysis suggests an additional factor encouraging married women to remain at home: their work in the home contributed significantly to the support of the family. They didn't need to enter wage labor as long as their home production provided sufficient goods for use and exchange.

By the beginning of the twentieth century, the expansion of capitalist production had essentially eliminated women's precapitalist economic roles in the home. Of course, this transition was a gradual process, and there was no dramatic and sudden surge of women into the labor force. In fact, there were a number of forces that tended to keep married women in the home despite economic dependence. First, as in the nineteenth century, ideology was unambiguous that married women belonged at home; patriarchal attitudes of husbands and fathers no doubt reinforced this message on a personal level. Second, although the birthrate was dropping, women continued to have total responsibility for child care and housework, with few alternative services offered by society. Third, protective legislation and blatant discrimination severely limited the pool of jobs available to women; in 1900 almost 29 percent of all women in the labor force were private household workers (Oppenheimer, 1976: 220). Fourth, to the extent that male workers had won pay increases to achieve a "family wage" (i.e., enough to support a family on one paycheck), married women weren't *forced* into the labor force by economic necessity. There is reason to question, however, the extent to which male workers *had* achieved the family wage: Hartmann (1979: 30, fn 39) suggests that it had largely been won by them by the early twentieth century, but some writers argue that for many workers it was never more than an ideological myth (Barrett and McIntosh 1980; Fox 1980).[8]

Finally, it is precisely in the nature of the latent reserve army to *remain* latent until the growth of capital requires a new pool of labor. Women were not likely to enter the labor force en masse as long as the demand for their labor was limited. What was needed for their labor force participation to be actualized was a sharp increase in the demand for labor—and more particularly in the demand for labor in *female* occupations. Occupational segregation by sex has a long history in the United States. It predates industrialization but was rigidified and reinforced during the 1800s through the actions of both capital and organized labor.[9] An increase in the demand for women's labor, then, could come in one of three ways: through a growth in occupations already defined as female, through the creation of new female occupations, or through the redefinition of a previously male occupation as female.

The movement of women into the labor force largely coincided with the latter creation of demand: clerical work, in particular, which had in the nineteenth century been a relatively small and characteristically male occupation, became redefined as a female occupation in the twentieth century at the same time that it began a process of phenomenal growth (Davies 1974). The rapid growth in the demand for clerical workers has been associated with the increasing concentration of capital:

> As business operations became more complex, there was a large increase in correspondence, record-keeping, and office work in general. This expansion created a demand for an expanded labor force. (Davies 1974: 150)

The growth in demand for clerical workers and the characterization of clerical work as a female occupation were both striking and coordinated: the 1880 census reported a total of 5,000 stenographers and typists, of whom 40.0 percent were female; by 1900 there were 112,600 stenographers and typists, 76.7 percent female; by 1930 there were 811,200 stenographers and typists, of whom 95.6 percent were female (Davies 1974: 255). The period since 1930 has seen yet more phenomenal growth in employment in secretarial and other clerical work, which has continued since that period to be an essentially all-female occupation: in 1979, the roughly comparable category of secretaries and typists employed about 4.7 million workers, of whom 98.6 percent were women (Bureau of Labor Statistics 1980: 10). Beside clerical work, women are also concentrated in service work, another occupational category that has expanded rapidly, partially in the postwar period. In 1979 clerical and service occupations together accounted for 52 percent of all employed women (Bureau of Labor Statistics 1980:10).

Thus, the demand for women workers increased, and increased sharply, quickly outrunning the supply of young, unmarried women who had constituted the female labor force in the nineteenth and early twentieth centuries. The pool of single women aged 18 to 34 had actually *declined* by 2.8 million, or 46 percent betwen 1940 and 1960 (Oppenheimer 1976: 17), due to a combination of the low birthrate during the Depression and the high marriage rate in the postwar period. Where, then, were to be found the "great masses of [wo]men" to be thrown "on the decisive points without injury to the scale of production in other areas" (Marx 1967: 632)? Obviously, from among the latent pool of married women.

It would be an oversimplification, however, to attribute the increased labor force participation of married women solely to the removal of production housework and production for exchange from the home and the increase in demand for women workers. Clearly, other factors played a role. Demographic factors were probably significant: women finished bearing children earlier than they had in the past, so they completed their childrearing well before old age. Many of the married women in the labor force in the 1950s and 1960s had reentered paid work after children were grown. Whatever other factors were involved, however, it seems clear that one important component of married women's movement into the labor force was the change in their work in the home, which made them a latent reserve army, ready to be drawn into the labor force as the need arose.

IMPLICATIONS OF THE ANALYSIS FOR
FEMINIST POLITICAL ECONOMY

A number of implications arise from this argument, perhaps the most important being that women have become part of the *permanent* labor force or, as Braverman (1974: 385, 390) expressed it, women have left the latent pool to join men in the floating and stagnant reserve army of labor. Many feminists (including myself in an early paper) have argued that women serve as a marginal labor force for capitalism, to be taken into wage labor when needed and sent back to their primary role in the home when no longer required (Beechey 1977; Trey 1972). However, the removal of women's work for production and exchange from the home makes this a much less viable alternative for capitalism. Economic stagnation or worse in the 1980s may fuel the "New Right" rhetoric that women should go back to the home, and nonenforcement of affirmative action and antidiscrimination legislation may severely hamper women's ability to improve (or even maintain) their economic position, but the fact is that women's production work in the home is no longer available for them to do. They can be unemployed, of course, or employed temporarily or sporadically, but they cannot, in any meaningful numbers, just be sent "home"—the latent reserve army, once it has been activated, can never become *latent* once again.

Failure to distinguish between production and maintenance housework masks this reality. Anthias (1980: 59), for example, argues that women cannot be seen as a latent pool of labor because housework cannot be analyzed as task specific, and because women continue to produce use-values in the home once they are in the labor force. By pooling all of housework as the production of "use-values," Anthias fails to recognize the historic invasion of the production of subsistence by capitalism. The implication is that the "use-values" remain at home for women to perform; if they are removed from the labor force they can simply increase production of domestic "use-values." As I have argued, this option is not open to women, not because there is a lack of *work* to be done in the home, but because that work does not provide an alternative source of support for the family. A return to home production is not feasible because of a lack of access to land and because goods can be produced more cheaply in the capitalist sector. Maintenance housework can economize the household's need for commodities, by making them last longer; however, these savings are not an adequate substitute for women's earnings, especially as women continue to perform maintenance tasks *even when* they work for pay. In addition, maintenance work in the home is not a meaningful alternative to wage labor for women.

This argument has a number of implications for our understanding of the dynamic of capitalist development as it relates to the economic oppression of women. In particular, it points to the possibility of contradictions between capitalism and patriarchy. One school of feminist thought, represented in particular by Heidi Hartmann and Zillah Eisenstein, argues that there exists a "partnership" (Hartmann 1979b), a "mutual accommodation" (Hartmann 1979a), or a "mutual dependence" (Eisenstein 1979) between capitalism and women.[10] In brief, men control women's labor within the home and, through their demands for household services, limit women's ability to seek market work. Capitalism hires women only for sex-segregated, low-paid, dead-end work and, perhaps, pays women less than the value of their labor power (Beechey 1977). Thus, even when women do work for pay, they remain economically dependent upon men and are forced, essentially, by economic pressure to marry and, once married, to provide household services for their husbands. This provision of services for the husbands also benefits capitalism, since it insures that women will continue to produce and reproduce the labor force within the home. Further, patriarchal relations within the home reproduce hierarchical gender identities, useful to capitalism in its superexploitation of women.

While the description of this dynamic illuminates the dual pressure faced by women under patriarchal capitalism, there are two theoretical problems that tend to arise from this approach. First, there is a tendency for such an analysis to be static, posed in terms of an historic struggle, perhaps, which developed the "partnership"; but once the partnership was established, it is seen as abiding. The possibility of contradiction between capitalism and patriarchy may be acknowledged, but the analysis seems to lead not into an investigation of the possibility of contradiction but into an assumption that such contradictions, if they exist, cannot be sufficiently fundamental to threaten the partnership. Thus, an area of what I believe is crucial investigation is in effect closed off.

Second, the analysis tends to deemphasize women's labor force participation as a determinant of their condition, arguing that the low wages paid to women, combined with their continued responsibility for housework and child care, mean that patriarchal relations within the home remain the key determinant even when women work for pay. The focus of the analysis, therefore, tends to remain on the family, with less attention paid to the possibility that changes in women's labor force experience may affect changes in their overall experience and in the dynamic between capitalism and patriarchy.

For example, Hartmann points out that even though married women have entered the labor force in large numbers, they are occupationally segregated into specific low-status, low-wage jobs, largely in clerical and service occupations. Women continue to earn about 60 percent of male earnings for full-time, full-year work. It is occupational segregation and pay differentials, Hartmann argues, that maintain patriarchy even while families come to depend on two earners for their support:

> The "ideal" of the family wage—that a man can earn enough to support an entire family—may be giving way to a new ideal that both men and women contribute through wage earning to the cash income of the family. The wage differential, then, will become increasingly necessary in perpetuating patriarchy, the male control of women's labor power. The wage differential will aid in *defining* women's work as secondary to men's at the same time as it necessitates women's actual continued economic dependence on men. The sexual division of labor in the labor market and elsewhere should be understood as a manifestation of patriarchy which serves to perpetuate it. (Hartmann 1979b: 19; emphasis in original)

Yet, surely there is a difference in the possibility of forcing women to submit to patriarchal authority in the home between a situation in which women were directly dependent upon men for survival (as when women were not legally entitled to own farmland and thus were essentially forced to marry in order to gain access to the means of survival, or to work sweatshop jobs at below subsistence pay) and a situation in which women work as wage laborers for capitalism, earning money *separate from* and *independent* of their husbands. Obviously, many women still cannot earn enough to survive, even poorly, outside marriage. This is especially true of unskilled workers in blue collar and service work, many of whom are nonwhite. This reality is reflected in the poverty of families in the United States maintained by women. In 1978, one-third were poor by official government standards, and many of the rest were just above the poverty line. By contrast, 1 in 18 families with a male present were below the poverty line (National Advisory Council on Economic Opportunity 1980: 17-18).

Nevertheless, the movement of married women into wage labor has created the *possibility* of their supporting themselves outside of marriage. The option of leaving an oppressive marriage or choosing not to make one is far greater because of women's labor force participation; the option of refusing to be coerced into providing unequal amounts of labor and remaining subservient in the home exists to an unprecedented extent because much of women's productive labor takes place outside of and independent from the home. Thus, by forcing married women into wage labor, capitalism may be undermining the material basis of men's ability to enforce patriarchy in the home, *even though* it relegates women to low paid "women's work" in the labor market. This is not to deny that patriarchy retains a powerful *ideological* presence even in households where material coercion is no longer a factor: patriarchy is deeply embedded in our ideological structure.

A further implication of this argument may be that the family wage never had an extensive actual (as opposed to ideological) existence. Certainly it is apparent that few working class families lived solely from the earnings of one male wage worker at least before the early part of this century. However, as married women began losing their ability to provide subsistence and cash at home, they began gradually entering the labor force, so that the family wage may perhaps at best be seen as a temporary or transitional phenomenon. Hartmann suggests that:

> . . . the expropriation of production from the home was followed by a social adjustment process creating the social norm of the family wage. . . . (T)his process occurred in the U.S. in the early 20th century. . . . The "family wage" resolution has probably been undermined in the post World War II period. (Hartmann 1979b: 30, fn39)

In this sense, the family wage may be seen as an almost meaningless concept, encompassing *at most* 40 years of precarious existence. However, the concept has had a powerful ideological life; it has been used historically to justify unequal pay, occupational segregation, and preferential hiring of men; to discourage women from identifying themselves as workers; and, presumably, to keep male workers under control because of their responsibilities as "breadwinners." Hartmann (Ibid.) argues that this ideological message continues unabated: "Yet whatever the *actual* situation today or earlier in the century, we would argue that the social norm *was* and *is* that men should earn enough to support their families."

This norm is upheld, in Hartmann's view, by occupational segregation and the extreme wage differentials between men and women. I would suggest that the reality of economic conditions over the past decade appears to have resulted in increasing awareness that the family wage no longer exists for most families. Certainly labor force participation is no longer seen as aberrant for married women; it is generally recognized as an economic necessity. This does not mean that it is seen as good or desirable, however; it is important to distinguish between a *norm* and an *ideal*. Whether many in the United States still cling to an ideal of man/breadwinner and woman/housewife is difficult to guess, but it does seem possible to argue that its ideological power is weakening.

CONCLUSION

In sum, this essay argues that the rapid and steady increase in the participation of married women in wage labor in the latter half of the twentieth century can be understood as the result of the invasion of their traditional production for use and exchange in the home by capitalist production, coupled with a rising demand for clerical and service workers in the capitalist sector. Women were "freed" into the latent reserve army of labor and have been gradually incorporated into active wage labor as capitalism has expanded.

This argument has implications for our understanding of women's historic economic roles, of the dynamic interaction between capitalism and patriarchy, and of the concept of the family wage. Women have always contributed significantly to the economic support of themselves and their families, but the source of that support has changed over time from production for use and exchange within the home to wage labor. Thus, the expansion of capitalist production may be undermining the material base of patriarchy within the home. By separating home from work, gradually removing production work from the home, and, finally, incorporating women into the wage labor force, capitalism has "tended to whittle away at the economic and ideological basis of patriarchy" (Rowbotham 1973: 119).

Understanding women's wage labor as an extension in another form of their historic economic contribution to the family, we can place women's current economic experience in historic perspective. Working class families have rarely been able to live from the earnings of only one person; women (and children) provided support first through home production and later through wage labor. Because home production is no longer an option for women, the trend toward wage work is irreversible. Despite occupational segregation and cutbacks in affirmative action, and despite conservative calls for a return to the (mythical) family of man-the-provider and woman-the-receiver (Gilder 1981), working class women have no choice but to continue to seek paid work.

This argument has implications for capitalism and for the interaction between capitalism and patriarchy. Capitalism may find women a less flexible segment of the labor force than in the past. Forced by economic necessity to seek wage work, and to stay in the labor force for most of their adult lives, women are increasingly coming to define themselves as workers and to act in opposition to low pay and occupational segregation. Since wage work will continue to be an objective necessity for women, their consciousness of the problem of inequality, and their opposition to it, is likely to continue to exert pressure on the economic system.

Does this mean that capitalism has set the stage for the destruction of patriarchy? No, I don't believe this is the case. There is no evidence that inequality in the labor force is decreasing, and inequality between men and women clearly continues in the family as well: for example, women continue to perform the vast majority of housework, whether or not they also perform wage labor (Power 1977). Whatever its historical origins (and whether or not patriarchy at one time had a separate material base), the oppression of women has become incorporated into the dynamics of capitalism, in a complex and contradictory fashion. It is the task of feminist political economy to investigate the nature of this interaction.

Acknowledgments. I wish to thank Yassaman Jalili for her research help and Nicholas Kozlov, Sue Himmelweit, Laurie Nisonoff, Peter Meyer, Nancy Breen, and the entire editorial board of the Review of Radical Political Economics for their helpful comments and criticisms.

NOTES

1. Census takers in 1920, for example, were instructed to *exclude* care of boarders as a form of employment, unless it was the principal means of support for the family (Jensen 1980:15).

2. For a more detailed description of the change from production to maintenance in the United States, see Power (1977). For similar investigations, see Oakley (1974), which focuses on England, and Tilly and Scott (1978), which examines England and France.

3. Since no time-use studies exist for preindustrial women's work, we must piece together an image of their work days, largely through diaries, letters, and household inventories. Beside Earle, see Cott (1977: ch. 1), Dublin (1979: ch. 1), Ulrich (1982: part 1), and Demos (1970: parts I and II).

4. Here we see an illustration of the material base of patriarchy. Because women's labor and—crucially—their ability to produce children were necessary for survival (and ideally accumulation) on these independent small farms, women were coerced into marrying and providing these services for men.

5. Even today, families may attempt to defray some of their survival costs through, for example, sewing clothes, growing vegetables, canning and freezing; but few provide more than a small proportion of their total needs in this way. Further, the amount of savings are rarely sufficient for this production work to be a *substitute* for wage labor; it represents, at most, a supplementary savings.

6. I am aware of the current argument about whether the working class family should be seen as a locus of struggle over patriarchy or as a unit unified in its struggle against capitalism.

I do not mean in this discussion to take a stand on this issue but, rather, simply to describe the economic significance of working class women's domestic production. It does seem clear *both* that the organization of the family was patriarchal *and* that women's domestic production cushioned the family's dependence on wage labor.

7. This last category requires more explanation. Family care largely consists of child care and was divided by these studies into physical care (including bathing, feeding, dressing, etc.) and nonphysical care (including helping children with lessons, chauffering children and other family members, etc.) Walker (1976: 106). Thus, the sharp increase in the time spent on family care could indicate more children per household in the Walker study, or more likely, a rise in the standards for child care, as an urban environment and new child rearing philosophies require women to spend more time supervising and chauffering their children.

8. Fox cites budget studies from the turn of the century through the 1960s that indicate that for most of the period a majority of families could not live in "health and decency" on the earnings of a male wage or salary earner alone. When women could not provide through work at home (as was increasingly the case, as we have seen), *children* were the main providers of supplementary income from paid work in the labor force in the first half of the twentieth century. By the 1950s, children were spending more time in school and less in the labor force, and increasing numbers of married women were working for pay. The percentage of households in the United States with three or more wage earners remained essentially the same between 1930 and 1970; the percentage with two or more wage earners remained the same from 1930 to 1950, after which it has increased. See Fox (1980: 198-202).

9. The question of how and why occupational segregation by sex has remained embedded in U. S. capitalism is important, but discussion of it would lead us far astray from the major arguments in this chapter. For the present purpose, I will simply take occupational segregation as given.

10. Eisenstein lables this view "socialist feminism," in distinction from Marxist and radical feminist analyses. According to Eisenstein, a socialist feminist analysis views the oppression of women as affected by both capitalism and patriarchy, systems with *separate* and at least partially *independent* material bases. Hartmann's analysis also begins with this basic premise, although she describes herself as a "marxist-feminist" and differs from Eisenstein on a variety of issues (including, possibly, the saliency of class in an analysis of the oppression of women). There is considerable analytic debate in the feminist literature about the relationship between capitalism and patriarchy: the relative importance of the two systems in determining the oppression of women, the dynamics of the interaction between capitalism and patriarchy, whether it is analytically correct to posit a separate material base for patriarchy, and even whether it is appropriate to use the term patriarchy at all in describing the transhistorical and transcultural subordination of women to men. This is a very important debate, and it forms the context for the questions examined in this essay. A detailed discussion of the debate cannot be included here; however, my argument suggests that the dynamic between capitalism and patriarchy is contradictory as well as complementary, that economic forces play a crucial role in determining the sex-gender system, and that insofar as patriarchy ever had a material base separate from capitalism, that material base has been continuously and substantially eroded by the expansion of capitalist relations of production. For further discussion of the debate over the relation between capitalism and patriarchy, see Power (1986); Sargent (1980); Rubin (1975); Kuhn and Wolpe (1978); and Barrett (1980).

REFERENCES

Anthias, Floya. 1980. Women and the Reserve Army of Labour: A Critique of Veronica Beechey. *Capital and Class* 10 (Spring).

Barrett, Michele. 1980. *Women's Oppression Today.* London: Verso Editions.

Barrett, Michele and Mary McIntosh. 1980. The "Family Wage": Some Problems for Socialists and Feminists. *Capital and Class* 11 (Summer).

Beechey, Veronica. 1977. Some Notes on Family Wage Labour in Capitalist Production. *Capital and Class* 3 (Autumn).

Bell, Carolyn Shaw. 1967. *Consumer Choice in the American Economy.* New York: Random House.

Braverman, Harry. 1974. *Labor and Monopoly Capital.* New York: Monthly Review Press.

Brown, Carol. 1981. Mothers, Fathers and Children: From Private to Public Patriarchy, In *Women and Revolution,* Lydia Sargent (ed). Boston: South End Press.

Bureau of Labor Statistics, U.S. Department of Labor. 1980. *Perspectives on Working Women: A Databook.* Washington, D.C.: BLS Bulletin 2080.

Cott, Nancy T. 1977. *The Bonds of Womanhood.* New Haven: Yale University Press.

Davies, Margery. 1974. Woman's Place is at the Typewriter: The Feminization of the Clerical Labor Force. *Radical America* (July-August).

Demos, John. 1970. *A Little Commonwealth.* London: Oxford University Press.

Dublin, Thomas. 1979. *Women at Work.* New York: Columbia University Press.

Earle, Alice Morse. 1910. *Home Life in Colonial Days.* London: Macmillan Co.

Easton, Barbara. 1978. Feminism and the Contemporary Family. *Socialist Review (May-June).*

Eisenstein, Zillah. 1979. Developing a Theory of Capitalist Patriarchy and Socialist Feminism. In *Capitalist Patriarchy and the Case for Socialist Feminism,* Zillah Eisenstein (ed). New York: Monthly Review Press.

Fox, Bonnie. 1980. Women's Double Work Day: Twentieth-Century Changes in the Reproduction of Daily Life. In *Hidden in the Household,* Bonnie Fox (ed). Toronto: The Women's Press.

Gilder, George. 1981. *Wealth and Poverty.* New York: Bantam Books.

Hartmann, Heidi. 1979a. Capitalism, Patriarchy, and Job Segregation by Sex. In *Capitalist Patriarchy and the Case for Socialist Feminism,* Zillah Eisenstein (ed). New York: Monthly Review Press.

———. 1979b. The Unhappy Marriage of Marxism and Feminism: Toward a More Progressive Union. *Capital and Class* 8 (Summer).

Jensen, Joan. 1980. Cloth, Butter and Boarders: Women's Household Production for the Market. *Review of Radical Political Economics* vol. 12 no. 2 (Summer).

Kuhn, Annette and Ann Marie Wolpe (eds). 1978. *Feminism and Materialism.* London: Routledge and Kegan Paul.

Lynd, Robert S. and Helen Merrell Lynd. 1929. *Middletown.* New York: Harcourt Brace.

Marx, Karl. 1967. *Capital,* vol. I. New York: International Publishers.

Milkman, Ruth. 1976. Women's Work and Economic Crisis: Some Lessons from the Great Depression. *Review of Radical Political Economics* vol. 8 no. 1 (Spring).

National Advisory Council on Economic Opportunity. 1980. *Critical Choices for the 80's* (Twelfth Report). Washington, D.C.: U. S. Superintendent of Documents.

Oakley, Ann. 1974. *Woman's Work.* New York: Random House.

Oppenheimer, Valerie Kincade. 1976. *The Female Labor Force in the United States,* Population Monograph Series, no. 5. Westport, Connecticut: Greenwood Press.

Power, Marilyn. 1977. *Housework as a Production Activity.* Unpublished Ph. D. Dissertation, University of California at Berkeley.

———. 1986. Unity and Division among Women: Feminist Theories of Gender and Class in Capitalist Society. *Economic Processes and Political Conflicts: Contributions to Modern Political Economy,* Richard England (ed). New York: Praeger.

Reid, Margaret G. 1934. *Economics of Household Production.* New York: John Wiley and Sons, Inc.

Rowbotham, Sheila. 1973. *Woman's Consciousness, Man's World.* Middlesex, England: Penguin Books.

Rubin, Gayle. 1975. The Traffic in Women: Notes on the "Political Economy" of Sex. In *Toward an Anthropology of Women,* Rayna Reiter (ed). New York: Monthly Review Press.

Ryan, Mary. 1979. Femininity and Capitalism in Antebellum America. In *Capitalist Patriarchy and the Case for Socialist Feminism,* Zillah Eisenstein (ed). New York: Monthly Review Press.

Sargent, Lydia (ed). 1980. *Women and Revolution.* Boston: South End Press.

Sen, Gita. 1980. The Sexual Division of Labor and the Working-class Family: Towards a Conceptual Synthesis of Class Relations and the Subordination of Women. *Review of Radical Political Economics* vol. 12 no. 2 (Summer).

Simeral, Margaret H. 1978. Women and the Reserve Army of Labor. *Insurgent Sociologist* (Fall).

Smuts, Robert W. 1971. *Women and Work in America.* New York: Schocken Books.

Tilly, Louise A. and Joan W. Scott. 1978. *Women, Work, and Family.* New York: Holt, Rinehart & Winston.

Trey, Joan. 1972. Women in the War Economy. *Review of Radical Political Economics* vol. 4 no. 2 (Summer)

Ulrich, Laurel Thatcher. 1982. *Good Wives: Images and Realty in Lives of Women in Northern New England, 1650-1750.* New York: Alfred A. Knopf.

Walker, Kathryn and Margaret E. Woods. 1967. *Time Use: A Measure of Household Production of Family Goods and Services.* Washington, D.C.: Center for the Family of the American Home Economics Association.

Wilson, Maud. 1929. *Use of Time by Oregon Farm Homemakers.* Portland, Oregon: Agricultural Experiment Station Bulletin 256.

Chapter 9

Unity and Division Among Women: Feminist Theories of Gender and Class in Capitalist Society

MARILYN POWER

There have been numerous attempts, primarily but not exclusively by Marxist feminists, to locate women within an economic class analysis. Such an analysis is useful for illuminating the changing patterns of women's economic experience, their relation to capital and to male workers, and also for suggesting possible areas of unity and division among women themselves. However, these theorists differ from each other in fundamental ways, and as a result their writings imply very different answers to these important questions. This chapter will survey and critically assess some of these theories of gender and class, with particular attention to their implications for relations among women. This issue is of continuing interest to the feminist movement because it explores the possibilities of organizing women as a group with common, unified goals. I will end with a statement of some general principles for developing a successful theory of gender and class and with a suggestion of some elements of such a theory.

Applying class analysis in an advanced capitalist economy is complicated by issues such as the distinction between productive and unproductive labor, divisions between manual and mental workers, and the role of ideology in defining class position. For women, the analysis is further complicated by the sex-gender system. Women perform two types of labor: wage labor and domestic labor (unpaid labor in the home). Within the labor force they are segregated into "female" occupations, which are given a particular character by the sexist ideology of the society. Sexism in general, as ideology and lived reality, affects society's view of women workers, women's consciousness about their own work, and the material conditions of work for women.

Feminist theorists analyzing the experience of women in advanced capitalism uniformly argue that to understand women's complex and continued oppression, a theory must incorporate *both* their wage labor and their domestic labor. However, after this initial point of agreement, the theories differ widely on such questions as the *relative* importance of domestic and wage labor in explaining women's position, the relation of domestic labor to capitalism, and the existence of patriarchy as a structure with a material base relatively independent from capitalism. In the discussion that follows, I will group theorists primarily by their position on these questions. In some cases, they present an *explicit* theory of class and gender; in others, it must be inferred from their analysis.

REPRODUCTION AS A SEPARATE MODE OF PRODUCTION

A number of theorists, most particularly among radical feminists, view women as a sexual class.[1] Shulamith Firestone (1970), for example, argues that the oppression of women by men was historically the first form of inequality and that it has continued across history and across modes of production. Thus, the oppression of women as a class has its base in patriarchy, a system of male dominance separate from capitalism. Although classes are normally seen in relation to a mode of production in Marxist analyses, Firestone does not attempt to apply such an analysis to patriarchy. A number of other writers, however, explicitly locate the oppression of women within a separate mode of production that coexists alongside capitalism and that is referred to variously as the housework, domestic, or family mode of production. These theories view women's performance of unpaid domestic labor, in this separate mode of production, as the primary determinant of their overall societal position.

Christine Delphy (1977), a French radical feminist writer, criticizes traditional Marxist analysis for seeing the oppression of women as a secondary characteristic of class struggle, with no material base outside of capitalism. Delphy argues that women's oppression has a material base in men's appropriation of women's labor within the family mode of production, which is separate from and somewhat independent of capitalism. Married women provide domestic service, childrearing, and certain other goods through their unpaid labor in the home. Men appropriate their wives' surplus labor and provide for their wives' subsistence. This "patriarchal exploitation" differs from capitalist exploitation in that the level of subsistence is not determined by the amount of labor performed, but rather by the "wealth and goodwill" of the husband (Delphy 1977: 14).

Since virtually all women are married at some point in their lives, and all married women must engage in domestic production, Delphy argues that women constitute a *class*. In addition, because they are destined to occupy their position in the family mode of production by birth, women are also a *caste*. If women enter capitalist production by performing wage labor, they acquire a second class position as members of the proletariat and within the proletariat they constitute a superexploited caste. However, patriarchal exploitation is the "common, specific, and main" oppression of women (Delphy 1977:14); the liberation of women requires the destruction of patriarchy through the mobilization of *all* women as a class.

Delphy's specification of women as a class is not very precise; in the course of a few paragraphs she describes women in the family mode of production as serfs, proletarians, and slaves. In addition, Delphy defines women as a class because their surplus labor is appropriated by men. But, as Molyneux (1979:14) has pointed out, classes are determined by relations of production, not merely by appropriation. The performance of surplus labor is not necessarily exploitative in and of itself.

John Harrison (1973) also develops an argument based on the existence of a housework mode of production. An economic system operating under a dominant mode of production will nearly always contain other modes of production as well. Harrison identifies three types of additional modes of production, which he calls the vestigial mode, the foetal mode, and the client mode. The vestigial mode is the remnants of the previous dominant mode; the foetal model is a forerunner of a future dominant mode of production. A client mode, however, is created or co-opted by the dominant mode to fulfill certain economic and social functions. Its reproduction is bound up with the reproduction of the dominant mode, and it has no independent existence. Harrison (1973:50) argues that housework constitutes such a client mode of production (as do large areas of state activity).

The producer in the housework mode of production is the housewife, and she performs three types of labor: the production of use-values for herself, use-values for her husband, and use-values for her children. The housewife performs surplus labor if her labor time exceeds that necessary for her subsistence, measured in a combination of wage goods and use-values. This surplus labor is appropriated by the capitalists through the payment to her husband of a wage below the value of labor power (Harrison 1973:43).

Thus, the housework mode of production serves the function for capitalism of contributing to the reproduction of labor power and, in the process, produces surplus labor, which is appropriated by the capitalist class as surplus value. Capitalism created the housework mode to fill this function, although housework could in fact be performed completely under capitalist production relations, or by the state. Housewives, as performers of housework, constitute a distinct class (Harrison 1973:50). If women perform both housework and wage labor, they occupy two class positions, housewives and proletarians.

Within political economy, classes are normally thought to exist in opposition to each other. Yet, in Harrison's housework mode of production there appears to be only one class, housewives. Capitalists appropriate the surplus labor of housewives, but, as Harrison notes, housework is not socialized as in capitalist production; nor do capitalists directly control the labor process (Harrison 1973:50). Men don't constitute a class in opposition to women. As husbands they are merely the vehicle through which capitalists get access to housewives' surplus labor; they appear to play no role at all in the social relations of the housework mode of production.

There are other theoretical problems with Harrison's model as well. Most fundamentally, as has been pointed out by several authors (cf. Molyneux 1979; Himmelweit and Mohun 1977), it is not theoretically possible for surplus labor from the housework mode to appear in *value* terms in the capitalist mode, a value with no material base in capitalist production. In addition, the analytic usefulness of the concept of a client mode of production is not clear since it is seen as dependent for its existence on the capitalist mode of production and changed by every change in capitalism.

In general, analyses of housework as a separate mode of production are useful in suggesting that social relations and dynamics within the household may be different from those of capitalist production and thus require a separate analysis. However, neither Delphy nor Harrison successfully develops an analysis of those social relations. For Delphy, women are "enslaved" by their husbands, but the basis for male domination is never established (is it genetic male aggression? something else?). In addition, the class analysis developed is rather awkward. Women are *always* a class in the domestic mode of production (and for Delphy men are always a class as well), but women also *sometimes* occupy class positions within capitalism. Thus, women may occupy class positions in two modes of production simultaneously (and virtually *all* men do, in Delphy's analysis). If a woman engages in wage labor sporadically, she is sporadically part of the proletariat, sporadically not.[2]

Finally, analysis of housework as a separate mode of production impedes our ability to understand the dynamics of the relationship *between* capitalism and domestic labor. Housework is clearly affected by the expansion of capitalist production. In fact, the invasion of the sphere of women's domestic production by capital is partially responsible for the movement of women into wage labor (Power 1983).

"DUAL SYSTEMS" ANALYSES

Dual systems analysts attempt to establish a material base for social relations between men and women separate from capital and, at the same time, to avoid the degree of division between the household and capitalist production implied by the domestic mode of production analysis. They do this by positing that women's position both in the home and in wage labor is determined by the interaction of two separate and relatively autonomous systems, capitalism and patriarchy.

Heidi Hartmann (1981) argues that any society requires both a mode of economic production and a mode of producing people, in the dual sense of biological reproduction and of inculcating social norms. Following Gayle Rubin (1975), Hartmann calls the mode of producing people the "sex/gender system," the system by which the biological sexes, male and female, are transformed into socially created genders, men and women (Hartmann 1981: 16). Hartmann labels the present sex/gender system in capitalist societies "patriarchy," which she defines as "a set of social relations between men, which have a material base, and which, though hierarchical, establish or create interdependence and solidarity among men that enable them to dominate women" (Hartmann 1981: 14). The material base of patriarchy lies in men's control over women's labor power, which they maintain by excluding women from access to productive resources and by restricting women's sexuality. Monogamous heterosexual marriage, in which women are primarily responsible for housework and child care, is a "relatively recent and efficient form" (Hartmann 1981: 15) both for controlling women's labor and for reproducing patriarchal social relations across generations.

Patriarchal relations, according to Hartmann, are present not only within the family, but in the sphere of production as well. Patriarchy and capitalism have potentially conflicting interests, as both would like to control women's labor power. Hartmann suggests that historically this conflict has been resolved through the forging of a mutually beneficial "partnership" between capitalism and patriarchy in which women serve as a low-wage labor force for capitalism while continuing to provide services for men in the home.

Hartmann does not explicitly analyze patriarchy as a mode of production separate from capitalism. Indeed, given her assertion that both a mode of economic production and a sex/gender system are necessary in any given society, it may seem that such a separation is analytically impossible. Yet, her understanding of patriarchy as a system with a separate material base and its own social relations strongly implies that it is a mode of production. This impression is reinforced by the fact that patriarchy is seen as relatively independent from capitalism. While affected and modified by its relation to capitalism, patriarchy evidently predated it and may continue under socialism as well. It cannot be seen, however, as a free-floating version of Harrison's "client" mode of production (that is, a client mode that can attach itself to any of a number of dominant modes). Sex/gender systems and economic systems are *mutually* dependent: hence, it is not possible to find "pure" capitalism or "pure" patriarchy, but rather only patriarchal capitalism (or patriarchal feudalism, etc.).

Thus, the position of women is determined *dually* by the partnership of patriarchy and capitalism. One could read this argument as implying that women's position is the outcome of two intertwined class systems, one in which women are a class and one in which class is determined by their individual relations to wage labor. Hartmann does not, however, develop an explicit theory of classes from her dual systems analysis. She does argue that patriarchal social relations divided the working class (which is not defined) by "allowing one part (men) to be bought off at the expense of the other (women)" (Hartmann 1981: 21).

This ambiguity over the implications of the analysis for an understanding of gender and class are symptomatic of the ambiguities in the dual systems analysis in general. As Hartmann notes, the term patriarchy in her work is more descriptive than analytic. She raises questions for further study (1981:30), including: Are there laws of motion of a patriarchal system? What are the contradictions of the patriarchal system? and What is their relation to capitalist contradictions? These questions once again imply an analysis of patriarchy as a mode of production.

In particular, the assertion that patriarchy has a material base needs more discussion: To say that men maintain patriarchy by keeping women economically dependent and ideologically inferior is insufficient—that is *how* patriarchy reproduces itself, but not *why*. It is undeniable that men have some form of material interest in maintaining male privilege and that they have been unwilling to relinquish their control over women's labor (and their general position of ideological dominance). In order to have a material base, however, patriarchy must be not just something (some) people *want*; rather, it must be materially necessary to the society's mode of production and reproduction. This was certainly the case in the preindustrial agricultural family, in which children were productive resources and control over women's reproductive capacity was the key to family survival. It is less clear now that patriarchy has a material base. This is not to deny that it has a powerful ideological base. Further, the ideology of patriarchy (as well as the legal basis for it) has been continually reproduced by capitalism, which has found patriarchy not only easier to accommodate than to fight but also quite useful for capitalist production and reproduction.

The ambiguity about specification of the "system" of patriarchy, and its material base, is heightened in the work of Carol Brown (1981), who argues that there are in fact *two* aspects, or systems, of patriarchy: private patriarchy and public patriarchy. Private patriarchy involves the control individual husbands have over their wives and children; public patriarchy is "the control of society—of the economy, polity, religion, etc.—by men collectively, who use that control to uphold the rights and privileges of the collective male sex as well as individual men" (Brown 1981: 240). According to Brown, monopoly capitalism weakened private patriarchy by moving the tasks of reproducing labor power outside the home. In the process, conditions were set for the predominance of public patriarchy, manifested in an increase in the power of "higher level" men over all women and a decrease in the power of "lower level" men over any women (Brown 1981: 244). In this argument, patriarchy seems to have lost whatever material base and separation from capitalism it once had. Patriarchy's continued existence (in altered form) is simply assumed, without any attempt to establish a materialist explanation for it.

Another writer in the dual systems school, Ann Ferguson, develops the concept of patriarchy into an explicitly separate mode of production and produces, in effect, a "triple systems" analysis of the position of women. Ferguson argues that women, and men, can be characterized by three different class positions simultaneously in advanced capitalist patriarchal social formations: sex class, family class, and individual economic class. Sex classes are a result of the existence of a "family mode of childrearing, sexuality, and affection," which Ferguson calls "patriarchal sex/affective production" (Ferguson 1979: 281). Women are the exploited, and men the exploiting, class in this mode of production because there is unequal exchange between them: Women receive less of the goods produced than men, and spend more time producing them.[3] The material base of patriarchy, that is, male exploitation, is cultural and psychological; the fact that women are childrearers creates male and female personalities and expectations that perpetuate the sexual division of labor in the family (Ferguson 1979: 298, 298f, 299). In addition, Ferguson (1979: 301) suggests that males' control over the paycheck affords them the power to appropriate the "surplus: surplus wages, surplus nurturance, and sexuality."

Beside their sex class, says Ferguson, individuals have an economic class position defined by their relations to production. Persons who do not have a direct relation to capital have their class position defined indirectly, for example, housewives by their husbands' relations to production and children by their parents'. Finally, everyone has a family economic class, determined by the relations of the family's "breadwinner(s)" to production. Ferguson recognizes that ambiguity could enter this last definition if husbands and wives are in different individual relations to capital. She offers an essentially intuitive solution to this ambiguity: class identification involves "historical and cultural self-identity"; hence, family class cannot be seen as simply "an additive function of the individual economic relations of husband and wife." Ferguson offers no rigorous means of determining family class, but simply an example: if a man owns a small grocery store, the "cultural implications of . . . (his) . . . position and money" determine that the family class is likely to be petit bourgeois, whether the wife is a housewife or a factory worker (Ferguson 1979: 282).

Historically, family has usually taken precedence over sex as a determinant of women's class identification, according to Ferguson. However, in advanced capitalism there are increasing contradictions between the social relations of capitalist production and the social relations of patriarchal sex/affective production in the family (Ferguson 1979: 303).[4] In particular, wage labor and welfare allow women to live separately from men, and inflationary pressure on family income causes women to seek wage work even when married. These conditions have resulted in increased instability in patriarchal nuclear families, which, Ferguson suggests, will make it likely that women will find their prime identity as a sex class rather than within family class. As a result, women can be seen as a potentially revolutionary class, with the ability to disrupt both patriarchy and capitalism.

There are a number of difficulties with Ferguson's analysis, including the ambiguity discussed above in the determination of family class. In particular, her specification of the social relations of the family mode of production leaves many loose threads. Once again, class is defined largely in terms of appropriation, rather than relations of production; and in this case the "exploitation" is discovered in a relation of unequal exchange, in which "the man is able to appropriate more of the women's labor time for his own use than she is of his" (Ferguson 1979: 296). Ferguson bases her argument about the existence of sex classes additionally on men's greater power and autonomy within the family, which allows them to appropriate women's nurturance and sexuality as well as their labor time.[5] The bases of men's ability to enforce this unequal exchange seems to be an inadequately specified combination of biology, culture, psychologically produced role expectations, and greater access to wages.

Unequal exchange (whether of material or psychological goods) is not an adequate indication of the existence of classes, however. In addition, the psychological and cultural factors she points to can be more plausibly explained as *effects* than as causes of inequality. Finally, given the crucial role wage labor plays in determining relations within the family in her argument, she has not clearly established sex/affective production as a separate mode of production from capitalism.

In general, both dual systems and domestic mode of production analyses are based on some valid and important observations and intuitions. Relations of production within the home are different from those in capitalist commodity production: for example, the labor is unpaid and *appears* voluntary, and the immediate products are for use, not exchange. Women's roles in unpaid domestic labor seem crucially tied to their subordinate position within the home, not just economically, but sexually, psychologically, and culturally as well. And the "product" of domestic labor is unlike the product of capitalist production; abstractly, from the capitalist point of view, the product is labor power, but concretely the product is *people*. Finally, men as a group derive certain material benefits from the subordination of women, in terms of services in the home and less competition in the labor force.

However, attempts to establish housework as a separate mode of production, or patriarchy as a system with a separate material base, do not seem to have succeeded in rigorously establishing these separations. Incorporating the sex/gender system into a class analysis undoubtedly raises the level of complexity; however, these attempts just cited are simultaneously unduly complex and unduly simple. That is, we are confronted with the possibility of women occupying two (or three) class positions within two different modes of production simultaneously, a conception that may be more confusing than it is clarifying. And at the same time, the separation of housework from capitalism conceptually may divert our attention from the complex and continuous interaction between the two. In short, I must conclude that the conceptualization of women as a sexual class, solely or in combination with other class locations, has not been persuasively established and, in addition, obscures more than it clarifies. Further, none of these analyses encourages an investigation of possible *divisions* among women; as a sex class they are united, and as wage laborers they are assumed to be uniformly "superexploited."

WOMEN DEFINED BY THEIR RELATION TO CAPITAL

A number of writers argue that domestic labor is not separate from, but directly linked to the capitalist mode of production. Susan Himmelweit and Simon Mohun, for example, acknowledge that housework is private production, performed outside the sphere of capitalist commodity production and under completely different social relations. Because it is not commodity production, domestic labor "is of no direct concern to capital" (Himmelweit and Mohun 1977: 16). Nevertheless, it is crucially important to capital, because domestic labor produces the use values that are necessary to maintain and reproduce labor power.

Housework is not wage labor, but it is part of capitalism and necessary to its functioning. The form domestic labor takes is "specific to and part of the capitalist mode of production" (Himmelweit and Mohun 1977: 23), not separate from it. Himmelweit and Mohun do not draw conclusions for class analysis from their argument. They do suggest, however, that women who perform domestic labor are a major component of the industrial army and that capitalism has an inherent tendency to draw them into wage labor. This tendency is potentially destructive for capitalism, as it may create a more unified working class. The absorption of women into wage labor has its limits, however, because capitalism requires "free" laborers who are produced *outside* commodity production. This (biological) reproduction by women must be performed outside the sphere of wage labor.

Jean Gardiner (1977) directly confronts the question of determining women's class position through a combination of their roles in wage labor and domestic labor. She begins by noting that there is not a simple, one-dimensional way of defining class. Some writers define the working class very broadly (cf. Freedman 1974) or very narrowly (cf. Poulantzas 1974); but however narrowly it is defined, there will always be further subdivisions, both material and ideological. Gardiner's solution is to accept a broad definition of the working class as those dependent upon the sale of labor power for survival, "with a commitment to examine and give political weight to the divisions and subdivisions within class" (Gardiner 1977: 156).

Gardiner emphasizes the relation of the *family* to the class structure because she believes it is important in understanding the specific positions of women and men. The family unit helps reproduce the capitalist class structure because it is the economic unit for the generational reproduction of classes; because it reproduces the class structurally, socially, and culturally; and because the family plays a key role in the daily maintenance of the working class through both redistribution of wages and domestic labor. The family has played a direct role in facilitating the creation of a wage labor force. The unpaid domestic labor of women has lowered the average wage capitalists have had to pay. In addition, because the family supports nonwage earning members, it has facilitated the creation of a reserve of unemployed workers, both women and men, and it has aided the reproduction of classes across generations by supporting children and childrearers (i.e., women).

Looking at the working class family in this light, Gardiner notes that "the relationship of the mass of people to the system of social production is considerably more complex than the wage labour relation as normally described" (Gardiner 1977: 157). The working class at any one time will include *both* those selling their labor power *and* those dependent upon that sale: for example, housewives, children, the unemployed, the sick, and the old. However, while members of the working class, nonwage earners have a "vicarious relationship to the sale of labour power which must affect their position both materially and ideologically" (Gardiner 1977: 158).

Women have entered wage labor in growing numbers since World War II, but most women do not earn enough to be self-supporting. As a result they continue to be economically dependent on marriage. Within marriage women continue to be responsible for housework and child care;[6] this responsibility in turn facilitates a sexual division within the labor force, in which women are drawn into low paid, routine work in positions subordinate to men. An understanding of women's two roles requires a "new approach" to class analysis. Women have a "dual relationship" to the class structure: a *direct* relationship through their own wage labor and a relation to class *mediated* by the family, their dependence on men, and domestic labor (Gardiner 1977: 159).

Because men and women have different relations to wage labor, they may have divergent interests, both within the family and within the labor force. Women's consciousness of class, and the forms of their involvement in class struggle, will be different; for example, they may stress the need for child care and social services.

Gardiner's conception of women's dual relationship to class is helpful in allowing us to incorporate both domestic and wage labor within a single mode of production analysis. In addition, Gardiner reminds us that the working class consists not only of those directly engaged in wage labor, but also those dependent on that wage[7]—and that this dependence is specific to (created by) the dynamics of capitalist production. Capitalism draws workers into wage labor, but it also expels them as the unemployed, the disabled, and the old. And, as Himmelweit and Mohun point out, the creation of new generations of workers must take place outside capitalist production. Thus, the structure of the working class family is directly affected by capitalism, and domestic labor cannot be understood separate from it.

Gardiner's work is also useful for its recognition that complexity and division inevitably exist within a class; they are not signs that we should abandon class analysis or seek to create a plethora of classes.[8] However, her concept of women's "mediated" class position, while useful, is undefined; a more exact specification of that mediation is needed. In addition, Gardiner's extremely broad definition of the working class tends to obscure differences among women workers. She does acknowledge that women whose education allows them to support themselves independently from men are in a "distinct economic position from the majority of women workers," but that difference is not at all antagonistic. Common interests can be established, for example, around reproductive rights, child care, and discrimination (Gardiner 1977: 162). This is a valid point. However, material economic differences of interest may exist among these women as well (not to mention ethnic and racial divisions, which Gardiner does not raise).

Finally, Gardiner doesn't explore the origins of women's subordination to men. She suggests that the material base of their subordination lies in women's continued economic dependence on men, which is connected to the sexual division of domestic labor. She does not seek to explain the forces that established and reproduce that sexual division historically. Michèle Barrett (1980) notes that no theory has established that the sexual division of labor would be *automatically* reproduced by the reproduction of the class system. She suggests that it can be better understood as "a product of an ideology of gender division that was incorporated into the capitalist division of labor rather than spontaneously generated by it" (Barrett 1980: 138). Thus, an understanding of women's experience cannot be *wholly* incorporated within an analysis of capitalist class dynamics.

CLASS DIVISIONS AND STRATIFICATION IN THE LABOR FORCE

Lastly, a number of theorists focus exclusively on women's position in wage labor. Labor market segmentation theorists, for example, view the working class (broadly defined) as divided into segments that seek jobs in separate labor markets and experience different labor processes (cf. Gordon, Edwards, and Reich 1982). Within each major segment there is further segregation by factors such as race and sex. The segments of the working class are divided from each other along economic, political, and cultural lines; sex and race segregation exacerbate this process of "divide and conquer."

Labor market segmentation is seen as growing out of the historic development of capitalism. However, sex and race segregation are not historically explained; they are taken as "givens." Indeed, while segmentation is seen as a twentieth century phenomenon, the sexual division of labor was present from the onset of capitalist production. Thus, women frequently become an "exception" to the historical analyses (Gordon, Edwards, and Reich 1982: 120-21). In addition, labor market segmentation theorists have yet to examine divisions *among* women workers. In general, as Michèle Barrett notes, such theories see class and gender as cumulative factors (that is, a woman's economic position is determined by her class position *plus* her gender), which can be empirically divided and measured. The problem with such an approach, according to Barrett, is that it gives us no insight into the interaction *between* the variables, and as a result, it "cannot throw any light on the theoretical problems of analysing class, race and gender in terms of reproducing a divided labor force" (1980: 128-29).

From another viewpoint, Jackie West (1978) agrees with most feminist theories that it is necessary to understand both women's wage labor and their unpaid labor in the home. However, she believes that the first step is to examine wage labor rather than to try to incorporate both areas of work into theory simultaneously. West argues that the implications of women's employment for their class position has been largely ignored and that it is necessary to examine this question *before* creating a class analysis that integrates women's wage labor with their domestic labor. Focusing exclusively on women's "dual role" may "suggest more ambiguity and complexity in the position of women than may in fact exist" (West 1978: 222).

Ambiguity about women's class membership stems less from their dual role, according to West, than from the fact that they are largely employed in white-collar labor, which has been a "grey area" in Marxist analyses of class (1978: 235). In particular, there is dispute about whether women white-collar workers are part of an expanded proletariat (Braverman 1974) or of the new petit bourgeoisie (Poulantzas 1974). This question is the focus of West's discussion. Historically, the distinction between mental and manual work has constituted a major factor dividing white-collar from blue-collar workers. However, there is "considerable agreement" that white-collar work is being transformed; women's service and clerical jobs in particular are becoming deskilled, routinized, and increasingly similar to manual work (West 1978: 235-37). Nevertheless, West disagrees with Braverman that the office is not *entirely* analogous to the factory, because she believes the distinction between productive and unproductive labor is still germane.

Poulantzas' solution to the productive/unproductive labor question is to argue that women engaged in unproductive labor are part of the new petit bourgeoisie but, for the most part, polarized toward the working class (Poulantzas 1974: 316). West does not find this categorization useful. She argues that low-level office and clerical workers in fact do not fit Poulantzas' criteria for the new petit bourgeoisie (e.g., agents of subordination of the working class) and that the labor process in clerical work is coming increasingly to resemble that of manual work. West argues that the lowest levels of nonproductive sales, service, and clerical workers have been proletarianized, while higher levels remain in the petit bourgeoisie. This does not mean that these proletarianized workers will necessarily have a working class consciousness: their functions as unproductive workers may continue to create differences between them and productive workers.

Hence, women's class position can be determined, West argues, without any reference to the sexual division of labor. However, a *full* analysis must include sexual divisions since they "affect the class structure by accounting for (as well as being descriptive of) women's monopoly of certain positions" (1978: 246). Here West incorporates women's role in the home back into the analysis. Women are channelled into certain positions in the labor force because they are a source of "cheap, flexible and disposable labour power," and this characteristic "stems fundamentally from their actual and assumed role in the family" (1978: 248). Women's specific class position, then, is an outcome of the interaction of capitalism with the sexual division of labor in the home (i.e., women as the primary houseworkers and childrearers, combined with the ideology that women should be economically dependent on men).

West's analysis avoids much of the theoretical confusion that seems to arise when writers try to incorporate women's domestic and wage labor simultaneously into the analysis. And she demonstrates that it is possible to say a great deal about women's class position by reference to their wage labor alone because the *pattern* of women's wage labor participation is reflective of their domestic, cultural, and ideological positions. It is striking that most feminist writers do not focus much of their attention on concrete analyses of women's position in the labor force, despite the rapid growth in this area of women's work.

I would agree with West that Poulantzas' characterization of women clerical and service workers as petit bourgeois is not very helpful. However, by merging clerical and service work in her analysis, West fails to recognize some crucial differences between these two groups of women workers. Clerical work has been traditionally viewed as "mental" work and, because it requires literacy, historically attracted "native" white women from upper working class and petit bourgeois backgrounds in the United States. Service work, however, is largely "manual" work and was traditionally allocated to nonwhite and "ethnic" white women. Some of these distinctions are beginning to break down, as I will discuss shortly, and the potential significance of this change is lost if clerical and service work are not clearly distinguished in the analysis.

PRINCIPLES FOR A THEORY OF GENDER AND CLASS

Implicit in my critique of these theories of class and gender are five basic principles that seem to me necessary components of a successful analysis:

1. The family has a history *somewhat* independent from capitalism but deeply and intimately tied to it. It is not appropriate to theorize the family as a separate mode of production. Nor is it useful to view women as simultaneously occupying two class positions.
2. The sexual division of labor in the home and in the labor force means that women have somewhat different concerns from working class men and, importantly, some concrete points of conflict with them. This does not, however make women a *class*.
3. Women's experience in wage labor is increasingly important in determining their class position.
4. Within the labor force there are divisions among women workers on issues such as status and autonomy, mental versus manual work, and racial/ethnic differences. There are currently trends toward both greater unity and greater division among women workers.
5. Sexual oppression and women's role in the family shape women's experience, but somewhat differentially by economic position. (Affluent women can, for instance, afford day care, full-time housekeepers, etc.) Nevertheless, there is potential unity among women over such issues as reproductive rights and sexual violence.

In the following section, I will pursue these last two principles and suggest the outlines of an analysis of divisions among women engaged in wage labor in the contemporary United States. It must be emphasized that this discussion constitutes only one piece of a comprehensive analysis of gender and class. It is for this reason that I will refer to "groups" of women workers rather than using class terminology.

CONCRETE ANALYSIS OF DIVISIONS AMONG WOMEN WORKERS

Understanding women's wage labor at the current moment is crucial for a number of reasons. First, women were a majority of new workers in the United States over the past decade: of the 22 million person increase in the labor force between 1970 and 1980, 12.6 million, or nearly 60 percent were women. Second, the process of incorporating *married* women into the labor force, which began in the early twentieth century, increased at a rapid pace during the 1970s; by 1980, over half of all married women with husband present were in the labor force. This increase in the participation of married women occurred particularly among women with children at home: by 1979, 51.9 percent of married women with children under 18 were in the labor force (compared with 49.4 percent of all married women). Among married women with preschool children, 43.2 percent were in the labor force, compared with 30.3 percent in 1970. These figures illustrate a clear trend: Capitalism is incorporating women into the permanent wage labor force. Wage labor is no longer temporary or supplementary for most women; they spend the greater part of their adult lives performing it (the Women's Bureau in 1978 estimated an average of 28 years), and it is necessary for the economic support of themselves and their families.

But studying women's wage labor is important for another reason as well. Trends in the 1970s in the location of women within occupations suggest the possibility of both growing divisions and growing homogeneity among women workers, trends with important implications for the possibility of political unity among women in years to come. These occupational trends and their possible implications form the focus of this section of my essay. In particular, I want to explore the possibility that women workers can be analyzed in three distinct economic groups, with some commonality of interest but also important material conflicts of interest among them:

- Group 1: women professionals and managers.
- Group 2: women clerical, service, and production workers (a majority of women workers).
- Group 3: women at the bottom of the economic hierarchy, many of whom cycle back and forth between welfare and low-wage labor.

Within each group there are both forces for unity and forces for division. In addition, there are potential conflicts and potential alliances across group lines. Sexism affects all women but differentially across groups and segments of groups. I will illustrate these observations briefly.

Group 1

Around 17 percent of all women workers in the United States are in professional and technical occupations. Of course, the majority of women in this category are located in the traditional female professions of nursing, noncollege teaching, and social work, occupations that are high-skilled but low paid and with limited possibilities for advancement. However, over the past decade, there has been a marked movement of women into such nontraditional fields as accounting, law, medicine, computer science, and even engineering: two-thirds of new accountants were women, one-third of new computer specialists, and one-fourth of new lawyers and physicians. Women managers are far more likely to be health administrators and office managers than corporate executives. Nevertheless, half of all new managers and administrators over the past decade were women (see table 9-1).

These occupations offer women unprecedented and very real opportunities for income, power, and prestige. As a result, women in group 1 who have entered traditionally male fields may have some real, material conflicts of interest with other women workers. They have tended to benefit from Reagan's conservative economic policies, gaining from 1981 personal tax cuts considerably more than they lost in social services.

Women at this end of group 1 tend to espouse a highly individualistic, "free market" ideology, with an emphasis on learning to play the game and making it to the top individually. In these ways, women in traditionally male, group 1 occupations may identify their interests with those of capital.

TABLE 9.1. Representation of Women in Selected Traditionally Male Professional and Managerial Occupations, 1972 and 1982

Occupation	Percent Female 1972	Percent Female 1982	Change in # Women ÷ Change in # Workers
All occupations	38.0%	43.5%	68.7%
Professional & technical	39.3	45.1	57.2
• lawyers & judges	3.8	15.4	27.3
• physicians	10.1	14.8	24.5
• engineers	0.8	5.7	17.1
• computer specialists	16.8	28.5	35.2
• accountants	21.7	38.6	63.8
Managers & administrators	17.6	28.0	52.1
• bank officials & financial	19.0	37.1	52.1

Sources: United States Department of Commerce (1978); United States Department of Labor (January 1983)

This identification with capital must be emphatically qualified, however, on a number of fronts. First, these women are likely to support affirmative action, clearly a point of disagreement with the Reagan administration. Second, on social issues such as abortion, violence against women, and pornography, women from the top of group 1 are more likely to find a commonality of interest with other women. These are potentially the most unifying issues.

The rest of the women in group 1 (that is, women in traditionally female professions) have considerably more commonality of interest with women in group 2 in pay, status, and ideology. The potential for alliances between women in such traditionally female occupations as nursing and women in group 2 is very great.

Group 2

One-third of all women workers in the United States are clerical workers, and one-fifth are service workers, while less than 15 percent work in blue-collar jobs. Historically, there have been a number of divisions between clerical and service workers. When clerical work became a female occupation at the turn of the century, it was considered genteel work, and because it required literacy, relatively high in status and pay. Clerical workers were likely to be "native-born" white women, frequently from petit bourgeois backgrounds (Davies 1974). Service work, in contrast (then largely domestic work) was considered menial, manual rather than mental, and was poorly paid. Service workers were generally foreign born or black. Thus there were a number of aspects to this division: mental/manual distinctions, pay differentials, and racial/ethnic differences.

All of these divisions between clerical and service work are still present, but over the past decade they have diminished markedly for two reasons. First, black women have moved out of service work and into clerical work in large numbers (see table 9-2). And second, mechanization and rationalization of office work have continued and accelerated a trend toward deskilling of clerical work, thereby eliminating highly skilled and relatively well-paid jobs from the top of the clerical hierarchy and opening up less skilled and low paying jobs at the bottom.[9] Without minimizing the continuing differences within group 2, there seem to be concrete and significant reasons for arguing that there is a *tendency* toward homogeneity within this group of women workers.

Women from group 2 tend to be alienated from women at the top of group 1. "Lifestyle-feminism" particularly offends them, because of its emphasis on making it alone and because they perceive it as antifamily. Women from group 2 are often strongly attached to the nuclear family, not least because they would face grave difficulty trying to support themselves and their children without it.

TABLE 9.2. Distribution of Black and White Women over Selected Occupations, 1972 and 1982

	White Women		Black Women	
Occupation	1972	1982	1972	1982
Clerical workers	36.3%	35.1%	23.3%	29.7%
Service workers	19.3	18.1	42.0	29.7
(private household)	(3.0)	(1.9)	(15.2)	(5.4)
(other service)	(16.2)	(16.3)	(26.8)	(24.4)
Operatives, nontransport	12.5	8.2	15.0	13.5

Source: U.S. Department of Labor, Bureau of Labor Statistics, Employment and Earnings, January 1973 and January 1983.

Group 2 members may also be alienated from those in group 3, perceiving them as a threat for a number of reasons. Women in group 3 serve as a continuous reminder of what could happen to any but the most secure group 2 worker, in case of divorce, illness, or unemployment. Group 3 women may also serve to depress wages for women workers by competing for jobs at the low end of the female job ladder.

Group 3

These are women in poverty. They are disproportionately black and frequently raising children alone. They tend to survive through a combination of work, welfare, and kin networks. Not all women who receive welfare payments belong in group 3. Many women who receive welfare, perhaps a half, use it as a temporary support in an emergency. They are generally on welfare for less than two years, then leave the system and never return (Rein and Rainwater 1978). Group 3 women, by contrast, are chronically marginalized at the bottom of the economic ladder. They cycle between low-paid, dead-end jobs and welfare. Often when they do work, their wages fail to lift them out of poverty. In the past they have frequently received supplemental welfare while working but it is precisely these supplemental payments that were the primary focus of the Reagan Administration's brutal welfare cuts in the early 1980s.

In general, group 3 is bearing the brunt of Reagan's cuts in social programs. Despite official rhetoric, the "safety net" has been removed, and for many group 3 women and their children, simple survival is in jeopardy. Many of these women are engaged in a desperate scramble for a job, any job, which may well pit them against women at the bottom of group 2.

Women in group 3 are not in general unified with each other, except for kin. Welfare rights organizations, for example, are not strong, and the dismantling of the federal poverty program further diminishes sources of unity. Thus, not only are group 3 women likely to have difficulty aligning themselves with other women workers, they are also likely to have difficulty developing cohesion with each other.

By dividing women workers into three groups, then, we can see clear, material bases for division as well as unity among them. Women do not play a homogeneous role in the labor force, and they cannot be viewed as uniformly oppressed by wage labor. It would be a mistake to presume that we can draw any *simple* conclusions about women's political behavior from these observations—for example, that women in traditionally male professions will align with capital or that women clerical and service workers will begin to organize together. Historical and ideological factors intervene between material class position and political consciousness. In addition, for women more than men, the class positions of other family members affect class identification. For example, a secretary (female) married to a professor (male) is less likely to identify herself as a member of the working class than a secretary (female) married to a factory worker (male). Finally, the material differences among women in their performance of wage labor must be balanced against their *common* experience of social, ideological, and indeed, physical oppression by a sexist society. These qualifications notwithstanding, it is clear that an analysis of women's class position must include an understanding of the dynamics and complexity of their role in wage labor.

CONCLUSION

I have argued that analyzing women in class terms in twentieth century United States capitalism requires an examination both of the wage labor they perform and their domestic labor. A successful theory of class and gender should provide insight into women's relation to men and to capital. And it should suggest the potential forces for division and unity among women. It should do all of this within a dynamic framework that allows for contradiction and change and that draws our attention to the forces that reproduce the class structure.

The theories examined in this chapter have provided many valuable insights into this process, but a great deal more needs to be done. I have suggested the outlines of a concrete examination of women's labor force experience, which I believe must be part of a theory of gender and class. As such, my argument about trends toward unity and division among women workers is just one fragment of a comprehensive analysis of gender and class, because it does not address the role of domestic labor or of women's relation to the family and to men.

Finally, I have emphasized that there is no simple and direct relationship between material class position and political consciousness. Thus, even if we could successfully "locate" all women within an objective class analysis, we could not draw any *simple* conclusions about the likelihood of organizing a unified political movement among women, or the possibilities for unionizing clerical workers, or strategies for uniting women who work steadily with women on welfare.

In the end, of course, it is precisely these political questions that are important. The debate over the analysis of class and gender has been motivated by such questions since its inception. It must never degenerate into a simpleminded quest for a taxonomy into which women can be "fit."

NOTES

1. Liberal feminists of the nineteenth century also considered women a sexual class, insofar as law, custom, and religion uniformly oppressed women and gave privileges to men (Eisenstein 1981: ch. 7).

2. That women may occupy two class positions at once is not a problem for Harrison, who argues that dual class positions are not uncommon. Someone who owns stock and also engages in wage labor, for example, is both a capitalist and a proletarian, according to Harrison (1973: 50).

3. The goods produced by sex/affective production are domestic maintenance, children, nurturance, and sexuality.

4. For further development of this argument, see Ann Ferguson and Nancy Folbre (1981).

5. Ferguson presents five criteria for the determination of classes: exploitation relations (defined as expropriation of the surplus), political relations, historical cohesiveness, domination relations, and autonomy.

6. Gardiner implies this is due to their continued economic dependence, which keeps them subordinate to men; but she doesn't pursue this point.

7. Jane Humphries (1977) makes this same point.

8. On the other hand, in her 1976 article, Gardiner suggested housewives may be seen as a class. Her 1977 approach seems to be more fruitful.

9. For example, the number of stenographers declined by 61,000 from 1972 to 1981, while the number of computer and peripheral machine operators (e.g., typists on word processors) increased by 326,000 (*Employment and Earnings* January 1982; *Statistical Abstracts of the United States* 1978).

REFERENCES

Barrett, Michèle. 1980. *Women's Oppression Today*. London: Verso Editions.

Beneria, Lourdes amd Sen Gita. 1982. Class and Gender Inequalities and Women's Role in Economic Development—Theoretical and Practical Implications. *Feminist Studies* 8 (Spring).

Braverman, Harry. 1974. *Labor and Monopoly Capitalism*. New York: Monthly Review Press.

Brown, Carol. 1981. Mothers, Fathers and Children: from Private to Public Patriarchy. In *Women and Revolution*. Lydia Sargent (ed.) Boston: South End Press.

CSE Sex and Class Group. 1982. Sex and Class. *Capital and Class* (Spring).

Davies, Margery. 1974. Woman's Place is at the Typewriter: The Feminization of the Clerical Labor Force. *Radical America* (July-August).

Delphy, Christine. 1977. *The Main Enemy*, London: Women's Research and Resources Centre Publications.

Eisenstein, Zillah R. 1981. *The Radical Future of Liberal Feminism*. New York: Longman.

Ferguson, Ann. 1979. Women as a New Revolutionary Class. In *Between Labor and Capital*. Pat Walker (ed.) Boston: South End Press.

Ferguson, Ann and Nancy Folbre. 1981. The Unhappy Marriage of Patriarchy and Capitalism. In *Women and Revolution*. Lydia Sargent (ed.) Boston: South End Press.

Firestone, Shulamith. 1970. *The Dialectic of Sex*. New York: Bantam Books.

Freedman, Francesca. 1975. The Internal Structure of the American Proletariat: A Marxist Analysis. *Socialist Revolution* 26 (October-December).

Gardiner, Jean. 1976. Political Economy of Domestic Labour in Capitalist Society. In *Dependence and Exploitation in Work and Marriage*. Diana Leonard Barker and Sheila Allen (eds.) London: Longman.

––––––. 1977. Women in the Labour Process and Class Structure. In *Class and Class Structure*. Alan Hunt (ed.) London: Lawrence and Wishart.

Gordon, David M., Richard Edwards, and Michael Reich. 1982. *Segmented Work, Divided Workers*. Cambridge: Cambridge U. Press.

Harrison, John. 1973. The Political Economy of Housework. *Bulletin of the Conference of Socialist Economists* (Winter).

Hartmann, Heidi. 1981. The Unhappy Marriage of Marxism and Feminism: Towards a More Progressive Union. In *Women and Revolution*. Lydia Sargent (ed.) Boston: South End Press.

Himmelweit, Susan and Simon Mohun. 1977. Domestic Labour and Capital. *Cambridge Journal of Economics* vol. I.

Humphries, Jane. 1977. The Working Class Family, Women's Liberation, and Class Struggle: The Case of Nineteenth Century British History. *Review of Radical Political Economics* 9 (Fall).

Molyneux, Maxine. 1979. Beyond the Domestic Labour Debate. *New Left Review* no. 116.

Poulantzas, Nicos. 1973. On Social Classes. *New Left Review* no. 78.

––––––. 1974. *Classes in Contemporary Capitalism*. London: Verso Press.

Power, Marilyn. 1980. Capitalism, Patriarchy, and the Oppression of Women: Theories of Sexism. Unpublished manuscript. University of New Hampshire, Durham.

––––––. 1983. From Home Production to Wage Labor: Women as a Reserve Army of Labor. *Review of Radical Political Economics* XV (Spring).

Rein, Martin and Lee Rainwater. 1978. Patterns of Welfare Use. *Social Service Review* 52 (December).

Rubin, Gayle. 1975. The Traffic in Women: Notes on the "Political Economy" of Sex. In *Toward an Anthropology of Women*. Rayna R. Reiter (ed.) New York: Monthly Review Press.

U.S. Department of Commerce, Bureau of the Census. 1978. *Statistical Abstract of the United States*.

U.S. Department of Labor, Bureau of Labor Statistics. *Employment and Earnings*, various issues.

Vogel, Lise. 1981. Marxism and Feminism: Unhappy Marriage, Trial Separation or Something Else? In *Women and Revolution*. Lydia Sargent (ed.) Boston: South End Press.

West, Jackie. 1978. Women, Sex, and Class. In *Feminism and Materialism*, Annette Kuhn and Ann Marie Wolpe (eds.) London: Routledge and Kegan Paul.

PART 5
Labor, Capital, and the State

Chapter 10

Capital Accumulation, Class Struggle, and School Finance Reform

RICHARD W. ENGLAND

Over the course of the past century, there have been striking changes in both the scale of public education in the United States and also its mode of financing. In 1880, there were fewer than 10 million pupils enrolled in public elementary and secondary schools in this country. By 1980, the number had risen to 41.5 million, more than a fourfold increase during those ten decades. Even more impressive has been the growth of public secondary education. In 1880, there were only 110,000 pupils enrolled in public secondary schools in the United States. By 1980, the number had grown to more than 13.5 million students, a 124-fold increase over the course of the century (U.S. Bureau of the Census 1975a: 368-69; 1981: 147). This explosion in public secondary schooling was especially rapid during the years from 1910 to 1930, a period Martin Trow has identified as the one in which mass secondary education emerged in this country (Trow 1977).

This expansion of the public schools has entailed, in turn, a rapidly growing commitment of funds to finance their construction and operation. In 1890, the U.S. public school system required the expenditure of $566 million, measured in 1958 prices. By 1970, real spending on public elementary and secondary education had grown to $30.1 billion. As a result, public school spending, which had been slightly more than 1 percent of GNP in 1890, rose to more than 4 percent of GNP by 1970 (U.S. Bureau of the Census 1975a: 244, 373-74).

Accompanying this historic growth in pupil enrollment and financial expense has been a substantial shift in the mode of financing the public schools of this country. As recently as World War I, the federal government played practically no role in funding the public schools. By the end of World War II, the federal government still provided less than 1.5 percent of the receipts of public elementary and secondary schools. By the end of the

1970s, however, that federal share was nearly 10 percent (U.S. Bureau of the Census 1975a: 373; 1981: 153).

The role the various state governments have played in financing the public schools contrasts sharply with that played by the national government. Before the turn of the century, state governments routinely provided, on average, more than one-fifth of the funds needed to pay for public schooling. Between the turn of the century and the Great Depression, that state share fell below 20 percent. But by 1950 it had risen sharply to nearly 40 percent and had surpassed 45 percent by the end of the 1970s (U.S. Bureau of the Census 1975a: 373; 1981: 153).

Hence, in the space of one century, public schooling in the United States has undergone a variety of radical transformations. Whereas secondary education used to be reserved for an affluent minority, it is now nearly universal in scope.[1] The percentage share of national output devoted to public schooling has risen fourfold since 1890. The distribution of the fiscal burden of public schooling has shifted dramatically toward the federal and state governments. As a consequence, public school finance, although still heavily dependent upon local property taxation, has become increasingly dependent upon income, sales, and other centralized forms of taxation during recent decades.

These observations are, of course, mere historical description. How can one begin to interpret and comprehend these dramatic changes in the scale and mode of financing of U.S. public education? In order to understand these developments, one needs a theoretical framework with which to interpret historical data and events. One such framework is provided by the neoclassical theories of human capital and public finance, both of which have been used to analyze developments in the educational sphere.[2] Although less widely known in the United States, Marxist political economy constitutes a serious theoretical alternative to the neoclassical approach.[3] In the remainder of this chapter, I will argue that, although its results to date are incomplete, the political economic approach is certainly the more promising of the two.

A BRIEF EXPOSITION OF THE MARXIAN APPROACH

The Marxian approach to analyzing public education and school finance begins by insisting that educational developments are firmly rooted in the contradictory and antagonistic nature of capitalist society as a whole. According to Marxian political economy, capitalism faces two problematic tasks as it grows and develops: accumulation of capital and reproduction of the social relations of production. Capital accumulation requires, in the first instance, that capitalists be able to hire workers with appropriate skills and in requisite numbers. Having purchased the laboring capacities of those workers, the owners of capital must then try to organize production in such a fashion that the commodities produced have a value greater than the value of the labor power and physical means of production consumed during their production. After having extracted this surplus value during the labor process, capitalists then face the rigors of competition in the marketplace and the task of realizing surplus value in the form of money profits, interest, and rents. To the extent they succeed, capitalists can then accumulate their pecuniary gains as additional capital, and another cycle of capitalist production and exchange can begin (Marx 1967: part VII).

This recurring cycle of production, exchange, and capital accumulation could not continue, however, if the social relations of capitalist society were not simultaneously being reproduced. That is, the social class divisions that characterize capitalism must somehow be maintained, albeit on an expanded scale:

> [What] distinguishes it as a mode of production is its social organization; the great majority of producers do not own what they need to secure their livelihood. . . . This group, wage labour, has no claim on the product of its work; nor does it exercise any direct control over the choice of commodities to be produced, technologies to be used, or organization of work . . . The expansion of the capitalist mode of production—the accumulation process—is accompanied by the recruitment of new wage workers. (Bowles 1978: 785)

Analyzing in detail how these class divisions get reproduced is beyond the scope of this brief essay. What needs to be emphasized at this point, however, is the contradictory and antagonistic character of this dual process of capital accumulation and social reproduction. During the infancy of capitalism, for example,

> The extension of capitalist production, and particularly the factory system, undermined the role of the family as the major unit of both socialization and production. . . . Having risen to political power, the capitalist class sought a mechanism to ensure social control and political stability. The outcome, in virtually all capitalist countries, was the rise of mass education. (Bowles 1972: 38-40)

More generally, capital accumulation, which is central to the expansion and development of capitalist society, tends to undermine its social reproduction by creating a large, potentially class-conscious army of wage workers (Bowles and Gintis 1975: 78).

As James O'Connor has pointed out, this dual process of accumulation and reproduction has its reflections in the evolution of the state. More specifically,

> The capitalistic state must try to fulfill two basic and often mutually contradictory functions—*accumulation* and *legitimization*. . . . This

> means that the state must try to maintain or create the conditions in
> which profitable capital accumulation is possible. However, the state
> also must try to maintain or create the conditions for social harmony.
> (O'Connor 1973: 6).

In O'Connor's view, the rapid growth of the government sector during the
twentieth century and the simultaneous centralization of political power at
the federal level of government are both a cause and consequence of the
emergence of monopolistic industries organized by large-scale capital.

This is not to argue, of course, that the state either appears to be or is,
in fact, an instrument firmly in the grasp of monopoly capitalists. In a
liberal democracy, the state certainly appears at first glance to represent the
"general will." Beyond the realm of simple appearances, however, the state
actually exists as a "relatively autonomous" entity and cannot be reduced to
a mere tool of the dominant social class. As Shapiro (1980: 326) has put the
question,

> [The] political is [not] a mere reflection of the economic realm. . . . The
> policies of the state, at least in the short run, may indeed diverge from
> the interests of the dominant economic classes. In addition, the conflict
> among [and within] the dominant classes themselves requires a state
> that operates with some degree of autonomy.

What, precisely, is the role of public schooling in capitalist society?
There is no unanimity of opinion among Marxist political economists in
answer to this question. James O'Connor's account of the emergence of
monopoly capital in the United States during the present century emphasizes "the reorganization of the labor process and the free availability of
masses of technical-scientific workers, [which] permitted the rapid accelera-
tion of technology." Although O'Connor concedes that the rapid substitution of machines for workers during recent decades has created the need for
"education programs which . . . [help] to legitimate the system," his
theoretical emphasis is clearly on "technical-administrative knowledge" as
an increasingly important form of labor power and on public schooling as
the prime source of that expertise.[4]

Samuel Bowles and Herbert Gintis, on the other hand, certainly
recognize that schools transmit cognitive skills, but they argue that public
education is even more important in capitalist society as a means to
legitimate social inequality in all its forms, especially class divisions between owners and workers:

> Thus the educational system does much more than produce human
> capital. It segments the work force, forestalls the development of work-
> ing class consciousness, and legitimates economic inequality. . . .
> (Bowles and Gintis 1975: 77-78)[5]

This assessment of the legitimating role of public schools was not shared by Nicos Poulantzas, the late Marxist structuralist. According to Shapiro (1980: 324),

> Poulantzas, in fact, rejects the proposition that political and ideological socialization is restricted to certain specialized institutions such as the school, though he does see the school as particularly important in this respect. . . . Indeed, he says, for many it is the organization of work (not school) that effectively inculcates an acceptance of hierarchical social relations.

It is clear, then, that contemporary Marxists have not yet reached a consensus about the exact role of schooling in capitalist society. However, I believe there are several dicta political economists should observe as they pursue additional research on capitalism and schooling. First, public education must be viewed as one arena among several in which class struggle takes place and in which capitalist crises periodically erupt.[6] Second, in order to grasp concrete events and trends within the educational sphere, one needs to go beyond a simple two-class view of capitalist society. That is, one has to take account of shifting political coalitions among social classes and strata of classes in order to understand the historical evolution of public schooling. Third, as Sarup (1978: 176) and Giroux (1983: 257-60) have pointed out, one needs to view parents, students, and educators as *active* agents within the schools, not as passive components of an educational system that reproduces capitalist relations.[7] Finally, public education must be seen not just as a site for the reproduction of labor power but also as a major use of state revenue. This recognition suggests that tax politics plays a role in the evolution of public schooling. Let me illustrate these points by sketching an analysis of the school finance reforms that took place in the United States during the 1930s, a period of acute social and economic crisis that clearly revealed the antagonistic character of capitalist social relations.

SCHOOL FINANCE REFORM AND THE GREAT DEPRESSION

Over the course of the 1930s, public schooling in the United States underwent some striking changes, as the data in table 10-1 attest. Although total enrollment in U.S. public day schools remained almost the same from 1930 to 1940, there was a 50 percent increase in public secondary school enrollment during the decade. Accompanying this stagnation in total enrollment and shift toward secondary schooling were some significant developments in school finance. Over the course of the 1930s, real spending on public schools grew by only 14 percent. However, federal and state

TABLE 10.1. U.S. Public Schools during the 1930s

	1930	1940
Total enrollment	25.68 million	25.43 million
Secondary enrollment	4.40 million	6.60 million
Real spending (1958 dollars)	$4.70 billion	$5.34 billion
School employment	1.173 million	1.327 million
Pupil-teacher ratios		
• elementary	33.2	32.7
• secondary	20.6	22.0
State aid share	16.9%	30.3%
Federal aid share	0.4%	1.8%

Sources: Calculated from U.S. Bureau of the Census (1975a: 224, 368, and 373; 1975b: 1104).

grants to help finance local public schools grew substantially in relative importance during the Depression years. In 1930, the federal and state shares of public school revenues averaged 0.4 and 16.9 percent, respectively. Ten years later, the federal share had risen to 1.8 percent, whereas the state share had risen sharply to 30.3 percent. Hence, although federal aid to public education did expand during this period, it was educational grants from state governments to local districts that grew more dramatically.

These decennial data do not reveal, however, the acute crisis that confronted U.S. public education at the beginning of the New Deal. Between 1932 and 1934, real spending on public elementary and secondary schools dropped precipitously from $5.41 to $4.08 billion per year, a drop of nearly *one-quarter* in only two years.[8] During that same period, total enrollment grew slightly, and hence real expenditure per student dropped from $206 to $154 per annum, measured in 1958 prices. This fiscal contraction was accompanied by reduced employment in public education. Not surprisingly, then, average class size rose at both the elementary and secondary levels of public schooling between 1932 and 1934, as reported in table 10-2.

What sense can Marxian political economy make of these educational trends? In order to answer that question, one must look briefly at several important developments in U.S. capitalism prior to the Great Depression. Perhaps the most important of these developments was the emergence of large, monopolistic corporations around and after the turn of the century. As Richard Edwards (1975: 429) has pointed out,

TABLE 10.2. Fiscal Crisis of U.S. Public Schools, 1932–1934

	1930	1940
Total enrollment	26.28 million	26.43 million
Secondary enrollment	5.14 million	5.67 million
Real spending (1958 dollars)	$5.41 billion	$4.08 billion
School employment	1.171 million	1.145 million
Pupil-teacher ratios		
• elementary	33.0	33.5
• secondary	22.2	24.9
State aid share	19.9%	23.4%
Federal aid share	0.4%	1.2%

Sources: Calculated from U.S. Bureau of the Census (1975a: 224, 368, and 373; 1975b: 1104).

> [Big] business has passed through two quite different phases. The initial period . . . (roughly 1890 to 1920) was a time of considerable instability for big corporations. By the early twenties—certainly by 1923—the system had "stabilized," and relatively little change [in the identity of the leading corporations] has occurred since then.

This entrenchment of large, monopolistic corporations by the 1920s had profound implications for the contours of social life in the United States. It contributed, for example, to dramatic changes in urban form:

> The first major expansion of downtown central business districts occurred in the 1920s. Downtown office space in the ten largest cities increased between 1920 and 1930 by 3,000 percent. . . . Huge corporations had not consolidated their monopoly control over their industries until after World War I. Once they gained stable market control, they would begin to organize that control [and] . . .separate administrative functions [spatially] from the production process itself. (Gordon 1978: 51).

That is, the advent of a corporate stage of capital accumulation entailed the growth of far-flung bureaucracies to oversee the production and exchange of a growing mass of commodities.

The increasingly bureaucratic character of capital accumulation during the early part of this century induced, in turn, a rapid change in the structure of occupations. Between 1910 and 1930, for instance, the number of clerical workers in the United States more than doubled, increasing from roughly 1.9 million to 4.25 million employees. As a result of this rapid employment growth, clerical workers constituted 9 percent of the labor force in 1930, compared to 5.1 percent in 1910 (Glenn and Feldberg 1979: 55).

During that same era, a constellation of occupations that some theorists have identified as a "new middle class" or "professional-managerial class" also grew quite rapidly. According to the estimates of Val Burris (1980: 23, 30) this corporate army of managers, supervisors, technicians, and sales personnel tended to supplant self-employed farmers, artisans, and other independent producers at a rapid pace between World War I and the Great Depression. In 1910, the self-employed accounted for 29.2 percent of the U.S. labor force, whereas the "new middle class" constituted only 7.3 percent of the work force. By 1930, on the other hand, the percentages were 23.2 and 11.3, respectively. Just as important, the absolute number of members of the "new middle class" more than doubled between 1910 and 1930, from 2.5 to 5.3 million employees.[9]

These dramatic shifts in occupational structure required, in turn, the rapid expansion of public elementary and secondary education in the United States during the two decades prior to the Great Crash. As noted earlier in this chapter, secondary enrollment exploded between 1910 and 1930, from 915,000 to 4.4 million pupils in only two decades. During that same interval of U.S. history, elementary enrollment expanded a bit more modestly from 16.9 to 20.6 million students. This enrollment growth reflects demographic trends during that era to some degree. The number of U.S. residents between the ages of 5 and 14 years grew from nearly 19 million in 1910 to more than 24.5 million in 1930. However, the fraction of young people between the ages of 5 and 17 attending school also rose during that period, from roughly 80 to 90 percent (U.S. Bureau of the Census 1975a: 10, 368). This increase in the school enrollment rate presumably reflected the dramatic shifts in the social class and occupational composition of the U.S. population during that era.[10]

This rapid expansion of public schooling was financed by a massive increase in real educational expenditure. In 1918, real spending on U.S. public elementary and secondary schools stood at $1.52 billion, measured in 1958 dollars. By 1932, that figure had more than tripled to $5.41 billion. School expenditures dramatically outpaced the expansion of gross national product during that same period, rising from 1.0 to 3.75 percent of GNP (U.S Bureau of the Census 1975a: 224, 373).

The mode of financing this enormous increase in educational outlays reveals a great deal about the balance of class forces in the United States from the end of World War I to the Great Depression. In contrast with a prewar period of trade union militancy and aggressive socialist politics, the U.S. working class was generally on the defensive during the 1920s. For example,

During the 1920s and the early 1930s membership in labor unions in the United States diminished to the point where contemporary observers were seriously asking whether the union movement would survive another decade. . . . The American Federation of Labor had for the first time failed to grow during a period of [relatively rapid capital accumulation and] prosperity. . . . (Yates 1981: 220-21, 236fn.)

In fact, AFL membership fell from around 4 million in 1921 to about 2 million by 1933.

The generally defensive posture of the U.S. working class during the 1920s helps to explain the particular mode of financing that was used to expand public schooling during that period. With the passage of the Smith-Hughes Act in 1917, one might have expected a greatly expanded role for federal aid to public education in subsequent years. In fact, there were legislative initiatives in the U.S. Congress that tried to do precisely that:

> Some additional support for federal aid to education was gained as a result of the Red Scare during and after World War I. Many conservatives believed that . . . support for the communist movements in Europe was caused in part by a high level of illiteracy among immigrants and native American workers.

This perceived threat from radical ideologies helped to motivate the Smith-Townsend Federal Aid to Education Bill, variants of which were submitted to the Congress between 1918 and 1925. The bill was never reported out of committee, however, in part because of spirited opposition by the U.S. Chamber of Commerce and other business lobbying groups (Owen 1974: 121-22).

This capitalist opposition to federal aid to public education probably reflected a distaste for progressive reforms in the federal tax system, which had been enacted just before and during World War I, largely in response to populist and socialist political agitation. The federal tax on corporate profits began in 1909 and was soon followed by federal levies on individual incomes and estates in 1913 and 1916, respectively. As King has pointed out, these taxes had explicitly redistributive implications:

> America's [1917] entry into the war. . .supplied the pretext for an enormous expansion of the income tax. . . . [T]he dominant political coalition in the Congress. . .was concerned primarily with preventing war profiteering and with forcing the wealthy to bear a just share of expenses. . . . There was still considerable feeling in the country that this was a rich man's war, entered into for imperialist gain and windfall profits. The example of the Russian Revolution was a caution for those who wished that. . .the cost of the war [could be] shifted downward. (King 1983: 20-22)

As a result of these radical popular sentiments, the federal tax on individual incomes was steeply progressive in 1918: Whereas wage earners paid little or no tax, the effective rate levied on those with $1 million of net income exceeded 70 percent (see table 10-3).

TABLE 10.3. Effective Federal Tax Rates on Individual Incomes

	Net Income Group			
	$3,000	$10,000	$100,000	$1,000,000
1918	1.2%	7.8%	35.0%	70.3%
1920	0.8	5.6	31.2	66.3
1922	0.0	4.6	30.1	55.1
1924	0.0	1.4	22.5	43.0
1926	0.0	0.8	16.0	24.1
1928	0.0	0.8	15.7	24.1
1930	0.0	0.8	15.7	24.1
1932	0.0	4.2	30.0	57.1
1934	0.0	3.4	30.2	57.1
1936	0.0	3.4	32.0	67.8

Note: Four exemptions are assumed. Effective tax rate = tax liability divided by net income.
Source: U.S. Bureau of the Census (1975b: 1112).

The end of World War I witnessed a vigorous capitalist campaign to reduce federal income and profit taxes. As two contemporary analysts of the fiscal politics of that period later recalled,

> The issue [of tax revision] was really pushed. . .by business men who began forming organizations to spread their ideas, chiefly in opposition to the [wartime] excess-profits tax. One of the first of such groups was the Business Men's National Tax Committee which had as its goal the substitution of a sales tax for the excess-profits tax. (Blakey and Blakey 1940: 190)

Several years later, an organization known originally as the American Bankers' League, but later renamed the American Taxpayer's League, began "to spread propaganda against the federal estate tax" (Blakey and Blakey 1940: 253-54).

Despite these capitalist initiatives, which were frequently under the political leadership of Treasury Secretary Andrew Mellon, there was no fiscal counterrevolution during the 1920s. Over the course of the decade, there was indeed a steady erosion of the progressivity of the federal income tax, as table 10-3 documents. However, the conservative plan to enact a national sales tax was defeated, and the federal taxes on incomes, profits, and estates were retained. On the eve of the Great Depression, the bulk of federal tax revenues were still collected by taxing individual incomes and corporate profits, and the income tax was still essentially a levy on the wealthy.[11] Hence, although many capitalists favored the rapid expansion of public schooling after World War I in order to combat "subversive" ideologies and to train the clerks, managers, and technicians required to staff burgeoning corporate empires, they probably also feared the use of a relatively progressive federal tax system to fund that educational expansion. Since the working class was on the political defensive during the 1920s, its organizations and representatives were in no position to demand increased federal funding of public education. Thus, the federal share of local public school receipts remained below one-half of one percent as late as 1932.

What means were employed, then, to finance the educational expansion that preceded the Great Depression? A combination of increased local taxation and additional educational aid from state government provided most of the funds. In 1918, state grants and local revenues provided $243 million and $122 billion, respectively, to local public school budgets (measured in 1958 dollars). By 1930, state aid and local taxes contributed $738 million and $3.50 billion, respectively, in dollars of comparable value (U.S. Bureau of the Census 1975a: 224, 373).

Upon whose shoulders did these state and local taxes fall? Answering that question requires a brief look at the typical state and local tax systems of the time. Although some state governments did levy taxes on corporate profits, individual incomes, and gifts or bequests of wealth during the 1920s, those relatively progressive taxes averaged less than 30 percent of state tax revenues during that decade. Levies on retail purchases and payrolls, on the other hand, provided 37 percent of state revenues in 1922 and nearly 51 percent in 1927. State property taxes provided another 33 percent, on average, in 1922 and over 21 percent in 1927.[12] Throughout the period, the overwhelming bulk of local taxes to support public schooling came from property taxation (Musgrave and Musgrave 1976: 207).

TABLE 10.4. **Sources of Federal Tax Revenue (billions of current dollars)**

	Total Revenue	Individual Income	Corporate Income	Excises
1929	$2.94	$1.10	$1.24	$0.54
1930	3.04	1.15	1.26	0.57
1931	2.43	0.83	1.03	0.52
1932	1.56	0.43	0.63	0.45
1933	1.62	0.35	0.39	0.84
1934	2.67	0.42	0.40	1.29
1935	3.30	0.53	0.58	1.36
1936	3.52	0.67	0.75	1.55

Source: U.S. Bureau of the Census (1975b: 1107).

Analyzing the exact incidence of these taxes among various income groups and social classes raises a host of theoretical and empirical issues that cannot be pursued in this chapter. However, one can speculate that additional federal taxes on high personal incomes, estates and gifts, and corporate profits would have been borne largely by the owners of monopoly capital.[13] State and local taxes on payrolls, consumption, and real estate, on the other hand, were ultimately paid by industrial and office workers, farmers, shopkeepers, and other petty proprietors to a great extent.[14] Hence, because of the political weakness of the working class and independent producers during the 1920s, it is highly probable that monopoly capitalists managed to impose much of the expense of educational expansion upon subordinate social classes, thereby facilitating monopolistic accumulation of capital.

The onset of the Great Depression in 1929, however, brought this process of capital accumulation to a virtual halt. At the bottom of the Depression in March 1933, industrial production had fallen 37 percent from its 1929 level, business investment spending had nearly ceased, and measured unemployment stood at 25 percent of the civilian labor force (Naples, Riddle, and Rose 1981: 17). In addition to these oft-cited developments, tenant evictions, farm foreclosures, and cuts in industrial wage rates also affected masses of U.S. citizens as well.

These calamitous economic events eventually resulted in a fiscal crisis for local public education. According to one contemporary observer,

> During the first two years of the depression the schools did business about as usual. By September, 1931, the strain was beginning to tell. Salary cuts [for teachers] were appearing even in large towns, and the number of pupils per teacher had definitely increased. Building programs had been postponed. In a few communities school terms had been considerably shortened. . . . During 1932-33 the deflation gathered momentum so rapidly that many communities had to close their schools. By the end of last March [1933] nearly a third of a million children were out of school for that reason.

Hundreds of other school districts would have been forced to close as well if their teachers had not accepted (often worthless) tax anticipation warrants instead of cashable paychecks (Shannon 1960: 94-95).

This financial crisis of public education reflected the high degree of dependence of school budgets on state and, especially, local property taxation. Because of falling farm incomes, numerous business bankruptcies, mass unemployment, and pervasive wage cuts, many taxpayers simply did not have sufficient money income with which to pay their property tax bills. Testifying before a U.S. Senate subcommittee in 1933, Professor Sumner Slichter pointed to "a steadily rising ratio of delinquent [property] taxes throughout the country. In fact, delinquency ratios of from 20 to 30 percent are not unusual" (Shannon 1960: 37). Hence, the general economic crisis of the early 1930s resulted in widespread nonpayment of property taxes, which, in turn, led to a severe fiscal crisis for public schooling in the United States.[15]

This fiscal crisis of public education was particularly acute in Chicago, where the near collapse of industrial production resulted in an unemployment rate of roughly 50 percent by 1932. A group of local bankers and industrialists formed the Committee on Public Expenditures to lobby for severe cuts in the city's school budget. Under capitalist pressure, the Chicago school board acted in July 1933 to cut public educational costs:

> [It] voted to discontinue the city's junior college, [and] to abolish the junior high schools. . . . [and] 50 percent of the district's kindergartens. . . . [The board also] dismissed 1,400 teachers from the system. . .and the high school teaching load was increased to seven classes a day. (Wrigley 1982: 218)

In addition, the salaries of all teachers were to be cut by shortening the school year by a month.[16]

According to Julia Wrigley (1982: 267), there is evidence that business groups in other cities also mobilized to cut school budgets, presumably to reduce their property taxes during a period of severely depressed profitability. The U.S. Chamber of Commerce called for 20 different educational cutbacks, including shortening the school day and school year, increasing class sizes, abolishing kindergartens, cutting teachers' salaries, and imposing fees on public high school students. These cuts in the quality and even the availability of public schooling during the early 1930s would not have posed an immediate problem for U.S. capitalism if producing more graduates had been the only responsibility of local school systems. After all, the Depression itself had swollen the ranks of the reserve army of the unemployed, so there was no current need for large numbers of fresh graduates to fill job vacancies. There were large numbers of chemists, engineers, teachers, and even business executives who had been trained in earlier years and who were seeking work in the early 1930s (Shannon 1960: 90-92).

The fiscal crisis that confronted public education in 1933 required action, not because shortages of educated labor were imminent, but rather because the legitimacy of capitalist social relations was coming into question. During the winter of 1931, for example, crowds of hundreds of unemployed workers looted grocery stores in Minneapolis and Oklahoma City. During the summer of 1932, World War I veterans marched on Washington to demand federal bonus payments. At the same time, militant farmers in the upper Midwest tried to block food shipments in an attempt to raise depressed farm prices (Shannon 1960: 119-120, 123). In Ohio and Pennsylvania, the

Unemployed Leagues fought tenant evictions and claimed 150,000 members in early 1933 (Rosenzweig 1975; 58-60). By 1934, two years before the Congress of Industrial Organizations was formed, a wave of labor strikes occurred, often with communist leadership (Naples, Riddell, and Rose 1981:18). As David Shannon (1960: 111) has assessed that period,

> Fear of a revolution was widespread during the last several months of President Hoover's administration, and much of the politics of the period can be understood fully only by viewing political events against the background of anxiety about violent revolt. The vigor with which the army dispersed the Bonus Expeditionary Force from Washington in the summer of 1932, for example, had its roots in revolutionary fear.

However, it was not simply general unrest among small farmers, unemployed workers, and veterans that prompted school finance reform during the 1930s. There was also popular resistance to the *particular* educational cutbacks that some business leaders were seeking. This resistance was very well organized in Chicago, for example:

> [R]epresentatives of about 40 civic associations met to create a . . . committee to organize . . . against the [school] board. The new committee . . . included members from the Women's City Club, . . . the Chicago Bar Association, [and] the Cook County League of Women Voters. . . . The crisis of the budget cuts brought the teachers and the civic associations together. . . . [They] worked together to blanket the city with . . . nearly two million leaflets . . . [and] called a mammoth rally nine days after the board announced the cutbacks. An estimated 25,000 people jammed into the Chicago Stadium. (Wrigley 1982: 227-28)

The Chicago Federation of Labor also denounced the board's budget slashing. As a result of these protests by labor and professional organizations, the school board was forced to rescind some of its planned cuts in educational services.[17]

With general unrest in much of the country and particular instances of resistance to educational cutbacks, the state had to take action to relieve the acute fiscal crisis facing public education. Although the means to resolve this crisis of educational finance were not predestined, it appears that members of the ruling class had already outlined a strategy for doing so immediately after the Great Crash. In 1930, the National Industrial Conference Board had published a critique of state and local property taxation that recommended less dependence on that particular source of government revenue.[18] In the eyes of the Conference Board (1930: 8-9),

> The general property tax system has obviously and seriously broken down on the administrative side. . . . [No] system has yet been devised whereby substantially all intangible property can be placed on the

> assessment rolls. . . . [A] most serious factor . . .is the failure of state legislatures to provide for competent and adequately supported [tax] administration. This administrative defect is particularly evident when local officials without necessary technical training are required to place values on interstate railways and other complicated corporation properties.

The disdain these wealthy industrialists harbored for "the local point of view in assessment and collection of the local property tax" was not just a result of the alleged technical incompetence of assessors and tax collectors, however. The Conference Board's report also mentioned serious *political* issues involving state and local property taxation, especially the classification of taxable properties into different categories and the application of differential tax rates to those categories.

Throughout much of the nineteenth century, the principle that the values of all nonexempt properties should be taxed at a uniform rate had governed property taxation in most sections of the country. By 1930, however, only 17 states, most of them nonindustrial, had embodied that uniformity principle in their constitutions (Conference Board 1930: 95). By 1927, on the other hand, 31 states had adopted constitutional provisions that permitted at least partial classification of property (Benson 1965: 63). This erosion of property tax uniformity must have been threatening to the ruling class during an era of increasing popular militancy and resentment against monopoly capital: There was a risk of popular initiatives to raise more local tax revenues and thereby relieve the fiscal crises of municipal governments and school districts by taxing corporate properties at punitive rates.[19]

It is not surprising, then, that the Conference Board proposed "that less reliance be placed on these taxes in the future" and advocated "administrative centralization with provision for central supervision and control of local [tax] administrators." These proposed reforms amounted to less than a complete repudiation of local property taxation, however. In fact, opined the Conference Board's tycoons,

> Property taxation may be too important as a revenue producer to disappear from the fiscal systems of state and local government. . . . Property taxes must continue to occupy an important place in the systems of the future. (Conference Board 1930: v, 10)

This commitment to property taxation probably reflected an awareness that classification, and even exemption, of various categories of property would be to the *advantage* of monopoly capital once the contemporary political mobilization of industrial workers and small farmers had subsided.[20]

Three years after the Conference Board tabled its recommendations on property tax reform, the National Survey of School Finance published its final report in 1933. Originally funded in early 1931 by the U.S. Congress, the Survey was funded during its last two years by the Rockefeller-endowed General Education Board.[21] The report of the National Survey correctly observed that,

> In all but a few states the actual minimum status of education is determined by the economic ability of local districts to support schools rather than by social needs for education. This fact has resulted in vast areas in American education where the educational offering is distinctly inferior. (Mort 1933: 3)

After conceding that enormous fiscal disparities among local school systems resulted from reliance on local property taxation, the report's author went on to blame "lack of state action" for the persistence of those inequalities. That is, the National Survey did not envision a major increase in *federal* aid to local public education in order to ease its fiscal crisis or reduce inequalities in public school finance. Rather, concluded the Survey's final report,

> The task ahead is not to bring all states into the same pattern of practice. It is rather to have each sovereign state accept responsibility for meeting attainable standards acceptable to its own people and for meeting those standards in ways which are in harmony with their thinking. (Mort 1933:3)

Thus, the National Survey called for state aid programs generous enough so that local school districts within each state could afford to provide some minimum standard of public schooling to their pupils.

Although federalist political philosophy may have played some role in forming these recommendations, the prospective mode of financing expanded state aid programs probably played a more significant role. During the Great Depression, state legislatures were under competitive pressure to make regressive tax concessions in an attempt to keep private capital within their borders. Because of the combined effect of these tax concessions and the direct impact of the Depression on business profits, state taxes became even more regressive by the end of the 1930s. Between 1927 and 1940, for instance, the proportion of state tax revenue from levies on corporate profits fell from 5.3 to 3.5 percent. At the same time, state duties on estates and gifts fell from 18.9 to 10.3 percent. Even more dramatically, state property tax revenues fell from 21.2 to 5.9 percent of total receipts. State sales and excise tax revenues rose, however, from 42.8 to 51 percent by 1940 (Musgrave and Musgrave 1976: 207).

At the federal level of taxation, however, political developments during the early 1930s were far more threatening to monopoly capital. A congressional bill to reduce the federal deficit by enacting a national sales tax was defeated in 1932, largely because of opposition from the agrarian wing of the Democratic Party (King 1983: 30-31). The Revenue Act of 1932 imposed a graduated gift tax, doubled the rates on the estate tax, and doubled the effective tax rate on high personal incomes. The Revenue Act of 1934 raised the levies on estates and gifts once again and lowered the tax rates on middle-income households (Blakey and Blakey 1940: 332-34, table 10.3). Tax measures such as these were certainly not a source of comfort to the wealthy.[22] Hence, monopoly capital preferred resolution of the fiscal crisis of local public education by increasing state aid programs rather than by initiating federal aid programs.

Over the course of the Great Depression, the strategy for school finance reform formulated by monopoly capital was the one actually put into practice, but not without some political struggle. By 1934, more than 25 bills calling for more federal aid to public education had been introduced in the U.S. Congress. In 1935 alone, 30 to 40 such aid bills were filed, but all were successfully defeated by conservative opponents despite political support for additional federal aid from such mass organizations as the American Legion, American Farm Bureau Federation, and National Education Association (Munger and Fenno 1962: 28-29; West 1980: 11).

The political victory of monopoly capital is reflected in the evolution of public school budgets after 1933. Between 1934 and 1940, local funds increased from $1.37 billion to $1.54 billion, a 12.5 percent gain. During that same period, educational aid to local school districts from state governments increased from $423 million to $684 million, a gain of nearly 62 percent. Federal aid, on the other hand, remained a paltry source of public school funds, rising from $21.5 million in 1934 to $39.8 million in 1940 (U.S. Bureau of the Census 1975a: 373). The reasons for this political victory of monopoly capital are not transparent. Perhaps states differed substantially in the *severity* of the educational crises they faced and in the degree of political mobilization of farmers, professionals and workers. To the extent those interstate differences existed, popular efforts to increase federal aid must have been blunted and school finance reform in particular states encouraged.

In any event, the fiscal recovery of public education in the United States after 1933 was financed by a partnership between state and local governments, not by an expanded role for the federal government. Federal financing of public schools was not to become a significant factor until the 1960s, by which time the federal tax on corporate profits had been weakened by investment tax credits and other "reform" measures and the federal income tax had been converted into a mass tax falling primarily on wage and salary earners.

CONCLUSION

Let me end with a succinct conclusion. American society has gone through several periods of history when major changes in the scale, organization, and mode of financing public education took place. Those historial periods have usually been marked by political conflict and by fundamental changes in economic structure. Orthodox economists have tried to grasp those developments by applying concepts such as "human capital" and "external benefits," which were originally conceived by neoclassical theorists. These interpretive efforts have largely failed, however, because of the methodological and conceptual flaws of neoclassical economics.

Marx's method of historical materialism, on the other hand, provides a superior foundation upon which to construct an interpretation of the evolution of public school finance, or of any other social phenomena for that matter. Rather than relying on notions of static equilibrium and the abstract individual, Marxian political economy focuses on the social relations that link concrete individuals and the contradictory character of those relationships. As Marx himself (Tucker 1978: 4) put the issue,

> [Legal] relations as well as forms of state are to be grasped neither from themselves nor from the so-called general development of the human mind, but rather have their roots in the material conditions of life. . . . The mode of production of material life conditions the social, political and intellectual life process in general.

Once this methodological premise has become more widely accepted, real progress will be made in understanding school finance reform, in particular, and social evolution, in general.

NOTES

1. This is not to deny, of course, that the *quality* of secondary education enjoyed by students varies enormously by region, race, and social class.

2. For examples of this theoretical approach, see Becker (1975) and Break (1980).

3. For examples, see O'Connor (1973) and Bowles and Gintis (1976).

4. O'Connor (1973:101, 111-15). In this respect, O'Connor's analysis of education sounds similar to that of the human capital theorists. In fact, he refers to state expenditure on public schooling as a social investment in "human capital," apparently not recognizing the unscientific character of that concept.

5. For additional examples, see Bowles (1978: 784) and Bowles and Gintis (1976: 11, 102-3).

6. On education as an arena of class struggle, see Bowles and Gintis (1976: 11-13). For two critiques that argue that they sometimes forget the centrality of class struggle, see Featherstone (1977: 139-49) and Gorelick (1977: 20-36).

7. To quote Giroux (1983: 257-59): "[R]adical educators have argued that the main functions of schools are the reproduction of the dominant ideology, its forms of knowledge, and the distribution of skills needed to reproduce the social division of labor. . . . But . . . [r]eproduction theorists have overemphasized the idea of domination in their analyses. . . . By downplaying the importance of human agency and the notion of resistance, reproduction theories offer little hope for challenging and changing the repressive features of schooling."

8. These figures were calculated from U.S. census data on nominal spending levels and GNP deflators for corresponding years. Since the price level for all goods and services included in the GNP probably varied in a fashion different from the cost of educational services, these figures should be seen as approximations.

9. Whether these salaried occupations, which staff corporate and state bureaucracies, constitute a distinct social class or not has been a topic of keen debate among contemporary Marxists. Compare the various essays in Walker (1970).

10. To what extent this rising school enrollment rate reflected political initiatives by corporate leaders who needed a growing pool of educated labor and to what extent it reflected a growing popular awareness that clerical and professional occupations offered opportunities for future employment is not immediately obvious. Miriam Cohen (1977: 120-43) reports that Italian-American women in New York City "were attending school on a more regular basis [by the 1940s,] and larger numbers were staying on into the high-school years. In the late thirties, a decline in truancy took place both in the poorest neighborhoods and in the more economically stable communities. . . . [I]t seems likely that Italians were beginning to understand the changing [occupational] situation and acted accordingly by keeping their daughters in school so that they could train for white-collar work."

11. See tables 10-3 and 10-4. The reasons for the slow pace of fiscal reaction during the 1920s are unclear and deserve additional research. One apparent reason is that the business community was sometimes divided on issues of fiscal "reform." Whereas the Business Men's National Tax Committee favored a national sales tax, for example, other groups such as the U.S. Chamber of Commerce and National Association of Retail Grocers opposed such a plan. Another probable reason is that, although they were declining economically during the 1920s, small farmers were still a potent political force in the United States. They led the fight, for instance, to retain the excess-profits tax after World War I (Blakey and Blakey 1940: 190-91).

12. There were, of course, some notable exceptions to these national averages, and *differences* among the states in tax structure would have to be taken into account in order to fully analyze the school finance trends of the 1920s and 1930s. In 1929, for example, New York collected over 17 percent of its revenues from income taxes, whereas the comparable fraction for all state governments was only 4.6 percent. Texas, on the other hand, raised more than 2 percent of its revenue by *poll taxes*, whereas the comparable national average was practically zero (U.S. Bureau of the Census 1933: 6-7). Detailed analysis of these interstate differences in tax structure is beyond the scope of this chapter, however.

13. This assumption about the incidence of the tax on corporate profits is debatable. However, as Tresch (1981: 376) has concluded,

> A large number of researchers have tried to determine, empirically, the incidence of the U.S. corporate income tax. Their results could not possibly be more divergent, ranging all the way from Richard Musgrave's finding that the tax is borne *at least* 100 percent by the consumers of corporate output to Arnold Harberger's estimate that . . . corporate shareholders almost certainly bear virtually the entire burden of the tax.

In the absence of a scientific consensus on this question, I believe one must recognize the historic opposition of corporate leaders to profits taxation. This hostility probably reflects *ex ante* apprehension on the part of individual capitalists that they will be unable to shift corporate tax liabilities to workers and consumers, whatever the *ex post* outcome in the aggregate turns out to be.

14. Evidence in support of the hypothesis that farmers and other landowners bore a substantial share of the growing property tax burden of the 1920s can be found in Jensen (1931: 69-73): "[So] far as the evidence goes, it supports the hypothesis that the increases in taxes between 1919 and 1924 were rather completely capitalized. . . . [When] the taxes increase, the capital value is depressed so that the net current return, clear of taxes, remains at 2.3 percent."

15. There is some evidence that property tax delinquency ratios had been rising before 1929, one reflection of the contradictions in the accumulation process of the 1920s, which eventually culminated in the Depression (Jensen 1931: 319). Wrigley (1982: 208) reports that Chicago's property tax system was already in crisis at the time of the Great Crash.

16. The educational crisis in New York City was also quite severe. According to Hoffman (1983: 49), "The greater cuts in city employment were between 1932 and 1934, when the [municipal] labor force was trimmed by 6 percent. The greatest cuts were in the areas of education and health. . . ."

17. How widespread these forms of popular resistance were and how political coalitions to resist budget cuts differed from place to place are areas for future research. Julia Wrigley's case study of Chicago is a fine model for research on other cities and regions.

18. In the preface to this study, the Conference Board (1930: vi-vii) acknowledged "the co-operation and suggestions of its Advisory Committee on Taxation and Public Finance, composed of men of special knowledge and broad experience in this field. . . ." They included a Yale political economy professor; representatives of the National Lumber Manufacturing Association, the National Manufacturers Association, and the New York State Farm Bureau; and top executives of Prentice-Hall, Union Carbide, General Motors, General Electric, and the Delaware and Hudson Railroad.

19. One piece of evidence to support this point is the almost obsessive attention the authors of the Conference Board report paid to the property classification scheme that had been adopted in Minnesota in 1907 and that was still effective in 1930. It provided for assessment of mining company properties at 50 percent of full value but all other properties at various assessment ratios below that level. This and other tax laws aimed specifically at the mining companies resulted in what the Conference Board termed "a peculiarly burdensome system of supertaxation" (Conference Board 1930: 18-19, 25).

20. After having commented nervously on the property classification schemes of Minnesota, Montana, and North Dakota, the authors of the Conference Board report then mentioned uncritically that at least eight states exempted manufacturing establishments from either state or local property taxation (Conference Board 1930: 29-30).

21. The direct role of capitalists in drafting this report is less obvious than that of the Conference Board. However, the Survey's Board of Consultants included a banker and a railroad president in addition to seven university professors, four educational administrators, three state budget directors, and the research director of the National Education Association (Mort 1933: iii).

22. On the other hand, one should not exaggerate the extent to which changes in the federal tax system during the early 1930s were actually progressive. As King (1983: 31-33) has emphasized, federal receipts from income and profit taxation fell because of shrinking tax bases, whereas federal *excise* revenues grew sharply during those years. (See also table 10-4 in this chapter.) However, as Blakey and Blakey (1940: 366-68) have pointed out, President Roosevelt was under political pressure from populists such as Senator Huey Long to adopt the *rhetoric* of income and wealth redistribution during the midst of the Depression. In a 1935 tax

message to the Congress, Roosevelt stated, "Our revenue laws have operated in many ways to the unfair advantage of the few, and they have done little to prevent an unjust concentration of wealth and economic power."

REFERENCES

Becker, Gary S. 1975. *Human Capital*. Chicago: University of Chicago Press.

Benson, George C.S. 1965. *The American Property Tax: Its History, Administration, and Economic Impact*. Claremont, California: Institute for Studies in Federalism and the Lincoln School of Public Finance.

Blakey, Roy G. and Gladys C. Blakey. 1940. *The Federal Income Tax*. New York: Longmans, Green and Co.

Bowles, Samuel. 1972. Unequal Education and the Reproduction of the Social Division of Labor. In, *Schooling in a Corporate Society*, Martin Carnoy (ed.), pp. 36-64. New York: David McKay.

———— . 1978. Capitalist Development and Educational Structure. *World Development* June; 783-96.

Bowles, Samuel and Herbert Gintis. 1975. The Problem with Human Capital Theory—A Marxian Critique. *American Economic Association Proceedings* May: 74-82.

———— . 1976. *Schooling in Capitalist America.*. New York: Basic Books.

———— . 1980. *Financing Government in a Federal System*. Washington: Brookings Institution.

Burris, Val. 1980. Capital Accumulation and the Rise of the New Middle Class. *Review of Radical Political Economics* Spring: 17-34.

Cohen, Miriam. 1977. Italian-American Women in New York City, 1900-1950: Work and School. In *Class, Sex, and the Woman Worker*, Milton Cantor and Bruce Laurie (eds.) pp. 120-43. Westport, Connecticut: Greenwood Press.

Conference Board. 1930. *State and Local Taxation of Property*. New York: National Industrial Conference Board.

Edwards, Richard C. 1975. Stages in Corporate Stability and the Risks of Corporate Failure. *Journal of Economic History* June: 428-57.

Featherstone, Joseph. 1977. Commentary: Symposium on Schooling in Capitalist America. *History of Education Quarterly* Summer: 139-49.

Giroux, Henry. 1983. Theories of Reproduction and Resistance in the New Sociology of Education: A Critical Analysis. *Harvard Educational Review* August: 257-93.

Glenn, Evelyn Nakano and Roslyn L. Feldberg. 1979. Proletarianizing Clerical Work: Technology and Organizational Control in the Office. In, *Case Studies on the Labor Process*, Andrew Zimbalist (ed.). New York: Monthly Review Press.

Gordon, David M. 1978. Capitalist Development and the History of American Cities. In, *Marxism and the Metropolis*, William K. Tabb and Larry Sawers (eds.). New York: Oxford University Press.

Gorelick, Sherry. 1977. Undermining Hierarchy: Problems of Schooling in Capitalist America. *Monthly Review* October: 20-36.

Hoffman, Joan. 1983. Urban Squeeze Plays: New York City Crises of the 1930s and 1970s. *Review of Radical Political Economics* Summer: 29-57.

Jensen, Jens Peter. 1931. *Property Taxation in the United States*. Chicago: University of Chicago Press.

King, Ronald F. 1983. From Redistributive to Hegemonic Logic: The Transformation of American Tax Politics, 1894-1963. *Politics & Society* 12 (1): 1-52.

Marx, Karl. 1967. *Capital, volume 1*. New York: International Publishers.

Mort, Paul R. 1933. *State Support for Public Education*. Washington: American Council on Education.

Munger, Frank J. and Richard F. Fenno, Jr. 1962. *National Politics and Federal Aid to Education*. Syracuse, New York: Syracuse University Press.

Musgrave, Richard A. and Peggy B. Musgrave. 1976. *Public Finance in Theory and Practice*. New York: McGraw-Hill.

Naples, Michele, Tom Riddell, and Nancy Rose. 1981. The Crisis in Perspective. In, *Crisis in the Public Sector: A Reader*, Economics Education Project (eds.). New York: Monthly Review Press and Union for Radical Political Economics.

O'Connor, James. 1973. *The Fiscal Crisis of the State*. New York: St. Martin's Press.

Owen, John D. 1974. *School Inequality and the Welfare State*. Baltimore: Johns Hopkins University Press.

Rosenzweig, Roy. 1975. Radicals and the Jobless: The Musteites and the Unemployed Leagues, 1932-1936. *Labor History* Winter: 52-77.

Sarup, Madan. 1978. *Marxism and Education*. London: Routledge & Kegan Paul.

Shannon, David A. 1960. *The Great Depression*. Englewood Cliffs, New Jeresey: Prentice-Hall.

Shapiro, H. Svi. 1980. Education and the State in Capitalist Society: Aspects of the Sociology of Nicos Poulantzas. *Harvard Educational Review* August: 321-31.

Tresch, Richard W. 1981. *Public Finance: A Normative Theory*. Plano, Texas: Business Publications, Inc.

Trow, Martin. 1977. The Second Transformation of American Secondary Education. In, *Power and Ideology in Education*, Jerome Karabel and A.H. Halsey (eds.). pp. 105-17. New York: Oxford University Press.

Tucker, Robert C. 1978. *The Marx-Engels Reader*. New York: W.W. Norton.

U.S. Bureau of the Census. 1933. *Census of Agriculture: Taxes on Farm Property in the United States*. Washington: U.S. Government Printing Office.

_____ . 1971. *People of the United States in the 20th Century*. Washington: U.S. Government Printing Office.

_____ . 1975a. *Historical Statistics of the United States, Colonial Times to 1970*, part 1. Washington: U.S. Government Printing Office.

_____ . 1975b. *Historical Statistics of the United States, Colonial TImes to 1970*, part 2, Washington: U.S. Government Printing Office.

_____ . 1981. *Statistical Abstract of the United States: 1981*. Washington: U.S. Government Printing Office.

Walker, Pat (ed.). 1979. *Between Labor and Capital*. Boston: South End Press.

Weisbrod, Burton A. 1969. External Effects of Investment in Education. In, *Economics of Education*, volume 1, Mark Blaug (ed.). Baltimore: Penguin.

West, Allan M. 1980. *The National Education Association: The Power Base for Education*. New York: The Free Press.

Wrigley, Julia. 1982. *Class Politics and Public Schools: Chicago, 1900-1950*. New Brunswick, New Jersey: Rutgers University Press.

Yates, Michael D. 1981. Public Sector Unions and the Labor Movement. In, *Crisis in the Public Sector: A Reader*, Economics Education Project (eds.). New York: Monthly Review Press and Union for Radical Political Economics.

Chapter 11

Scientific Management, Human Relations, and the Class Struggle: The Evolution of the Labor Process in the United States

RICHARD W. HURD

In recent years radical scholars have begun to look carefully at the organization of work in advanced capitalist societies. Harry Braverman's monumental work *Labor and Monopoly Capital*, has stimulated a decade of research, discussion, and debate (Braverman 1974). While this focus on the labor process is welcome, the research is lacking in certain respects. Braverman's analysis concentrates almost exclusively on Scientific Management and its impact on the organization of work, and most other radicals follow his lead. While this focus is reasonable because of the primary role payed by Scientific Management, it is important that we not ignore the other weapons in capital's arsenal.

Because of the emphasis placed on Scientific Management, the analysis of Braverman and other radicals implies that management pursues a single-minded strategy, namely, to wring every possible ounce of productivity out of workers through tight supervision and careful control. In reality, the management of work is more varied and flexible than this. All workers know that some bosses are worse than others. Managers who are friendly, give workers a bit more influence, and allow them to set their own pace (within limits) will often gain both greater respect and higher productivity from the workers under their supervision.

In actuality, then, the management of work has been influenced by two competing philosophies, Scientific Management and Human Relations. Scientific Management adherents have argued that the best way to improve productivity is to study work systematically, design efficient production systems, and enforce production standards. The essence of Scientific Management is the dictatorial control of the labor process by management. The Human Relations advocates retort that the production standards of Scientific Management are meaningless if workers are not motivated. They propose a behavioral science approach to the management of work, concentrating on the worker's psyche and attempting to devise techniques to improve worker effort. The Human Relations philosophy is to subtly manipulate the labor process to create an illusion that the needs and problems of workers are being given proper consideration by management.

The representatives of these two schools of thought, operating in academia and consulting firms, have competed for the attention of capitalists, and each viewpoint has gained a degree of influence. The common practice has been for industrial engineers and production managers to use the techniques of Scientific Management to design production systems that maximize productivity and control. Human Relations consultants, personnel managers, and line supervisors have been expected to deal with the problems of motivation within this framework. Although Human Relations had had a rather minor impact on the organization of work per se, it has profoundly influenced the environment in which work is performed. Thus the Human Relations school is worthy of careful study if we are to understand the labor process in its entirety.

The first aim of this chapter is to assess the impact of Human Relations management on the labor process. To provide background for the analysis, I will review the origins of Scientific Management and its role within capitalism. Next, I will summarize the Human Relations approach to management and then discuss the influence of Human Relations on the thinking of the proponents of Scientific Management. Finally, I will propose a conceptual distinction between the two sometimes contradictory aims of the management of work—*control* of the labor process and *seduction* of workers into a state of submission.

The second aim of the chapter is to demonstrate the influence of the class struggle on the management of work. I will argue that the relative influence of control and seduction will vary with the form and intensity of the class struggle. The chapter's concluding section traces the history of the management of work in the United States, shows how worker response to management initiatives helps to mold future management decisions, and assesses the relative influence of Human Relations management and Scientific Management over time.

THE DIVISION OF LABOR AND SCIENTIFIC MANAGEMENT

In 1776 Adam Smith expounded upon the advantages resulting from the division of labor. The division of the production process into a series of distinct steps would increase labor productivity because: (1) less time would be lost by workers changing from one task to another, (2) the repetition of a single task would increase the worker's skill and dexterity in performing that task, and (3) repetition would suggest to workers possible innovations in tools and machinery (Smith 1937: 3-12).

It was not until 1832 that Charles Babbage added to this list what is probably the most essential contribution of the division of labor: " . . . the processes, each requiring different degrees of skill and force, can purchase exactly that quantity of both which is necessary for each process" (Babbage 1970: 15).

At the beginning of the twentieth century, Frederick Taylor's Scientific Management extended the principle of the division of labor by establishing a system for determining the precise degree of skill and force required for each operation. Taylor postulated that maximum productivity would be obtained when each worker knew what to do, how to do it, and in what time. In order to specify these parameters he suggested that human work should be studied systematically and analyzed scientifically. Taylor's goal was to design work systems efficiently in order to improve worker productivity (Taylor 1970: 27-32).

Since Taylor's pioneering work, increasing attention has been paid to measuring various components of human work and setting standards for the performance of specific tasks. Furthermore, the profession of industrial engineering has emerged, and its members have developed sophisticated techniques for applying the principles of Scientific Management to the design of production systems.

Braverman has shown that the major concern of Scientific Management is control of the labor process. With the rise of the factory system in the nineteenth century capital wrested control of production from workers. The role of Scientific Management was to extend and perfect that control. As Braverman (1974:86) observes, "Scientific Management, so-called, is an attempt to apply the methods of science to the increasingly complex problems of the control of labor in rapidly growing capitalist enterprises . . . . It enters the workplace not as the representative of science, but as the representative of management masquerading in the trappings of science."

The key principles of Scientific Management, as Braverman interprets them, are: (1) the dissociation of the labor process from the skills of the workers; (2) the separation of conception from execution, whereby mental labor becomes the province of management while physical labor is delegated to workers; and (3) the use of management's monopoly over knowledge to control each step of the labor process and its mode of execution (Braverman 1974: 112-3, 118).

Braverman concludes that the application of the principles of Scientific Management has clear-cut results: workers' skills are degraded and craftsmanship is destroyed, workers are treated as machines, and the resulting dehumanization of labor breeds dissatisfaction. Workers express their discontent in a number of ways, including sabotage, cooperative restriction of output, indifference towards their jobs, and other forms of rebellious behavior.

THE HUMAN RELATIONS SCHOOL OF MANAGEMENT THOUGHT

Recognizing that workers will react negatively to the dehumanizing impact of Scientific Management, management philosphers and practitioners have devised a variety of strategies to reduce discontent. These have included: (1) industrial psychology, which has attempted to create an environment in which dissatisfaction is minimized and worker productivity is maximized; (2) the human relations approach to management, which preaches that managers should treat workers with human respect and understanding in order to secure their cooperation; (3) personnel departments, which have been created to attend to the specific problems of workers; and, most recently, (4) job enrichment schemes, which have been designed to increase worker commitment by enlarging the content of jobs or increasing workers' decision-making authority. These various behavioral approaches are referred to collectively as "Human Relations" in this chapter.

The basic message of the proponents of Human Relations is that if management treats workers more humanely, then workers will respond positively and their productivity will improve. This philosphophy can be traced to the paternalism of many nineteenth century capitalists. It was not until the early twentieth century, however, that this paternalism was translated into a coherent philosophy of worker management, most notably by Henry Gantt, Hugo Munsterberg, Mary Parker Follett, and Elton Mayo.

Gantt was the most prominent disciple of Frederick Taylor, joining him in 1887 during the early experiments at the Midvale Steel Works and working with him until 1901. Gantt is perhaps best known for developing the "daily balance chart" used to measure the amount of time required to perform a particular task. But he is also remembered as an early proponent of a more humanitarian approach to management (George 1968: 100-1). Writing in 1919, Gantt (1970:46) observed,

> . . . It is undoubtedly true that the "efficiency" methods, which have been so much in vogue for the past twenty years in this country, have failed to produce what was expected of them. The reason seems to be that we have to a large extent ignored the human factor and failed to take advantage of the ability and desire of the ordinary man to learn and to improve his position. Moreover, these "efficiency" methods have been applied in a manner that was highly autocratic.

Munsterberg was the first to argue effectively that psychological techniques should be applied in industry in order to determine the appropriate worker for each job and to help identify the environment that would be most likely to induce maximum effort (George 1968: 174). Follett argued that it is management's responsibility to harmonize and coordinate the group efforts of the workers, rather than to autocratically force workers to perform their assigned tasks (George 1968: 131).

The person most commonly associated with the birth of the Human Relations is Elton Mayo, who presided over the renowned Hawthorne experiments conducted in the late 1920s. Based on his research, Mayo concluded that management should recognize workers as humans with wants, motives, drives, and goals that need to be satisfied. Managers could not hope to maximize worker effort unless they sought to help workers fulfill some of these subjective desires (Mayo 1971: 215-29). Mayo's ideas were extended and expanded by a number of managerial philosophers in the 1930s and 1940s.

In recent years, the Human Relations banner has been carried by the organizational behaviorists, who preach trust and communication as the most effective solutions to hostility between management and workers. Perhaps most well known is Frederick Herzberg, who has observed that workers will be more productive if their jobs are challenging and provide opportunities for advancement and recognition (Herzberg 1968). Herzberg and other contemporary proponents of Human Relations have been largely responsible for the discussions of work humanization and the resulting proliferation of job enrichment experiments that we witnessed during the 1970s. The influence of the Human Relations school has varied over time and from one establishment to another, but is has undoubtedly affected management's approach to workers. In his authoritative treatise, *"The History of Management Thought,* Claude S. George, Jr., notes, "[In] industry today, no manager would consider a system of supervision not incorporating the ideals and concepts of sound human relations" (George 1968: 174).

Although in management circles Human Relations has long been recognized as influential, Braverman and other radicals have discounted its importance. Braverman views Human Relations-inspired responses to worker hostility with disdain. He proclaims them to be diversionary tactics with little, if any, influence on the labor process. As Braverman (1974:143) puts it, "These schools and theories have succeeded one another in a dazzling proliferation of approaches and theories, a proliferation which is more than anything else testimony to their failure." He goes on to conclude,

> . . . [The] behavioral sociological schools . . . have yielded little to management in the way of solid and tangible results. . . . From their confident beginning as "sciences" devoted to discovering the springs of human behavior the better to manipulate them in the interests of management, they have broken up into a welter of confused and confusing approaches . . . with little impact upon the management of worker or work. (Braverman 1974: 145)

Braverman's cynicism concerning Human Relations is well founded if directed at the potential for meaningful improvements in the conditions of work within capitalism. However, his total dismissal of this management strategy is unwarranted. By ignoring or belittling the Human Relations approach to management, Braverman and his disciples have diverted our attention from this crucial component of the management of work. We need to improve our understanding of all management techniques in order to expose their role within capitalism.

Not all radicals have been comfortable with Braverman's framework, however. Maarten deKadt's review of *Labor and Monopoly Capital* posits that Human Relations is an alternative form of control of labor that is underestimated by Braverman (deKadt 1975). Perhaps a more telling indictment comes from Susan Porter Benson. She concludes that,

> It is critical to understand . . . the limits of the application of scientific management, its differential effects on men and women, and the importance of other types of management reform, particularly personnel work and human relations. In many occupations, the impact of a more wholesome work environment may have been greater than that of Taylorism . . . .(Benson 1978: 53)

While we need other detailed studies of workers in particular occupations and/or industries to confirm this thesis, Benson's observation that both approaches to management have had an important influence on the work environment of women sales clerks can in all likelihood be generalized to cover a wide range of work settings.

The following section demonstrates that although industrial engineers and their management counterparts are indeed concerned with efficiency and control, they are also aware that workers are human and therefore quite capable of resisting management directives. This "human element" is given explicit attention by the proponents of Scientific Management, reflecting the influence of the Human Relations school of thought.

THE HUMAN RELATIONS INFLUENCE ON SCIENTIFIC MANAGEMENT

For decades academic proponents of Scientific Management and Human Relations have engaged in heated debate with each other over appropriate management practices. As the debate has taken shape, those who argue for Scientific Management take on the role of the pragmatists, while the defenders of Human Relations appear to be the idealists. On the surface, at least, Scientific Management is more consistent with the logic of capitalism and therefore easier for capitalists to comprehend. The deduction does not follow, however, that Human Relations advocates are engaged in a fruitless philosophical exercise with little influence on the labor process.

In fact, Human Relations proponents have made an important contribution to the suppression of worker unrest and the undermining of working class consciousness. The arguments of the Human Relations school have even influenced the thinking of their nominal opposition—industrial engineers, production managers, and others commonly associated with Scientific Management.

For example *Time and Motion Study*, published in 1940 and authored by three highly respected industrial engineers, makes it clear that the techniques of Scientific Management cannot be implemented without considering the response of workers. Industrial psychologists are viewed as helpful in selecting appropriate workers for specific jobs. There is also considerable discussion in the book of ways to approach workers so that their trust might be gained. This issue is given special attention in the preface: "The authors have long recognized that labor has a right to be informed on the subject of time and motion study, and that this work should be done with the interests and problems of labor in mind" (Lowry, Maynard, and Stegemerten 1940: 9).

Maurice Kilbridge, a production management specialist, reminds us that certain aspects of work, particularly the effort exerted, *cannot* be determined by Scientific Management: " . . . the question of what constitutes a fair day's work cannot be answered by 'scientific investigation' alone but must remain 'a subject to be bargained and haggled over'" (Kilbridge 1960: 10). Kilbridge's article implies that the roles of the personnel department and labor unions in determining the structure of work are crucial ones. Work rules included in virtually every union contract clearly limit management's authority to control the assignment of workers and the pace of work. Even in nonunion settings management must reach some accommodation with workers regarding the effort required of employees.

To look at another example, the *Industrial Engineering Handbook*, last published in 1971, focuses on the most up-to-date Scientific Management practices, with articles on "Stopwatch Time Study," "The Measurement of Repetitive Work," "Administrative and Control Procedures" "Office Cost Controls," etc. Even here, the editor-in-chief concedes the influence of the Human Relations school: " . . . Advances have been made in other disciplines which . . . [are] of great interest to the industrial engineer. Behavioral scientists, for example, have long been critical of the philosophies and activities of the industrial engineer, yet many industrial engineers are ready and even eager to use any findings of the behavioral scientists which they judge to be practical and useful in achieving their own industrial engineering goals" (Maynard 1971: xviii).

H.B. Maynard's Production, compiled by the European offices of a leading industrial engineering consulting firm in 1975, is a vivid illustration of this point. This volume begins with the revealing declaration that the application of the principles of Scientific Management has gone too far, and further that " . . . the division of labor is in the end self-defeating" (Maynard 1975: 7). Pointing to the problems created by discontented workers, the authors suggest "more solid and creative industrial engineering" (Maynard 1975: 37). Calling on their colleagues to learn from the Human Relations advocates, they argue that more consideration should be given to workers when designing production systems.

In an article on productivity in *Industrial Engineering*, Serge Birn (1979:39) echoes the H.B. Maynard position. As a result of fragmentation, Birn argues, " . . . we now have too few idiots to fill idiot-proof jobs." Thus many workers find themselves holding jobs that do not challenge or interest them, and labor productivity sags. After reviewing how the techniques of Human Relations can be incorporated into the industrial engineering framework, Birn (1979:43) observes, "These are not just gimmicks of psychologists to make people happy. On the contrary, these are most effective tools for hard-boiled profit-conscious management. Tools it should put to use to increase productivity and reduce costs."

Human Relations and Scientific Management practitioners alike are now talking about merging their efforts in designing new "socio-technical production systems" (Maynard 1975: 16), that is, designing production systems with worker motivation in mind. The rising acceptability of this approach in Scientific Management circles was underscored at the May 1979 meetings of the American Institute of Industrial Engineers, where the keynote panel discussed "Productivity and Quality of Working Life Centers." Among talks delivered at other sessions were "A Human Approach to Motivation and Productivity," "Labor-Management Cooperation in a Manufacturing Environment," and "The Rebirth of Beverly—A Quality of Worklife Program" (American Institute 1979).

Even the defenders of Scientific Management, then, recognize that the management of work involves more than dictatorial control over the production process. Simply telling workers what to do, how to do it, and in what time, as prescribed by Taylor, is insufficient. Employees must also be persuaded to perform up to these standards. Only the most docile of workers thoroughly imbued with the work ethic could possibly measure up to the Scientific Management ideal of "the superskilled operator . . . (whose) motions are steady and quick as those of a machine . . . (performing) the task like an automaton" (Lowry, Maynard, and Stegemerten 1940: 212-23). Because workers are not machines, management has been forced to develop practices that have served to acclimate workers to the drudgery of their jobs, reduce their opposition to management initiatives, and increase their identification with the employing company. The techniques adopted have included the payment of higher wages and the mutual determination by management and workers of certain production standards as part of the "effort bargain." Management strategies to win worker cooperation have been profoundly influenced by the Human Relations school.

CONTROL VS. SEDUCTION

Although the management of work involves Scientific Management and the specification of tasks, it also involves Human Relations-inspired attempts to reduce worker alienation, to increase worker identification with the company and dedication to the job, and even to help with the personal problems of workers. There are thus two aspects of the management of work—one is *control*, the other is motivation or, more appropriately, *seduction*. It is important for management to organize work in the most "efficient" manner possible, which to management means maximizing control over the production process. But management is also concerned with maintaining an atmosphere of harmony in the workplace.

Seduction, then, includes all management tactics that tie workers to the firm, such as pensions, paid vacations, seniority privileges, and profit sharing. It also encompasses tactics designed to reduce worker antagonism towards management, including job enrichment schemes, company parties, suggestion boxes, and so-called work humanization.

Implementation of these tactics has paid off. A majority of workers have been seduced into a state of resignation; most workers accept management control of production as a fact of life, looking to higher wages as a consolation prize and to membership in their unions or their "company families" as an alternative to pride in their own work.

The distinction between the control and seduction aspects of worker management is drawn so that we might gain a more complete understanding of the operation of the capitalist economy. The influence of the Human Relations school and the practice of seduction are not, of course, indications that capitalism can be modified to effectively meet the needs of workers. In fact, the contrary is true. Whether we are talking about Scientific Management and control or Human Relations and seduction, the essence of the management of work is the same. The goal of Scientific Management is to maximize the contribution of workers to production and thereby increase the surplus value, while Human Relations attempts to minimize worker opposition and the development of class consciousness. The application of Scientific Management techniques has led to the fragmentation of work and the degradation of skills, while the Human Relations aproach has helped to reduce worker opposition to fragmentation and degradation. In spite of the success of Human Relations, the inevitable result of the continuing application of the principles of Scientific Management is alienated labor. But this need not signal the fall from grace of the industrial engineer or the end of capitalism. As one seduction technique wanes in effectiveness, others are developed.

THE EVOLUTION OF THE MANAGEMENT OF WORK —
A HISTORICAL OVERVIEW OF THE U.S. EXPERIENCE

Although the control and seduction aspects of management have been with us at least as long as capitalism, their relative influence has changed over time. Prior to the 1930s control clearly dominated, but since then management's reliance on seduction has increased, especially in the last decade.

From 1800 to 1930

The switch from craft to factory production in the early 1800s gave capitalists the opportunity to gain control of the labor process by exploiting the division of labor more effectively (Marglin 1974). Although workers reacted violently at times to the new highly regimented factory life, they were unable to generate a unified working class movement and so wielded little influence on the organization of work. During this era of competitive capitalism, the management of work was based on the whims of the individual capitalist and hired supervisor rather than on any coherent philosphy. In some cases harsh autocracy prevailed, while in others a paternalistic attitude was evident. Under this erratic system of supervision, many skilled workers still exerted a fair amount of control over their jobs.

As monopoly capital emerged late in the nineteenth century, there was a noticeable trend towards large factories and even larger bureaucratic corporations. Faced with the problems of managing an expanding enterprise and work force, capital sought some systematic way to control the labor process. Scientific Management was the answer, giving capital both a rationale and a method for extending and perfecting the control of the labor process.

Workers reacted violently to the imposition of Scientific Management, however. The Industrial Workers of the World (IWW) led strikes protesting work rationalization in McKees Rocks (PA), Lawrence (MA), Paterson (NJ), Detroit and other eastern industrial centers (Davis 1975: 74-76). The International Association of Machinists, the Amalgamated Clothing Workers, and other socialist unions took outspoken positions opposing Scientific Management (Palmer 1975: 41-43). Even the conservative American Federation of Labor (AFL) officially condemned Taylorism and called on the government to legislate against its use (Taft 1957: 299-300).

This worker revolt led to a two-pronged response from capital: (1) counterattack with the aid of the state and (2) revision of management practices to disguise Scientific Management. The counterattack began with mass arrests of those opposed to World War I, effectively decimating the IWW and greatly weakening the socialist unions (Rayback 1966: 280-89). In the aftermath of the war, capital launched a frontal attack on workers through its new antiunion mouthpiece, the National Association of Manufacturers (NAM). NAM's American Plan effectively painted every worker uprising as communist inspired. Put on the defensive, the AFL cooperated with capital by conducting its own witch hunt to rid the labor movement of communists (Boyer and Morais 1973: 209-17).

With the labor movement effectively weakened and the AFL serving as the junior partner of management, a revised Scientific Management dominated the labor process. The first signs of concession to the Human Relations approach appeared when many of the large corporations created personnel departments. The duties of the personnel departments were to hire and train workers, institute new fringe benefit plans, and establish company-dominated unions to channel workers' complaints into nondestructive outlets. A key element in capital's strategy to undermine worker discontent was Henry Ford's high wage doctrine. As implied by the name, the idea was to pay workers enough money to keep them quiet (Bernstein 1966: 170-88).

H. B. Maynard's Production aptly refers to the era before the 1930s as "decide and order" (Maynard 1975: 134, 139). For most of this period, workers' attempts to challenge capital were thwarted. Because concessions were unnecessary, control clearly dominated the management of work.

The 1930s to the 1970s

The economic crisis of the 1930s forced capital to abandon the high wage doctrine and cut wages, eliminate fringe benefits, and reduce the size and duties of personnel departments. In addition to these cost-cutting measures, capital took actions designed to increase productivity, primarily through work intensification and the speedup. Stripped down to its essence, the true anti-working-class nature of Scientific Management was revealed in its rawest form.

For the first few years of the Depression, while the unemployed expressed their anger in mass demonstrations and other forms of struggle, those lucky enough to have jobs did little to fight back against speedups and wage cuts. By 1934, however, workers had taken all they could stomach. A general strike in San Franscisco, an East Coast textile strike involving 376,000 workers, a teamsters strike that shut down Minneapolis, and an industrial strike in Toledo supported by mass demonstrations of the unemployed foreshadowed the rest of the decade (Bernstein 1971: 217-317).

The class struggle intensified as the crisis continued. In 1935, eight industrial unions split from the AFL to form the Congress of Industrial Organizations (CIO). The CIO immediately launched organizing campaigns in rubber, steel, autos, and other mass production industries affected by the Scientific Management mentality. With the CIO riding the crest of the wave of worker militance, capital was put on the defensive. Company unions were infiltrated and then taken over by the CIO; wage cuts were met with mass walkouts, speedups with sit-down strikes (Bernstein 1971: 432-634). It was the sit-down, a tactic popularized by the IWW 25 years earlier, that best reflected workers' unwillingness to accept the autocratic authority of their supervisors. From September 1936 to June 1937 one-half million workers staged sit-downs, which affected almost every major industry and all parts of the country (Rayback 1966: 354).

The immediate response of capital was to fight back. Leading the counterattack were the "Little Steel" companies (Bethlehem, Inland, Republic, and Youngstown), which " . . . used every weapon: citizens committees to support intimidation, back to work movements, special police which attacked picket lines and routed union leaders out of headquarters with tear gas, local police who made mass arrests, militia which protected strikebreakers" (Rayback 1966: 352). After initial successes, however, capital's strong-arm tactics failed. By 1941, the Little Steel companies and most other major corporations were unionized. Union membership increased from 2.9 million in 1933 to 14.8 million in 1945 (Reynolds 1970: 327).

Faced with the harsh reality of dealing with unions on a daily basis, capital came to recognize that the era of "decide and order" had ended. It had become obvious that untempered application of the principles of Scientific Management no longer served the interests of capital because such behavior engendered violent reaction from workers. The Human Relations approach began to gain influence.

In a discussion of the 1930s, Claude George (1968:173) observes:

> Business itself was held responsible by many for the economic breakdown in our system. Communications between labor and management were nonexistent or poor. . . . Grabbing at straws, [management] started trying the human relations approach. In fact, any gimmick that worked would have been acceptable. But what started out as a gimmick turned out to be profound.

An integral element of the evolving management strategy was recognition that advantages might be gained by dealing with union leaders who were pro-capitalist, rather than continuing the practice of attempting to crush every workers' movement, regardless of its political posture. As I have noted elsewhere, "Capital spent much of the (1930's) groping for a new strategy for its confrontations with labor. The increased militance of workers made the outright repression of earlier periods ineffective. A growing number of capitalists were beginning to see the advantages of collective bargaining" (Hurd 1976: 38). Two prominent capitalists espousing this view were Gerald Swope of General Electric and Cyrus Ching of U.S. Rubber (Bernstein 1971: 601-3). It was not until the 1940s, however, that the advantages of Human Relations' collective bargaining were accepted by most capitalists.

During World War II, with the class struggle subdued by patriotic appeals and by War Labor Board-imposed strike controls, capital devised a strategy to recoup their losses of the 1930s. Once again, capital swung a two-edged sword, attacking the left wing of the union movement, on the one hand, while adopting a more conciliatory approach towards employees and conservative unions, on the other.

The attack on radical unions began with labor law reform when U.S. Chamber of Commerce and National Association of Manufacturers lawyers assisted in the drafting of the 1947 Taft-Hartley Act. Taft-Hartley placed far-reaching restrictions on union strike and boycott activity, made it difficult for unions to lend support to each other, and required all union officials to sign a noncommunist oath (Hurd 1976: 38-40). In short, Taft-Hartley attempted to outlaw worker solidarity and class consciousness, and, in the process, it laid the backdrop for the more direct attack on labor radicals that was conducted during the McCarthy era of the 1950s. The Chamber of Commerce helped to orchestrate the direct attack as well, publishing "Communists Within the Labor Movement" and other pamphlets. With nonradical union bureaucrats in both the CIO and the AFL conducting purges of alleged communists, the post-World War II "red scare" had its designed effect (Boyer and Morais 1973: 329-70).

With the left wing of the union movement eliminated, capital accepted the wisdom of Ching, Swope, and the Human Relations philosophers and settled comfortably into the era of "mature collective bargaining." Under mature collective bargaining, capital accepts unions as legitimate, grants them a limited sphere of influence, and negotiates with union representatives "in good faith." In return, unions agree to concentrate primarily on improving the economic position of their members through wage and fringe benefit improvement, formally recognize "management's right to manage" (including mechanization decisions and most aspects of the organization of work), and agree not to strike during the life of collective bargaining agreements.

Since 1945, capital has conceded to workers and their unions a clearly defined (and limited) role in decision making, reinstated fringe benefits, expanded the personnel function, and openly adopted Human Relations practices. Even in nonunion workplaces, capital often sets up formal grievance procedures, invites employees to offer suggestions, distributes employee newspapers, sponsors employee social functions, provides cafeterias, and sometimes adopts profit-sharing plans. In short, capital has recognized the usefulness of giving attention to reducing worker resistance to its formal prerogatives. *Seduction* now complements *control* in virtually every major corporation. Although management still makes all crucial decisions, worker reactions are now considered systematically. H.B. Maynard and Co. refer to this approach as "decide and persuade" (Maynard 1975: 173). From the mid-1940s to the mid-1970s this approach fulfilled capital's needs.

The Current Situation

A crucial concession made by the union movement in order to gain its status as a legitimate institution of capitalist society was the acceptance of Scientific Management. In contrast to their violent opposition earlier in the century, unions have accepted Scientific Management since the 1950s on the condition that resulting productivity improvements lead to higher wages (Gomberg 1973). Unions have interfered with the application of Scientific Management only by formalizing the rules governing internal labor markets (Doeringer and Piore 1971: 34-39). Work rules are perceived as protective by unions and workers because they clearly define limits to specific jobs and establish job ladders that guarantee opportunities for advancement. In spite of these advantages, however, many work rules simultaneously serve capital by increasing hierarchy, dividing workers into categories, and reducing workers' awareness of their collective interest.

As John and Barbara Ehrenreich have observed, the division of labor in detail, the application of Scientific Management, and the dehumanization of work have contributed to an atomized w⌃·king class that does not exhibit class consciousness. Furthermore, work hierarchies and the separation of conception from execution have dulled workers' senses and general intelligence (Ehrenreich and Ehrenreich 1976).

In the 1960s and 1970s, with collective spirit diminished and unions increasingly bureaucratic, workers responded to their repression individually. *Work in America* and a number of other studies described the decline in the work ethic and revealed that the workers of the 1970s respected authority less than their predecessors. No longer willing to accept dehumanized, deskilled, and degrading jobs, workers expressed their frustration through sabotage, absenteeism, turnover, and resistance to authority (U.S. Department of Health, Education, and Welfare 1973). In short, workers generally eschewed a collective response to the oppressive character of the labor process and adopted an individualized, anarchistic response instead.

In this setting, capital began to reevaluate the management of work, and a new set of seductive techniques evolved. Under the rubric of "job redesign," capital is now attempting to overcome individual worker resistance to authority and reinstitute the work ethic by improving the "quality of working life" (QWL). Capital has adopted such schemes as job rotation (periodically switching workers from one job to another), job enlargement (combining two or more low-skill jobs), flexible working hours (within strict limits workers set their own schedules), and quality control circles (workers participate in monitoring quality and recommend improvements in the production system).

The QWL experiments, however, are merely window dressing. They are based on the teachings of the contemporary Human Relations disciples, organizational behaviorists. Organizational behavior suggests that management should find out what employees are thinking and what they want. Armed with this information, management can devise the response most likely to motivate (seduce) their employees. Such responses can be as simple as creating more effective communication channels, or as complex as building a new factory designed to encourage individual worker initiative. The most common approach is job redesign within existing facilities.

Organizational behavior has had a major impact. Management officials charged with motivating employees now enjoy increasing influence and higher salaries than ever before. Even their title has been upgraded from "personnel manager" to "human resources executive." *Business Week* notes that "Managers who deal with the so called 'people' issues in a company . . . are rising in power and influence. . . . Today he—or in may cases she—reports directly to the chief executive officer and plays a crucial role in making strategic business decisions" (Hoerr 1985: 58).

The new seductive techniques of organizational behavior are especially appealing to capital because they offer a strategy for weakening or avoiding unions without engendering a militant reaction from workers. Capital has learned how to wage class war peacefully. Rather than launching a frontal attack on unions, management carefully selects the appropriate seduction techniques, then sets out to create an environment that encourages workers to reject union organizing attempts or to decertify existing unions.

Management consulting firms are offering advice to capital on how to most effectively conduct such antiunion campaigns. For example, in the spring and summer of 1979, Professional Seminars Associates offered two-day seminars at seven locations across the United States. The title speaks for itself, "Avoiding Unions: A Seminar Designed to Help the Business Community Establish and Maintain a Non-Union Environment." The subjects covered were straight out of the Human Relations school: "communications as the key to union avoidance," "how to develop an effective grievance procedure," "constructive discipline," "how to help employees modify their behavior," etc. (Professional Seminar Associates, Inc. 1979). The willingness of capital to listen to such advice was underscored by a *Business Week* report, "The Antiunion Grievance Ploy." Hundreds of corporations have implemented grievance procedures for their nonunion employees, including TWA, Singer, and McDonald's (*Business Week* 1979: 119-20). The complete union avoidance program recommended by the consulting firms, usually referred to as "positive labor relations," offers unorganized workers most of the benefits of unionism including high wages, good fringe benefits, and seniority protections (Freeman and Medoff 1984: 230-32).

In August 1978, Peter Pestillo, then a Human Resources executive with B.F. Goodrich, noted that,

> The structure imposed by a union limits opportunity to provide such devices as job rotation to improve both the workplace and productivity. . . . In nonunion facilities the whole supervisory force has usually had more training in human relations than in older plants. There is extensive and open communication between all levels of supervision and the workforce. There is . . . a functioning system for the resolution of disputes. Frankly, without a conflict resolution system . . . you just don't stay unorganized long. (Pestillo 1978: 235, 238)

Subsequently, Pestillo moved to Ford Motor Company as vice-president for industrial relations. In this position, he negotiated a contract with the United Automobile Workers that established a jointly sponsored QWL program called Employee Involvement (EI).

A stinging critique of the EI program by UAW activist Mike Parker accurately exposes its antiunion implications. Parker argues that EI, specifically, and QWL, generally, are harmful to unionism because: (1) QWL erodes union consciousness by encouraging individual initiative and cooperation with management; (2) QWL breaks down solidarity among workers by fostering quality and productivity competition between workers in different plants, companies, and nations; (3) QWL is used by capital to extract information from workers about how work is performed, information capital uses in order to increase productivity and, ultimately, surplus value (Parker 1974).

Of course, not all companies have instituted quality circles or other QWL programs. Some employers still focus on Scientific Management-inspired control techniques, and cases of blatant union busting are all too common. The point is that the QWL approach is increasing in popularity among important segments of capital in the United States. *Business Week* recently described the influence of QWL in an article entitled "Beyond Unions," pointing to a trend that "involves reorganizing work and giving workers more control over their jobs. The movement is taking place in thousands of factories, stores, and offices, and it is likely to become a permanent part of the U.S. industrial relations system" (*Business Week* 1985: 75). In the contemporary United States, *seduction* influences the labor process more than ever before.

CONCLUSION

For a complete understanding of the labor process under capitalism, we must consider both Scientific Management-inspired control and Human Relations-inspired seduction. Scientific Management is a more convenient target because it blatantly exposes the true objectives of capital. Human Relations is more elusive, holding out the promise that workers and capital can function cooperatively. Because of this, it is extremely important that we devote more attention to Human Relations-inspired seduction techniques. In recent years, capital has become increasingly adept at seduction, convincing workers that individualism is superior to collective action and that cooperation with management is the best route to individual improvement. Dismissing Human Relations out of hand, as Braverman does, is an insufficient response to this highly effective tool of capital.

So long as they are not challenged, quality of work life programs and other Human Relations-inspired modifications of the labor process will continue to undermine the potential for the development of working class consciousness. For a progressive working class movement to attract broad support, workers must be convinced that they have more to gain through collective action than through cooperation with management.

Acknowledgments. Constructive criticism was offered by many participants of the Labor and Political Economy Workshops at the University of New Hampshire, most notably Marc Herold, Bob Horn, and Kent Klitgaard.

REFERENCES

American Institute of Industrial Engineers. 1979. Annual Conference and Productivity Engineering Show: Complete Program and The Antiunion Grievance Ploy. *Business Week* (February 12): 119-20.

Babbage, Charles. 1970. On the Division of Labor. In *Source Book in Production Management,* Robert G. Brown (ed.), pp. 12-22. Hinsdale, Illinois: Dryden Press.

Benson, Susan Porter. 1978. The Clerking Sisterhood. *Radical America* (March-April): 41-55.

Bernstein, Irving. 1966. *The Lean Years.* Baltimore: Penguin Books.

———. 1971. *Turbulent Years.* Boston: Houghton Mifflin.

Birn, Serge. 1979. Productivity Slump: Broader IE's Needed. *Industrial Engineering* (February): 39-43.

Boyer, Richard and Herbert Morais. 1973. *Labor's Untold Story*. New York: United Electrical Radio and Machine Workers of America.

Braverman, Harry. 1974. *Labor and Monopoly Capital*. New York: Monthly Review Press.

Business Week. 1979. The Antiunion Grievance Ploy. *Business Week* (February 12): 117-20.

_____. 1985. Beyond Unions. *Business Week* (July 8): 72-77.

Davis, Mike. 1975. The Stop Watch and the Wooden Shoe: Scientific Management and the Industrial Workers of the World. *Radical America* (January-February): 69-95.

De Kadt, Maarten. 1975. Management and Labor. *Review of Radical Political Economics* (Spring): 84-90.

Doeringer, Peter and Michael Piore. 1971. *Internal Labor Markets and Manpower Analysis*. Lexington, Massachusetts: D.C. Heath.

Ehrenreich, John and Barbara Ehrenreich. 1976. Work and Consciousness. *Monthly Review* (July-August): 10-17.

Freeman, Richard and James Medoff. 1984. *What Do Unions Do?* New York: Basic Books.

Gantt, Henry. 1970. Democracy in the Shop. In *Source Book in Production Management*, Robert G. Brown, (ed.), pp. 43-47. Hinsdale, Illinois: Dryden Press.

George, Claude. 1968. *The History of Management Thought*. Englewood Cliffs, New Jersey: Prentice Hall.

Gomberg, William. 1973. Job Satisfaction: Sorting Out the Nonsense. *AFL-CIO American Federationist* (June): 15-17.

Herzberg, Frederick. 1968. One More Time: How Do You Motivate Employees? *Harvard Business Review* (January-February): 53-62.

Hoerr, John. 1985. Human Resources Managers Aren't Corporate Nobodies Anymore. *Business Week* (December 2): 58-59.

Hurd, Richard. 1976. New Deal Labor Policy and the Containment of Radical Union Activity. *Review of Radical Political Economics* (Fall): 32-43.

Kilbridge, Maurice. 1960. The Effort Bargain in Industrial Society. *The Journal of Business* (June): 10-20.

Lowry, Stewart, H. B. Maynard, and G. J. Stegemerten. 1940. *Time and Motion Study*. New York: McGraw-Hill.

Marglin, Stephen. 1974. What Do Bosses Do? *Review of Radical Political Economics* (Summer): 60-112.

Maynard, H. B. 1971. *Industrial Engineering Handbook*. New York: McGraw-Hill.

_____. 1975. *Production: An International Appraisal of Contemporary Manufacturing Systems and the Changing Role of the Worker*. New York: John Wiley and Sons.

Mayo, Elton. 1971. Hawthorne and the Western Electric Company. In *Organization Theory*, D. S. Pugh (ed.), pp. 215-29. Middlesex England: Penguin Books.

Palmer, Bryan. 1975. Class, Conception and Conflict: The Thrust for Efficiency, Managerial Views of Labor and the Working Class Rebellion, 1903-1922. *Review of Radical Political Economics* (Summer): 31-49.

Parker, Mike. 1984. *Inside the Circle: A Union Guide to QWL.* Detroit: Labor Notes.

Pestillo, Peter. 1978. Learning to Live Without Unions. *Industrial Relations Research Association Proceedings* (August): 233-39.

Professional Seminar Associates, Inc. 1979. "Avoiding Unions."

Rayback, Joseph. 1966. *A History of American Labor.* New York: Free Press.

Reynolds, Lloyd. 1970. *Labor Economics and Labor Relations.* Englewood Cliffs, New Jersey: Prentice Hall.

Smith, Adam. 1937. *The Wealth of Nations.* New York: Modern Library.

Taft, Philip. 1957. *Time of Gompers.* New York: Harper and Brothers.

Taylor, Frederick. 1970. The Principles of Scientific Management. In *Source Book in Production Management,* Robert G. Brown (ed.), pp. 27-32. Hinsdale, Illinois: Dryden Press.

U.S. Department of Health, Education, and Welfare. 1973. *Work in America.* Cambridge, Massachusetts: M.I.T. Press.

Chapter 12

State Strategies of Control in the Public Sector

ROBERT N. HORN
JOSEPH M. TOMKIEWICZ

Critics of monopoly capitalism generally argue that the primary function of the state consists of providing and maintaining an environment conducive to the accumulation of capital and the reproduction of capitalist relations of production. In order to accomplish this task, the state must not only enact policies that promote the interests of capital but also make those policies palatable to labor in order to minimize worker militancy. One of the tactics that the state has at its disposal is the passage and enforcement of labor laws that, on the surface, appear to be neutral between labor and capital but that, in fact, exist to promote the welfare of the latter. Rick Hurd (1976), for example, has argued that labor law enacted during the New Deal was not as progressive as most students of labor relations contend, but, in fact, was a necessary step by the state to control the rise of militancy among industrial workers.

In this essay, we argue that the enactment of a progressive sounding labor law in the public sector (Pennsylvania Act 195) was similarly an attempt by the state to stem labor unrest by the state's public employees, especially the teachers. We begin with a brief review of the law that Act 195 replaced and indicate why it had ceased to function as an effective control mechanism. We then present some of the more important provisions of the new law and discuss the administration of the law and its impacts on Pennsylvania teachers. We conclude with some comments on the need for public sector workers to develop alternative strategies to gain some measure of control over their work lives.

THE PENNSYLVANIA NO STRIKE LAW AND THE RISE OF TEACHER MILITANCY

The Pennsylvania Public Employee Relations Act (Act 195) was conceived and enacted because existing legislation, the Pennsylvania No Strike

Law (Act 492), had ceased to function as an effective mechanism of social control in the public sector. Two circumstances contributed to the "need" to replace Act 492 with a more comprehensive set of regulations to administer workplace relations in the public sector: (1) the inability or unwillingness of the courts to uphold the existing statute and (2) the rise of militancy among teachers and other workers in the public sector.

The No Strike Law had been in effect since 1947. Under this legislation, public employers were not obliged to recognize or bargain with worker organizations. Strikes were prohibited. In the event of a strike in the public sector, the law stated that a "striking public employee (1) [shall] be terminated, (2) if re-employed, shall not receive a raise in pay for three years, and (3) shall be on probation for five years and serve without tenure at the pleasure of the appointing officer or body" (Bureau of National Affairs 1971: 80). Given that collective bargaining was not mandatory, and that strike activity was prohibited, it was obvious that when an employer refused to recognize an employee bargaining unit, there was virtually nothing employees could do to make their voices heard and still remain within the confines of the law. The effectiveness of this law, in practice, was suspect:

> All penalties for violation of the 1947 law were applied to employees. Because of this, and because of the significance of some of the penalties assigned under the law, the courts generally refused to uphold the provisions of the law. Thus the 1947 law became unenforceable. (Pennsylvania School Boards Association 1973: 173).

The Hickman Commission, established in early 1968 by Pennsylvania Governor Raymond Shafer to study alternatives to Act 492, believed the prohibitions against public worker rights present in the No Strike Law were weaknesses that no longer were tenable, especially with the "great increase over the years in the number of public employees and their work load" (Pennsylvania Department of Labor and Industry 1974: 5).

The realization that Act 492 had, in fact, ceased to be an effective control mechanism is evidenced by the increase in strike activity by teachers during the late 1960s. Teachers, although aware of possible state reprisals against militant activity, did not hesitate to close the schools when contract talks failed to meet their expectations. The increase in strike activity, documented in table 12-1, clearly indicates the disregard on the part of Pennsylvania teachers for the existing legislation. The courts, for the most part, did not uphold the mandated sanctions against striking teachers. In fact, to prevent further strike activity, the state issued a teacher amnesty law granting teachers amnesty from the penalties cited in the No Strike Law.

Teacher militancy was not an anomaly when viewed within a larger social context. On the contrary, it may be said that the heightening of strike activity by teachers to assert their demands grew from an unrest permeating

TABLE 12.1. Strike Activity: Pennsylvania Teachers

Year	Number of Strikes	Average Duration (in days)	Faculty	Pupils
1960-66	0	0	0	0
1966-67	5	1.6	188	6,209
1967-68	5	6.2	412	20,286
1968-69	22	3.7	200	5,070
1969-70 (part year)	10	11.0	250	5,677

Source: Pennsylvania State Education Association Research Department Communication.

society in general during that period. Stanley Aronowitz (1973: 250) points out that the latter part of the "sixties and the opening of the 1970s marked the reawakening of rank-and-file militancy." He goes on to note that

> . . . among public workers, a wave of union organizing and strike movements took place. This wave was led by teachers and hospital workers. The impact of public employee organizing was peculiar because every strike by this group of workers is, perforce, a strike against the state. In many cases, the pent up frustration of these workers . . . caused widespread disrespect for laws prohibiting strikes by public employees and court injunctions aimed at enforcing the law. (Aronowitz 1973: 250)

During the 1960s, civil disobedience became a widespread and effective strategy pursued by various groups to achieve their goals. Teachers could not help observing the successes of other groups who were willing to oppose the "establishment." In Pennsylvania, the establishment at that time was represented by the state in the form of Act 492. The widespread nature of civil disobedience, however, was not enough in itself to encourage teachers to break the laws created to keep them in check. Two other circumstances arose that gave impetus to "illegal" teacher activity: adverse trends in salaries and education quality.

Throughout the 1960s, teachers became acutely aware that workers who were organized into unions and exerted various forms of bargaining power had achieved a greater measure of success in improving their wages and working conditions than unorganized labor. Teacher salaries lagged behind most other occupational groups. For example, in 1969 the median salary for male secondary school teachers was $9,247, placing them 150th on the list of occupations devised by the U.S. Department of Labor, despite the fact that they possessed higher educational achievement than 89 percent of those ahead of them in the salary list (Sommers 1974: 37).

In addition to displeasure over low salaries, teachers were growing more dissatisfied with the schools themselves, due in part to the refusal by many school administrators to recognize teachers as professionals who could and should have a significant role in policy formulation. Thus, three factors were working simultaneously and interrelatedly: the rise of civil disobedience as a "tool" in achieving collective goals, the impetus toward such actions precipitated by displeasure over salaries, and the mode of operation of the schools.

The power establishment within Pennsylvania was not ignorant of the events that seemed to be threatening their "ideal" of state sovereignty. Act 492 was becoming less viable as a tool to keep teachers' (and other public workers') aspirations under control. What was needed was a new way to control the "explosion" of teacher awareness and willingness to act on their own behalf while making such controls palatable to the controlled.

David Berlo (1975: 17) has observed that "the traditional control system is force and authority based on the potential use of force." Such a control system "preaches the morality of hard work and submissive compliance and defends the justice of a class system in which some are instructors [the state, in this case] and some are instructees [public workers and labor in general]." Such a philosophy of control was embodied in Act 492.

The passage of Act 195 was a reaffirmation, by the state, of force as a control mechanism. However, such force was now clothed under the guise of persuasion. As Berlo (1975: 17) points out, "persuasion makes a tacit recognition of voluntary compliance, but uses language to lead people to positions predetermined by the persuader as in his or her best interest. It is a form of external control, often having the appearance of cooperation and voluntariness, but, in fact, being a surrogate for force power."

Berlo's analysis of workplace relations is quite similar to James O'Connor's (1973: 6) view that a basic function of the state under capitalism is to legitimize the existing social relations of production, often by promoting the perception that the system is equitable. Thus, labor law, administered under the guise of fairness and impartiality between labor and management, in effect serves the interests of the latter but tries to make the workers feel they are getting a fair share. In what follows, we assert that the administration of Act 195 confirms both Berlo's and O'Connor's views of the role of the state. The passage of the Act was an attempt to harness militant workplace relations while making the teachers believe that the state was acting in their collective best interests.

Three issues can help demonstrate that Act 195, instead of providing a new freedom for teachers to organize, bargain, and even strike, merely provided a different route for the state to control their activities. The three issues referred to are: (1) the scope of bargaining, (2) bargaining unit determination, and (3) the 180 day rule and its debilitating effect on the right to strike. Prior to discussing these issues, a brief interlude to discuss the main provisions of Act 195 seems appropriate.

THE PENNSYLVANIA PUBLIC EMPLOYEE RELATIONS ACT:
THE NEW CONTROL MECHANISM

The Pennsylvania Public Employee Relations Act rendered it "lawful for public employees to organize, form, join or assist in employee organizations or to engage in lawful concerted activities for the purpose of collective bargaining" (Act 195: article IV, section 401). That workers in the public sector were given the right to bargain collectively and that employers were obligated to accept an elected representative as a recognized bargaining agent constituted a marked improvement over the earlier No Strike Law. However, the state mandated that only certain areas were subject to bargaining. Article VII, section 702 specifies bargainable items: "Wages, hours, and other terms of employment" are deemed negotiable. What is *not* negotiable is any matter relating to "inherent managerial policy," such as budgets, organizational structure, and selection and direction of personnel.

Section 702 is, in effect, a management's rights clause. In education, it serves to "uphold the property rights which school boards have in their school district" (Williams and Yates 1975: 175). In other words, the "inherent managerial policy" clause serves as a means to maintain and preserve management's control over the workplace and to limit bargaining to those select areas with which management has historically been most able to cope. It quite simply carries over into the public sector the "pure and simple" brand of business unionism that characterized the rise of the American Federation of Labor and that continues to be the dominant mode of bargaining in the private sector.

Pennsylvania was not the first state to permit collective bargaining in the public sector, but it was the first industrial state to permit and legalize strikes by publice sector workers. The law grants public workers a limited right to strike, but only after a long impasse procedure has been effectively exhausted. The impasse procedure, described in article X, is a protracted affair, in which the opposing parties are required to call in the services of the State Board of Mediation and the Pennsylvania Labor Relations Board (PRLB) once negotiations have reached a stalemate. All in all, the rank and file must sit back and wait over 100 days while the impasse procedure runs its course under the watchful eyes of state labor bureaucracies. Strikes and related job actions, which may serve to show the intensity of worker support for an issue on the bargaining table, are prohibited and are legally enjoinable during the impasse procedure.

If, at the end of the entire process, labor and management have not come to terms, strikes are permitted providing such a strike does not create "a clear and present danger or threat to the health, safety or welfare of the public" (article X, section 1003). In such cases, which are determined by the courts in the jurisdiction where the strike occurs, management can resort to appropriate injunctions and "shall be entitled to relief if the court determines the strike creates a clear and present danger. . . . " (article X, section 1003). As we will see, school boards have frequently made use of this provision in order to enjoin strike activity by teachers, claiming the injunction is justified in order to protect the interests of the general public. Having looked at Act 195, we can now proceed to show how its institution was, in fact, an attempt by the state to regain control over the public sector.

THE ADMINISTRATION OF ACT 195:
NEW LEVELS OF CONTROL

Article VII of Act 195 deals with the issue of scope of bargaining. Both employer and employee groups have the obligation to confer in good faith over wages, hours, and other terms of employment. Employers, however, have no obligation to bargain over any matter of "inherent managerial policy." Unfortunately for teachers, many school districts attempted to limit bargaining to only wages, contending that few other items did not touch upon managerial policy. Clarence Morrison, staff legal counsel of the Pennsylvania State Education Association (PSEA) said:

> We do not contend that school boards have to grant or agree to every item, but we feel that they should not be given the opportunity to close-off negotiations simply by stating that certain items are non-negotiable under inherent managerial rights. (Williams and Yates 1975: 127).

The resistance by school boards to any broadening of the scope of bargaining led to frustrations for teacher groups and tended to demonstrate that, in many ways, the freedom to bargain granted under Act 195 was illusory.

The landmark State College case convinced many teacher groups that their freedom to bargain depended on the arbitrary discretion of school boards. If a school board decided that an item presented by a teacher organization was one it would rather not bargain over, it simply invoked the provisions of section 702. In the State College case, both the Court of Common Pleas and the Pennsylvania Commonwealth Court ruled that 21 items presented by the State College Education Association were matters of inherent managerial policy and thus nonbargainable.

This decision was appealed to the Pennsylvania Supreme Court, at which time the PSEA argued that all the items defined as nonbargainable by the lower courts had actually been negotiated and were present in contracts in many districts throughout the state. After deliberating for over a year, the Pennsylvania Supreme Court handed down its decision in 1975. The court decided that teachers could present a wide range of items on the bargaining table. However, any item a school board objected to on the basis of managerial policy would be remanded for final arbitration to the PLRB. Thus, discretion for scope of bargaining rested solely with school districts, while teachers could only present their demands and "hope."

The administering of article VII thus led to an ironic situation. Prior to the enactment of Act 195, terms or subjects open to negotiations could be worked out on the local level between the school board and the appropriate union. There was no specification of boundaries of bargainable items. These circumstances existed in spite of Act 492. After the "liberating" legislation of Act 195, these circumstances quickly evaporated.

Section 604 of article VI deals with another crucial issue: bargaining unit determination. This provision of Act 195 has allowed school boards additional opportunity to impede teacher organizing attempts. The definition of a bargaining unit is not negotiable. The local school board determines which positions are supervisory and confidential (and thus excluded from bargaining units) by the way the employer assigns authority and responsibility. Even after a unit determination is made by the PLRB, a position may be removed at any time should the school board decide to alter the work assignment or job description so that the position is "converted" to a supervisory or confidential one.

School boards have attempted to exclude as many employees as possible from bargaining units. They have challenged the inclusion of such professionals as guidance counselors, department heads, school nurses, subject matter supervisors, psychologists, head teachers, and assistant principals. They have fought the inclusion of so many positions "that if they were to succeed, there would be hardly any members left in the bargaining units" (Pennsylvania State Education Association 1975: 8). Such obstructionist school board attitudes, "have created artificial barriers between personnel who are said to supervise or administer and personnel who teach" (PSEA 1978: 4). Section 604 is another example of the law being used, not to encourage the freedom of teachers to organize and bargain, but on the contrary to impede and disrupt these legislated "guarantees."

The functioning of the educational system in Pennsylvania falls under the Public School Code of 1949. Section 1501 of this law requires that there must be a minimum school year of 180 days of instruction. Teacher organizations believed that this requirement coupled with the limited right to strike afforded by Act 195 would provide them with a measure of bargaining power. If a work stoppage did take place, school boards could remain recalcitrant only until that time when a continued stoppage would make meeting the 180-day requirement impossible. Thus, teachers reasoned, school districts would be motivated to negotiate meaningfully and not stonewall the teachers' union.

Unfortunately, teachers were again disappointed in the reality of act 195. The courts shifted all discretion for the decision to meet the 180-day requirement to the school boards. In the case of *Root vs. Northern Cambria*

School District (1973), the Pennsylvania Commonwealth Court ruled that a school district could not be forced to remain open 180 days. The court interpreted section 1501 of the School Code as requiring school districts to make an attempt to provide 180 days in order to retain state subsidies. If, however, the district found it impossible or impractical to meet the requirement because of a teacher strike, the district could not be said to have broken any laws.

In the case of *Bristol Township School District vs. Bristol Township Education Association* (1973), the Pennsylvania Commonwealth Court stated that "when a strike lasts so long that the 180-days requirement cannot be met, there is a clear detriment to the public welfare and the teachers must be enjoined from continuing it." In this particular instance, an injunction was issued against striking teachers that enjoined their work stoppage.

In effect, these decisions granted school boards the legal power to completely emasculate teachers' right to strike. School boards could withstand a strike by teachers, confident that when agreement was reached they could ignore the 180-day requirement and thus cost teachers a loss in pay and provide a boon for the school district treasury in the form of saved teacher salaries. However, if the whim so pleased the school boards, they could seek injunctive relief against strikes by arguing "detriment to the public." In fact, one school district rescheduled its opening day from September 1 to October 15 on the supposition that if teachers attempted to strike, the school board would seek an immediate injunction under the supposition that even a one-day stoppage would not allow a full 180-day school year. Again, the promise of Act 195 was to be dissipated as quickly as the state courts could render their "in the public's interest" decisions. Apparently, teacher rights were not included as part of the public's interest.

CONCLUSION: THE NEED FOR ALTERNATIVE STRATEGIES

In this essay we have developed the hypothesis that although most groups of organized labor in the state supported Act 195, the Act was in effect an attempt by the state to regain control over the public sector by placing negotiations into the straight jacket of legalistic impasse procedures and narrowly defined areas subject to bargaining. On paper and in comparison with statutes in most other states, the Pennsylvania law appeared to be a progressive one—granting both collective bargaining and the right to strike. However, "labor law generally, including Act 195, has tended to favor management. . . . Historically, the courts of the U.S. have leaned to reactionary rulings in cases in which there was even a slight hint of violation of property rights. . . . " (Williams and Yates 1975:127).

We have shown that public school boards are no less determined than private capital to maintain exclusive control over the administration of the workplace. As in the private sector, the courts have been willing to act on behalf of the property rights of school boards in their attempts to maintain control over the public schools. Court actions interpreting scope of bargaining, unit determination, and the 180-day instruction provision are clearly supportive of school board views concerning the sanctity of private property.

We are forced to conclude that teachers must develop alternative strategies in order to achieve some degree of control over their work lives. Labor cannot rely upon the state to act as an impartial mediator in the struggle between workers and management. Passage of Act 195 and its interpretation by the courts demonstrates once again that meaningful progressive labor law reform is simply not consistent with the operation of a capitalist economic system. Act 195 merely repositioned the bolts of oppression—it did not loosen them.

REFERENCES

Aronowitz, Stanley. 1973. *False Promises: The Shaping of American Working Class Consciousness.* New York: McGraw-Hill.

Berlo, David. 1975. Morality of Ethics? Two Approaches to Organizational Control. *The Personnel Administrator* 20(2): 16-19.

Bristol Township School District vs. Bristol Township Education Association. 1973. Commonwealth Court of Pennsylvania.

Bureau of National Affairs. 1971. *Labor Relations Handbook, 1971.* Washington, D.C.

Hurd, Richard. 1976. New Deal Labor Policy and the Containment of Radical Union Activity. *The Review of Radical Political Economics* 8(3): 32-43.

O'Connor, James. 1973. *The Fiscal Crisis of the State.* New York: St. Martin's Press.

Pennsylvania Department of Labor and Industry. 1974. *Pennsylvania Labor Relations Board Report for the Calendar Years 1970, 1971, 1972, and 1973.*

Pennsylvania School Boards Association, Inc. *Act 195, third printing.* Harrisburg, Pennsylvania: Pennsylvania School Boards Association, Inc.

Root vs. Northern Cambria School District. 1973. Commonwealth Court of Pennsylvania.

Sommers, Dixie. 1974. Occupational Rankings for Men and Women by Earnings. *Monthly Labor Review* 97(8): 34-51.

Williams, Bruce and Mike Yates. 1974. Concerning State College's "Unbargainable Items." *Pennsylvania School Journal* 122(3): 126-28.

PART 6
Transition to Socialism

Chapter 13

Heavy Industrialization: The Algerian Experience

EL-HACHEMI ALIOUCHE

INTRODUCTION

Most underdeveloped nations have attempted to break their ties with economic backwardness and engage in a process of economic development. Many strategies have been devised to reach these objectives. In this essay, the experience of one such country, Algeria, is analyzed. The cornerstone of Algerian ideology is that economic independence is imperative if a developing country wants to achieve its development goals.

This chapter is divided into three parts. In the first part, the reasons that led Algeria to choose a strategy of economic development involving heavy industrialization are presented. The theoretical foundations of this strategy are summarized, and how this strategy was applied in Algeria is described. In the second part, the experience of the first decade after this strategy was put into effect is evaluated. And, finally, the reforms introduced in the early 1980s are discussed. 1980 marked the end of the first phase of industrialization and the beginning of a new phase characterized by greater emphasis on economic efficiency.

THE ALGERIAN STRATEGY OF DEVELOPMENT

Socioeconomic Background

To a large extent, the postindependence Algerian strategy of economic development was a reaction to the historical situation resulting from 132 years (1830–1962) of brutal colonization. It was a situation of profound underdevelopment. During the colonial period, the Algerian economy, mainly agrarian, was characterized by a dualist structure. Two sectors coexisted: a modern sector and a traditional one. The modern sector was controlled by a few French families and companies that owned the best lands in the country. Using labor-saving techniques and equipment extensively, they mainly produced cash crops for export. The traditional sector had lands of much poorer quality and used primitive tools and techniques. This sector had very low yields, and yet it supported the vast majority of the indigenous population. There was little interaction between these two sectors. In fact, until 1959, "the symbiosis is greater between the economy of France and the modern sector of Algeria than between this latter and the economy of the Algerian countryside" (Benissad 1979:10). Algeria was so deeply dependent on France, the colonizing power, that "without France, the Algerian economy would not survive" (Benissad 1979:17). An indication of this dependence was trade. In 1960, France took 80 percent of all Algerian exports and accounted for 75 percent of Algerian imports (Farsoun 1975:7).

Industrial production was low, and whatever industry existed was concentrated in the light industry sector. The food industry alone contributed 45 percent of total industrial production (Benissad 1979:16). Income distribution was very unequal, with a handful of individuals owning vast wealth, while the majority of the population lived in miserable conditions. In 1951, out of 8 million Algerians, 5.4 million earned an average of $45 per year (Farsoun 1975:4). Health conditions were poor, with a high death rate (20 per thousand) and a low life expectancy at birth (47 years). The situation in education was no better. Only 46 percent of the school-age children attended primary school, and 90 percent of the adult population was illiterate (World Bank 1981).

Before the war of independence (November 1954 to July 1962) conditions in Algeria were already distressing. The war further devastated the country. What little industry there was, was disrupted; productive investments vanished and production declined to the point where in 1963 it was only 65 percent of what it had been a few years before (Farsoun 1975:4). By the end of the war, over one million people had been killed (out of a total population of less than ten million!), two million people were released from regroupment camps, and five hundred thousand refugees and four hundred thousand orphans had to be resettled. Unemployment in the industrial and service sectors rose to at least two million, while private civilian consumption dropped by 25 percent between the years 1954 and 1961 (World Bank 1981).

The eight hundred thousand French (and other European) colons in Algeria had monopolized the technical, managerial, medical, and all other professional fields. In 1962, there were only 1,700 Algerian teachers (*Le Monde* July 1982:11), less than 2,000 students in higher education (*Le Monde Diplomatique* November 1982:34–35), and less than five Algerian agricultural engineers (Benissad 1979:28). The sudden and massive departure of most of the colons in 1962, many of whom destroyed records and equipment as they left, brought Algeria to the brink of collapse.

Karen Farsoun (1975:3) summarizes Algeria's colonial experience in the following way:

> [Algeria's] own history serves as one of the most extreme examples of the profound destruction and deprivation of which colonialism was capable, and also serves as an example of the strength and endurance that a colonized people can muster in their task of overthrowing the yoke of the colonizers.

Choice of Development Strategy

The colonial experience, and especially the war of independence, had a profound and lasting effect on all Algerians who lived through that period. Since 1962, the paramount concern of successive Algerian governments has been the consolidation of national independence. This concern was reflected in the choice of the strategy to be followed for economic development.

As early as 1960–62, *El-Moudjahid*, the newspaper published by the Front de Liberation Nationale (FLN, the party leading the struggle for independence), outlined the basic components of that strategy. This involved the "building of an authentic and integrated national economy" by means of "destructive and constructive" actions (Benissad 1979:18). The destructive actions were aimed to eliminate the ties of dependence, particularly those with France, to destroy the mechanisms by which foreign interests exploited Algeria, and to remove the internal barriers to an autonomous economic development. The constructive actions were designed to build an introverted economy using the nation's resources. Since independence, these objectives have been consistently reaffirmed by the Algiers Charter, in presidential speeches, and in the 1976 National Charter.

When Algeria gained its independence in 1962, a period of political instability followed. It was not until 1967 that a comprehensive and coherent strategy of economic development emerged. The primary concern was the achievement of economic independence in the longrun. However, in Algeria economic independence is not an end in itself. Rather, it is the necessary condition for the achievement and the preservation of other major economic and social objectives, such as the building of socialism and the eradication of poverty and unemployment.

Because Algeria inherited from colonialism an economy characterized by archaic structures and a lack of an industrial base, a "veritable Industrial Revolution" was thought to be necessary to achieve these goals (Front de Liberation Nationale 1976:79). Industrialization's main role was to provide the country with the means to achieve an autonomous and integrated development by supplying the national economy with most of its needs in capital and consumer goods. Heavy industry was to form the foundation of the economy for two strategic reasons (Front de Liberation Nationale 1976:167). First, the existence of heavy industries in Algeria itself would guarantee the independence of the national economy and therefore the independence of the country. Heavy industries such as the steel industry, the hydrocarbons and petrochemical industries, the mechanical engineering branches, the electronics and electrical industries, the shipbuilding industry, and the chemical industry would act as a shield against external manipulations by providing most of the necessary inputs to the rest of the economy. Second, the existence of these heavy industries would provide the county with the capability to produce the military equipment it needs for its national defense and will therefore reinforce its independence.

In Algeria, then, the choice of heavy industrialization as the national economic development strategy resulted primarily from the belief that such a strategy is the one that contributes best to the preservation and reinforcement of national independence. Heavy industrialization, by developing the capital goods sector and by fostering the development of the productive forces, promotes socialism, makes rapid economic growth possible, and helps the establishment of an integrated and introverted national economy.

Theoretical Foundations

In their quest for an economic development strategy that would satisfy the political leadership's overriding objective of national independence, Algerian planners were inspired by two theoretical models: the Feldman model and the "industries industrialisantes" theory. These two models are outlined here, the Feldman model very briefly since it has been widely discussed elsewhere, the "industries industrialisantes" theory in more detail.

The Feldman Model

The Feldman model (1964) is an extension of the Marxian expanded reproduction scheme. In the Feldman model, the economy is divided into two departments. Department I produces capital goods that can be either installed in department I to make more capital goods or put in department II to produce more consumer goods. Department II produces consumer goods. Once the capital goods are installed, they cannot be transferred from department to department.

Basing his thinking on this two-sector division of the economy, Feldman used a dynamic analysis to study the growth rates of the total and departmental outputs and their interdependence. He came up with two important conclusions, one concerning the ratios of the capital stocks in the two departments, the other the allocation of investment between the two departments. He first concluded that to have a high rate of growth of the economy, a large share of the product of department I should be injected back into department I. Second, he found that to maintain a steady rate of growth, investment should be allocated between the departments in the same proportion as the capital stock. These two propositions are illustrated in table 13-1, which shows that the higher the proportion of the capital stock in department I (i.e., the greater Kp/Kc is) and, correspondingly, the higher the proportion of new investment in department I (i.e., the greater dKp/dK is), the higher the rate of growth of the economy will be. Thus, the Feldman model strongly supports the view that giving priority to heavy industry will result in a high growth rate of the economy. However, this will come about only at the cost of a low growth in consumption in the short-run. In the long run, however, consumption (and the economy in general) will grow faster than if a lower priority is given to heavy industry.

The Feldman model has several shortcomings. For one thing, Feldman's division of the economy into two sectors is rather crude. Though it may be attractive theoretically, this model has only a limited empirical meaning. Further, Feldman assumes the economy to be a closed system. In today's world where underdeveloped countries can trade their natural resources and buy capital goods, the applicability of the Feldman model is sharply reduced.

The "Industries Industrialisantes" Theory

The model of "industries industrialisantes" as developed by G. Destanne de Bernis (1966) is closely related to the Feldman model and the Mahalanobis (1955–56) model. It also presents many similarities with the

TABLE 13.1. Feldman's Two Propositions

Kp/Kc	dY/dt	$dKp/(dKp+dKc)$
0.106	4.6% per year	0.096
0.2	8.1	0.167
0.5	16.2	0.333
1.0	24.3	0.5

Notes: Kp = capital stock in department I,
Kc = capital stock in department II,
Y = total putput, and
K/Y = 2.1, by assumption.
Source: Ellman 1979:123.

work of Rosenstein-Rodan (1943) and Hirschman (1958). De Bernis was initially inspired by F. Perroux (1965) and his theories of "growth poles" and
"firme motrice." A firme motrice

> is a production unit that exerts asymmetric and irreversible effects on
> the social and institutional activities situated forward and backward of
> its own production. (Benissad 1979:129)

An "industrie industrialisante" is such a "firme motrice." It is located in
the capital goods sector because it is from this sector that economic growth
is initiated and new structuration of the economy progressively takes shape.

De Bernis (1966) sets out to find the best way for an underdeveloped
country to reach an autonomous development of an (ultimately) integrated
economy. He refuses to see the problem in terms of "agriculture versus industry" and "heavy industry versus light industry." Rather, he sees the
economy as an ensemble of potentially complementary sectors. His aim is
to determine an investment criterion that maximizes external economies and
minimizes external diseconomies. Hence, the problem comes down to the
determination of the sectors or industries that are particularly potent in
starting a chain reaction through the capture of external economies, that is,
sectors or industries that have strong forward and backward linkages. De
Bernis calls these sectors or industries with strong linkages "industries industrialisantes." He includes in this category the steel industry, the
hydrocarbons and petrochemical industries, the mechanical engineering
branches, and electronics and electrical industries, and the chemical industry. These "industries industrialisantes" have three principal features:

1. They have large dimensions to take advantage of economies of
scale.
2. They are in the capital goods sector because only industries in this
sector have the direct effect of restructuring techniques and the social and
economic structures.
3. They are highly capital-intensive to maximize output and to create
the propitious conditions for technological development.

When an industry with strong backward linkages is established, a
market for its inputs is created. This will encourage the emergence of new
industries that cater to its input needs. Similarly, when a new industry with
strong forward linkages is established, it will stimulate the creation of new
industries to use its output. Thus, the "industries industrialisantes" start a
chain reaction in the economy that will ultimately result in an integrated
economy having the means to develop autonomously. However, this will
not be the case if reliance on imports, especially of capital goods, persists or

if raw materials and intermediate goods are readily and continuously exported, thereby forfeiting the potential linkages.

For agriculture to develop, two steps are crucial: reorganization of the production structures, or "progresses in organization," and introduction of modern equipment, or "progresses in equipment." The first is imperative for it prepares the ground for the introduction of modern equipment. As De Bernis (1966:440) puts it, "Without the progresses in organization, nothing can be done that is efficient."

The aim of the reorganization of the production structure is to create new relations of production and a new mode of production that will allow a rapid technical evolution. The progress in organization will result in an increase in productive employment and also in higher average productivity. This in turn will spur the peasants' demand for modern equipment like tools, fertilizers, and cement, all goods that can be produced by the "industries industrialisantes." Thus, agriculture needs for its own development the existence of the steel industry, the chemical industry, and the cement industry, as well as other heavy industries. Moreover, agriculture encourages the creation of such industries for two reasons. First, it provides them with an important and ready market. Second, it can contribute to their financing through the mobilization of the surplus created initially by the progresses in organization and later by the introduction of modern equipment. Agriculture and industry are therefore complementary. The development of one of them encourages the expansion of the other.

The "industries industrialisantes" stimulate the development of the industrial sector in two ways:

1. The "industries industrialisantes," through their effects on agricultural productivity, expand the financial resources available for the expansion of the industrial sector.

2. They provide the capital goods necessary for the expansion of the industrial sector.

Thus, the "industries industrialisantes" encourage the veritable industrialization of the country.

An implication of the Feldman model is that giving a high priority to heavy industry will result in the shortrun in a slow growth of consumption. De Bernis disagrees and explains that such a conclusion was arrived at because Feldman ignored two essential factors: the role of the traditional subsistence sector and the industrialization effects set in motion by the "industries industrialisantes" of the capital goods sector. When these two factors are taken into consideration, "at no time is consumption slowed by a policy of high (priority to heavy industry)" (De Bernis 1966:465).

De Bernis distinguishes two periods after a program of "industries industrialisantes" is launched. In the first period, lasting about a decade during which the "industries industrialisantes" are built, the progresses in organization will be the main source of employment creation. At the end of this first period, the effects of the "industries industrialisantes" should start to be felt. These industries should have created the conditions for a rapid development of the entire industrial sector. With numerous new industries coming continuously on stream, unemployment will be eradicated.

For de Bernis, the rapid building of "industries industrialisantes" constitutes the way out of underdevelopment and the condition for an effective strategy of economic development. However, the success of such a program depends on two crucial conditions:

1. Since it can not be assumed that the propagation of the effects of the "industries industrialisantes" through the economy will occur spontaneously, central planning is necessary. Also, a certain number of radical sociopolitical transformations will have to be carried out.

2. Since the "industries industrialisantes" necessarily have large dimensions, they can be successfully implemented only in countries with continental dimensions or within the framework of regional economic cooperation between several smaller countries.

De Bernis' theory displays several weak points. This theory is completely pertinent only for countries with continental dimensions or within the framework of regional cooperation. It is not so relevant for most underdeveloped countries, which for the most part do not have the required size (except perhaps China, India, and a few others) and in most cases do not enjoy the internal and regional political stability necessary for regional economic cooperation.

Progresses in organization form the basis of several important conclusions reached by de Bernis. Yet, he does not define in any clear and concrete manner the nature of these progresses, or how they will be brought about, or how they will interact with the social and economic environment to improve it.

De Bernis advocates the use of capital-intensive techniques and advanced technology. Given the abundance of unskilled labor and the shortage of capital and highly skilled labor in most underdeveloped countries, it is doubtful that most of these countries can build "industries industrialisantes" without relying heavily on foreign sources of capital and technology and maintaining a high rate of unemployment, at least in the short run.

The Algerian Model of Economic Development

The National Charter, published in 1976 by the FLN following several months of popular debate, states explicitly the essential objectives of development in Algeria. This is, on the one hand, to accelerate the elevation of the Algerian people to living conditions in accordance with the norms of modern living and, on the other hand, to provide the country with an economic base freed from underdevelopment (Front de Liberation Nationale 1976:119). However, to achieve these objectives, true independence must be gained. For this reason, as the National Charter states,

> the development of Algeria is based on the quest for and consolidation of economic independence which postulates a constant action to avoid any hold, under any form, of the world imperialist system on the life or the future of the Nation. True independence postulates economic independence, which is based essentially on the recuperation of the natural resources, the appropriation by the collectivity of the major means of production, balance in foreign trade, the financial independence of the State, the creation of a national market, and the mastery of technology. In other words, it is a question of undertaking an integral development, including all aspects of the national life, based fundamentally on the popular will and on the necessity for the Nation to rely first on itself to accomplish the conditions of its effective independence, political as well as economic. (Front de Liberation Nationale 1976: 121-22)

To attain these objectives, an economic development strategy was progressively developed. This strategy is what came to be known as the "Algerian model of economic development." This model is heavily influenced by the Feldman model and, especially, by the "industries industrialisantes" theory. The major features of this model, as it was put into application over the period 1967-77, are: (1) nationalization of all foreign capital, (2) socialization of the major means of production, (3) creation of "industries industrialisantes," and (4) import substitution, whenever possible.

Nationalization of Foreign Capital

Nationalization of all foreign capital is, in the Algerian view, a condition for economic and political independence. It is also necessary because of the need to maximize the financial resources required by an ambitious development program.

Following independence in 1962, all lands owned by the *colons* were nationalized. In 1966, the mining companies were taken over by the state. This soon was followed by the nationalization of foreign banks, insurance companies, manufacturing operations, and all vacant property left by the *colons*. After the June 1967 Middle East war, most of the U.S. oil companies were expropriated. In February 1971, after months of fruitless negotiations, Algeria unilaterally took over 51 percent of the oil operations, 100 percent of the natural gas concessions and operations, and 100 percent of the oil and gas transport facilities of the remaining French companies.

In April 1971, a new law was passed restricting severely foreign direct investment in the country except in special cases, where it would be allowed only in the form of joint ventures with state corporations, with the latter controlling at least 51 percent of the joint venture.

Socialization of the Major Means of Production

For Algeria, "national liberation and social liberation are fundamentally interdependent" (Front de Liberation Nationale 1976:24). That is, upon independence Algeria chose the socialist path. Socialism's appeal is that it not only makes possible the acquisition of the most advanced techniques and scientific methods, but it also allows the organization of society on principles of rationality, equality, and humanity. In Algeria, the objectives of socialism are essentially threefold: (1) the consolidation of national independence; (2) the establishment of a society free of exploitation; and (3) the promotion of the Algerian people (Front de Liberation Nationale 1976: 22–23). However, socialism in Algeria has to be specifically Algerian. It has to be in tune with the historical and cultural realities of the country:

> Socialism in Algeria does not originate in any materialistic metaphysics and is not connected to any dogmatic conception alien to our national character. Its building is associated with the development of Islamic values which are a fundamental basic element of the personality of the Algerian people. (Front de Liberation Nationale 1976: 24)

Furthermore, as the late president Houari Boumediene said, Algeria

> is a country where the dictatorship of one class is not conceivable because our revolution is basically a peasant revolution and the proletariat does not exist yet. (Benissad 1979:22)

State control over the mineral resources and the major means of production was an important step toward socialism. By the early 1970s all the major means of production, the natural resources, the financial sector, the external trade, and the wholesale trade were nationalized and taken over by state companies and agencies. Algerian socialism, however, tolerates the existence of private property. A distinction is made between "exploiter private property" and "non-exploiter private property":

> The exploiter private property is that where the ownership of capital allows the exploitation of others and the enrichment to the detriment of the workers. The non-exploiter private property includes the property that an individual may need for his work, his housing, his culture, his health, his leisure and, in a general manner his personal and family use. (Front de Liberation Nationale 1976:30)

The exploiter private property is to be eliminated, whereas the "non-exploiter" private property is protected by the law as long as it does not constitute an obstacle to the building of socialism. But the private sector will always constitute a potential danger for socialism (Front de Liberation Nationale 1976:31). For this reason, several measures are taken to control it: limitation of its size and of its fields of activities, control over its earnings, dependence upon the socialist sector, and protection of the workers. Given that it is adequately controlled, the "non-exploiter" private sector has a useful role to play in the national economy. It can produce goods and services that the state companies and agencies can not provide at this state of their development, and it can also create jobs.

"Industries Industrialisantes" Form the Foundation of the Economy

The major goal of the Algerian strategy of economic development is to create almost from scratch a fully integrated, introverted economy with the means to develop autonomously. Algeria has large reserves of natural resources such as oil (more than 8 billion barrels of reserves), natural gas (10 percent of world proven reserves), and iron ore (5.3 billion tons of reserves). The challenge is to use these resources to build a fully developed economy before they run out. The Algerian development strategy has three main facets. One seeks to extend the sources of surplus and maximize them. This is an additional reason why it was imperative to nationalize the natural resources. Once these resources are in the hands of the state, the task is to maximize the revenues derived from them. Since it joined OPEC, Algeria has consistently pushed for higher oil prices. It also has waged a battle with its main gas customers (Western Europe, the United States, and Japan) to raise the price of its natural gas to the level of oil prices. Furthermore, it has tried as much as possible to sell its foreign-currency-earning goods, mainly oil and gas, not in the form of raw materials but in the form of more expensive refined products.

A second key facet of the country's development strategy is the use of revenues generated through exports to build a heavy industry that will form the backbone of the economy. Given the abundance of oil, natural gas, and iron ore, the hydrocarbons and the petrochemical industries and the steel industry, industries eminently "industrialisantes," are to be the "engines of development" around which other "industries industrialisantes" such as the mechanical engineering branches, the electronics and electrical industries, and the chemical industry will evolve.

The third main aspect of Algeria's development program is to organize exchanges between agriculture and industry. On the one hand, agriculture is to provide a market for the output of industry and later be a source of surplus for further industrialization, while, on the other hand, industry is to provide the equipment and materials necessary for agriculture to progress from a primitive to a modern state. But a condition for a successful agriculture-industry exchange is the reorganization of agriculture. This was one of the purposes of the Agrarian Revolution that was launched in 1971.

This multifaceted strategy was put into action through multiyear investment plans. The first plan, appropriately labeled "Pre-Plan" (1967–69), was designed to prepare the ground for more ambitious plans: First Four-Year Plan (1970–73), Second Four-Year Plan (1974–77), and so on. (See table 13-2.) These plans have a number of principal characteristics. One is that industry has priority over agriculture. Investment in industry represented over 56 percent of total investments in the Pre-Plan versus only 16 percent for agriculture. During the First and Second Four-Year Plans, the comparable data were 57 versus 13 percent and 64 versus 4.7 percent, respectively. Within industry, heavy industry has priority. This sector was allocated 89.3 percent of total industrial investments during the Pre-Plan, 94.7 percent during the First Plan, and 93.3 percent during the Second Plan.

The Plans also give investment priority over consumption. The share of gross planned investment of the public sector (the state and the public companies) in the gross domestic product grew from 27.8 percent in 1969 to 55.3 percent in 1977. If the private sector is included, the gross national planned investment represented close to 60 percent of the GDP in 1977 (Palloix 1980a:535).

Investments have been concentrated in the hydrocarbons and petrochemical industries and the steel industry, since they are to act as the "engines of growth" in the economy. Over the 1967–77 period, these sectors received, respectively, 46.5 percent and 14.6 percent of total industrial investments (Palloix 1980a:540). The plants in the heavy industry sector are large, use capital-intensive techniques and advanced technology, and are highly integrated. Integration rates of 70–80 percent are not uncommon.

Each sector of the industry is monopolized by one state corporation. Examples are the hydrocarbons and petrochemical industries (Sonatrach), steel industry (Sns), mechanical engineering branches (Sonacome), electronics

TABLE 13.2. Algerian Investment Plans, 1967–1977

	1967–69		1970–73		1974–77	
	Amount (billions of dinars)	Share (%)	Amount (billions of dinars)	Share (%)	Amount (billions of dinars)	Share (%)
Hydrocarbons	2.7	28	9.8	27	36	30
Capital goods	2.2	22	9.7	27	33	29.8
Consumption goods	0.45	6	1.3	3	5	4.3
Total industry	5.4	56	20.8	57	74.2	64.1
Agriculture	1.6	16	4.6	13	5.8	4.7
Infrastructure and others	2.7	28	11.3	30	40.8	33.3
Total	9.7	100	36.7	100	120.8	100

Source: Benachenhou 1982:48.

and electrical industries (Sonelec), and chemical industry (Snic). Foreign direct investment is usually not allowed. Construction of the plants and factories is to be mainly on a turnkey or a "produit on main" basis. In the Second Plan, turnkey and "produit on main" contracts accounted for 77 percent of the industrial contracts finalized (Temmar 1983:192).

Import Substitution

In order to reduce reliance on external markets and to economize on foreign currency, a policy of import substitution was actively pursued. Whenever possible, products were to be produced in Algeria instead of imported.

Agriculture has an important role to play, but it is industry that will have the most impact on the reduction of imports:

> By assuming an ever larger cover of the national needs for consumption and investment goods from national production, industrialization comes to reduce imports, and practically limit them to some goods that determined factors do not allow to obtain in the country, i.e. certain types of equipment, some raw materials and a series of finished and semi-finished goods. (Front de Liberation Nationale 1976:126)

With the importance of outside markets for the national economy thus reduced, economic independence will be enhanced.

In the beginning, only products requiring a low technology content and locally available inputs were affected by this policy. These products were mainly concentrated in the light industry sector, especially in the textile, leather, and food industries. For example, the ratio of imports over total national supply of textiles and leather goods dropped to 6.6 percent in 1974 from 29.5 percent in 1969 (Benissad 1979:136). As new industrial complexes go into production, more and more products previously imported, including capital goods requiring advanced technology, will be manufactured in Algeria.

EVALUATION OF THE ALGERIAN EXPERIENCE OF HEAVY INDUSTRIALIZATION: THE FIRST PHASE (1967–79)

Though it can be argued that a decade is not a long enough period of time for an in-depth evaluation of strategy that aims at long-term structural change, it nevertheless is sufficient for an evaluation of the first results and the comparison of those results with official objectives. The long-run objective of Algerian economic development is the establishment of an independent, socialistic, and integrated economy. In this section, Algeria's progress towards these goals is evaluated.

Evidence

Economic Independence

In Algeria, economic (and political) independence is the paramount priority. This is understandable in a country that throughout its history suffered so much at the hands of foreign powers. In the Algerian view, the attainment of this aim is contingent upon the successful carrying out of a certain number of actions designed, on the one hand, to minimize the hold of external interests on the national economy and, on the other hand, to increase the country's capacity to implement the policies it chooses. These actions are recuperation of the national resources, socialization of the major means of production, balance in foreign trade, financial independence of the state, mastery of technology, and creation of a national market to supply the inputs and final goods to the country, especially food.

The first two of these actions were discussed earlier, and it was shown that by the early 1970s they had been successfully implemented. Let us turn now to the remaining four actions, beginning with foreign trade.

After the program of "industries industrialisantes" was launched in 1967, Algeria's foreign trade experienced a tremendous growth, increasing from a total of $613.2 million in 1967 to $7,122 million in 1977. In 1977, its foreign trade represented 82.9 percent of its gross domestic product, up from 41.5 percent in 1967 (Schnetzler 1980:456). Furthermore, its foreign trade remained overwhelmingly directed toward the industrialized capitalist countries, as shown in table 13-3. By the end of the 1970s, the industrialized capitalist countries were the main trading partners of Algeria. In 1979 they purchased 96.2 percent of Algeria's exports and accounted for 90.8 percent of its imports. Concurrently, the role of the socialist countries was almost negligible: 1.78 percent of exports and 2.84 percent of imports in 1979. Looking at individual nations, the role of France had drastically declined. In 1967, France represented 61.3 percent of Algerian exports and 72.6 percent of imports. By 1979, these figures had dropped to only 10.8 percent for exports and 25.3 percent for imports. The role of the United States, however, had grown markedly, especially in exports. Exports to the United States, which represented only 0.40 percent of total Algerian exports in 1967, jumped to 52.9 percent by 1979.

Thus, by 1979, Algeria had come to depend almost exclusively on the industrialized capitalist countries for its foreign trade. Algeria also depended on a few primary commodities for its exports. In 1979, the share of primary commodities (almost exclusively oil and gas) represented 99.6 percent of total exports (United Nations 1981). Over the first phase of industrialization, then, Algeria relied heavily on foreign trade with the industrialized capitalist countries. One of its objectives, namely, diversification of foreign trade, was not achieved even though important progress was made toward its goal of diversification away from France. These developments were partly the result of political as well as geographical considerations, but to a large extent they stemmed from Algeria's strategy of heavy industrialization.

In assessing the official goal of financial independence, one notes that Algeria's ambitious development plans were partially financed through

TABLE 13.3. Direction of Algerian Foreign Trade (in percent)

Region	1967		1974		1979	
	Exports	Imports	Exports	Imports	Exports	Imports
Industralized capitalist countries	94.3	92.2	84.3	84.9	96.2	90.8
• United States	0.4	5.9	23.4	12.0	52.9	5.3
• France	61.3	72.6	19.2	27.9	10.8	25.3
• West Germany	14.9	3.4	20.5	12.9	16.5	16.2
• Italy	4.6	3.5	5.8	8.2	5.1	14.1
Socialist Countries	—	—	3.9	5.5	1.8	2.8
• Soviet Union	—	—	1.7	2.8	0.5	0.6
Others	5.7	7.8	11.8	9.6	2.1	6.3
Total value (in $ millions)	780	613	4,687	4,247	9,380	8,419

Source: International Monetary Fund.

TABLE 13.4. Public External Debt, 1971-78 (in millions of dollars)

Source	1971	1973	1975	1978
Official sources	1,068.8	1,637.1	2,112.1	3,420.2
Suppliers and others	1,043.9	1,297.9	3,665.9	5,714.7
Financial markets	128.5	1,981.4	3,812.8	9,978.5
All lenders	2,241.1	4,916.4	9,590.8	19,113.4

Source: Frieden 1981:414.

external borrowing. The amount of external debt accumulated to finance the country's economic development is shown in table 13-4. By 1978, Algeria's external debt reached almost $20 billion. This external source of capital represented 28 percent of the total investment funds in 1977 (see table 13-5). At the end of 1975, according to the *Bulletin du FMI*, Algeria was ranked first in terms of external debt per capita among the developing countries with public debts exceeding $5 billion, and it was fifth in terms of total amount of public debt (Schnetzler 1980:456n). Also, the debt service ratio jumped disturbingly from 3.2 in 1970 to 25.6 percent in 1979 (World Bank 1981).

Since the "industries industrialisantes" program was launched, the role of foreign firms as suppliers of technology has expanded significantly. These firms became involved in all aspects of Algeria's industrial development (Thierry 1980:478). One indicator of the growing reliance on foreign sources of technology was the rapid increase in the imports of technological goods and services (see table 13-6). In 1978, Algeria imported 90 percent of its mechanical and electrical equipment, and more than two-thirds of total engineering activities were performed by foreign firms (Thierry 1980:479-80).

After the launching of the "industries industrialisantes" program, Algerian agricultural production was increasingly unable to meet national

TABLE 13.5. Share of External Finance in Total Investment Capital (in percent)

Year	1971	1972	1973	1974	1975	1976	1977
Share	26.0	22.4	19.8	31.6	24.1	33.0	28.0

Source: Adapted from Palloix 1980a: 546-47.

TABLE 13.6. Algerian Imports of Technology (billions of dinars)

	1973	1974	1975	1976	1977	1978
Machinery and equipment imports	3.53	5.77	9.75	10.59	13.13	n.a.
Spending on technical assistance	n.a.	2.7	4.7	5.0	6.6	8.6

Sources: MPAT 1979:297; Benachenhou 1982:87.

consumption. Local cereal production, which in 1969 satisfied 73 percent of consumption, covered only 41 percent in 1977 and less than 40 percent in 1979. In the late 1970s, local production met only 10 percent of sugar needs, 50–60 percent of milk needs, and 25 percent of fats needs. This prompted the government to turn increasingly toward imports to fill the gap. Imports of agricultural products, which in 1970 totalled only $173.6 million, rose to $974 million in 1976 and to $2,240 million in 1980. During the same period, exports of Algerian agricultural products dwindled. The share of food in total Algerian exports dropped from 20 percent in 1970 to only 1.1 percent in 1979. Even in absolute value, food exports declined. In 1976 they amounted to $149 million and dropped to $118 million in 1980, representing, respectively, 15.3 percent and 5.3 percent of agricultural imports for those two years (Food and Agriculture Organization 1981).

Building of Socialism

Earlier we noted that the state took over the major means of production and had a monopoly over foreign trade and wholesale trade. Using centralized planning and fiscal control bodies, the state directly set production quotas, regulated resource allocation, fixed prices, and undertook the marketing of most major commodities. These actions are clear indications of progress toward socialism. However, these actions by themselves are not enough to build socialism. For this reason, it is important to look at some other criteria to see what other progress was achieved toward that end.

The satisfaction of the fundamental needs of the popular masses is a major objective of Algerian socialism. In general, there was a significant improvement in the basic welfare of the vast majority of Algerians after 1962. On the average, they lived longer, had better access to medical care, ate better, were more educated, and had more access to modern goods than ever before (see table 13–7). Just as importantly, the benefits of economic development in Algeria were shared by all sectors of society. Education was democratized and made accessible to all Algerians. In 1974, medical care was socialized and became free. Prices of basic foods were heavily subsidized so as to make them universally affordable, while prices of luxury durables were steeply taxed. Rents for public housing, electricity rates, and prices of heating and cooking gas were kept low, thus bringing these goods within the reach of even the poorest segments of society.

TABLE 13.7. Social Conditions in Algeria

	1960	1970	MRE[a]
Demographic Characteristics:			
• Crude birthrate (per thousand)	51.0	49.0	48.0
• Crude death rate (per thousand)	20.0	16.0	13.0
• Life expectancy at birth (in years)	47.0	53.0	56.0
Health and Nutrition:			
• Population per physician	7,930	7,860	5,560
• Population per hospital bed	280	340	370
• Calorie supply per capita (percentage of requirements)	73.0	78.0	89.0
Education:			
• Number enrolled in primary school as a percentage of age group	46.0	75.0	89.0
• Number enrolled in secondary school as percentage of age group	8.0	11.0	19.0
• Adult literacy rate	10.0	26.0	35.0
Housing and consumption:			
• Access to electricity (as a percentage of total dwellings)	—	34.0	57.0[b]
• Radio receivers per thousand people	54.0	—	198.0
• Energy consumption per capita (kilogram of coal equivalent)	252.0	342.0	729.0

Notes: [a]Most recent estimate (between 1974 and 1977).

[b]This figure was taken from Le Monde Diplomatique, November 1980:26.

Source: World Bank 1981:444, 450–51.

Thus, in terms of medical care, education, and basic consumption, the welfare of the average Algerian generally improved. A person who visited Algeria in the 1960s and then again in the late 1970s could see the improvements. But there remained some dark spots, housing being one of them. During the first phase of industrialization, the supply of housing lagged markedly behind demand. With one of the highest population growth rates in the world, the breakup of the traditional extended family, and the low cost of housing, demand for housing soared. In the late 1970s demand for housing in the urban areas was estimated at 100,000 new units a year, but a total of only 100,000 new urban and semiurban units were built over the 1964–78 period (Schnetzler 1980:459). Overcrowding resulted. In 1966, an average of 6.8 persons inhabited a 65-square meter living space. By 1977, that figure had increased to 8.3 persons (Osterman 1982:29).

The most important basic need that was not met adequately was the provision of jobs. Though the number of wage earners more than doubled from 1,060,000 in 1966 to 2,210,000 in 1977 (Palloix 1980:558), unemployment remained high at between 18 and 28 percent (Benachenhou 1982:220–21). Although, as seen earlier, per capita basic consumption generally improved, per capita real global private consumption deteriorated. Global private consumption (in current Algerian dinars AD) rose from AD 9.2 billion in 1967 to AD 36.6 billion in 1976 (Benissad 1979:149). When the rate of inflation and the increase in population are taken into account, one finds that per capita real consumption actually declined. Thus, as far as the satisfaction of basic needs is concerned, the first phase of industrialization ended with mixed results. Important progress was made, but in some areas (employment, per capita consumption, and housing), the results were not satisfactory.

It is hard to assess the impact of industrialization on social inequalities, since good data on income distribution in Algeria are scarce. Still, some information is available that gives some indication on how income distribution evolved over the first phase of industrialization. Several sources suggested that over the period being considered the differences in salary between the highest paid workers and the lowest ones declined (Osterman 1982, Palloix 1980b, Nellis 1983). Table 13–8 documents the evolution of industrial salaries between 1968 and 1976. It indicates that increases in salaries occurred in such a way that the higher the salaries the smaller the increases, and the lower the salaries the larger the increases. The result was a reduction in the wage differential between the highest and lowest salaries. Also, there was an official ceiling on salaries to which even the salaries of the very highest officials were subjected. This ceiling was AD 2,400 (approximately $600) a month in 1975 (Nellis 1983:385).

In 1971, the Agrarian Revolution was launched. One of its major goals was a more equitable income distribution in the rural areas. The large

TABLE 13.8. Evolution of Industrial Salaries, 1968 to 1970 (Algerian dinars per month)

Type of Worker	1968	1976	Average Annual Growth (% per year)
Engineers, managers	1,700	2,400	4.40
Technicians	1,200	1,700	4.45
Skilled workers	870	1,200	4.63
Unskilled workers	450	670	5.10
Average	750	1,066	4.49

Source: Palloix 1980(b):560.

estates were nationalized and distributed to the poor peasants. Furthermore, a ceiling was put on the amount of land a family could use.

Can we conclude, then, that income distribution was made more equitable? The evidence presented here is not detailed enough to justify such an interpretation. First, by 1977, implementation of the Agrarian Revolution was still limited and affected only a small portion of the rural areas. Second, even though data on salaries point to a narrowing of wage differentials, this information loses much of its significance when one knows that many engineers, managers, and officials received, as supplements to their salaries, bonuses and material advantages such as cars and housing. Third, the existence of a private sector made it possible for some individuals to accumulate large amounts of money.

A final criterion for judging progress towards socialism is popular participation. Over the 1967–79 period, Algeria established a set of institutions designed to involve the popular masses in local government matters, national policy initiation and review, and choice of political representatives at the local and national levels. Centrally controlled national organizations articulating the interests of workers, peasants, women, and youth, as well as a mass mobilizing political party, elected local councils, and an elected National Assembly were all instituted. In addition, elected committees at the level of the workplace (in all industrial units of the parastatal sector, on all self-managed farms, and in every rural cooperative) were put in place. An average Algerian became entitled to participate in elections at the workplace, at the communal, daira (county) and wilaya (province) levels, in party elections, in his or her mass organization, and in a variety of national elections. Over an eight-month period in 1976–77, Algerians voted four times: for the National Charter, for a new constitution, for the president of the Republique, and for the National Assembly.

Thus, over the 1967–79 period the number of participatory opportunities increased substantially in Algeria. Some people have pointed out the limited nature of this popular participation, but in Algeria these options were seen as an important step toward socialism:

> These bodies are the tutorial laboratories in which a basically uneducated population is learning the skills necessary for the proper functioning of participatory decentralized local government. (Nellis 1983:389)

Economic Integration

The use of input-output tables is, in principle, helpful to get a clear idea about the degree of integration of the different sectors of an economy. By comparing input-output tables at different points in time, an idea of the progress toward economic integration can be obtained. In the case of Algeria, M.E. Benissad, an Algerian economist, has compared the input-output tables of 1968 and 1970 and concluded that some progress toward economic integration was achieved (Benissad 1979:141–46). In 1977, a new table was drawn for the year 1974; unfortunately, it cannot be compared to the earlier ones because it used a different methodology.

For lack of better data, we will rely on some information giving at least a general feeling on the evolution of economic integration in Algeria. Though the production of raw materials, intermediate goods, and manufactured goods substantially increased, exports of these goods dropped, with the exception of oil and gas products, thus reducing leakages and fostering a more intense interaction between the different sectors of the economy. The industries with the highest forward and backward linkages and that exert strong and positive effects on economic integration (the hydrocarbons and petrochemical industries, the steel industry, the mechanical engineering branches, the electronics and electrical industries, the chemical industry, and the construction materials industry) experienced a fast growth over the first decade of industrialization.

By 1977, the hydrocarbons sector supplied 100 percent of the energy needs of the country (which expanded fourfold over the period 1965–77). In 1965, wood and coal represented 19 percent of the country's total consumption of energy. The petrochemical industry gave birth to the fertilizer industry, which, by 1978, was able to satisfy 58 percent of the total demand for agricultural fertilizers, a demand that grew at a rate of more than 25 percent a year (Mekideche 1980:518–21). The petrochemical industry also produced such items as methanol, synthetic resins, ammonia, urea, and polyethylene. Most of this output was used domestically to produce finished and semifinished goods. Plants in Algiers, Setif, and elsewhere transformed this output into plastic products, synthetic fibers, and other goods for agriculture and other sectors of the national economy.

The steel industry progressed from the basic conversion of iron ore into pig iron, which was mostly destined for exports, to the production of a varied array of iron and steel products for domestic use. The steel complex at El-Hadjar produced 300,000 tons of steel in 1976. This included steel pipe, steel tubing, seamless pipe, cold roll steel, and tin plate (U.S. Department of Commerce 1977:3). With the rapid expansion of the economy and the ensuing growing demand for steel products, the steel industry was able to meet only 40 percent of domestic demand in 1978 (Bouchema 1980:497). For this reason, a further expansion of the steel industry was planned to boost the capacity of the El-Hadjar steel complex to 2 million tons a year. Long-term plans for a 10-million tons a year steel complex started to be discussed.

The mechanical engineering branches, which depend closely on the steel industry, expanded significantly. Between 1967 and 1977, 17 new industrial complexes were built for this sector alone, producing diesel engines, motorcycles, farm machinery, machine tools, and heavy construction equipment. Sonacome, the state monopoly in the mechanical engineering branches, covered 50 percent of the needs of agriculture in mechanical equipment.

The supply of electric power progressed rapidly. In 1970, only 38 percent of all Algerian homes used electricity. This rate increased to 57 percent in 1977. Numerous other accomplishments in the electrical and electronics industries, the chemical industry, the construction materials industry, and the light industries testified to the fact that industrialization was becoming a reality and that economic integration was progressing.

The policy of the state companies that required foreign contractors to build the industrial complexes according to an optimal rate of integration contributed to reducing leakages and thereby stimulated economic integration. Each industrial complex produced a large portion of the goods necessary for its own final output. The portion not produced in the complex itself was to be acquired in the other sectors of the national economy. Only in cases where the goods were not available locally were imports allowed. By the end of the 1970s, national production was able to satisfy an appreciable share of national demand, as is shown for some products in table 13-9. Thus, the available evidence suggests that during the 1970s the development of a self-centered and integrated economy progressed.

Heavy Industry and Progress toward an Independent, Socialistic and Integrated Economy

The evidence presented thus far supports the point that over the first phase of industrialization Algeria's reliance on foreign capital, technology,

TABLE 13.9. Domestic Production as Percent of Algerian Demand, Selected Products, 1980

Mechanical equipment for agriculture	60%
Commercial vehicles	49
Equipment for train services	20
Machine tools	10
Electromechanical equipment	20
Construction equipment	19
Cables	56
Lamps	87
Metallic frames	50

Source: Benachenhou 1982:296.

food supplies, and trade increased and that some progress toward socialism and economic integration was achieved. These results stem, to a large extent, from the strategy of heavy industrialization.

Heavy industrialization is an expensive undertaking. Since it was launched, Algeria's investment expenditures soared from an average, in Algerian dinars (AD), of 3.04 billion a year in the 1967–69 Pre-Plan to an average of AD 27.6 billion a year in the 1974–77 Second Plan. A single gas liquification plant at Arzew cost $2.5 billion, and Algeria built several such plants (Mekideche 1980:511n). Once a decision to follow a strategy of rapid heavy industrialization was made, a certain reliance on international financing was inevitable given the massive scale of investment resources needed and the reluctance, for political reasons, to allow foreign direct investment in the country.

The vital importance of foreign trade to the Algerian economy was also a reflection of the ambition of the heavy industrialization program. When the program was initiated in 1967, a capital goods sector was nonexistent in the country; therefore, all the capital goods needed for industrialization had to be imported and on an increasing scale as the Plans became more and more ambitious. (See table 13–10.) Not only did the physical quantities of capital goods increase substantially, but the prices of those goods went up significantly as a result of international inflation. The evolution of the costs of the industrial complexes in Algeria reflects this trend. As an example, the price of a gas liquification plant increased fourfold between 1970 and 1978 (Mekideche 1980:518). The increased quantities and the higher prices combined to drive the imports bill from a total of AD 3.15 billion in 1967 to AD 29.6 billion in 1977. On the exports side, more and more oil and gas had to be produced and exported in order to pay for the imports.

The structure of Algeria's foreign trade was to a certain extent the result of political and geographical considerations, as noted earlier, but it

TABLE 13.10. Composition of Algerian Imports, 1967 to 1977 (in millions of dinars and percentage shares)

| Year | Consumer Goods | | Intermediate and Capital Goods and Raw Materials | |
	Amount	Share of Total Imports (in percent)	Amount	Share of Total Imports (in percent)
1967	1,634	51.8	1,520	48.2
1970	1,164	18.7	5,049	81.3
1974	4,661	26.6	12,857	73.4
1977	8,198	27.8	21,336	72.2

Source: Benissad 1979:181.

was mainly the consequence of certain features of the heavy industrialization strategy. In most cases, Algerian industrial complexes used capital-intensive techniques and advanced technology. Algerian planners believed the best source of this technology, especially in the hydrocarbons, petrochemical, electronic, and mechanical engineering sectors, was the advanced capitalist countries. Algeria's exports consisted mainly of oil and gas, products that neither the Arab world as a whole nor the socialist world as a whole needed to import but that the capitalist world required. This explains the overwhelming share of Algerian exports going to these latter countries.

The choice of technology cannot be separated from the investment allocation decisions in different sectors of the economy. The choice of technology becomes very limited once the investment allocation decisions have been made. For instance, once a decision has been reached to give investment priority to heavy industry, the use of capital-intensive techniques and advanced technology becomes inevitable (Wilber 1969). Algeria, having opted for a strategy of economic development involving heavy industrialization, had to deal with the problem of technology supply. As a country where skilled labor and domestic technology supplies were extremely scarce, both a legacy of colonization, it had no choice but to rely massively, at least in the short run, on foreign sources of technology.

Agriculture suffered badly from the very high priority given to industry. Its share of total investment expenditures dropped from 19 percent in the Pre-Plan to only 4.7 percent in the Second Plan. This allowed the industrial sector to attract the youngest and the ablest managers and workers, and to deflect toward industrial use lands and water resources previously used for agricultural purposes. The result was a regression in food production, which fell to 97 percent of its 1969–71 average by 1978, according to

FAO data. At the same time, demand for agricultural products expanded rapidly under the pressures of a very high population growth rate and a fast increase in incomes. This led Algeria to reduce its already small food exports and to import large quantities of agricultural products.

Hence, Algeria became increasingly dependent on the outside world after the start of the "industries industrialisantes" program, a result seemingly at odds with its professed objective of economic independence. Can one conclude that this objective was compromised? This would be a hasty conclusion. Economic independence can only be a long-term objective for a country like Algeria, which began its development program extremely dependent on the former colonial power and which had insufficient domestic productive forces. The objective pursued was not to be completely self-sufficient. Rather, the aim was to develop domestic productive forces to a point where no external force would be in a position to inflict harm on the Algerian economy for political or economic gain. Algeria, therefore, did not reject interdependent relationships as long as they were equally beneficial to all parties involved. Nevertheless, it is true that over the short run Algeria became dangerously dependent on the industrialized capitalist countries, a group of countries with which it had serious ideological disagreements. This situation was reluctantly accepted as a necessary evil to be eliminated as soon as possible. The crucial point was that in the short run and medium run, the bases for autonomous development had to be established. There is evidence suggesting that such bases were, in fact, being achieved.

First, as shown earlier, Algeria succeeded in creating a modern industrial sector that was becoming increasingly integrated during its First and Second Plans. Second, there is evidence supporting the view that bases for long-run autonomous technological development were being laid. The most significant is the vast effort in education. Investment expenditures in education represented AD 2.89 billion (8.7 percent of total investments) in the 1970-73 Plan and AD 9.95 billion (9.0 percent of total investments) in the 1974-77 Plan. Education expenditures during the 1974-77 Plan amounted to more than the total investment expenditures during the 1967-69 Pre-Plan. This translated into a steep increase in the number of people attending school and a mushrooming of educational facilities across the country, as table 13-11 shows. Between 1974 and 1977, the number of students enrolled in primary schools as a percentage of age group increased to 89 percent, up from 46 percent in 1960 (World Bank 1981).

It has been estimated that the state firms generally reserved at least 10 percent of their total investments funds for the training of their manpower (Said-Amer 1981:82). Each industrial complex had a training school where the new recruits, generally unskilled, spent between two months and two years learning a skill. In addition, each state firm offered numerous

TABLE 13.11. Evolution of Algerian School Enrollments

	1962-63	1970-71	1977
Primary schools	777,636	1,851,416	2,782,044
Secondary schools	50,784	227,207	493,005*

Note: *Data for school year 1975-1976.
Source: Benachenhou 1982: 341-242.

scholarships to high school and college graduates to study in Algeria or abroad. During the 1970s, at least some of the state firms were able to establish the nucleus of an autonomous technological base. An indication of this is that by the late 1970s the number of Algerian technicians and engineers engaged in industrial research and development was 5,000, as compared to only 1,381 in 1970 (Thierry 1980:479).

There are other factors that permitted Algeria to keep control of its economy, even though it had become extremely dependent on the outside world. Though the industrialized capitalist counties played a key role in its industrialization efforts, Algeria was not overwhelmingly dependent on any one country. Moreover, it instituted some procedures that prevented any foreign power from getting to a position where it would acquire political or economic leverage on Algerian affairs. For example, the construction of the El-Hadjar steel complex was divided up among several competing foreign groups: Italians, Russians, British, French, East Germans, West Germans, Swedish, and Japanese. This practice was typical in the major industrial complexes.

In addition to its short-term effect of greater external dependence, Algeria's "industries industrialisantes" program also affected the basic welfare of the average Algerian. Over the 1967–77 period, the consumer goods sector, especially housing, received little attention from Algerian planners. The low growth in consumption as evidenced by the decline in per capita real private consumption seems to confirm Feldman's conclusions and contradict those of de Bernis.

The low growth in employment resulted from decisions that favored capital-intensive techniques and advanced technology throughout the economy. During the early stages of their development, the Soviet Union and China were able to achieve higher growth rates in employment. The Soviet Union, which emphasized capital-intensive techniques and advanced technology in heavy industry, also relied on labor-intensive techniques in subsidiary processes such as maintenance, intraplant transport, and material handling. China also used labor-intensive techniques and low technology whenever possible. In Algeria, no such efforts were made. Algerian planners believed that Algeria could not use dual techniques as in the Soviet Union and China, because of its reliance on foreign firms for its technology and the training of its labor force (de Bernis 1971:552).

Not only were dual techniques not used in heavy industry, but Algerian state firms systematically preferred capital-intensive techniques even in light industry. Table 13-12 shows the relatively high average costs of job creation in some plants in the light industry sector. By contrast, the average cost of job creation in the private sector was AD 13,744 for 86 industrial private firms in the Oran region during 1968-73 (Bouziane 1982:282). This shows that poor results in job creation were not direct results of the priority given to heavy industry, but, rather, they were the consequence of a feature of the "industries industrialisantes" model as applied in Algeria, namely, the systematic preference given to capital-intensive techniques in both heavy and light industries.

RECENT DEVELOPMENTS: THE SECOND PHASE OF INDUSTRIALIZATION

At the end of the Second Four-Year Plan in 1977, no new plan was initiated for the following two years. Instead, the government paused to take stock of the record of the past decade of industrialization. Many party members and government officials criticized the excessive reliance of Algeria on foreign markets and the "excessively predominant place accorded the hydrocarbons sector essentially oriented to the world capitalist market." Many were not impressed by the growth in industrial production, which lagged well behind what could have been expected from the massive investment efforts. Indeed, a large number of the new industrial production units ran at less than 50 percent of their capacity.

In order to preserve the long-run objective of the establishment of an independent, socialist, and integrated economy, corrective measures were deemed necessary. Starting in 1980, a number of reforms that were to be implemented in the 1980-84 and 1985-89 Five-Year Plans were introduced

TABLE 13.12. Average Cost of Job Creation in Algerian Industry, 1972-73

Plant	Average Cost of Job Creation (in Algerian dinars)
Furniture (Boufarik)	73,400
Grouped mills (Bouira)	159,000
Shaving blades (Algiers)	31,000
Plastic bags (Setif)	140,000

Source: Benissad 1979:54.

(see table 13.13.) Industry was still to take the lion's share of total investment expenditures: 38.6 percent in the 1980–84 Plan and 31.6 percent in 1985–89 Plan. However, industrial priorities shifted and light industry was given more attention. The sectors that would get more consideration were construction materials, textiles, and food processing in order to alleviate the frequent shortages of these goods.

Furthermore, labor-intensive techniques were favored over capital-intensive ones, whenever possible. Agriculture was to receive growing attention compared to previous plans: AD 47.1 billion ($12.3 billion) or 11.7 percent of total investment expenditures were earmarked for this sector in the 1980–84 Plan and AD 79 billion or 14.4 percent in the 1985–89 Plan. Reforms were introduced in the agricultural sector to increase production and thereby reduce the country's food dependence, which was deemed "intolerable." The marketing of fruits and vegetables produced by the state sector (which controls half the agricultural area) was liberalized; the self-managed domains were restructured and broken up into "economically viable and humanly masterable units"; the gap between agricultural and nonagricultural incomes was reduced; the use of production inputs such as seeds and fertilizers was intensified; a large effort in water development for

TABLE 13.13. Algerian Investment Plans, 1980–89 (in billions of dinars)

	1980-89		1985-89	
	Amount	Share (%)	Amount (AD bns)	Share (%)
Productive Sectors:				
• Industry	154.5	38.6	174.2	31.6
• Production enterprises	20	5	19	3.5
• Agriculture-water	47.1	118	79	3.5
• Transport	13	3.2	16	2.7
• Storage-distribution	13	3.2	15.85	2.9
• Telecommunications	6	1.5	8	1.4
Basic Infrastructures and Social Sectors:				
• Economic infrastructures	23.2	5.8	45.5	8.3
• Housing	50	15	86	15.7
• Education-training	42.2	10.5	45	8.2
• Health	7	1.7	8	1.4
• Collective equipment	9.6	2.4	44	8
Total	400.6	100	550	100

Note: Totals may not be exact because of rounding.
Source: Afrique Expansion February-March 1985:87.

agriculture was undertaken; and technical recruitment for agriculture would be more than doubled, with the intention of providing one engineer or technician for every 80 farmers.

Measures were taken to bolster economic efficiency. The state firms, some of which had become giants and formed "states within a state" (the hydrocarbons company, Sonatrach, alone employed 100,000 people), were split into several smaller and presumably more manageable units. In addition to their productive activities, the state firms also marketed their products and provided various social services to their employees. They also ran consumer cooperatives and built employee housing. The object of the "restructuration" of the state firms was to separate production and distribution activities and to improve productivity through a clearer definition of management responsibility. Fifty-one state firms were broken up into more than 350 new companies. Sonatrach was split up into 13 financially independent companies, each specializing in one area of the oil and gas industry such as refining, distribution, or plastics. In an effort to stimulate greater productivity, wages were raised by up to 15 percent, and productivity bonuses and worker profit-sharing schemes were introduced.

The satisfaction of social needs was also given a higher priority. In fact, the motto of the government for the 1980–84 Plan became; "for a better life." Investment spending on social services was substantially increased. Social spending was allocated AD 128 billion ($33.4 billion), or 32 percent of total investment expenditures over the 1980–84 Plan, second only to industry. Housing alone received AD 60 billion ($15.7 billion), or 15 percent of total investment spending. The 1980–84 Plan called for the construction of 700,000 housing units (450,000 by the state sector and 250,000 by the private sector) over the duration of the Plan.

The "non-exploitive" private sector, which already accounted for about one-third of the gross domestic product, was encouraged to play a greater role in the nonstrategic sectors of the economy, especially in farming, commerce, tourism, and light industry. The purpose was to create more jobs and to improve the domestic supply and quality of scarce goods and services. Private firms became eligible for financial and fiscal incentives, as well as assistance in accounting, management, and the preparation of investment applications. The state would provide bank loans, investment grants, and tax benefits if a private firm's project was in line with government development objectives.

In an attempt to obtain a more effective transfer of technology, foreign firms were encouraged to set up joint ventures as minor partners with the state companies, especially in the hydrocarbons, construction, public works, and mechanical industries. The foreign partners were to get a five-year tax break, reduced taxes on reinvested profits, repatriation of earnings, and royalties on technology transfers. In an attempt to reduce the external debt burden, all external commercial borrowing was halted from the end of 1979 to mid-1983. The aim was to bring down the debt service ratio to below 10 percent by 1990. A set of 15 measures was adopted to encourage nonhydrocarbons exports, including subsidies, greater use of barter arrangements, and setting up of Algerian dinar-convertible accounts for exports. The products promoted include ceramics, construction equipment, electrical fittings, telephone exchangers, phosphates, petrochemical products, and various agricultural goods.

It may be too early to evaluate the effects of these reforms. Nevertheless, some preliminary remarks can be made. Algeria is now more open to foreign direct investments than before. However, foreign investors are still closely controlled since they can be only minority partners with state companies. The importance of trade with the industrialized capitalist countries has remained very high. In 1983, 83.1 percent of Algeria's exports went to the nations of the European Economic Community and to North America (MPAT 1984). Exports are still overwhelmingly composed of hydrocarbons products, accounting for 98 percent of total exports in 1984. But the hydrocarbons exports are more highly diversified. The share of crude oil (close to 90 percent in 1973 and 72.3 percent in 1979) dropped to 23.4 percent by 1983, while the share of condensates, LNG, natural gas, refined products, and LPG increased (*Revolution Africaine* 23 November 1984:9).

Algeria has had a surplus in its balance of foreign trade since 1979, with a peak of $2.6 billion in 1981. This and the moratorium on external borrowing from 1979 to 1983 helped lower its debt burden. By 1982, external debt dropped to $15.4 billion. It was not until mid-1983 that Algeria went back to the Euromarket for two new loans totalling $1.45 billion, a move motivated by the increasingly uncertain oil market and repayments on the external debt. Debt service payments rose to an estimated $3.8 billion in 1982 and then to about $4.3 billion in 1983 when principal repayments peaked at around $2.5 billion, thereby driving the debt service ratio to over 30 percent. This ratio has since started to decline, and both the external debt and debt service ratio are expected to fall significantly by the late 1980s.

Algeria's technological potential has continued to expand. Over the 1980-84 period, there were 42,900 new graduates from higher education. This is a remarkable achievement when this number is compared to the 32,500 new graduates over the much longer 1963-80 period. For the 1984-85 schoolyear, 78 percent of the teachers in higher education were Algerian nationals, as compared to 67 percent in 1979-80 and 52 percent in 1968-69.

Economic integration has progressed even further during recent years. An indication of this improvement is the larger place in the national economy of the industries with the strongest integrative effects (the steel industry, the mechanical engineering branches, and the electrical and electronics industries). The share of this group in industrial labor and amortizement charges, which stood at 9.4 percent in 1969, increased from 15.8 percent in 1977 to 25.1 percent in 1981 (MPAT 1979, 1984). Industrial output also grew at 10 percent a year in 1982 and 1983, mainly because of a more intensive utilization of the nation's productive potential.

The government attitude toward private enterprise has changed from tolerance to encouragement, and consequently many private firms have expanded rapidly. For example, Alfreix, an Algerian private firm specializing in the production of automobile spare parts and accessories, has been so successful that it has expanded to other countries. Recently, it signed contracts to build manufacturing plants for at least two African countries, Mali and Senegal. As a result of economic liberalization, a national bourgeoisie is rapidly emerging.

Satisfaction of the basic medical, nutritional, and educational needs of the people has continued to improve. However, the crisis in the housing sector has not abated. One reason is that only 60 percent of the housing construction program of the 1980–84 Plan was actually realized. Popular participation in decision making has continued to be high. In 1984–85, the citizens of Algeria were called to elect the president of the Republique and to renew the popular assemblies at the commune and daira levels. Since mid-1985, popular debates have been taking place all over the country for "the deepening and the enrichment" of the National Charter.

CONCLUSION

Algeria's major objective since it gained political independence has been the establishment of an independent, socialist, and integrated economy, with economic independence being the paramount priority. A program of "industries industrialisantes," financed mainly through hydrocarbons exports, was initially chosen as the national strategy for economic development because it was expected to create heavy industries and, in principle, stimulate rapid economic growth and industrial integration leading to autonomous development. After more than a decade of the program, much progress was made, especially in terms of satisfying the basic needs of the population, education, technological development, and economic integration. However, the very high priority given to heavy industry and the consequent neglect of agriculture, social services, and light industry threatened the very goal of economic independence the Algerian development strategy was designed to promote. Algeria became excessively reliant on external sources for its capital, technology, and food needs. This danger was recognized when, at the end of the Second Four-Year Plan in 1977, the government paused to take stock of a decade of heavy industrialization.

Reforms were introduced, on the one hand, to satisfy popular demands for better living conditions and, on the other, to increase production and reduce dependence on external markets. It is too soon to judge the effectiveness of these reforms. But, on the basis of early indications and past performance, one is inclined to be optimistic about the future prospects for higher economic growth, generally better living standards, and more economic independence. Unfortunately, this may come at the cost of increased income and class differentiation.

REFERENCES

Benachenhou, Abdelatif. 1982. *L'experience algerienne de planification et de developpement 1962–1982*. Algiers: Office des Publications Universitaires.

Benissad, Mohamed. 1979. *Economie du developpement de l' Algerie-sous-developpement et socialisme*. Algiers: Office des Publications Universitaires.

Bouchema, Ali. 1980. Elements pour une approche des problemes de productivite de la siderurgie algerienne. *Revue Tiers-Monde* no. 83.

Bouziane, Semmoud. 1982. Croissance du secteur industriel prive en Algerie dans ses relations avec le secteur national. *Revue canadienne des etudes africaines* 16(2).

De Bernis, G.D. 1966. Industries industrialisantes et contenu d'une politique d'integration regionale. *Economie Applique* no. 3–4.

_____ . 1971. Les industries industrialisantes et les options algeriennes. *Revue Tiers-Monde* no. 47: 545–63.

Ellman, Michael. 1979. *Socialist Planning*. Cambridge: Cambridge University Press.

Farsoun, Karen. 1975. State Capitalism in Algeria. *MERIP Reports* no. 35.

Feldman, G.A. 1964. On the Theory of Growth Rates of National Income, Parts I and II. In *Foundations of Soviet Strategy for Economic Growth: Selected Soviet Essays, 1924–1930*, N. Spulber (ed.), pp. 174–99, 304–31. Bloomington: Indiana University Press.

Food and Agriculture Organization (FAO). 1981. *Trade Yearbook*. Rome: FAO.

Frieden, Jeff. 1981. Third World Indebted Industrialization: International Finance and State Capitalism in Mexico, Brazil, Algeria and South Korea. *International Organization* 35(3).

Front de Liberation Nationale. (FLN). 1976. *Charte Nationale*. Algiers: FLN.

Hirschman, A.O. 1958. *The Strategy of Economic Development*. New Haven: Yale University Press.

Mahalanobis, P.C. 1955–56. The Approach of Operational Research to Planning in India. *Indian Journal of Statistics* 16: 3–62.

Mekideche, M. 1980. Le secteur des hydrocarbures: quelle contribution au developpement economique and social de l'Algerie? *Revue Tiers-Monde* no. 83.

Messaoudi, A. 1984. Contribution a la reflexion sur le transfert de technologie et le developpement technologique en Algerie. *Les Cahiers du Centre de Recherche en Economie Applique* no. 3: 61–86.

Ministere de la Planification et de l'Amenagement du Territoire (MPAT). 1979. *Annuaire statastique de l'Algerie 1977–1978*. Algiers: MPAT.

_____ . 1984. *Annuaire statastique de l'Algerie 1982*. Algiers: MPAT.

Nellis, J.R. 1983. A Comparative Assessment of the Development Performances of Algeria and Tunisia. *The Middle-East Journal* 37(3): 382–88.

Osterman, Rigmar. 1982. L'Algerie entre le plan et le marche: points de vue recents sur la politique economique de l'Algerie. *Revue canadienne des etudes africaines* 16(1).

Palloix, Christian. 1980a. Industrialisation et financement lors des deux Plans Quadriennaux (1970–1977). *Revue Tiers-Monde* no. 83.

_____ . 1980b. Un essai sur la formation de la classe ouvriere algerienne (1963–1978). *Revue Tiers-Monde* no. 83.

Perroux, Francois. 1965. *Les Techniques Quantitatives de la Planification*. Paris: Presses Universitaires de France.

Rosenstein-Rodan, P.N. 1943. Problems of Industrialization of Eastern and South Eastern Europe. *Economic Journal* (June).

Said-Amer, Tayeb. 1981. *Le Developpement Industriel de l'Algerie*. Paris: Editions Anthropos.

Schnetzler, Jacques. 1980. Les effets pervers du sous-emploi a travers l'exemple algerien. *Revue canadienne des etudes africaines* 14(3).

Temmar, Hamid. 1983. *Strategie de Developpement Independent. Le Cas de l'Algerie: Un Bilan*. Paris: Editions Publisud.

Thierry, Simon-Pierre. 1980. Les biens d'equipement dans l'industrie algerienne: evolution passee et perspectives. *Revue Tiers-Monde* no. 83.

United Nations. 1981. *Statistical Yearbook*. New York: United Nations.

U.S. Department of Commerce. 1977. Marketing in Algeria. *Overseas Business Report* (November).

Wilber, Charles. 1969. *The Soviet Model and Underdeveloped Countries*. Chapel Hill: University of North Carolina Press.

World Bank. 1981. *World Development Report*. Washington: World Bank.

Chapter 14

Development in a Peripheral Socialist Economy: Grenada, 1979–83

MARC W. HEROLD

The Grenadian Revolution led by the New Jewel Movement (1979–83) was one of the most under-reported events of the past decade. In March 1979, a People's Revolutionary Government (PRG) under Prime Minister Maurice Bishop assumed power in Grenada and undertook the first experiment towards socialist transformation in the Commonwealth Caribbean. A central part of this process was a particular socioeconomic development project. Given the small size of Grenada, the dominance of peasant agriculture, the limited working class, and the openness of the economy, the PRG considered a strategy of gradual reforms and progressive "disengagement from imperialism" to be the appropriate development strategy. At the time of the U.S. invasion (October 1983), a meticulous bibliographic search by the author revealed a total of 14 articles and six books about the Grenadian Revolution (the "Revo"), and many of these were either collections of speeches or interviews. Such a dearth of information played directly into the hands of the Reagan regime bent on slandering the Revo.[1] This essay is a modest attempt both to fill that empirical void and to analyze the Revo's major *economic* achievements.

ANTECEDENTS TO REVOLUTION

It is the mid-1970s, you are black, a descendant of African slaves, and in your 20s (two-thirds of Grenada's population is under 29 years of age). You live in the countryside where over 80 percent of Grenadians live. You are one of five Grenadians still living on the island; your four brothers and sisters have emigrated to Britain or North America (Tobias 1980; Neumann 1982), having made the age-old choice between deprivation at home or emigrating. You are more than likely to be unemployed—overall

291

unemployment rates of 50 percent were common in the 1980s (with levels of 80 percent for women and people under 25 years of age)—and yet, over one-third of the island's arable land lies idle. Grenada spent $15 million in 1979 to import food, an amount that represented 40 percent of total imports (Jackson 1981: 37; Lynch 1981: 19). Economic growth had been dismal during the years of your young adulthood, with per capita gross national product falling at the annual rate of 1.8 percent between 1970–78 (Carlip, Overstreet, and Linder 1982: 222).

Your personal distress is simply a reflection of Grenadian society under the allegedly constitutional and democratic government of Sir Eric Gairy, your Prime Minister. Gairy had ruled the island for 18 years. A leading British journal aptly characterized the Gairy regime as "a very squalid and vindictive form of personal government." Corruption was legion. The patronage system seemed to know no bounds. Political repression at the hands of Sir Eric's Volunteers for the Protection of Human Rights (more commonly known as his Mongoose Gang) was the order of the day. In the fall of 1977, Gairy established close ties with Chile's dictator Pinochet, who supplied arms and training for the gang (Lynch 1981: 15). While it's likely you witnessed the daily violence and repression, it probably didn't touch you directly.

More relevant, you and thousands of Grenadians know that you had voted against Gairy in 1971 and then again in 1976. Yet Gairy, by then knighted by the British, was still on center stage, reputed to be one of the most repressive figures in the Caribbean. You knew that the national elections of 1971 had been rigged, with registration roles listing thousands of deceased Grenadians and polling stations often having at least two voter's lists (Augustine 1974: 181; Manning 1984: 80). Gairy's democracy was a "thinly-veiled camouflage for brutality and thuggery" (Davies 1979: 5), democracy at work in the Third World supported by Britain and the United States!

Economic development under Gairy was nicely summed up as being "Hurricane Gairy." Bernard Coard of the P.R.G. described the situation:

> Can you imagine a constant hurricane wind of thirty years? That is the situation we've inherited. Gairy left us an unbelievable mess. Millions upon millions of dollars of taxpayers' money raped from the treasury—disappeared. Can't be found anywhere. There are people who haven't seen water in their pipes for five years. Roads—terrible. Medical facilities—non-existent. No sheets or pillows on hospital beds, no medicines—not even aspirins, no qualified nurses, only three ambulances to cover the whole country and they didn't work. School buildings collapsing, no school books or uniforms. Half the population out of work and forty percent illiterate. (Lowther 1979: 339)

Upon assuming power in March 1979, the New Jewel Movement (NJM) discovered that Grenada's national accounts had not been audited for seven years and substantial foreign loans had simply disappeared!

Recall, you are unemployed and in your 20s, living in the country described above. Where would you have been on noon, March 13, 1979? In the streets rejoicing over the demise of Gairy and expressing your support for the youthful leadership of the NJM. The story of March 13th has been told elsewhere (EPICA 1982; Payne, Sutton, and Thorndike 1984; Manning 1984): It was a bloodless change of government with only three reported deaths. Some called it "the peaceful revolution." A Canadian weekly labelled it "a revolt in reggae time" (Lowther 1979: 4). The NJM knew it could count on the support of the people, but it faced a formidable task of social and economic reconstruction in a largely hostile regional environment.

THE REVOLUTIONARY PROJECT

On March 13, 1979, Grenada was shaken by the third revolution in Caribbean history—after those of Haiti in 1804 and Cuba in 1959. The Revo's leader, Maurice Bishop, saw

> the revolution as having three pillars: first, putting the people at the center, ensuring the needs of the people are always met, their views always heard, their grievances always addressed. Never tell lies to the people. Never hold back the facts. Second pillar: the national economy—agriculture, agro-industries, fisheries, and tourism. If we do not develop a vibrant economy, we will not have a surplus to use to bring benefits to the people. Third pillar: national defence. No revolution, in our view, has the right to call itself that if it cannot defend its people. We can't afford a standing army, so what we have to rely on is a strong militia. Our people in uniform are the ordinary citizens of our country. (Cockburn and Ridgeway 1983)

Bishop understood the need for a fourth pillar: owing to Grenada's limited defense capacity and the political complexion of its neighbors, the only real protection against U.S. imperialism was regional and international public opinion (Cockburn and Ridgeway 1983).

In the broadest terms, the Revos ought to involve the people in public and political life (through the creation of mass participatory organizations, the encouragement given to unionization, the community-based health and education centers, etc.), raise the peoples' standard of living through economic growth, and ensure Grenada's independence. Though major changes were made in the interests of the masses, the results by 1983 had not eroded the entrenched bases of capitalist penetration. Grenada's foreign policy stressed nonalignment and anti imperialism and sought closer relationships with the Third World and the socialist bloc. As such, Grenada could be called a state of socialist orientation (Ambursely and Winston 1983: 92; Mars 1984).

Theory and Planning

Claremont Kirton (1983:7), who worked in the Ministry of Planning, has stated that the Revo had four broad objectives. First, there was the necessity of actually transferring state power from an antidemocratic, pro-imperialist minority to the progressive forces led by the NJM, who would act in the interests of the masses. Second, there was the aim of altering the production relations and bringing the productive forces under the control and direction of the progressive forces. Third, there was the task of disengaging from international capitalism. Finally, there was the fundamental aim of raising the material levels of welfare of the country's population.

Programs were directed in the economic and social spheres covering a wide array of fronts. Nonetheless, they weren't components of an integrated national plan:

> [L]ong-term integrated planning does not yet exist in Grenada. Such planning depends upon two preconditions: an up-to-date data base, and an institutional framework for planning. The bureaucracy under Gairy had no mechanism for collecting or keeping statistics; at the time of the revolution even the size of the island's population was unknown. Nor was there any capability within the government for integrated planning. (EPICA 1982:76)

Preconditions for effective planning were said to include: a certain minimum level of state control (ownership) of the economy (achieved by expanding the state sector and through state investment); the existence of a technically competent cadre of people committed to planning; the establishment of organizational structures through which plan implementation could be carried out (a planning ministry and assorted organs but also the involvement of the masses in all aspects of plan preparation and implementation)[2]; and, lastly, the existence of a good statistical information base (Kirton 1983: 28–36). During 1981–83, a variety of surveys and censuses were completed that were to contribute to the formulation of a three-year plan in late 1983. The type of planning envisioned by the PRG was of an indicative or parametric nature with indirect controls exercised over the private sector, given its importance in the economy (namely, 70 percent of gross domestic product in 1982, Manning 1984: 78).

The Grenadian experience is an excellent illustration of accumulation/development in the peripheral socialist economy (PSE) as conceptualized by Fitzgerald (1982, 1985). Fitzgerald has argued that accumulation in the PSE involves replacing the traditional two-sector model (with a producer goods and consumer goods sector) by a three-sector one: producer goods (I), nonbasic consumer goods (II), and basic consumer goods (III). In the PSE, sector I becomes the "heavy industry" of such incomplete economies, providing foreign exchange for the import of productive inputs and equipment (Fitzgerald 1982: 4). This model brings to the fore the reality that socialism during the past three decades has come about in small (price-taking), underdeveloped, agricultural, and foreign-trade-dominated economies in which a significant private sector persists in sectors I and III. A critical planning decision becomes the relative importance given to investment goods versus popular (i.e., peasants' and workers') consumption. There is limited scope for depressing peasant incomes by manipulating the internal terms of trade (thereby saving scarce foreign exchange and allowing higher investment) without cutting the real wage in sector III and thereby encouraging the peasants' withholding of a marketable surplus (Fitzgerald 1982: 8). The proletariat is insignificant, and smallholders are assumed to supply basic needs (food). The constraint upon growth becomes foreign exchange rather than the supply of labor or wage goods.

The essential dynamic in the PSE is to achieve the requisite balances between different sectors: sufficient growth of sector II to provide incentive goods for producers in sectors I and III; sufficient growth of sector I to provide needed inputs (through international trade) for sectors I and II, which both have relatively significant imported inputs. A critical distinction is that sector I has plannable output but exogenously set prices (the external terms of trade); whereas sector III has plannable prices (the internal terms of trade), but production remains outside state control; and only in section II are prices and output plannable. Consequently,

> the articulation of these three departments with one another and the world economy is a key aspect of the P.S.E; indeed, the relations of exchange may be as important as the relations of production in such an economy. The planners of the P.S.E. can only obtain capital goods and wage goods by *trading* with two sectors outside their own direct control. (Fitzgerald 1982: 6)

The PRG's efforts were directed towards three critical areas: the social arena, economic development, and the political process. I shall examine the former pair of issues since the latter has been effectively dealt with elsewhere (Ambursley 1983; Henfrey 1984; Mandle 1985). Henfrey (1984: 25) observes:

what puzzles socialists, perhaps, is how to evaluate the fact that the P.R.G's quite marked success by conventional, that is capitalist, standards—the recovery of growth, balanced budgets, low debt, and high investment ratios—such that even the I.M.F. and World Bank as well as Cuba voiced their approval and went on lending.

Only the United States took a belligerent stance towards tiny Grenada, pursuing propaganda destabilization, blocking international loans, engaging in economic destabilization, and later intervening violently. (Searle 1983; Mars 1984).

The Social Arena

Achievements in the social sphere through popular mobilization allowed an increase in necessary consumption (the social wage) without deterring investment. Progress was made in providing education and health, in beginning to change the place of women in society, in creating a new army, and in introducing a new culture.

The aims in education were to reduce illiteracy, slash the family cost of education, and create a new infrastructure stressing popular participation in the educational process. In 1980, the PRG carried out a massive literacy and adult education campaign through the parish-level Centers for Popular Education (CPEs). Illiteracy was reduced from 40–45 percent to 2 percent during 1979–82 (see table 14–1). Grenada was the first eastern Caribbean

TABLE 14.1. Social Indicators of the Grenadian Revolution (at year end)

	1978	1979	1980	1981	1982	1983
Unemployment rate (total)		49%	35%	27%	12-14%	10%
Female unemployment rate		60%		21%		
Illiteracy rate		40-45%		6%	2%	
Rate of unionization of the work force	40%				80%	
Number of scholarships for foreign higher education	3	109		220+		
Educational allowance per child for parents of schoolchildren	$130		$241			
Fees for secondary education, per quarter	$13.89		$4.63	0	0	0

Sources: The Europa Year Book 1983 and 1985; Kirton 1983: 1; Jackson 1981: 36; Lynch 1981: 17 and 21; and Walker 1983: 24.

country to initiate a mass literacy campaign inspired by the models of Cuba (1961), Tanzania (1967–78), Mozambique (1975–80), and Nicaragua (1980).

The second phase of the CPEs' work involved the teaching of arts, languages, and mathematics under the slogan, "each one teach one, we learn together" (Jackson 1981: 36). These community education councils were to develop the awareness that education is a community pursuit involving the active participation of people, not merely knowledge gleaned from texts or an activity that took place behind the walls of educational institutions (Lynch 1981: 18). In May 1980, a work-study and teacher-training model was launched to combine agricultural-technical work alongside academic learning. Past divisions between work and study, theory and practice, were thereby to be eliminated.

The PRG sought to reduce private educational costs in order to make schooling available to all. By September 1981, no fees were charged for secondary education, a particularly significant benefit to the rural peasantry and urban working class. The first secondary public school to be built in Grenada in 90 years was inaugurated in 1980 (Jackson 1981: 36). At the level of higher education, the government increased the number of foreign scholarships and slashed the cost born by Grenadians attending foreign institutions of higher learning (see table 14–1).

New initiatives were launched in 1979 to provide basic paramedical services and assistance to the elderly and disabled. A system of social security payments was introduced for the first time ever in 1980. A national milk distribution program was instituted, and community-directed day-care centers were set up. In 1982, some 3,000 households benefitted from a housing-repair program that offered soft loans of up to $400 with repayment stretched over six years. A national insurance scheme was launched in 1983 (George 1983: 19).

A very deliberate effort was made at decentralizing medical attention and care, moving resources away from two urban hospitals (catering to 20 percent of the population) and into medical clinics in the countryside and at the parish level. As Maurice Bishop put it,

> these village health committees will also monitor the quality of health care and will be involved at the same time in collective hygiene, sanitation and education about basic medical problems. Obviously, that has tremendous social consequences, not to mention its democratic aspects. (Pagne 1980: 21)

The Revo also meant nearly doubling the number of doctors on the island (from 23 to 40), a health center set up in every parish for the first time, a dental clinic, and a public health antimosquito campaign. Much of the improved medical care, and especially the preventive aspect, was due to the internationalist solidarity of the Cuban people and government, which sent many doctors, dentists, and specialists to Grenada. Even the conservative *Financial Times* of London (May 21, 1981) had to concede that, "Cuba (also) sent many doctors and dentists who have revolutionized the standard of medicine on the island."

Serious efforts were made to elevate the position of women in Grenadian society (Jackson 1981; Walker 1983). The thrust was both to reduce past inequities (e.g., by legislating equal pay for equal work, by prohibiting sexual abuse at the workplace, and by passing a maternity law) and to open up new avenues of progress. For the first time in Grenadian history, women played leading roles in running the country. The National Women's Organization was established under the leadership of Phyllis Coard, a member of the Central Committee and also Deputy Minister of Tourism. A woman headed the CPEs, and Dessima Williams served as ambassador to the Organization of American States.

The new army was to be engaged in productive activities alongside its traditional task (Searle 1979: 183–84). After the revolution, various mass organizations formed the backbone of the militia, which supplemented the People's Revolutionary Army (trained and equipped by Cuba). Teachers, students, farmers, and trade unionists alike contributed one day per week to military service. The Revo also sought to stimulate pride for Grenadian cultural achievements and a rejection of the imported symbols of cultural imperialism (Kolmes 1982).

Economic Performance: Creation of a Mixed Economy Satisfying Basic Needs

Economic development in Grenada must be placed in the context of the global recession of the 1980s:

> The recession has been immensely important (for the Caribbean), for it has produced a significant fall in all major areas of economic activity: in tourism, in the prices of primary products both agricultural and mineral, in remittances, and in levels of investment from developed areas. This decline in economic activity has coincided with a general closure of the traditional avenues of emigration. (Halliday 1983: 14–15)

Against this ill-boding background, the economic program of the PRG involved establishing a mixed economy, meeting the masses' basic needs through increased production, and expanding the social wage. The latter was particularly important in a small open economy where money wages couldn't simply be arbitrarily hiked. Bernard Coard (People's Revolutionary Government of Grenada 1982: 101–3) elaborated upon the social wage:

Before the revolution there was 49 percent unemployment. Among women it was 70 percent. Since the revolution we have got that down to about 12 percent. Before the revolution there was absolutely no planning. Now we have developed the beginnings of a system of planning. Before the revolution people throughout the country did not have potable water. Less than 30 percent had pipe water in their homes. Today that proportion has been just about doubled. Now we have free health care, a free educational system. Illiteracy has been reduced to just two percent.

And lastly, in order to diminish the disruptive effects emanating from the world economy, the PRG pursued a "disengagement from imperialism," or the development of economic self-reliance. This involved establishing a state foreign trading corporation, encouraging the consumption of local foods, increasing the value-added locally, reducing imports, diversifying, and expanding exports and production within Grenada (EPICA 1982: 74).

Although the Grenadian economy is extremely open[3], it's also true that it does not rely upon one principal crop for its export trade. Historically, three crops (bananas, cocoa, and nutmeg) regularly accounted for over 90 percent of the island's exports (see table 14–2). Grenada's bananas were sold to Geest Industries (Britain), much of its cocoa crop was exported to World's Finest Chocolates and other U.S. companies, and the bulk of its nutmeg crop went to Holland for processing. The diversity of exports, nevertheless, endowed Grenada with a certain degree of flexibility: when one crop failed or its world price collapsed, the impact could usually be buffered by income from other agricultural exports (Carlip, Overstreet, and Linder 1982: 223).

TABLE 14.2. Trends in Grenadian Exports

	1977	1979	1980	1981	1982	1983
Merchandise exports in E.C. $ millions*	38.4	63.4	44.0	n.a.	50.1	
1. Nutmeg	13.1	12.0	8.6	8.1	8.2	
2. Cocoa	8.8	27.0	18.0	18.5	12.5	
3. Bananas	8.5	10.5	10.5	10.0	8.9	
4. Mace	1.4	2.5	1.8	1.7	2.5	
$\frac{1+2+3+4}{\text{total}}=$	82.8%	82.0%	88.4%	n.a.	64.0%	
Tourist receipts				17.3	14.7	
# tourist arrivals		143,100	145,900	87,200	72,900	82,676

Sources: The Europa Year Book 1981, 1982, 1983, 1984, and 1985; Kirton 1983: 19 ; and A Yearbook of the Commonwealth.

*Note: *E.C. $ 2.70 per U.S. $ 1.*

This is not to say that in recent times the Grenadian economy wasn't plagued by the instability of its export earnings arising from world price movements and adverse weather. The average price of nutmeg fell during 1978–83, from U.S. 87 cents to U.S. 55 cents (*Journal of Commerce*. 1984. September 21: 23B). On average, export prices fell 13 percent during 1980–82, while prices of imports rose by 15 percent (Payne, Sutton, and Thorndike 1984: 24). The ravages since 1975 of the banana disease, moko, combined with flooding in 1979 and hurricane storm damage in 1980 and 1981, damaged banana acreage. Record levels of nutmeg production in 1981–82, corresponded with worldwide overproduction and stockpiling, causing depressed international prices and consequently a reduction in Grenada's export income (*The Europa Yearbook* 1985: 1712). In 1983, nutmeg provided 35 percent of total exports (23 percent in 1982), helped by a five-year trade agreement signed with the Soviet Union in 1982. The Soviets agreed to buy 500 tons of nutmeg per year—one-fourth of Grenada's annual production—at stable prices, which would have brought stability to the island's 7,500 nutmeg producers. Tourist revenues fell as well during the tourist recession of 1981–83, compounded by concerted American and British efforts to discourage tourism to Grenada.

Since agriculture accounted for a major part of Grenada's economic activity—about one-third of the gross domestic product and the labor force and over 60 percent of visible export earnings in 1982 (Kirton 1983: 13)—any transformation had to begin there. Agricultural change was conceived within a framework emphasizing a state sector (with collective farms and state-run agro-industrial plants), a cooperative sector (consisting mainly of small coop farms that marketed their produce through a new national marketing board), and a private sector (made up of private commercial farms, trading firms, and hotels). The larger estates formerly belonging to Gairy were worked as state farms. The PRG sought to stimulate the coop sector, alongside the 8,202 private commercial farms (on 34,243 acres) and the public sector (with 33 state farms covering 4,100 acres) (Kirton 1983: 13).

An important part of the PRG's agricultural program was seeking to achieve greater food self-sufficiency (Payne 1980: 283) and changing the population's perception that consuming local foods was a sign of poverty. The legacy of colonialism was visible here: the country's economy was based on cash-crop export agriculture, and yet Grenada had a population whose diet included high-priced imported food. While import substitution in food was pursued for a variety of sound economic reasons (e.g., lesser pressure on the balance of payments and increased employment), the Grenadians were quite aware that complete self-sufficiency was impossible. The Minister of Agriculture stated in 1980:

. . .there are some products that we will always have to import, for instance, wheat flour. I think what we can do in the case of flour is to find a way of combining some of the local crops into the flour, for instance, manioc can be integrated into wheat flour: you can use between 5 and 10 percent cassava flour and 90 to 95 percent wheat flour to make flour of very good quality. At the same time, that would provide employment and income for farmers. (Pagne 1980: 33)

Import substitution through the development of agro-industries and fisheries remained a central component of PRG's economic strategy (*The Europa Year Book* 1983: 1619). The program met with some success: the value of imported food declined from over 33 percent prior to 1979, to 27.5 percent in 1982 (Brierley 1985: 51; Payne, Sutton, and Thorndike 1984: 23).

The NJM felt that the general principles of the Revo had to be rooted in the specific conditions of Grenada. Grenada had the highest percentage of peasant proprietorships in the Caribbean area: In 1982 98 percent of farmers operated 53 percent of the land, with average farm size being under two hectares. This material reality had direct bearing upon organizational forms to be developed in agriculture. Although the NJM had committed itself to nationalizing agriculture, a sizeable amount of Grenada's farmland still consisted of small holdings in 1981–82: about one-fifth of the 14,000 cocoa-producing acres, one-fourth of the 8,000 acres devoted to bananas, and one-half of the 6,500 acres in nutmeg (Carlip, Overstreet, and Linder 1982: 223). The fundamental question revolved around how to develop the spirit of cooperation in a countryside with such widespread private ownership and a miniscule land mass. The wide distribution of land among Grenadians simply obviated the possibility of applying "coercive economic and financial measures" to the land question (Pagne 1980: 20).

Agricultural development was to be promoted intensively, extensively, and through new cooperative agricultural forms. The program of the PRG was "to marry idle lands with idle hands." A central role was played by the National Cooperative Development Agency (NACDA), created in April 1980. The agency initially invited groups of unemployed people to identify idle land in their neighborhood and to suggest the manner in which they would be prepared to work it as a cooperative. Four thousand acres of idle land were thus identified (EPICA 1982: 79). While NACDA's land procurement team negotiated the purchase with the landowners, NACDA held training sessions for the future coop members. Once NACDA acquired the land, it was leased to the cooperative.

To ensure that groups which receive NACDA loans are viable and a good credit risk, NACDA requires prospective "cooperators" to meet rigorous requirements. A feasibility study is always performed to

> determine whether the venture is financially sound. Before registering as
> a cooperative, the group receives five days of intensive training in the
> principles and operation of cooperatives, accounting, business manage-
> ment, and record-keeping. The members must also show a commitment
> to the cooperative ideal and enough unity and dynamism to carry
> through with the venture. (EPICA 1982: 79)

NACDA thus provided the coop members with financing, training, and ac-
cess to land. Functioning coops by 1983 included the United Agricultural
Workers Cooperative, Grenfruit (run by women), the Grenada Banana
Cooperative, the Grenada Nutmeg Cooperative, the Minor Spices
Cooperative, and the Grenada Cocoa Association, as well as the fishing
cooperative.

The PRG's land reform program consciously drew upon characteristics
of the "maroon," a ritual with which many Grenadians could identify. In
such a communal undertaking, workers pitch in to finish a job; often the
project's sponsor provides food for the volunteer workers. "Maroons" were
used as a means of winning people's confidence towards collective forms of
labor.

By May 1981, 19 coops had been established in poultry and sheep raising, baking, jam making, crafts, children's clothing, macrame objects, etc.
(Lynch 1981: 20). Most of these were *production cooperatives* in which
members shared a plot of land or a fishing boat (means of production) and
worked collectively, pooling all their resources and realizing a shared profit. The other type of cooperative was the *service cooperative*, in which
members worked their own plots of land independently (or fished in their
own boats) but joined together to purchase supplies and/or market their
produce (EPICA 1982: 81).

The PRG admitted the agricultural inefficiency (e.g., idle land, low
worker productivity) associated with the 30 state farms. In a move designed
to centralize control, provide effective management, and increase production on these holdings, the PRG founded the Grenada Farm Corporation.
As a means of achieving greater productivity from state-farm employees, an
incentive schema was introduced whereby one-third of any state farm's profit would be divided amongst its workers (Brierley 1985: 47).

A performance assessment of the different types of agricultural units is
difficult to make. Mandle (1985: 37–38) suggests, on the basis of examining
commentary by PRG officials, that : (1) the state farms were not meeting
output targets because of low labor productivity, insufficient education,
primitive technology, management weakness, and a lack of specialization
on the units; and (2) that both youth and small farmers were resisting
cooperativization. More generally, the organizational dilemma facing the
PRG was the traditional one of choosing the appropriate agricultural unit:

small or large private farms, state farms or agricultural cooperatives? Mandle (1985: 38) argues that "with cooperatives resisted and with managerial incompetence hampering the state farms, the PRG decided to live with the status quo in the structure of the country's agriculture. It did so rather than adopt an agricultural reform strategy which would strengthen private farming in Grenada's agriculture." Living with the status quo as regards rural relations of production remained a hallmark of the PRG's four-year rule: A comparison with Cuba and Nicaragua reveals the extent of private agriculture (see table 14–3).

Despite this stalemate in land tenure, the PRG sought to increase the value-added in the Grenadian economy. This was *not* an easy task given the small size of the internal market—in 1974, there reportedly were merely six small factories producing beer and soft drinks (Coca-Cola) amongst other things (*The New York Times* 1974, February 6: 6). The new government gave priority to agro-industry and fishing. With the assistance of Cuba and the Soviet Union, a fishing school was set up in True Blue with a fleet of ten vessels donated by Cuba (*The Europa Year Book* 1985: 1712). In 1980, a fish processing plant was built, thereby reversing the absurd situation of Grenada importing salted and smoked fish (Pagne 1980: 33). In 1981, the government set up the National Fishing Company. By late 1979, a fisherman's cooperative had been organized, visible to all in St. George's with its huge banner proclaiming: "Let Those Who Labour Hold The Reins."

As mentioned, Grenada had a minuscule manufacturing sector. In 1982, it employed about 10 percent of the island's labor force and accounted for 2.7 percent of the gross domestic product (Kirton 1983: 18). The proletariat hardly extended beyond the docks of St. George's—the largest industrial employer was the local brewery with a labor force of 76 (Ambursley and Winston 1983: 199).

As part of its drive to develop agro-industry, the PRG established a number of enterprises: a plant producing hot sauces and chutney with beans originating both locally and from Guyana and Trinidad; a food processing

TABLE 14.3. Distribution of Cultivable Land According to Type of Agricultural Production Unit (percent acreage)

Country (year)	State Farms	Production Coops	Service Coops	Peasant Holdings	Peasant/ Capitalist
Cuba (1983)	80%	11%	—	9%	—
Nicaragua (1983)	24	6	16%	—	54%
Grenada (1982)	9		1.1*	51	39

*1.1 is the sum of Production and Service Coops.

plant using local fruit to manufacture juices, nectars, jellies, and jams; a fish processing factory that dries and salts fish; and an animal feed plant that produces high-protein animal food using as many local ingredients as possible. Moreover, an asphalt plant was built with Cuban assistance at the new international airport. The "Augosto Sandino" factory making prefabricated housing (500 units per year) began operations in early 1983 (again with Cuban assistance) (Kirton 1983: 21; Manning 1984: 21). Eggplant, onion, and lettuce farming were initiated in 1980, with lettuce being exported to Trinidad and West Germany. Trinidad was to become the major market for Grenadian vegetable exports.

Organizationally, the economy exhibited three forms of ownership in industry. The private sector played an important role in small-scale manufacturing (as well as agriculture). The cooperative sector was beginning to take hold in fishing, agriculture, and handicrafts. During 1979–83, the government expanded state ownership in the banking, trade, utilities, and tourist sectors, though about three-quarters of economic activity remained in private hands. Maurice Bishop (1981: 181) explained the rationale:

> the state sector alone cannot develop the economy, given the very low level of technology available, the limited human resources, the lack of capital, the lack of marketing enterprise, the lack of promotional capacity. So (government) must stimulate the private sector in business generally, but also of course in agriculture, and in particular among the small and medium farmers.

The PRG sought to promote agro-industry and industry based upon local raw materials (clay, sand, limestone, etc.) rather than the more import-intensive export manufacturing (Pagne 1980: 29).

No major controversial nationalizations were undertaken by the PRG. It simply acquired the three hotels and four restaurants owned by Gairy (Pagne 1980: 387). Foreign investment was encouraged in selected areas, while being prohibited in others (utilities, media, transportation). The private Coca-Cola franchise was nationalized in 1979 during a labor dispute (EPICA 1982: 63). The Canadian Imperial Bank of Commerce shut down its operations in Grenada in 1980. Holiday Inn sold out to a Canadian firm in the early 1980s. The major foreign corporate investors remaining in Grenada were: two international banks (Barclays Bank International and the Bank of Nova Scotia); Britain's Cable and Wireless (W.I.) Ltd., which owns the island's VHF communication network; and the Continental Grain Co., which reportedly owns a 51 percent equity stake in the island's flour mill (*Fortune*. 1984, February 6: 36). The government became a shareholder in the Grenada Sugar Factory Ltd. In mid-1981, it took over 51 percent of the island's power company, Grenada Electricity Services, from the Commonwealth Development Corporation, and, in 1982, it assumed full ownership. The PRG accused Commonwealth of plotting with ESSO and Barclay's Bank to sabotage Grenada's economy by running down the utility's equipment and finances (*Latin American Weekly Report*. 1981, June 5: 5). The Royal Bank of Canada sold its two Grenadian branches to the government during 1981–82, which formed the Grenada Bank of Commerce. In 1982, the government nationalized the Grenada Telephone Company (formerly co-owned by Continental Telephone (USA) and the government) in an amicable deal (*Latin American Weekly Report*. 1982, February 12: 6). Three Western firms were involved during 1982–83 on a contract basis in the construction of the international airport at Point Salines.

Selective encouragement of foreign direct investment found expression in a new investment code, adopted in 1983,

> that encouraged additional foreign investment by offering attractive tax exemptions and free trade zone provisions for light manufacturing. Unlike other Caribbean nations, Grenada under Bishop prohibited foreign investment in public utilities, media, transportation, and restaurants that were not part of hotels. The investment code also stipulated that foreign investment must transfer foreign capital to the country, use local raw materials when possible, and positively affect the country's standard of living. The government proposed to insure the investors' interests with regard to takeovers, disputes, industrial unrest, and losses arising from acts of the government (Barry, Wood, and Preusch 1984: 309)

The largest item in the PRG's capital budget was the construction (1980–84) of a $75 million international airport at Point Salines. Cuba provided 40 percent of the project's financing in the form of equipment and construction workers (*The Washington Post*. 1983, April 21). In 1979–80, the tourist industry accounted for 35 percent of Grenada's foreign revenues (down to 20 percent in 1981) and had historically been relied upon to offset a consistently adverse balance of merchandise trade. The airport represented the fulfillment of a 30-year dream and had been endorsed by the World Bank in 1976, the local and international tourist industry, and most significantly by the Grenadian people who within their modest means purchased "airport bonds" (EPICA 1982: 69–70). The airport was vital to the marketing of perishable nontraditional agricultural cash crops (e.g., eggplants, vegetables, mangoes). The skills learned in building the facility were generalizable (useable elsewhere in construction work). The airport was widely believed to lower transportation costs. It was, moreover, linked to agriculture, since more tourism meant greater demand for foodstuffs

(Pagne 1980: 28). The logic was a straightforward argument based on backward economic linkages:

International Airport → Tourism → Agriculture → Growth

Tourism was, moreover, to generate sufficient surplus for reinvestment in other productive areas such as agriculture during the first period of Grenada's development.

Other tourist-related projects were initiated by the PRG during 1980–83. In 1980, the government began studying a $60 million tourist development proposal for Grand Anse beach, put forth as a joint venture with the government by Canada's Carinex Resources (*Latin American Weekly Report*. 1980, November 14: 5). In 1983, the government acquired the island's largest hotel, a Holiday Inn, and renamed it the Grenada Beach Hotel (*Latin American Weekly Report*. 1983, April 22: 6). Besides encouraging capital expenditures on tourism, the PRG sought to increase the domestically produced inputs to the tourist sector—in the past, 90 cents of every tourist dollar spent in Grenada returned abroad—with hotels being strongly encouraged to utilize local foods and local entertainment and to sell local handicrafts. Needless to say, the whole idea of using tourism as a growth pole is fraught with problems, as pointed out by Mandle (1985: 23–33).

The program of economic recovery initiated by the PRG found strong support in most elements of Grenadian society. It is likely that the business community and certain strata of the middle class remained supportive of the PRG because the economic upswing more than compensated for their reservations regarding the NJM's political direction and rhetoric. Geoffrey Thompson, director of the chamber of commerce and St. George's leading businessman, observed, "it is a good time to invest for Grenadian entrepreneurs" (*The Los Angeles Times*.1983, August 3). Duncan Campbell, manager of a local hotel, added, "the revolution is getting people together and getting them working. Finally, after thirty years, we're getting an airport. It will make a big difference for the economy."

Even the World Bank in an internal report (dated August 1982) gave the PRG a valuable endorsement, which, while making no mention of the government's leftist orientation, described as sound the plans to transform the run-down economy inherited in 1979. As listed by the Bank, the government's aims were to rehabilitate industry and spur investment; stimulate productivity in both the private and public sectors, partly through stepped-up public investment; improve the efficiency of the public sector and maintain sound public finances; and emphasize agriculture and tourism. The report, in fact, raised the important question of *why Grenada achieved so much in three years, when conservative governments in the Caribbean were presiding over economic decline and stagnation.*

One reason is that Grenada was able to attract highly concessional international aid from Arab states, Latin America, and the socialist bloc (see table 14–4). Its debt servicing ratio remained a mere 4 percent of exports! (see table 14–5). In August 1983, the International Monetary Fund, not otherwise known for its leniency in lending to the Third World, approved a $14.1 million loan to Grenada (*The New York Times*. 1983, August 27: 36), with no strings attached. During 1979–83, Grenada received $150–200 million of foreign assistance from varied sources (see table 14–6). Because of the NJM's declared foreign policy of nonalignment (EPICA 1982: 124–25; Thorndike 1983), support in the form of loans, grants, and technical assistance came from both East and West (Manning 1984: 82). The United States, however, consistently sought to use its influence in order to bloc international credits for Grenada. It successfully blocked a $19 million, three-year IMF extended fund loan in early 1981, but was unable to later thwart a $4 million, one-year standby credit also from the IMF to be used for repairing damage caused to Grenada by Hurricane David in late 1979. And in

TABLE 14.4. Terms of Some Loans Received by Grenada

Date	Donor	Amount of Loan	Duration	Interest	Grace Period
June 1982	German Democratic Republic	$ 6 mn	10 yrs.	3.5%	1.5 yrs.
July 1982	Soviet Union	1.4	10	3	n.a.*
April 1982	OPEC	2	10	2	3 yrs.
August 1982	European Investment Bank	2.3	20	2	n.a.*
December 1982	Algeria	.7	4	6	3 yrs.
December 1982	Colonial Life	1.1	20	8.5	1 yr.

Sources: Compiled from various newspaper accounts.
Note: *Not available.

TABLE 14.5. Debt Servicing Ratios of Selected Countries in mid-1982 (debt service as percent of exports)

Argentina	179%
Mexico	129
Brazil	122
Chile	116
Venezuela	95
Colombia	94
Peru	48
GRENADA	3.7

Sources: Latin American Weekly Report. 1983, January 28 and March 18.

TABLE 14.6. Geographic Distribution of Identifiable International Assistance Received by Grenada, 1979 to 1983 (in U.S. $ millions and percent of total)

Source of Aid	Amount	Percent of Total Aid
Developed Countries		
• European Economic Community	$ 34.8 mn	21.5%
• Canada	7.3	4.5
• United States	1.7	1.0
• Socialist bloc	16.0	9.9
(subtotal)		(36.9%)
Less Developed Countries		
• Cuba	26.0	16.0
• North Africa, Middle East	33.7	20.8
• Venezuela	1.3	0.8
(subtotal)		(37.6%)
International Agencies		
• International Monetary Fund	18.1	11.2
• United Nations[a]	1.2	0.7
• Other	1.5	0.9
Private Companies[b]	20.6	12.7
Total aid received.................	$ 162.2 mn	100.0%

Notes: [a]Reported by the International Monetary Fund (1983:67).
[b]Largely supplier credits related to the international airport.
Sources: Computed by author from publicly available information. More details are available from the author upon request.

August 1983, Grenada obtained a $14 million loan from the IMF over U.S. objections (Manning 1984: 78).

The largest foreign donors included the European Economic Community, Arab states, Cuba, and the International Monetary Fund. Shortly after the 1979 Revolution, Cuba sent a 20-member medical team; it also provided assistance for fisheries, construction equipment and manpower for the Point Salines airport, weapons, and military advisers. The European Economic Community provided funds for the airport, road repairs, and community-based education and health centers (the CPEs). North Korea and Canada provided support for agriculture. Grenada's capital expenditure program of nearly $88 million over three years (1980–82) was almost completely foreign financed (Payne, Sutton, and Thorndike 1984: 25).

International aid flows approximately matched the cumulative deficits on the trade account, which totalled over $130 million during 1979–82 (see table 14–7).

While Grenadians welcomed foreign assistance in the form of money capital and more tangible assets, they were at pains to stress that in the final analysis, development depended upon far more than mere infusions of money. For example, between 1978 and 1979 capital expenditures were doubled from $8 to $16 million, but the key in boosting the economy's absorptive capacity was the large increase in voluntary labor (Pagne 1980: 24).

The economic achievements of the PRG are summarized in table 14–8. While overall economic growth (measured by gross domestic product) averaged minus 1.8 percent per year during 1970–78, it was plus 3.4 percent between 1979 and 1982,[4] making Grenada one of the few countries in the hemisphere to record positive growth. Income per capita rose from $450 in 1978 to $870 in 1983. The unemployment rate dropped from 49 percent in 1978–79, to 12–14 percent by 1982. The inflation rate was steadily reduced, so that in 1982 it was 7 percent (George 1983: 19). Reduced unemployment resulted primarily from the PRG's expansion of the armed forces and the development of youth and community projects (*The Europa Year Book* 1985: 1712). The major source of growth between 1979 and 1983 was the construction sector and, in particular, the new international airport.

Besides the airport, there were new roads, a new telephone system, new power generation facilities, and structures for various agro-industries. The increased relative importance of the construction and the services sectors was matched by a corresponding decline in agriculture and fishing's contribution to the gross domestic product (see table 14–9).

The longer-term goal of "disengaging from imperialism" took three forms: selective encouragement of foreign investment, the seeking of international aid from a variety of willing donors, and a redirection of international trade in such a way as to diversify trading partners. Table 14–10 indicates that Grenada lessened its trade dependence upon industrialized Western countries while increasing its exchanges with other developing countries. Trade with the socialist bloc remained insignificant. Clearly, Grenada exhibited an intense interest to continue its participation in the capitalist world economy.[5]

Some success was registered in developing nontraditional exports, and the share of food in total imports was reduced. The share of the four traditional export commodities dropped from over 80 percent in 1979 to under 64 percent in 1982 (see table 14–2). Export earnings of fruits and vegetables rose dramatically from $0.6 million in 1981 to $1.7 million in 1982, with the bulk exported to Trinidad & Tobago (Payne, Sutton, and Thorndike 1984: 23).

TABLE 14.7. Grenada's Merchandise Trade Account (in E.C. $ millions)*

	1970	1971	1972	1973	1974	1975	1976	1977	1978	1979	1980	1981	1982
Imports, c.i.f.	44.1	46.1	42.8	42.5	38.1	52.8	66.2	84.7	96.3	117.7	135.0	159.9	150.9
Exports, f.o.b.	10.5	9.3	9.9	13.6	17.8	26.9	33.0	38.4	45.8	63.4	44.0	51.1	50.1
Trade deficit =	33.6	36.8	32.9	28.9	20.3	25.9	33.2	46.3	50.5	54.3	91.0	108.8	100.9

Note: *To convert to U.S. dollars, use E.C. $ 2.375 per U.S. $1 for 1970-75, and E.C. $ 2.70 per U.S. $1 for 1976 to the present.
Sources: The Europa Year Book, various years; Kirton 1983:45; and *Latin American Weekly Report.* 1983. March 13, p.5.

TABLE 14.8. Summary Economic Indicators of the Grenadian Revolution

Year	Population in '000s	Population Growth Rate	Gross Domestic Product at Market Prices	Gross Domestic Product per Head	Average Annual Growth Rate of Gross Domestic Product
1972	95	1960-72: 0.6%	$ 40 million	$ 420	1960-72: 4.1% 1965-72: 5.0%
1974	98	1960-74: 1.2% 1965-74: 0.8%	40	330	1960-74: 2.2% 1965-74: 1.6%
1976	110	1960-76: 1.1%	50	410	1960-76: 1.9% 1970-76: -4.3% 1970-77: -3.2%
1978	106	1970-78: 1.6%	60	570	1970-78: -3.4%
1982	110.7	1.4%	109.8	992	1979: 2.1% 1980: 3.0% 1981: 3.0% 1982: 5.5%

Sources: World Bank Atlas, various years; Carlip 1982: 222; Kirton 1983: 45; and Latin American Weekly Report. 1983, March 18, p. 5.

TABLE 14.9. Grenada: Sectoral Origin of Gross Domestic Product

	1975	1977	1979	1980	1981	1982
Agriculture, fisheries, forestry	38.8%	33.2%	31.2%	27.5%	27.8%	25.2%
Manufacturing	2.8	2.8	2.7	2.6	2.8	2.7
Construction	2.5	2.7	2.2	4.5*	6.2*	7.3*
Transportation and communication	5.6	7.3	6.2	6.2	6.1	5.6
Hotels and restaurants	2.8	3.3	2.8	2.7	2.2	2.0
Government services	16.9	18.5	21.6	20.9	19.5	21.8
General services	17.0	15.6	16.9	19.4	19.1	19.1
Other	13.6	16.6	16.4	16.3	16.3	16.3
Total.....	100.0	100.0	100.0	100.0	100.0	100.0
Gross Domestic Product at factor cost (in E.C.$'s millions)	84.6	110.9	160.0	195.1	n.a.	n.a.

Note: *Largely the international airport.
Sources: South (February 1983) for 1975-79; Kirton, C., 1983, p. 14 for 1980-82.

Notwithstanding these considerable social and economic gains, certain material constraints remain immutably in place regardless of who is in power. These constraints include: the lack of energy resources; the small size of the Grenadian economy, which thwarts industrialization based on the home market with the implication that growth remains export-driven[6]; the country's limited land resources, which make it difficult to achieve food self-sufficiency; and the high degree of openness of the economy, making Grenada vulnerable to adverse developments in the international economy (Abbott 1980: 159; Neumann 1982). As Maurice Bishop once cautioned,

> . . . we happened to have achieved power at a period when the advanced industrial countries were going through a major international crisis, a major recession. This had a devastating effect on our economy. Of course a lot of the inflation in the country is imported inflation because we buy virtually all our manufactured items. We produce at this point virtually nothing in the form of manufactured goods. Indeed, even a considerable amount of food is still being imported into our country, and therefore the increases in prices abroad have been very, very tough on the economy.

Constraints upon Grenada's ability to borrow internationally arose both from U.S. opposition and from a peculiar, antiquated monetary structure. As a member of the Eastern Caribbean Currency Authority, Grenada does not have its own national currency. Its external dependence was worsened "by the existence of a virtual, anachronistic gold exchange

TABLE 14.10. Grenada: Direction of Trade, 1975-82 (in percent of total)

	Exports								Imports							
	1975	1976	1977	1978	1979	1980	1981	1982	1975	1976	1977	1978	1979	1980	1981	1982
Industrial Countries	89.2	93.1	86.6	88.5	91.6	83.4	83.2	69.6	42.8	59.0	47.2	47.1	46.5	35.7	19.7	37.3
• United States	5.3	4.4	3.8	2.9	0.5	—	—	—	4.7	10.4	—	—	—	—	—	—
• European Economic Community	79.6	84.4	78.8	82.3	85.1	79.8	76.9	63.2	27.6	34.3	46.3	45.4	44.0	30.5	15.6	31.3
Developing Countries	7.6	5.5	11.3	8.8	5.5	12.0	13.3	25.3	57.2	41.0	52.8	52.9	53.5	64.3	80.4	62.7
• Oil exporting	—	0.3	0.2	—	—	—	—	—	—	0.1	—	—	—	—	—	—
• Western hemisphere	5.7	4.7	7.3	7.8	4.9	11.9	13.3	25.2	57.2*	40.1*	51.8*	48.6*	49.2*	56.8*	76.9*	55.4*
• Other	1.9	0.5	3.8	1.0	0.6	0.1	0.1	0.1	—	0.7	1.0	4.3	4.3	7.5	3.5	7.3
Soviet Union, Eastern Europe	3.2	1.4	2.1	2.7	3.0	4.6	3.5	5.1	—	—	—	—	—	—	—	—
Total =	100	100	100	100	100	100	100	100	100	100	100	100	100	100	100	100

Note: *Especially oil from Trinidad & Tobago.
Source: Derived by author from International Monetary Fund, Direction of Trade Year Book, various years.

standard that equates the level and flow of domestic income to the availability of foreign exchange" (Kirton 1983: 11). Yet, international borrowing was urgent to finance the capital expenditure program and cover the merchandise trade deficits (see table 14–7).

In sum, the PRG's socioeconomic program resulted in: an increasing role of the state in the economy; rising levels of economic activity propelled by the construction sector, with consequent drops in unemployment levels; decreased, though still substantial, food imports as agriculture was diversified; rising exports of nontraditional crops; and a substantial diversification of both import and export markets, in particular a reduction in the overwhelming role once played by the Western industrialized countries. More generally, the PRG successfully raised the "social wage" as a means of generating political support and eliciting individual effort. A mixed economy was created that recognized the peculiar material reality of the island. And lastly, Grenada's sources of outside support were diversified. Grenada under the New Jewel Movement had become a state of "socialist orientation," a state moving towards eventual socialist development.

Given these realities, it was not the "economic loss" of Grenada that mattered to the United States—the country's markets, its exports, and its strategic military significance were insignificant. Rather, Grenada's importance lay elsewhere. Its very success was threatening, evoking the fear, as Noam Chomsky recently observed, that the "rot would spread," the rot of successful social and economic development (Chomsky 1985: 9). It is for this reason that the United States demonstrates extraordinary viciousness towards constructive developments in the marginal, resource-poor, backward countries of the Third World:

> In fact, the smaller and less significant the country, the more dangerous it is. So, for example, as soon as the Bishop regime in Grenada began to take constructive moves, it was immediately the target of enormous American hostility. (Chomsky 1985: 10)

Grenada could act as an inspiration to other forces challenging U.S. control in the region, as well as within the advanced countries through their large Caribbean emigré populations.[7] As Maurice Bishop noted,

> When people in neighboring islands hear about what is happening in Grenada, they ask questions of their own governments. The Americans are deadly concerned about that. (George 1983: 19)

POSTMORTEM ECONOMICS AFTER THE INVASION

The first invasion of revolutionary Grenada was by the U.S. military. The second comprised a clique of twentieth-century carpetbaggers and their

U.S. government sponsors under the Reagan Caribbean Basin Initiative. Grenada reverted to the proverbial status of just another formally democratic U.S. client state with a development strategy based on low-wage, export-oriented industries (e.g., wooden toys, candles, computer parts) and cruise-ship tourism. Its nutmeg crop was warehoused for lack of international sales outlets, and a part was sold to a monopsonistic U.S. firm, Caribbean Corporate Services, based on St. Croix (*The New York Times*. 1984. (January 22): III, 10).[8] Grenada's cheap labor ($ 4.50 per day) was unabashedly pedalled to prospective foreign investors, and unemployment returned to record levels of anywhere between 40 and 60 percent (*The New York Times*. 1984. (July 29): F8).

The installed free-market government proceeded to shut down many PRG projects, including the agro-industry plant, the Sandino prefab housing factory, the fisheries school, and the cooperatives. The new government also dismantled virtually all of the social and educational programs established between 1979 and 1983 (e.g., the centers for adult education, the milk feeding program for schoolchildren, scholarships for youth, etc.). The postinvasion regime attacked unions fostered during the Revolution and "reoriented" the union movement under the auspices of the American Institute for Free Labor Development (which works closely with the CIA to influence labor unions in Latin America and the Caribbean).

The governing party voted into office in 1984 had been nurtured and bankrolled by the United States as an alternative to Gairy's party and the remnants of the New Jewel Movement. Grenada along with other ministates of the Caribbean was increasingly militarized. The occupying American troops were set up in the former Holiday Inn, the Grenada Beach Hotel, until their departure in June 1984. And lastly, St. George's harbor became the winter base-camp for Courageous II, a U.S. entry in the 1987 America's Cup. Such developments appealed to the United States, which rewarded Grenada with the highest amount of U.S. aid per capita in the world in fiscal 1984 (*Journal of Commerce*, 1984. (May 10): 23).

All this led to a situation well described in a recent article in *Americas*:

> Grenada revisited: Grenada's 45 pristine talcum-fine beaches, its picture-perfect capital and inner harbor, and its hospitable people beckoning tourists again. . . .

It spelled for Grenadians a return to the status of: sellers of trinkets and "services" to tourists, employment in the legions of waiters, hewers of wooden toys (for Ingle Toys of New Jersey), and stitchers of canvas mailbags (for MacGregor Sporting Goods), in an environment dominated by the laws of the free market and Westminister-style democracy.

NOTES

1. The Reagan regime was quite successful in its propaganda war against Grenada, as recounted in SCAAN's publication (Stanford Central America Action Network 1983).

2. This was taken seriously: see the People's Revolutionary Government of Grenada (1982).

3. In 1982, the sum of exports, imports, and nonfactor services exceeded 80 percent of gross domestic product (Kirton 1983:2).

4. *The Journal of Commerce* (1983, June 13) reported that the cumulative rate of real growth between 1979 and 1982 was over 15 percent.

5. This is a general tendency among less developed countries noted by Feinberg (1983:109–14).

6. For a theoretical statement of such growth, see Fitzgerald (1982, 1985). In 1981, Grenada's export earnings amounted to a mere $19.6 million, barely enough to buy the tail section of a B-1 bomber.

7. One need only read the highly sympathetic articles on Grenada in such black journals as *Freedomways*, *The Black Scholar*, and *Sepia*, to understand the concern.

8. Needless to say, the new regime immediately abrogated the long-term trade agreement signed with the Soviet Union in 1982.

REFERENCES

Abbott, George C. 1980. Grenada: Maverick or Pace-Maker in the West Indies? *World Today* 36 (April) : 154–62.

Ambursley, Fitzroy. 1984. Grenada: The New Jewel Movement. In *Crisis in the Caribbean*, Fitzroy Ambursley and Robin Cohen (eds.). New York: Monthly Review Press.

Ambursley, Fitzroy and Winston James. 1983. Maurice Bishop and the New Jewel Revolution in Grenada. *New Left Review* 142 (November-December) : 91–96.

Augustine, Fennis. 1974. Mr. Gairy's Grenada. *The New Statesman* 87 (February): 181.

Barry, Tom, Beth Wood, and Deb Preusch. 1984. *The Other Side of Paradise. Foreign Control in the Caribbean*. New York: Grove Press.

Beckford, George. 1980. Socioeconomics Change and Political Continuity in the Anglophone Caribbean. *Studies in Comparative International Development* 15,1 (Spring) : 3–14.

――――. 1984. The Struggle for Grenada (six articles). *The Black Scholar* 15,1 (January-February 1984) : 1–59.

Bishop, Maurice. 1981. The Present Stage of the Grenada Revolution. In *Maurice Bishop Speaks: The Grenada Revolution 1979–83*. New York: Pathfinder Press.

Brierley, John S. 1985. A Review of Development Strategies and Programmes of the People's Revolutionary Government in Grenada, 1979–83. *The Geographic Journal* 151,1 (March) : 40–52.

Carlip, Vivian, William Overstreet, and Dwight Linder. 1982. *Economic Handbook of the World: 1982*. New York: McGraw-Hill.

Carrera, J. 1982. Grenada Has Chosen Its Road (interview with Maurice Bishop). *World Marxist Review* 25 (April) : 63–67.

Chomsky, Noam. 1985. Intervention in Vietnam and Central America: Parallels and Differences. *Monthly Review* 37,4 (September) : 1–30.

Cockburn, Alexander and James Ridgeway. 1983. The Four Pillars of Maurice Bishop. Grenada: The Island Reagan Hates. *The Village Voice* (June 28).

DaBreo, D. Sinclair. 1979. *The Grenada Revolution*. Castries (Sta. Lucia): Management Advertising and Publicity Services (MAPS).

Davies, Joan. 1979. Returning Democracy to the People. *The Canadian Forum* 59 (June) : 4–5.

Deere, Carmen D. 1984. Agrarian Reform and the Peasantry in the Transition to Socialism in the Third World. Amherst: University of Massachusetts, Unpublished manuscript.

EPICA Task Force. 1982. *Grenada. The Peaceful Revolution*. Washington D.C.: Ecumencial Program for Interamerican Communication and Action.

Feinberg, Richard. 1983. *The Intemperate Zone: The Third World Challenge to U.S. Foreign Policy*. New York: W.W. Norton.

Fitzgerald, E. Valpy K. 1982. The Problem of Balance in the Peripheral Socialist Economy. Unpublished manuscript (November) : 1–32. The Hague: Institute for Social Studies.

——— . 1985. The Problem of Balance in the Peripheral Socialist Economy: A Conceptual Note. *World Development* 13,1 (January) : 5–14.

Friedland, Jonathan. 1984. Grenada's Stab at Free Enterprise. *The New York Times* (July 29):III, 8–9.

George, Alan. 1983. Grenada: Island Socialism. *The New Statesman* 105 (March 25) : 19.

Hagen, Sue. 1983. Grenada: Revolution's Next Step Forward (report on Prime Minister Maurice Bishop's New Year's address). *Intercontinental Press* 21 (February 14) : 86–87.

Halliday, Fred. 1983. Cold War in the Caribbean. *New Left Review* 141 (September-October) : 5–22.

Henfrey, Colin. 1984. Between Populism and Leninism: The Grenadian Experience. *Latin American Perspectives* 11,3 (Summer) : 15–36.

International Monetary Fund. 1983. *Grenada—Recent Economic Developments* (August 11). Washington D.C.: The International Monetary Fund.

Jackson, Maurice. 1981. Grenada's Revolution: The First Two Years. *Political Affairs* 60,6 (June) : 34–39.

Jacobs, W. Richard and Ian Jacobs. 1980. *Grenada: The Route to Revolution*. Havana: Casa de las Americas.

Kay, F. 1971. *This is Grenada*. St. George's, Grenada: Carenage Press.

Kirton, Clarement D. 1983. Attempts at Economic Planning in the Early Stages of Transition: Some Notes on the Grenada Experience. (Unpublished paper (6–25 June) : 1–46. The Hague: Institute for Social Studies Policy Workshop.

Kolmes, Jo-Ann. 1982. Grenadian Culture: The People Wants to Get Up. *NACLA Report on the Americas* 16,5 (September-October) : 36–38.

Lowther, William. 1979. A Caribbean Coup: Revolt in Reggae Time. *McClean's Magazine* 92 (April 9) : 4–8.

Lynch, Charles. 1981. Education and the New Grenada. *The Black Scholar* 12 (July-August) : 13–24.

Mandle, Jay R. 1985. *Big Revolution Small Country. The Rise and Fall of the Grenada Revolution*. Lanham: The North-South Publishing Company.

Manning, Michael. 1984. Grenada Before and After. *The Atlantic Monthly* 253 (February) : 76–87.

Mars, Peter. 1984. Destabilization and Socialist Orientation in the English Speaking Caribbean. *Latin American Perspectives* 11,3 (Summer) : 83–110.

Mydans, Seth. 1984. Nutmeg Diplomacy in Grenada: The Aftermath of Invasion. *The New York Times* (January 22) : III, 10.

Neumann, A. Lin. 1982. The Pampered People's Republic, The Left Side of Paradise: Grenada Hosts Socialism. *The Boston Phoenix* (January 26).

Pagne, Lucien. 1980. Grenada: Towards a New Socialism? *The Courier Magazine* 64 (May-June) : 19–34.

Payne, Anthony. 1980. Revolutionary Politics in Grenada. *The Round Table* 280 (October) : 381–88.

Payne, Anthony, Paul Sutton, and Tony Thorndike. 1984. *Grenada: Revolution and Invasion*. New York: St. Martin's Press.

People's Revolutionary Government of Grenada 1982. *"To Construct from Morning." Making the People's Budget in Grenada*. St. George's: Fedon Publishers.

Prince, Rod. 1983. Clean Bill of Health for the Outcast of the Islands. *South* (February).

Searle, Chris. 1979. In the Wake of Hurricane Gairy. *The New Statesman* 98 (September) : 388–89.

Searle, Chris. 1979. Grenada's Revolution: An Interview with Bernard Coard. *Race and Class* 21,2 (Autumn) : 171–87.

———. 1983. *Grenada: The Struggle Against Destabilization*. London: Writers and Readers Publishing Cooperative Society.

Stanford Central American Action Network (SCAAN). 1983. *Grenada: Behind Reagan's Propaganda Victory: British and American Press Coverage*. Stanford: SCAAN (December).

Stoddart, Veronica. 1985. Grenada Revisited. *Americas* 37,5 (September-October): 8.

Thorndike, Tony. 1974. Grenada: Maxi-Crisis for Mini-State. *World Today* 30 (October) : 436–44.

———. 1983. The Grenada Crisis. *World Today* 39 (December) : 468–76.

Tobias, Peter M. 1980. The Social Context of Grenadian Emigration. *Social and Economic Studies* 29 (March) : 40–59.

Valenta, Jiri and Virginia Valenta. 1984. Leninism in Grenada. *Problems of Communism* 33,4 (July-August) : 1–23.

Walker, Annette. 1980. The New Jewel Revolution in Grenada. *NACLA Report on the Americas* 14,1 (January-February) : 40–43.

———. 1983. Grenada's Women Move Forward with the Revolution. *Freedomways* 23,1 : 23–28.

White, Gordon. 1984. Developmental States and Socialist Industrialization in the Third World. *Journal of Development Studies* 21,1 (October) : 97–120.

Index

Contributors

El-Hachemi Aliouche, is a doctoral student in economics at the University of New Hampshire at Durham.

Leigh Binford is an anthropology professor at the Hartford campus of the University of Connecticut.

Scott Cook is an anthropology professor at the Storrs campus of the University of Connecticut.

Valarie D. Ellis is a doctoral student in economics at the Durham campus of the University of New Hampshire.

Richard W. England is an economics professor at the University of New Hampshire at Durham.

Marc W. Herold is an economics professor at the University of New Hampshire at Durham.

Robert N. Horn is an economics professor at James Madison University.

Richard W. Hurd is an economics professor at the Durham campus of the University of New Hampshire.

Kent A. Klitgaard is an economics professor at New Hampshire College.

Nicholas N. Kozlov is an economics professor at St. Olaf College.

Marilyn Power is an economics professor at St. Olaf College.

Stephen P. Reyna is an anthropology professor at the Durham campus of the University of New Hampshire.

Joseph M. Tomkiewicz is a management professor at East Carolina University.

Benigno Valdés is a lecturer in economics at the Instituto Tecnologico Autónomo de México in Mexico City.